ALL THE FINE
YOUNG EAGLES

Other books by
David L. Bashow

Sting of the Hornet
Starfighter

ALL THE FINE YOUNG EAGLES

In the Cockpit with Canada's Second World War Fighter Pilots

David L. Bashow

Forewords by Lieutenant-General A. M. DeQuetteville
and Air Vice-Marshal J. E. Johnson

Stoddart

Published in 1996 by
Stoddart Publishing Co. Limited

Distributed in Canada by
General Distribution Services Inc.
30 Lesmill Road
Toronto, Canada M3B 2T6
Tel. (416) 445-3333
Fax (416) 445-5967
e-mail Customer.Service@ccmailgw.genpub.com

Distributed in the United States by
General Distribution Services Inc.
85 River Rock Drive, Suite 202
Buffalo, New York 14207
Toll free 1-800-805-1083
Fax (416) 445-5967
e-mail Customer.Service@ccmailgw.genpub.com

Cataloguing in Publication Data

Bashow, David L., 1946–
All the fine young eagles: in the cockpit with
Canada's Second World War fighter pilots

Includes index.
ISBN 0-7737-2976-3

1. World War, 1939–1945 – Aerial operations, Canadian.
2. Fighter pilots – Canada. 3. Canada. Royal Canadian Air Force –
History – World War, 1939–1945. 4. Great Britain. Royal Air Force –
History – World War, 1939–1945. I. Title.

D792.C3B37 1996   940.54'4971   96-931257-1

Cover design/illustration: Stephen Quick

Printed and bound in Canada

"Nor law, nor duty bade me fight,
Nor public men, nor cheering crowds,
A lonely impulse of delight
Drove to this tumult in the clouds."
— W. B. YEATS

CONTENTS

FOREWORD

BY LIEUTENANT-GENERAL A. M. DEQUETTEVILLE,
COMMANDER, CANADIAN FORCES AIR COMMAND

At the outset of the Second World War, thousands of young Canadians put their lives on hold and joined a crusade against tyranny. Almost a quarter of a million of them "did their bit" in air force blue, and of this number only a handful were selected to become fighter pilots. These individuals, from every province and territory in Canada, fought in the skies of many different nations and left an unparalleled legacy of courage and dedication for future generations. *All the Fine Young Eagles* is their story.

And a fine story it is! From a wide variety of sources, Dave Bashow has brought together the strands of countless separate tales and woven them into a fascinating history. Beginning with the handful of Canadians serving with the Royal Air Force in France in 1940, through the epic action of the Battle of Britain, and culminating with the achievement of air superiority in the skies over the German Reich, Bashow endeavours to bring the reader "into the cockpit" with the pilot. He achieves this aim remarkably well, combining historical narrative with the thoughts and words of the young Canadians who were actually there. The end result is an exciting book which deals with an important part of Canadian Air Force history.

All the Fine Young Eagles is a book which will have an appeal beyond the realm of historians and aviation enthusiasts. I believe that it will also be of interest and use to the current generation of Canadian fighter pilots, for it is first and foremost a fighter pilots' history. Even though the technology and the tactics of aerial combat have changed, the human factor has not. The manner in which these men, many still in their teens, dealt with the physical and mental demands of a merciless war in the air is worth considering by today's "crop" of pilots.

The deeds of the young men who flew during the Second World War will forever be a part of the Canadian Air Force. *All the Fine Young Eagles* puts a human face to these deeds and solidifies their contribution to our heritage. The airmen of today can only offer our thanks to those who have gone before and offer our appreciation for a job well done! *Per ardua ad astra.*

FOREWORD

BY AIR VICE-MARSHAL J. E. JOHNSON, CB, CBE, DSO (2 BARS), DFC (1 BAR)

During the early years of the Second World War, I knew several distinguished Canadian fighter pilots — Stan Turner, Dal Russel, Gordie McGregor, and Ernie McNab, all of Battle of Britain fame — but my real association with the Canadians began in the spring of 1943 when I was Wing Commander Flying of the Kenley Wing (403 and 416 Squadrons) and ended two years later when I left 127 Wing (403, 416, and 443 Squadrons). We were fortunate to fly the elegant Spitfire IX, whose only disadvantage was its lack of range; as a short-range fighter it had no equal.

We saw a fair amount of action, and I think the highlight of 1943 was escorting the B-17s of "The Mighty Eighth" as they fought their way deep into Germany. Before the arrival of the long-range Mustang — the most significant fighter of those days — the Americans took some hard knocks; but they pressed on and eventually won a great victory.

In the spring of 1944 I was appointed Wing Commander Flying of 144 Wing (441, 442, and 443 Squadrons), and on June 15, 1944, we made history when we were the first fighter outfit to move into Normandy at St-Croix-sur-Mer. From the beachhead our fighter-bombers — especially the Typhoons, flown by the bravest of the brave — stunned and paralysed the German armies.

After the great killing ground of Falaise, we began the long trek across northwest Europe, only to be halted by the Rhine and Montgomery's failure at Arnhem. By the following spring it was all over.

During these peregrinations I came to know many Canadian fighter pilots, and I knew the squadron commanders best of all because I saw and briefed them every day. The outstanding squadron commanders were Danny Browne, Hugh Godefroy, George Hill, Wally Conrad, George Keefer, "Buck" McNair, Dal Russel, and the greatest marksman of those days, Wally McLeod. They were good and trusted leaders who were always there in the tightest of corners. It was a privilege to be associated with such fighting Canadians, and here in Colonel David Bashow's outstanding and carefully researched narrative we meet again that gallant company:

> *"He that outlives this day, and comes safe home,*
> *Will stand a tip-toe when this day is nam'd."*
> — SHAKESPEARE, KING HENRY V

PREFACE

During the six years of the Second World War, Canadian fighter pilots flew and fought with great distinction in every theatre to which Commonwealth fighter forces were deployed. *All the Fine Young Eagles* attempts to capture the spirit and magnitude of the Canadian contribution, which began in Europe's Low Countries in 1940 and ended among the Japanese Home Islands in 1945.

A few words on the content and scope of the book are warranted. Since the Royal Canadian Air Force's aerial fighter contribution predominated over northwest Europe, a lot of my material relates to that theatre. A great many Canadian fighter pilots also served in Royal Air Force units, however, and deployed to all active theatres of British interest. Therefore, a substantial amount of text relates to operations in North Africa, Sicily, Italy, and the Far East. Home Defence fighter operations, including the Aleutians campaign, also form a significant part of the overall story.

Initially, I had intended to cover only day fighter, night fighter, and intruder operations, but I soon discovered that to provide a true representation of fighter actions, I would also need to properly recognize the army cooperation/fighter reconnaissance and fighter bomber disciplines. Though their respective missions did not primarily involve air combat, circumstances frequently demanded it, particularly during the last year of the European war.

A brief explanation of particular language in the book is also warranted. Some of the former pilots who have contributed personal accounts occasionally described or referred to their enemies in terms that by today's standards might be considered somewhat derogatory, although they were indeed household words during the war. I have felt from the outset that it was not part of my mandate to pass judgement on or tamper in any way with the veterans' contributions, and thus their stories appear just as they were presented to me.

All the Fine Young Eagles is not intended to be an exhaustive history, though a great deal of historical fact has been painstakingly researched and meticulously cross-checked for veracity before being incorporated into the text. The historical background is meant to serve as a supportive medium for the first-person recollections of the veterans themselves. While I have culled a substantial number of direct quotes from existing publications, I have done so because I feel that no better passages exist on a particular subject, or because the principals involved in a specific event have passed away.

To that end, I am grateful to the following individuals and organizations for granting me permission to quote from their previously published works: E. C. R. Baker, Donald L. Caldwell, Don Carlson, Tom Coughlin, "Stocky" Edwards, Hedley Everard, the late Adolf Galland, Hugh Godefroy, Hugh Halliday (from Orleans), Lloyd Hunt, "Johnnie" Johnson, Vic Johnson (*Airforce* magazine), the late Dave McIntosh, Brian Nolan, the late Bill Olmsted, the late Jeffrey Quill, Jackie Rae, *Reader's Digest* (Canada), Christopher Shores, and Allan Simpson.

Also, my profound thanks to the following veterans, who took the time and trouble to contribute their first-person recollections to me and, in so doing, provided what is in my opinion the very "soul" of this book: Noel Stansfeld, Arthur Deacon, Paul Pitcher, Hartland Molson, Bob Morrow, "Moose" Fumerton, "Stocky" Edwards, George Burroughs, Frank Hanton, "Duke" Warren, Rod Smith, Bert Houle, Karl Linton, Jackie Rae, Art Sager, Gordon Wilson, Noel Ogilvie, Cec Brown, Don Laubman, "Joe" Schultz, Bill Gould, Gord Ockenden, David Goldberg, Arthur Jewett, Dave Bockus, Russ Bannock, John Coupland, John Garland, Jim Prendergast, Chuck Darrow, Dick Reeves, Murray Lepard, and Don Sheppard.

Many other generous verbal and material contributions were made by a host of people along the way. Assistance ranged from financial help for research and the loan of photographs to the provision of specific suggestions and a great deal of advice and practical encouragment, for which I am extremely grateful. None were more supportive than Don Pearsons and Bill March of the Air Command Heritage Branch.

Finally, my deepest thanks to my dear wife, Heather, for her unflagging support and enthusiasm. She has again completely typed, edited, and proofread the entire manuscript, and also contributed many excellent suggestions for improving the structure and content of the text along the way.

I hope *All the Fine Young Eagles* helps to acknowledge the profound debt of gratitude Canada owes these veterans, one and all.

David L. Bashow
August 1996

INTRODUCTION

During the Second World War, Canada provided a formidable contribution of manpower and materiel to the prosecution of the air war against the Axis powers. Formal national representation by the Royal Canadian Air Force overseas ultimately consisted of forty-eight squadrons serving in all operational disciplines, the majority of which were concentrated in the European theatre. Large numbers of RCAF personnel, however, served while dispersed throughout the Royal Air Force, flying operationally in all theatres of war to which the RAF was deployed. As late as 1945, an estimated 60 percent of all RCAF aircrew were serving in RAF units, and, reciprocally, the designated RCAF operational units contained many Britons, other members of the Commonwealth, and other foreign nationals. Thus, any serious attempt to chronicle the contributions of Canadian airmen during the war years must recognize from the outset the diverse nature of that contribution.

When Great Britain declared war on Germany on 3 September 1939, there were over 1,000 Canadian aircrew serving on active duty with the Royal Air Force. They ran the spectrum of service time: some had remained with the RAF since the Great War and were now relatively senior, others had joined in the 1920s and were in intermediate ranks, while the vast majority had arrived on Britain's shores from 1935 onwards. Their reasons for enlisting were similarly diverse. Some undoubtedly saw little service future in the minuscule Royal Canadian Air Force of the 1930s, and others must have been caught up in the patriotic fervor of rearmament and the looming fascist threat. However, the majority were most likely driven by a

1

compelling sense of adventure. Few could have envisioned how long the "adventure" would keep them away from Canada. Many would not return for a great number of years; far too many would never return.

A small cadre of eighteen regular RCAF officers were also serving in various positions on exchange duties or on courses at the commencement of hostilities. One of them, Squadron Leader Fowler Morgan Gobeil, an articulate Royal Military College graduate and experienced pilot, would be chosen to lead 242 Squadron, the first distinctively Canadian fighter unit within the RAF.

To appreciate the nature of official Canadian representation in the RAF after the declaration of war by Canada on 10 September 1939, one must understand something of the prevailing national sentiment. In May 1939, King George VI and Queen Elizabeth visited Canada, marking the first time its reigning monarch had toured the country. Their quiet courage in the face of the impending threat moved the nation, stiffening the resolve of its citizens to help resist fascism in Europe. Canada had an equal resolve, however, never again to respond blindly to an arrogant, almost contemptuous assumption of support from Britain, as had occurred during the First World War. Canada had written her national identity in the blood of 60,000 war dead, and justifiably felt that she had earned the right to relative autonomy from Britain in foreign-policy decisions. That feeling was perhaps best exemplified by the nation's declaration of war on Germany on 10 September — a full seven days after that of Britain.

The RCAF's 242 Squadron owes its origins to the Canadian government's nationalistic desire to be represented by a distinctly Canadian unit at the earliest possible time after the outbreak of war. Since no RCAF formations were in a position to deploy immediately, the most logical solution was to cull suitable Canadian members from existing RAF units and holding pools and use those men to form a separate squadron. In fact, the British government was very pleased to have distinctively nationalistic Dominion squadrons serving within the RAF, viewing them as an excellent gesture to the world — particularly the fascist world — of Commonwealth solidarity. That view, formally presented by the British Air Council to the governments of Canada, Australia, and New Zealand on 26 September 1939, set in motion a chain of events which would culminate in the formation of a new squadron a little over a month later. The British Foreign Office was particularly enthusiastic about the propaganda value of a Canadian RAF squadron, and especially its forward deployment to the Continent. Accordingly, 242 (Canadian) Squadron came into being at Church Fenton, under the command of Squadron Leader Gobeil, on 30 October 1939.

The British government had made the mistake, however, of assuming that, even given the substantial contributions in terms of fighting units that would be made by the Dominions, the RAF would be the common service instrument for operational procedures, chain of authority, code of conduct, and disciplinary procedures. In mid-December, the Canadian minister of National Defence submitted a memorandum regarding the establishment of the British Commonwealth Air Training Plan. The memorandum stated that Canada, after consultation with Britain, would be permitted to establish Canadian units and formations overseas. Furthermore, these units and formations would subsequently be designated as elements of the RCAF, in accordance with RCAF regulations, procedures, and chain of authority. The British government immediately repudiated this proposition, stating that it was beyond the terms of the pending BCATP agreement. Nonetheless, the Canadian government held firm, and Prime Minister Mackenzie King was adamant that Canadian agreement to host the BCATP was tied to this proviso. Canada would not proceed further unless her sovereign rights were observed and respected. After further negotiations, which reworded the Canadian view slightly but not its sovereignty implications, the Chamberlain government relented and signed the BCATP into being, paving the way for full RCAF unit participation as elements of the RCAF later during the war.

The early deployment of British forces to the Continent had a significant impact on 242 Squadron's wartime contribution. When the requirement for a British Expeditionary Force on the Continent was determined necessary in the wake of the German annexation of Czechoslovakia in March 1939, planners were adamant that sufficient air protection be a part of that force. To that end, four of the modern Hawker Hurricane squadrons were detached from Fighter Command, an action which deeply concerned its commander, Air Chief Marshal Sir Hugh Dowding. Fighter Command would now be reduced to thirty-five squadrons, which by his calculations would be eleven squadrons below the minimum required for the air defence of Great Britain. But matters would only get worse as the government earmarked yet a further six fighter squadrons to the BEF.

After the declaration of hostilities, early air operations against the

Germans were flown almost entirely in the form of sporadic raids by Bomber and Coastal Commands. Poland had capitulated within a month, and while many of the cities in Britain that fall were still featuring Clark Gable and Vivian Leigh's feisty sparring in *Gone With the Wind*, the newsreel leaders painted an altogether more solemn portrait of Poland's demise and a portent of things to come. Then, in a strangely merciful way, free Europe settled in to endure the coldest winter on record for forty-five years, with frost reported all the way down to the Italian Riviera. The bitter winter weather was a godsend, as it delayed the German invasion of the Low Countries and allowed the British (and to a certain extent, her allies) precious time for buildup and training. It became known as the period of the Sitzkrieg, or "Phony War," in western Europe.

On 9 April, German troops overran Denmark, essentially without resistance, and also invaded Norway. Then, on 10 May, Germany turned its attention to the Low Countries. By that time, 67 (Hurricane) Wing had arrived for fighter support, consisting of 1 and 73 Squadrons. On the day of the German attack, 501 Squadron of the Auxiliary Air Force (AAF) joined the Wing with its two Regular Force squadrons and was in combat within the hour in support of the Advanced Air Striking Force (AASF) bomber and reconnaissance units.[1]

The RAF Component consisted of four squadrons of Hurricanes — two Regular Force and two AAF squadrons, which were still in a conversion process from Gloster Gladiators — and five squadrons of Westland Lysanders, used for army cooperation duties. At the commencement of hostilities against the Low Countries, the Luftwaffe possessed 4,500 operational aircraft.

By the end of the campaign's first day, incredible losses had been inflicted on the relatively puny (and neutral) Belgian and Dutch air forces.

What had happened, in fact, was the saturation of a battle area by air power on a scale that had hardly been dreamt of, with results which were not merely deeply gratifying to Hitler, Göring and the Luftwaffe leaders on account of their tactical value, but also, as the following days would show, psychologically devastating.[2]

The three Hurricane squadrons of the AASF flew forty-seven sorties and claimed six enemy aircraft destroyed while losing only two. The four squadrons of the RAF Component fared even better, flying

161 sorties and claiming thirty-six kills while also losing only two aircraft. On 10 May, two more Hurricane squadrons joined the RAF Component and were in turn followed by another the next day.[3] Thus, by 11 May, the seven fighter squadrons of the RAF Component, coupled with the three escort squadrons of the AASF, brought the total number of Hurricane squadrons in France to ten, the number promised by the government the previous year for the deployed British forces.

One of those ten Hurricane fighter squadrons was 242 Squadron, and its outstanding operational record in France would serve as a precursor to a much more significant contribution by Canadian airmen as day fighter, night fighter/intruder, fighter bomber, and fighter reconnaissance pilots in service with both the RCAF and the RAF throughout the entire Second World War.

---

1   John Terraine, *The Right of the Line*, p. 122
2   Ibid., p. 125
3   Ibid., p. 126

1

CURTAIN RISING

FRANCE 1940

*"The war in the air today makes shows like
Dawn Patrol look like Sunday School."*
— RUSS WIENS, 242 SQUADRON

15 JUNE 1940, NEAR LE HAVRE

Pilot Officer Noel K. Stansfeld of 242 (Canadian) Squadron was in
deep trouble. He and five Squadron mates had been patrolling eastward from their forward deployment base at Rennes over scattered
"popcorn" cumulus cloud at 18,000 feet when he spotted three
Messerschmitt Bf 109s 2,000 feet below them, streaking over the ver-
dant Norman countryside. Heart pounding, with an adrenaline rush
of exhilaration, and sensing the advantages of surprise and altitude,
Stansfeld waggled his wings to get his formation's attention, firewalled the throttle, and horsed his three-ton Hurricane I fighter over
in a slicing dive. Fiercely intent on closure, Stansfeld felt his initial
excitement change in a heartbeat first to surprise and then to abject
horror as some sixth sense told him to check his vulnerable tail area.
The sky was suddenly teeming with a far superior force of twenty
additional Messerschmitts.

With a sickening sense of despair, Stansfeld pushed the nimble sand-
and-spinach-camouflaged fighter into a steep dive and headed for the
security of a lower cloud. He could not warn the others because his
radio didn't work, but since the Hurricanes were scattering in all

directions, they had obviously seen this new threat. Fighting for his life, his snarling Merlin II engine producing nearly 1,000 horsepower at maximum revs, Stansfeld realized with gut-wrenching certainty that they had been suckered: the small, tempting formation he had seen below had been merely bait for a much larger enemy formation lurking above. After passing through the protective cloud he had so desperately sought, Stansfeld anxiously scanned the skies to reorient himself. He was shocked to find himself, as sometimes happens in the high-speed mêlée of aerial combat, suddenly alone in a sky that seconds earlier had been full of violently manoeuvring fighters.

While the good news was that no enemy aircraft were in sight, particularly in his vulnerable rear hemisphere, the bad news was that neither were any of his friends. Highly anxious for the collective security of his formation, and alone in hostile airspace and without maps or a clue as to his position relative to base, Stansfeld had to act quickly before indecision compounded his dilemma.[1]

Stansfeld selected what appeared to be a good landing spot in a field close to a village. The place was not as well-suited as he had guessed, for he narrowly missed dropping over the bank of a stream as he rolled to a stop. From all directions, French peasants converged upon him, waving assorted ancient rifles and muskets. They did not believe that he was a British pilot, and he could not clearly explain his presence. It appeared that he was going to be arrested if he was lucky, and shot if he was not.

At last, one man pushed through the crowd and effected a quick rescue. The person spoke good English; he had once been a cook in England. A brass compass and a Michelin road map were produced and the young Canadian was given directions to a French airfield where he might refuel. First of all, he had to take off from his improvised landing strip. The French beat down some of the wheat. Stansfeld then stood on the brakes, revved up the engine until he was in danger of nosing over, released the brakes and took off.

Having secured some gasoline, Stansfeld set course for Rennes, but again lost his way. Below was a railway line on which a train was carrying British troops and equipment. He resolved to land beside the tracks and ask for further directions. This time he was less fortunate. As the Hurricane touched down, it ran into a ditch, wiping out the undercarriage. A deafening roar filled the cockpit as an emergency horn went off. Somebody rushed up to render assistance; Stansfeld's first act was to borrow a knife and disconnect the horn. The aircraft was a write-off; he hitch-hiked from Blain (where he had crashed) to Nantes the next morning. No. 242 had by that time concentrated there for the defence of nearby St. Nazaire.[2]

All in a relatively routine day's work for the fair, good-looking Vancouver native, caught up in the maelstrom that was France that fateful spring. Little did Noel Stansfeld know that his war was just beginning.

On 3 November 1939, Squadron Leader Gobeil received the first of his new command's aircrew, in the form of his two Flight Commanders. They were Flight Lieutenants Donald R. Miller of Saskatoon, Saskatchewan, and John L. Sullivan of Guelph, Ontario, both of whom had joined the RAF in 1936. These two were soon followed by Flying Officer John W. Graafstra of Souris, Manitoba, and Pilot Officer Robert D. Grassick of London, Ontario. Grassick would become one of the most prominent and enduring personalities of 242 Squadron's Canadian phase.

On 6 November, the Squadron was deluged with new aircrew arrivals, the vast majority of the unit's initial complement: Flying Officer Lorne E. Chambers of Vernon, British Columbia, Pilot Officers Marvin K. Brown of Kincardine, Ontario, Arthur H. Deacon, Dale F. Jones, Hugh L. Niccolls, Joseph B. Smiley, and Russell H. Wiens, all prairie boys from Saskatchewan, John B. Latta of Victoria, British Columbia, William L. McKnight of Calgary, Alberta, Donald G. McQueen of High River, Alberta, Garfield A. Madore of Fort William, Ontario, and James W. Mitchell from Kirkfield, Ontario. The next day brought Flying Officer Richard Coe of Winfield, British Columbia, and finally, on 20 November, the last three of the initial cadre of pilots reported: Pilot Officers James. F. Howitt from Guelph, Percival Stanley Turner from Toronto, Ontario, and William A. Waterton from Camrose, Alberta. Turner, Latta, McKnight, and Grassick would all become particularly accomplished fighter pilots, with Willie McKnight destined to be the Squadron's unrivalled virtuoso in air combat until his death in 1941.[3]

These young pilots' backgrounds were as varied as their places of origin. Dark, intense Willie McKnight had been a medical student; the curly haired, pipe smoking Turner, a lifeguard; Sullivan, an RCMP constable; Smiley, a gold miner; Latta, a fisherman; and so on.

They represented a great proportion of the social, cultural, and geographical mosaic of the nation. United in their common love of flight and adventure, most had obtained at least some flight training prior to arriving in Britain.

The members of 242 Squadron were fortunate to be spared early operational employment. The delay of the German offensive worked to their advantage and bought them precious time for operational readiness training. By all accounts, Gobeil did a first-rate job during this period of moulding them into an efficient and effective fighting unit. Like any group of well-trained but inexperienced young warriors, they itched to test their new-found skills in combat once the German offensive started in earnest in May.

Dowding was now clinging tenaciously to his fighter reserves, and believed that the war in France held the potential for frittering away all of Britain's fighter assets, which would later be sorely needed for the defence of the United Kingdom. Although under intense pressure from all quarters, he never allowed any of his nineteen squadrons of coveted Spitfires to deploy to France. Continuous pressure, however, particularly from the French prime minister, forced the British government to relent somewhat, and Dowding had to commit thirty-two more Hurricanes and pilots — the equivalent of two more squadrons — to France on 13 May, the day the Germans breached the front at the Meuse River. On 14 May, Flight Lieutenant Sullivan, with Pilot Officers Grassick, McKnight, and Turner in tow as 242's contribution to the reinforcement effort, was sent to Vitry-en-Artois for augmentation service with 607 and 615 Squadrons. Sullivan's combat career would be tragically brief; he was killed on the very first day of action. For the others, their stay was brief though successful, with both McKnight and Grassick having claimed kills prior to their return to Britain on 19 May for a week's leave and rest.

Meanwhile, fuelled in no small measure by Prime Minister Winston Churchill's mistaken impression that only twenty-five fighter squadrons were required to adequately defend the United Kingdom, unrelenting pressure was brought to bear on Dowding to commit ten more of his precious fighter squadrons to the front. When the War Cabinet decided on 16 May to send a further ten Hurricane squadrons forward, Dowding sent a pivotal letter to the Air Ministry, essentially stating that his total number of fighter squadrons had *already* dwindled well below the minimum number of units required for the air defence of Great Britain. Reacting to this sharp jolt of reality, the Air

Ministry quickly had the deployment order for the ten additional squadrons rescinded. Nonetheless, eight half-squadrons were dispatched on 17 May and dispersed throughout the front as replacements, not reinforcements. This compromise was due to the unexpectedly rapid onslaught of the German Panzers against the retreating British and French armies.

As part of this new deployment plan, "A" Flight of 242 Squadron was sent to augment 85 Squadron at Lille/Seclin. This Flight, commanded by Flight Lieutenant Miller and consisting of Flying Officer Chambers and Pilot Officers Brown, Deacon, McQueen, and Wiens flew some uneventful patrols over the airfield on the seventeenth, but events would be far from quiet the following day. In the course of an early morning patrol in the Le Chateau area on 18 May, Brown, Chambers, and Wiens were all shot down! In a letter home, Wiens provides the following account of the action and gives graphic testimony to the terrible fighting conditions in France at the time:

I am at present in a hospital in England, and have been here for the past two weeks. Previous to that I completed an extensive tour of northern France which took in Lille, Valenciennes, Cambrai, St. Pol, Le Touquet, Etaples, Boulogne, and then home. I was shot down by a Messerschmitt 110, or rather by about four of them. We were out on patrol and ran into about twelve of them and did we have a scrap!

The war in the air today makes shows like Dawn Patrol look like Sunday School. It wasn't my first scrap but previous to that we never had such odds against us. We saw them first and went right in on their tail. I got one with my first burst and then followed a general mêlée. I was trying to manoeuvre for another one when a '110 nearly collided with me. The rear gunner and I had an argument, however. I gave him about 500 rounds and could see him fold up. I don't know whether the plane crashed or not, but if it did I have three.

My engine cracked up owing to bullets in the cooling and oil system. I did not parachute because it isn't safe anymore owing to parachute troops. The French pot them on the way down.

I crashed in a valley on top of some trees. I immediately wrote the plane off but got away with a bit of concussion and a stiff leg and a cut face. I was out for an hour or so and it is lucky she did not burn . . . The French found me first and thought I was a German. Three of them pulled guns on me and I thought I was done but I passed out again and woke up in British hands, so it was OK. I went from one hospital to another in this retreat. They were all bombed so you may well believe I am glad to be back.[4]

Brown had received leg wounds when he was shot down and ended up in the same ambulance as Wiens, heading for the coast, from where they were eventually evacuated to England. Chambers did not fare as well. Bailing out of his flaming Hurricane, he was badly burnt on the face, hands, feet, and right leg. Because he was left in a hospital in Cambrai, he missed the rapid evacuation to the coast and was taken prisoner the next day.

The nineteenth of May was a day of relentless advances for the Germans, forcing 85 Squadron to retreat to Merville in great haste, burning documents and abandoning equipment. Don Miller flew three patrols, the last in pursuit of a Heinkel 111 bomber force that was actively bombing his airfield at Lille as he scrambled to engage them in an aircraft still battle-damaged from his preceding sortie. Art Deacon went one better, flying four sorties that day after only two hours' sleep the night before. On the second patrol he destroyed one of the He 111s that had bombed the airfield, while on the third patrol he attempted to recharge his sleep batteries from that which he had missed the night before: "Deacon's third patrol of the day lasted 75 minutes. He was so exhausted that he fell asleep in his cockpit three times while over enemy territory!"[5]

After a fourth sortie, the exhausted survivors of "A" Flight were ordered back to Church Fenton via Manston — a return trip of nearly three hours. Even the return to Britain was not without incident, as Deacon recalls:

I remember that Don Miller's aircraft had been hit in the oil tank, and in order for the three of us to get back to England, he just jammed rags into the holes, filled up the tank, and then we took off for England, landed at Biggin Hill, put in some more oil, and then headed on up to Church Fenton. I said to the CO, "Well, now I have to get some leave, because I lost everything in France and have no clothes." He said no, because we were all supposed to go down to Biggin Hill in the morning. As we were taxiing out the next day, Bev Smiley's aircraft had a problem and he told the CO he would have to go back in. I then asked the boss how it would be if I brought Smiley's machine back in and he took my aircraft, and I would in turn take his when it was fixed. He said that was OK. As it turned out, the weather was bad the next day, and I couldn't take off, so I went into Leeds to see my girlfriend. The second day, it was the same thing . . . Thursday I got off and got down to Biggin, and a fellow jumped on the aircraft and said that Smiley had been killed that morning. I said, "That's too bad, but when there's bad luck, sometimes there's good luck. Open up the gun wells and see if there is a parachute bag in there." He did, and sure enough there was, with some pyjamas, and shaving stuff, and clean underwear, and some clean shirts. This was the way we used to carry our kit when we were moving around from one station to another. Anyway, I got a change of underwear and a change of shirts, but it was only a few days after that that *I* was shot down.[6]

Though official written records of this period of 242 Squadron's history are practically nonexistent, digests of Deacon's letters, printed in the *Calgary Herald* that summer, give a brief glimpse of his hectic lifestyle:

On one occasion he was forced down when his engine stalled and while he endeavoured to fix it he was machine-gunned by German fliers. He crawled under the plane until the attackers withdrew, and managed to escape uninjured and take off in his plane again. On another occasion he was forced down to land, somewhere in France, and had an embarrassing time trying to convince a mob of angry peasants that he was not a German flier. Fortunately, he said, his high school French pulled him through . . .

He said that during the six days he hardly had time to eat, never washed and never took his clothes off. "Sleep was an hour here and there," he said. During this time he also was engaged twice with German fighters, but managed to get away.[7]

In their brief two days of combat, the Flight had lost almost half their number, though their loss rate was generally representational of other RAF Hurricane squadrons on deployment. Also, the Squadron had been operating from behind a secure British perimeter. During their next visit to France, things would be significantly different. On 20 May, the balance of the surviving fighters of the Air Component returned to the United Kingdom, and by the twenty-first, the only British fighter squadrons still in France were the three of the AASF.

The withdrawal of the RAF Component augmented Fighter Command by seven original and eight half-squadrons of Hurricanes, although those squadrons were sorely depleted after their action on the Continent.

Canadians in the RAF were scattered throughout the deployed fighter squadrons, and not confined to 242 Squadron. Rolly Dibnah, then a lowly Pilot Officer who would later complete three operational fighter tours and rise to the rank of Squadron Leader, was one of their number. Dibnah was in the thick of it in France, was then wounded in the leg, and, after many adventures, was evacuated to England, where he would live to fight again.

From memory I remember sharing a '109 with "Hilly" Brown in early May, before the shooting started on the 10th; I shot down a Dornier 17 from about 500 feet near Boos, after we had returned from an anti-dive bomber patrol behind the retreating British army. The remainder of the France fiasco is a blur of '109s; being bombed on the ground on the afternoon of May 10th, the Squadron moving and moving and always back; taking off without knowing where you would land; being lost over Paris at night and finally finding Le Bourget; rearming and refueling our own aircraft; feeling sorry at losing a friend; being bone weary; a feeling that survival was the only thing, and that you probably wouldn't make it; the shock of being hit and upside down; the false euphoria of blood loss; the shock of hitting the ground; the hissing and crackling of the engine when the aircraft came to rest; not having the strength to get out of the cockpit; a French doctor in britches and muddy boots with a blood-stained smock clamping on an aluminum ball-shaped thing with a mask to cover my nose and mouth, and saying "Breeze deep"; 39 French officers and myself crying like babies after having our dressings changed in one ward at Bar-le-Duc, all because they were too rushed to bother to soak them off; the bliss of a cup of hot tea on arrival at the British Hertford Hospital in Paris, their very first war wounded; the pleasure of a few lungfuls of Nitrous Oxide, to sleep while they changed my dressings and applied a wire boot; the unending kindness and sympathy from the English nurses; my night nurse, Betty, wheeling my bed out onto a balcony so we could enjoy a mild, clear night; listening to the guns coming closer; the rush of three of the nurses to carry me in from the garden during a sudden rain of flak shrapnel; shrapnel fragments on the balcony, putting an end to nightly chats; one night in a British field hospital at Le Mans, seeing a British tank man brought in, burned to a black crisp, and howling; being picked up at the race course in Le Mans by the Squadron "Maggie," after getting away from an ambulance convoy at the rail yards; the reunion with the Squadron at Chateaudun; the ribald ruderies about my being so stupid as to get myself damaged; the quiet and peaceful flight from Chateaudun to Hendon, the next day, as one of the two passengers aboard a "Flamingo"; the pilots wanting to land at Jersey for a cup of tea, but deciding not to, because the starboard engine was acting up; leave and signing the papers, when, almost out the door, the doctor decides to examine my leg; back to the hospital for nearly a month and a half . . .[8]

The returning survivors of "A" Flight from 242 Squadron were promptly granted seven days of leave commencing on 20 May, then just as quickly had that leave cancelled due to the Dunkirk crisis. At mid-day on 21 May, along with Gobeil and the rest of 242, who were on standby at Church Fenton, they were ordered forward to RAF Biggin Hill. With the Germans rapidly driving for the coast and the BEF and French armies in full retreat, Prime Minister Churchill reluctantly concurred with Dowding and Newall that, despite the pleas of the French, Britain did not possess a "bottomless pit" of fighter resources. Instead of further deployments to the Continent, air support forces for the retreating armies would be in the form of patrols from British bases. 242 Squadron celebrated its first offensive patrols on the twenty-second with two confirmed kills of Henschel 126 reconnaissance aircraft without loss. The next day, however, would be another story.

On 23 May, during a morning reconnaissance mission escort near Ypres of Great War fame, the Squadron was bounced by eighteen Bf 109s. Flying Officer Graafstra and Pilot Officer Madore were both shot down and killed, while Pilot Officer Smiley was shot down and taken prisoner. Later that day, Squadron Leader Gobeil engaged a lone Bf 109 at 2,500 feet near Boulogne. Though the results were inconclusive, the event was significant in that this marked the first engagement of an enemy aircraft by a member of the RCAF during the Second World War. The next day, Pilot Officers Hill (an Englishman) and Mitchell were lost on a patrol over the Dunkirk-St-Omer-Boulogne area; apparent victims of a mid-air collision. On the twenty-fifth, as if to avenge the recent losses, Gobeil opened the scoring for the RCAF in the war with a confirmed kill over a Messerschmitt Bf 110.

The next day, 242 was back to relative strength with the return of Turner, Grassick, and McKnight, but the week's casualties had been a considerable drain, and first light on the twenty-seventh (the first day of Operation Dynamo, the Dunkirk evacuation) found the unit with only twelve pilots available for operations. Each day, starting on 27 May, 242 would deploy forward to Manston on the coast, fly two or three patrols, and then return to Biggin Hill at dusk. Its simple yet essential task was to provide air cover to the evacuating ground forces between Dunkirk and Furnes, engaging any Luftwaffe aircraft that attempted to attack the retreating columns in this vital, shrinking pocket of resistance. While the patrols on the twenty-seventh were uneventful, Pilot Officer Jones was killed on the twenty-eighth when five Hurricanes led by Miller were bounced by a force of sixty Messerschmitts. Deacon was shot down also and taken prisoner. He recalls his experiences over Dunkirk and shortly thereafter:

After a few days of patrolling over Dunkirk, I was shot down. You know, we were often outnumbered . . . We might have eight air-craft [in a formation] and we would run into twenty-five or thirty German fighters. They would get into a defensive circle, and the only way you could get at them was to join the circle and try to shoot one of them down, then get out. I tried this. Whether I got my German or not, I'll never know, but then I got hit. It was just off the French coast, so I threw the hood back and undid my harness, but then thought that maybe I could get to land and crash land somehow. We had had a couple of fellows shot in their parachutes in France, so I thought that if I could make land, maybe I wouldn't have to jump. So I just made the coast, pulled back on the stick, and as there was nothing there, I went straight in. When I came to, I had been thrown out of the aircraft and was in a potato patch, right alongside a hospital. People from the hospital came out, took me in and patched me up, but when I asked if they could get me back to the British lines, they said no, since they claimed they (the French) had capitulated that day.[9]

After further adventures, Deacon was picked up by the Germans in Antwerp, where he tried to get some follow-up medical attention for his wounds. From an old castle POW compound near Laufen in southern Germany, he picks up his story again:

> Some three months later, I was sitting out in the courtyard with nothing on but my shorts, thinking that I was in a hell of a position, when a fellow came along and tapped me on my shoulder. I looked up, and it was Smiley, who said, "What the hell are you doing wearing my underwear?" I said, "Well, I was sitting here, thinking I was in hell; and now I know it because you were killed three months ago." So Smiley and I were together in prison camp for the next five years. Life in the prison camp wasn't easy, but when you think of what the alternative was, I realize how lucky I am. I've had fifty-three years of life that many of my buddies didn't have, and although things were tough at times, you think of the fellowship and the good people that you met there.[10]

Adolf Galland was a young German fighter pilot with fighting experience in Spain prior to a very distinguished combat and staff career during the Second World War. Within eighteen months of the fighting over Dunkirk, he would be the ranking German ace with ninety-four kills, holder of the Diamonds to the Knights Cross of the Iron Cross, the nation's highest award for gallantry, and General of the Fighter Arm. A Captain and squadron commander fighting over the Dunkirk beaches, Galland would form very strong opinions as to why the evacuation was considered such a great success from the British viewpoint:

> Although Dunkirk was a heavy blow for England and had a political rather than a military effect on her French ally, for Germany it was nothing like a total victory. Göring decided upon the destruction of the encircled British expeditionary force. After the victories over the Polish and French air forces he was more than ever a partisan of Douhet's Stuka idea. The army was amazed and alarmed by the irrevocable order given to the Panzer columns to halt their advance on Dunkirk. Some even thought that Hitler intended to spare the English foe in order to arrive at an honorable peace with Great Britain after the fall of France.
>
> In addition to political grounds, there were those of a military nature. In spite of the initial German successes, Hitler still retained from World War I a great respect for his French antagonist.

Therefore it was conceivable that he did not trust his own success. In any case he feared a threat to his armored divisions as they wheeled to the west and to the northwest from French forces, should they suddenly attack from the southeast — an intention [General] Gamelin actually nursed although he was never able to carry it out. Hitler's knowledge of the battlefields of Flanders also originated from World War I. He regarded them as unsuitable for large-scale tank operations and saw in these fens a possible grave for his armored divisions. Ultimately it may have been Göring who was responsible for the fatal order to stop the advance. General Warlimont, Chief of Operations at German GHQ, in a conversation with Captain Liddell Hart on this subject, informed him that he had heard Göring's reply to Hitler: "My Luftwaffe will complete the encirclement and will close the pocket at the coast from the air." Guderian remarked, "I believe it was Göring's vanity which caused Hitler to make this momentous decision."

In any case, after this any sparing of the British enemy was out of the question. On the contrary, Göring made the greatest effort to solve this problem with his Luftwaffe. It merely proved that the strength of the German Luftwaffe was inadequate, especially in the difficult conditions for reinforcement created by the unexpectedly quick advance and against a determined and well-led enemy who was fighting with tenacity and skill. Dunkirk should have been an emphatic warning for the leaders of the German Luftwaffe.[11]

The entire twenty-ninth of May was a continuous blur of operations, as the Germans had come to the realization that the BEF was making a successful bid for freedom. They therefore concentrated the weight of two Air Fleets over the beachhead area. While official Luftwaffe losses of nineteen versus official RAF losses of eighteen on the day suggest equal give and take, it was a major victory for the British since over 50,000 soldiers were successfully evacuated. Willie McKnight, whose air combat career was really beginning to blossom, had a particularly rewarding late afternoon patrol:

I turned sharp right and opened fire at point blank range, the enemy rolling over on his side and diving into the sea from a height of about 5000 feet. Turning away I dived on an Me 109 chasing a Hurricane and after a very short burst he began smoking and dived steeply for the shore. I followed but was unable to catch him and on turning to return I sighted a Do 17 above and to my right. I climbed sharply and attacked from the port rear quarter. My first burst disabled his port engine and with my last burst he began smoking and crashed about 9.5 miles east of Dunkerque. My ammunition being expended I returned to base.[12]

Grassick, Turner, and Latta also claimed kills in this engagement. All told, 242 did exceptionally well for the day, with five enemy aircraft destroyed, three probables, and two damaged on the afternoon patrol alone, all without loss.

While the thirtieth brought an early respite in the form of uneventful patrols due to bad weather, a late-afternoon patrol resulted in a bomber force interception off Dunkirk and a red-letter day for the Canadians. McKnight flamed one of the Messerschmitt Bf 110 escort, which promptly broke into another Bf 110, *both* aircraft going down in flames! Plinston, Turner, and Latta all scored, as did none other than Pilot Officer Noel Karl Stansfeld, who had joined the Squadron in February. The Squadron lost Pilot Officer G. M. Stewart, who had just arrived three days earlier.

The first of June brought the heaviest overall fighting in the air during Operation Dynamo, with Fighter Command's aircraft flying eight separate sweeps over the beachhead as the Germans made a last-ditch attempt to foil the evacuation. In continuous combat from dawn to dusk, the RAF lost thirty-one aircraft, while the Luftwaffe lost nineteen bombers and ten fighters. In a late-afternoon engagement, Stansfeld and McKnight waded into a force of fifteen Junkers 87 Stukas that were dive-bombing shipping just off the beaches. Stansfeld probably destroyed one, but McKnight was particularly successful. He quickly destroyed two of the bombers, probably destroyed two others, and then, ammunition exhausted, carried out a number of feint attacks on the enemy formation, driving off several more Stukas. His victories, coupled with those of Stansfeld and a Bf 109 victory by Turner, resulted in another highly profitable day for 242. The day's fighting essentially broke the back of German resolve to halt the evacuation, and patrols were generally uneventful for the last three days of the withdrawal. Willie McKnight's torrid kill rate could no longer go unrecognized. He became the first Squadron member to be decorated when, on 4 June, an immediate award of the Distinguished Flying Cross was announced. The award was presented to him personally by King George VI three days later.

The Squadron had done very well during the Dynamo operations, destroying twenty-one enemy aircraft, probably destroying another seven, and damaging a further eight; these victories added to at least six during their first sojourn on the Continent. Though six pilots had been killed, and both Smiley and Deacon were POWs, the greatest majority of the losses had occurred prior to the commencement of Dynamo. Once the pilots picked up their initial combat experience, their confidence increased and so did their fighting efficiency.

There was some concern that the Squadron would lose its Canadian identity through the replacement postings of non-Canadian pilots, and this did inevitably come about, since relatively few Canadian RAF pilots were completing fighter training at this time. The plain fact was that with the utter rout taking place in France, the RAF simply hadn't the time to stroke the Canadian national ego, although they did send replacement Canadians to 242 both during and after Dynamo.

The chaotic and rapid evacuation of the bulk of the BEF from Dunkirk had left the covering First French Army in the lurch. While some 50,000 of their number were eventually evacuated, over 30,000 of them were forced to surrender after putting up a particularly valiant resistance to the Germans. Furthermore, two British divisions were still stranded in France. Undoubtedly somewhat fuelled by a sense of guilt, the British government reluctantly made the decision to send a further two divisions to France to augment the British ground forces already there and to aid their French allies in their new campaign south of the Somme and southwest of the Seine.

By 5 June, the three fighter squadrons of the AASF were reduced to only eighteen serviceable aircraft and forced to fly as many as four sorties each per day. Numbers 17 and 242 Squadrons were therefore deployed once again to the Continent. Though they would be the last RAF fighter units to actually deploy, seventeen British fighter squadrons would be engaged in combat over France between the Dunkirk evacuation and the return of the last Hurricanes on 18 June — four days before the capitulation of France. These further combats would cost the AASF fifteen Hurricanes, while Fighter Command would lose one Spitfire, twenty-six Hurricanes, and three Blenheims.[13]

For its part in this last, bitter phase of the campaign, 242 Squadron flew to Le Mans on 8 June, landing in three-plane "vic" formations on the racetrack there, and then flew on to Chateaudun, near Orleans, the same day. From there, housed in large bell tents, they would begin patrolling the next day from forward deployment fields. Noel Stansfeld remembers this very short-lived and hectic period of the campaign: "I recall that when we passed one another on the airfield, we would humorously salute and say, 'Heil Hitler, in case we lose.' This was not appreciated by the senior officers!"[14]

On 9 June, a seven-aircraft formation over Reims was jumped by fifteen Bf 109s, and McQueen was killed. Turner, however, was quick to avenge his friend, gunning down the man who killed McQueen and rapidly dispensing with another Bf 109.[15] All Squadron pilots were extremely active, flying an average of three patrols daily, but a lot of time was consumed flying from Chateaudun to the forward deployment airfields each morning. Most of the missions were either bomber escort duties or flying patrols over the BEF embarkation port of Le Havre.

By the evening of 13 June, the advancing German forces were seriously threatening the field at Chateaudun. By the fourteenth, Paris had fallen, and it was clear that the rest of the country would soon follow suit. The challenge now was to get as much of the force as possible back to England. Thus, the Squadron's hard-working groundcrew were sent to St-Nazaire on the Atlantic coast to await evacuation. After many harrowing experiences, most escaped on the sixteenth on the Polish liner *Sobieski*, reaching England two days later.

Meanwhile, fighting continued to be heavy for 242 Squadron's pilots. The fourteenth of June was particularly busy, with McKnight, Grassick, and Stansfeld successfully adding to what were becoming increasingly impressive victory scores. The next day, 242 moved to Nantes. From there the Squadron flew an average of two to three patrols each day, which turned out to be relatively anticlimactic, although confusion and fear of sabotage reigned supreme at the airfield. On 18 June, when it was obvious that they could do no more, the Squadron returned in various formations to Britain, Stansfeld downing a Heinkel 111 on the way home.

Totally accurate scoring results from this portion of 242's history have never been ascertained, as no precise records were kept. It would appear, however, that McKnight, Stansfeld, and Turner all added at least two confirmed kills to their scores, and the Squadron total may well have been higher. These successes were counted against the loss of only McQueen in action. The unit had been bruised and battered, but they had acquitted themselves well in France and over Dunkirk, acquiring invaluable combat experience and confidence in their own abilities, which would prove so vital in the coming summer months. Stan Turner recalls that by the time 242 arrived in Nantes, they were absolutely exhausted. The Squadron had performed admirably, downing thirty enemy aircraft, but had also taken its own share of casualties. Seven pilots had been killed and two others wounded, while yet another had suffered a nervous break-down. On top of everything else, their CO was missing in action. Most of their combat patrols were being led by either Turner or the feisty twenty-one-year-old Willie McKnight.

After the Dunkirk evacuation we'd been sent to France to operate from an airfield south of Paris. The battle by then was so confused it was often difficult to tell friend from foe. One evening, just before dusk, my wingman and I went after a Dornier bomber. It was too far ahead to catch, but by the time we turned back, we didn't have enough fuel to reach our base at Chateaudun. We landed in a wheat field and, as we climbed out in the dim light, a bunch of French farm workers sprang out of the hedgerows and came at us, yelling and brandishing scythes and sticks. It was touch-and-go to convince them we were on their side. Another night we had trouble with fifth columnists. A couple slipped past our guards and turned on the yellow lights in the Hurricane cockpits. We couldn't see the glow from the ground, but it was visible from the air. Jerry came over and dropped incendiaries, but fortunately there was no damage.[16]

After arriving at Nantes on 14 June, coincidentally the day the Germans staged an elaborate victory parade through the streets of Paris, 242's primary tasks were to provide protective air cover over the Allied evacuation ports of Bordeaux and Brest, to track German troop movements, and to destroy enemy supply dumps as well as other targets of opportunity. Since their groundcrew had already been evacuated, the pilots performed all their own servicing, took turns on guard duty, and slept alfresco under the wings of their aircraft. One evening they were sniped at as they exited a bar in Nantes, which Turner speculated was probably the work of yet another fifth colum-nist. Returning to base, they found the canteen tent deserted but full of liquor, so being resourceful fighter pilots, they decided to have a party. Turner recalls that McKnight refused to drink from a glass. Instead, whenever he felt like a drink, he would grab a bottle, smash it open at the neck, and down it straight without further ceremony.

The day France surrendered, French soldiers set up machine guns along our runway. "All aircraft are grounded," an officer told us. "There's to be no more fighting from French soil." We saw red. A brawl was threatening when I felt a tap on my shoulder. Behind me was a British Army officer, who had come out of the blue. "Go ahead and take off," he said. "I'll look after these chaps." He pointed to his platoon which had set up machine guns covering the French weapons. The French officer shrugged and left.[17]

By one o'clock in the afternoon, they had been told to return to the United Kingdom, becoming in the process the second to last RAF squadron to leave France. Prior to departing, they destroyed several Hurricanes that were not airworthy and set fire to the canteen, lamenting the loss of all their fine liquor. Scruffy and wild-looking, and feeling angry, bewildered, and emotionally deflated by the cataclysmic events which had recently befallen them, they climbed exhausted into their aircraft and set course for the British Isles.

———————

In all, the RAF lost 453 front-line fighter aircraft during the Battle of France, of which 386 were Hurricanes and 67 were Spitfires. However, only 75 were lost in air-to-air combat; the remainder were either destroyed on the ground or under repair in a time of fallback and had to be abandoned.

Though the Hawker Hurricane performed yeoman service for the RAF in France, if any one aircraft emerged as outstanding it was Willi Messerschmitt's nimble little Bf 109E. Tests done on a captured '109 at the Royal Aircraft Establishment at Farnborough verified what many RAF pilots already realized:

. . . [analysis] confirmed the already widely-held opinion that the Hurricane, even when fitted with the Rotol three-blade constant-speed airscrew, was inferior to the German fighter in all respects with the exception of low-altitude maneuverability and turning circle at all altitudes. In so far as the Spitfire I was concerned, when fitted with the two-pitch airscrew — and at that stage of the war virtually all Spitfires were fitted with such airscrews as priority in the supply of constant speed units had been allocated to bombers — this was also bested from virtually every aspect of the Bf 109E-3, although [the Spitfire's] inferiority was markedly reduced by the application of a constant-speed airscrew with which the average production Spitfire was only marginally slower than its German contemporary at rated altitudes. It was ascertained that the Messerschmitt could outclimb the Spitfire up to 20,000 feet, above which altitude the British fighter possessed an edge, but the German fighter could always elude the Spitfire in a dive, the float carburetor of the Merlin engine of the latter placing it at a distinct disadvantage. However, the Spitfire possessed a definite superiority in maneuverability at all altitudes as a result of its lower wing loading, a smaller turning circle, and enjoyed a distinct advantage above 20,000 feet.

The consensus of opinion among RAF pilots who had an opportunity to evaluate the Bf 109E-3 in flight was that it provided a formidable opponent to be treated with respect.[18]

In the upcoming months, ample opportunities would exist to test this rather succinct analysis in that most practical laboratory of all, the life-or-death world of air combat over the British Isles. The Battle of France was over; the Battle of Britain was about to begin.

1   Noel Stansfeld, letter to author, March 1993
2   Hugh Halliday, *242 Squadron: The Canadian Years*, p. 75
3   John Terraine, *The Right of the Line*, p. 16
4   Hugh Halliday, p. 38
5   Ibid., p. 40
6   Arthur Deacon, tape to author, March 1993
7   Hugh Halliday, p. 40
8   Lloyd Hunt, *We Happy Few*, p. 40
9   Arthur Deacon, tape to author, March 1993
10 Ibid.
11 Adolf Galland, *The First and the Last*, p. 7
12 Hugh Halliday, p. 56
13 John Terraine, p. 161
14 Noel Stansfeld, letter to author, March 1993
15 Hugh Halliday, p. 69
16 Stan Turner, *The Canadians at War 1939/45*, Second Edition, p. 34. © 1986 The Readers' Digest Association (Canada) Ltd. Reproduced with permission.
17 Ibid., p. 35
18 John Terraine, p. 165

2

CLOSE CALL

THE BATTLE OF BRITAIN

*"The ideal age for a fighter pilot in the Battle of Britain was
nineteen years; after that, you had more sense . . ."*
— PAUL PITCHER, 1 (RCAF) SQUADRON

What happened after Dunkirk would provide a very brief breathing
space and a fortuitous period of rejuvenation for Fighter Command,
for its squadrons had taken a dreadful mauling during the French
campaign. While the loss of 453 fighters was a significant cause for
concern, the British aircraft industry would replace them in the
month of June alone. In fact, total fighter production for the months
of June and July combined would be in excess of 940 first-line aircraft, Spitfires and Hurricanes. Of far greater concern was the loss of
362 combat-ready fighter pilots. It would be some time before
BCATP graduates started to swell the personnel coffers, and the
throughput at the Operational Training Units had its limits.

From the French capitulation on 22 June until the first full thrust
of the Luftwaffe against England on 13 August, encounters between
the two air forces were sporadic and indecisive. Hitler strongly
believed that England could be brought to her knees over time
through the slow strangulation of her sea supply lanes. Thus the
German High Command had spent very little time preparing invasion plans. In fact, it was only the British attack on the French fleet
at its anchorage at Mers-el-Kebir in Oran on 3 July, coupled with
increasing signs of Soviet belligerence and independence of purpose

in Romania and the Baltic States, that convinced Hitler of the need for a decisive and urgent campaign against the United Kingdom.[1] It would be mid-July before his planners could lay before him a detailed concept of operations for the invasion of Britain — codenamed Operation Sealion. Had he been prepared to carry on the momentum of attack immediately following his victory over France, that narrow margin of resource sufficiency which ultimately assured the success of Fighter Command in the Battle of Britain would have been significantly reduced.

What then were the relative strengths and weaknesses of the two adversaries that summer of 1940? Though numerically far superior, the size of the Luftwaffe must be put into the perspective of an attacker versus a defender. A fairly well entrenched maxim of war states that a force on the offensive should possess a firepower ratio of at least three to one over its adversary. According to that thinking, the Luftwaffe and Fighter Command of the RAF were relatively evenly matched. On 20 July the combined serviceable and ready-for-action strengths of *Luftflottes* 2 and 3 on the Continent, augmented by the long-range assets of *Luftflotte* 5 in Norway, totalled 656 single-engine fighters, 202 twin-engine fighters, 248 dive bombers, and 864 bombers. On a 7 July stocktaking, Fighter Command possessed 644 serviceable fighter aircraft and 1,259 combat-ready pilots. The British assets were organized in three (eventually four) groups of fifty-two squadrons — a considerable surplus over the forty-six fighter squadrons for which Dowding had struggled ceaselessly since the Munich crisis. Of those combat-ready squadrons, nineteen were Spitfire units and twenty-five were equipped with the doughty Hurricanes.

Both sides had clear advantages. During the Great War, scout pilots had learned to fly in line-abreast formations with 150-to-200-foot lateral separation, which allowed them to concentrate on lookout against attack and to search for the enemy without fear of collision. It also allowed them a sufficient turning radius to defeat an enemy attacking from the stern, since the lateral separation distance represented the turning radius described by a hard, defensive, break turn at combat speeds in the scouts of the day. During the golden years of peace of the 1920s and 1930s, almost all nations had forgotten this invaluable lesson. They had reverted to very close formations, usually in vics of three; pretty at airshows, but tactically unsound.

The Luftwaffe had relearned the virtues of the pair of fighters as the minimum fighting unit when they sent the Condor Legion to the aid of Generalissimo Franco during the Spanish civil war. Through trial and error, they developed the two-ship *rotte* or element, with one member of the formation the designated leader and attacker, the other the designated wingman and protector of the leader. These aircraft flew as close to line-abreast as possible (i.e., the wingman within 30° of the leader, providing good cross-cover to the vulnerable rear quadrant). The wingman, however, had to collapse to a 45°–60° "fighting wing" position on the leader during a hard-manoeuvring combat attack phase, with the proviso that he reassume his near-line-abreast positioning for lookout and search as soon as the dynamics of combat permitted. Although some lookout and protective cover could be provided by a good wingman in "fighting wing," his lookout productivity was much greater in the near-line-abreast position. The lateral separation of the two fighters in the *rotte* had increased from First World War numbers to around 600 feet — a reflection of the increased combat turn radii which were generated by the higher combat speeds of the new fighters.

The Germans also learned to combine two *rottes* into a four-ship basic formation called a *schwarme*, with lateral distance across the *schwarme* increasing to 1,800 feet. Vertical displacement between the two *rottes* was also considered tactically viable, since it gave one of the elements an altitude advantage, made the overall formation harder to detect because the aircraft were not all in the same horizontal plane, and afforded some detection capability to an attack from out of the sun. Furthermore, the Germans practised formation tactics with *schwarmes* grouped together as squadrons.

The RAF, on the other hand, had devised very stereotyped set-piece tactics based on the three-ship close vic formation with all its drawbacks. This was due to an almost exclusive concentration on attacks against a massed bomber fleet, flying in a straight line and not manoeuvring against attacking fighters. Thus, RAF combat manoeuvres were predicated upon a highly predictable, non-manoeuvring enemy. By tailoring their tactics to this perceived threat, Fighter Command became sadly predictable in its own right. Attack formation tactics were reduced to a series of six rigid formation attacks which assumed no fighter escort for the enemy bombers — a fatal assumption for far too many young RAF fighter pilots in 1940. The typical transit formation was the tight, three-plane vic, or "vee," with or without the addition of a single "weaver" above and behind the formation theoretically to protect it from attack from astern. In reality, the weaver was himself highly vulnerable and provided little additional security for the formation. The attack phase would consist of either a highly predictable "peeling off" for individual firing passes from the same direction, or a repositioning to close line astern for turns, and a further repositioning to close vic for the attack phase. Not only was the vic formation highly vulnerable to attack from above and behind, but three or more aircraft in close line astern became the epitome of vulnerability! To make matters worse, the complex attack manoeuvring called for slavish use of radio commands — a bad dependency, since British radios of the period were notoriously unreliable. In the highly dynamic world of aerial combat, with many people using and abusing the same radio frequency, the chances of a successful transmission of commands occurring and being understood by all members of the formation were remote. The prewar RAF was absolutely convinced that dogfighting had died as an art form in the Great War. Pathetically little fighter-versus-fighter practice was conducted, and when it was done, it was on a one-on-one basis, diametrically opposed to the German practice of formation tactics whenever possible. In fairness to the RAF's fighter leaders during the Battle of Britain, it must be noted that many were quite quick to discard the rigid vic formations and set-piece attacks, adopting some variant of the more open German attack formations and "pairs" tactics.

Both the Luftwaffe and Fighter Command possessed recent combat experience, and almost all their units had at least a core of battle-hardened veterans. Sadly for the RAF, the valuable combat lessons learned in blood over France were not immediately passed on to the fighter Operational Training Units. There, novice fighter pilots were taught merely to fly their high-performance aircraft rather than fight with them. The urgent need to pass on the experiences of the veterans to the tyros had not yet been grasped.

Since most of the impending air combat would occur over British territory, a sizeable number of Fighter Command pilots either making successful crash landings or parachuting to safety would be able to fight again. Luftwaffe aircrew in similar circumstances were lost for good. The same held true for crashed RAF aircraft on British soil, many of which could be repaired or rebuilt for later service. Luftwaffe aircraft carcasses not used for comparative evaluation and study simply went into the aluminum melting pot to be recycled as Spitfires and Hurricanes.

The "jewel in the crown" for Britain, however, was its radar warning network. The British plan centred on the all-out effort to stop the

Luftwaffe before they bombed, and not afterwards. Though the Germans possessed primitive radar of their own in 1940, they had dangerously underrated the British capability, and their intelligence network made no mention of the twenty-one highly visible and vulnerable "Chain Home" (CH) fixed-mast stations, supported by thirty "Chain Home Low" (CHL) rotating antenna stations and fixed antennas, which tracked both enemy shipping and aircraft. The fragile masts of the CH stations in particular, arranged systematically along Britain's coasts, were impossible to hide and pathetically open to air attack.

Another electronic advantage possessed by the British was the radio monitoring, or "Y Service," which provided continuous surveillance of German operational frequencies. While not technologically mature enough to be of extensive tactical value, it was often helpful in determining the units of the airborne German raiders, and thus in predicting return courses to home bases. This was in turn useful for vectoring RAF fighters onto interception courses. Due to a certain laxness on the Germans' part regarding radio silence, the Service was also useful in predicting enemy intended actions once airborne, as well as their altitude, which was not provided by the radar of the day. The delays in getting rapid warning to airborne friendly fighters were, however, often heartbreaking, as Section Officer Morris of the Service recalls:

There were occasions when we would intercept a message from a German formation approaching RAF fighters . . . having spotted our aircraft before they themselves were observed. We were then likely to hear: "*Indianer unten funf Uhr, Kirchturen 4, Aufpassen.*" (Bandits below at five o'clock, height 4000 meters, look out.)

In those days, we were unable to get this information through in time for it to be of tactical use, and we would get hopping mad that we had no means of warning our fighters that they were about to be jumped. Then "*Angreifen!*" (Attack!) the formation leader would yell, and we would know that the German fighters were diving on their target.

I would often hear one of the WAAF [Women's Auxiliary Air Force] operators murmuring, "Oh God . . . oh God . . . please . . . please look up . . ." and I knew how helpless she felt.[2]

All the radar, radios, and Air Observer data was channelled to Bentley Priory, Sir Hugh Dowding's headquarters, and into its underground

Operations Room. From this nerve centre, the air battles were centrally controlled with data and orders, then disseminated downwards to the various Group Operations Rooms, and from there to the Sector Operations Rooms, which held tactical control over the friendly fighters.

———•••••———

But what of an official RCAF unit presence in Britain during this prelude to the battle? The first RCAF formation to set foot in the U.K. was Number 110 Army Cooperation Squadron under Squadron Leader W. D. Van Vliet, arriving on 25 February 1940. This unit was equipped with Lysanders and, due to operational training requirements, was too late to see service (perhaps fortuitously) in France. A second Army Cooperation Squadron, Number 112, arrived at the end of May, with the first true RCAF fighter squadron disembarking on 20 June, coincidental with the fall of France. This unit, Number 1 (RCAF) Squadron, under the command of Squadron Leader E. A. McNab, would form the vanguard of a highly distinguished representation by RCAF fighter units in the European air campaign. After a brief operational training period, its members would acquit themselves admirably later in the battle. Paul Pitcher, an eventual luminary of Number 1 Squadron, recalls the origins of the unit and its early days in England:

> The core of Number 1 (RCAF) Squadron in August and September of 1940 consisted of former members of Number 115 Auxiliary Squadron from Montreal, which was formed in 1935 and merged at the outbreak of war with Number 1, a permanent force Squadron. As a result, most of us were professionals or businessmen in our late twenties and early thirties, some married, and quite conscious of the validity of the then-current philosophy that, "the ideal age for a fighter pilot in the Battle of Britain was 19 years; after that, you had more sense."[3]

Meanwhile, 242 Squadron, bloodied but unbowed, was regrouping at Coltishall in Norfolk. Squadron Leader Gobeil, who had not been a universally popular commander, had been hastily and unceremoniously returned to Canada, and the remaining veterans of 242 were not made to feel particularly welcome at Coltishall. Though their self-confidence was high, their morale was low, and they lacked firm, caring leadership. All that was about to change when, on 24 June, a short, dynamic Englishman with a very pronounced, lurching gait arrived to take command of the Squadron. The man was Squadron Leader Douglas Robert Steuart Bader. After having lost both legs in a dreadful crash in 1931, Bader was invalided out of the Service. Through persistent badgering and the sheer force of his indomitable will, he was able to convince an RAF medical review board, and subsequently the Central Flying School, that he could fly just as well as any man with legs, and was thus reinstated to flying duties. He got his first confirmed kill at Dunkirk, the first of twenty-two and a half confirmed victories that he would score prior to having a mid-air collision over France and becoming a prisoner of war in 1941.

In 1979, Sir Douglas recounted his impressions of the earliest days with 242 for *Airforce* magazine:

242 had already seen action in France in the early part of 1940, and had fought gallantly under impossible conditions, taking off from airfields which had been over-run by the Germans while the Squadron was in the air, so that they had to land even farther back. Then the pilots were rearming and refueling in preparation for the next operational sortie. From the general shambles of defeat in France, the pilots finally flew their Hurricanes back to England in twos and threes, while the remnants of groundcrew came back under the leadership of their splendid Adjutant, Flying Officer Peter Macdonald, MP.

It had been at Coltishall for a short time without a Squadron Commander — with one Flight Commander, an Englishman, and only the clothes they wore, the rest having been lost in France. At Coltishall were 242 (Hurricanes) and 66 (Spitfires) Squadrons. The Station Commander — a non-operational disciplinarian — had not received 242 with much enthusiasm, particularly as one of his first contacts with them was when Stan Turner fired his revolver into the ceiling of the Mess one evening!

The truth was that 242 had arrived back from operational duties in France into the chaos which surrounded the remnants of the British Army and the Royal Air Force, which had been sent to France at the end of 1939/beginning of 1940, and were now back home in a hurry. England was unprepared for them, as France had fallen too quickly. Air Vice-Marshal Leigh-Mallory, AOC 12 Group, had sent for me and told me to take over 242 and had said:

"They are 90% Canadians, pretty rough and lacking in discipline; they've had a bad time in France." He added: "Good luck in your first command, and ask for anyone you want."

When I arrived at 242 Squadron, I found a collection of sullen, brassed-off pilots and groundcrew who did not welcome their new CO with any degree of enthusiasm. There was nothing wrong with their morale — they were just bloody-minded.

I was most sustained by Peter Macdonald and Bernard West, the Squadron's Engineer Warrant Officer. West was a regular of the best type, with twenty years service behind him. I got rid of one or two pilots who clearly disliked flying in the face of the enemy, and imported two outstanding Flight Commanders, both English, Eric Ball, and George Powell-Sheddon. Eric won a DFC in the Battle of Britain, was shot down in the Western Desert later in the war, and was killed flying a Meteor soon after he returned from being a POW. George Powell-Sheddon, DSO, DFC, retired from the RAF as a Group Captain some years ago. George had a hell of a stutter which went into treble crescendo when he got excited. No squadron has ever broken up more quickly than did 242 one day in August, 1940. The R/T silence was suddenly shattered, as we climbed, by a high-pitched scream: "The th-th-th-thousands on our left." When we finally got back into formation, it was discovered that George had seen some barrage balloons glinting in the sun. He was never allowed to forget it.[4]

Number 1 Squadron under Ernie McNab had moved to Croydon airfield, just south of London, to get operationally ready for its impending baptism by fire. Along with McNab, the initial complement of pilots consisted of Flight Lieutenants V.B. Corbett and G.R. McGregor, Flying Officers E.W. Beardmore, C.E. Briese, E. de Brown, B.E. Christmas, J.P.J. Desloges, R.L. Edwards, G.G. Hyde, J.W. Kerwin, T.B. Little, P.W. Lochnan, W.B.M. Millar, H. de Molson, A.D. Nesbitt, R.W. Norris, J.D. Pattison, O.J. Peterson, P.B. Pitcher, E.M. Reyno, B.D. Russel, R. Smither, W.P. Sprenger, C.W. Trevena, and A.M. Yuile. Many of Number 1's "originals" would eventually become very distinguished fighter leaders. While they were non-operational for the initial engagements of the Battle of Britain, they would make their presence felt very forcibly as the summer progressed.

From early July until mid-August, the Luftwaffe, in an attempt to lure Fighter Command into the air in force, launched a preliminary round of probing attacks known as *Kanalkampf* (Channel Battle) against British ports and coastal shipping. The first engagement of significance occurred on 10 July, when a large convoy was bombed off the Dover coast. A huge dogfight involving more than a hundred aircraft developed over the Channel, and Fighter Command accounted for eight of the Luftwaffe while losing only one of its own. 242 Squadron was in the thick of it. Sub-Lieutenant Gardner, a Fleet Air Arm transplant and representative of the progressive "de-Canadianization" of the Squadron, doggedly pressed home multiple attacks on a Heinkel 111 that was bombing the convoy. Later in the day, John Latta severely damaged another Heinkel, but for the next seven weeks, combat pickings for 242 were lean. Though the Squadron was kept busy on convoy patrols, scrambling after elusive, probing raiders and patrolling the airfield, only seven actual combats would occur between 10 July and 30 August, resulting in the confirmed destruction of five enemy raiders. This was largely because Coltishall, on the northern flank of the battle arena, was well off the main route of the German attacks. The brief respite gave Bader and his pilots a chance to hone their formations and tactics. Though there was no time to rewrite the tactics manuals, and the four-ship spread formations used by the Germans had not yet gained widespread acceptance, Bader significantly widened the vic formations and installed two or three weavers to protect the vulnerable tail area of the battle flights.

On 11 July, the second day of *Kanalkampf*, Canada suffered her first fighter pilot casualty of the battle. Pilot Officer D. A. Hewitt from Saint John, New Brunswick, serving with 501 Squadron, fiercely attacked a Dornier 17 bomber but drew accurate return fire from the rear gunner. Spewing smoke and flames, his battered Hurricane plunged vertically into the Channel. Duncan Alexander Hewitt would be the first of twenty Canadian fighter pilots to die during the Battle of Britain.

Towards the end of July, Hitler told Luftwaffe chief Göring to be ready to launch the main air offensive against Britain on twelve hours' notice. Göring begged for a reprieve, since his plans were incomplete. Unfavourable attack weather then played into his hands. Throughout *Kanalkampf*, the Germans had grasped the importance of radar to the British defences, although they had seriously underestimated its capability.

Hitler's *Führerdirectiv* No. 17 of 1 August had authorized Göring to attack at his convenience anytime after the fifth. After two weather delays, Luftwaffe forecasters predicted a period of fair weather starting on 13 August, a date that would later acquire historic significance as *Adlertag* (Eagle Day). On 12 August, elite Luftwaffe units made a concerted attempt to blind Britain through elimination of the precious radar sites while simultaneously attacking some forward airfields. Though some radar sites were hit hard, only the Ventnor radar on the Isle of Wight was put off the air, and then for only three days.[5] The concept of the attacks had been well thought out, but the execution fell short of expectations and no permanent damage was done. Furthermore, although the Germans somewhat understood the importance of the radar, they failed to grasp the significance of the fighter direction system to which it was tied, such as the Sector Operations Rooms, and their failure to pursue these vital targets would cost them dearly.

Poor weather and muddled German signals made the greatly anticipated *Adlertag* on 13 August highly anticlimactic. Some primary objective British airfields were damaged but the day's scoresheet was decidedly in favour of the RAF. Forty-five Luftwaffe aircraft were lost, compared with only thirteen from Fighter Command, and many of the RAF pilots survived. After a bad weather day on the fourteenth, the Luftwaffe attacked once more in great strength on the fifteenth, with the airfields and production facilities again receiving priority attention. Luftwaffe intelligence seriously underestimated available British fighter strength, however, and though once again some of the fighter airfields were damaged, Göring's air fleets took a dreadful mauling, losing seventy-five aircraft compared to thirty-four from Fighter Command. Number 1 (RCAF) Squadron felt the impact of this day's raids when a group of fifteen Bf 110 fighter-bombers made a determined low-level attack on the airfield at Croydon, inflicting serious damage. On the plus side, all of the attackers were shot down. Number 1 Squadron was deployed to the other side of London at Northolt on gunnery training and missed the action, but Squadron Leader McNab, attached to an RAF squadron to gain combat experience, drew first blood for the RCAF in Britain when he shot down a Dornier bomber over Kent. After this raid, 1 Squadron became a lodger unit at Northolt and would remain so until early October.

In the wake of the raids on 15 August, Luftwaffe Intelligence again seriously underestimated the strength of Fighter Command. By the

Luftwaffe's reckoning, Fighter Command should by now have been reduced to an average of 300 serviceable aircraft. Fighter Command actually had nearly twice that number of serviceable Spitfires and Hurricanes at readiness. In fact, nearly 700 fighters had been turned out of British factories since the end of June. These numbers are somewhat misleading, however, as Dowding was forced to disperse them throughout a great deal of the country at any given time, thus often ensuring a numerical advantage for the escorting Bf 109s on any given raid. Nonetheless, that numerical advantage was often more than offset by the flexibility provided by the radar sites, allowing Fighter Command excellent fuel reserves, while the German fighters were operating near their maximum radius of action.

Concerned over bomber losses, Göring further hamstrung his fighter pilots by tying them to very close escort of the bombers. Adolf Galland recalls some of the frustrations associated with minimal fuel and bomber escort:

> With additional fuel tanks, which could be released and discarded after use, as employed later by both sides and which we had already tried successfully in Spain, our range could have been extended by 125 to 200 miles. At that time, this would have been just the decisive extension of our penetration. As it was, we ran daily into the British defenses, breaking through now and then, with considerable loss to ourselves, without substantially approaching our final goal.
>
> Failure to achieve any noticeable success, constantly changing orders betraying lack of purpose, obvious misjudgment of the situation by the Command, and unjustified accusations had a most demoralizing effect on us fighter pilots, who were already overtaxed by physical and mental strain. We complained of the leadership, the bombers, the Stukas, and were dissatisfied with ourselves. We saw one comrade after the other, old and tested brothers in combat, vanish from our ranks. Not a day passed without a place remaining empty at the Mess table. New faces appeared, became familiar, until one day these too would disappear, shot down in the Battle of Britain.
>
> The reproaches from higher quarters became more unbearable. We had the impression that, whatever we did, we were bound to be in the wrong. Fighter protection created many problems which had to be solved in action. As in Spain, the bomber pilots preferred close screening in which their formation was surrounded by pairs

of fighters pursuing a zigzag course. Obviously the proximity and the visible presence of the protective fighters gave the bomber pilots a greater sense of security. However, this was a faulty conclusion, because a fighter can only carry out this purely defensive task by taking the initiative in the offensive. He must never wait until he is attacked because he then loses the chance of acting. The fighter must seek battle in the air, must find his opponent, attack him, and shoot him down. The bomber must avoid such fights and he has to act defensively, in order to fulfill his task: war from the air. In cooperation between bomber and fighter, these two fundamentally different mentalities obviously clash. The words of Richthofen expressed during World War I, summarizing the task of the fighters, often came to our lips. Fundamentally they are still valid today. "The fighter pilots have to rove in the area allotted to them in any way they like, and when they spot an enemy they attack and shoot him down; anything else is rubbish."

We fighter pilots certainly preferred the "free chase during the approach and over the target area." This in fact gives the greatest relief and the best protection for the bomber force, although not perhaps a direct sense of security. A compromise between these two possibilities was the "extended protection," in which the fighters still flew in visible contact with the bomber force but were allowed to attack any enemy fighter which drew near to the main force.[6]

Through 18 August, the Luftwaffe continued its policy of widespread attacks on various installations, hoping to drive Dowding's fighter squadrons to exhaustion. When a late-evening mission on the eighteenth met fierce opposition over the Thames Estuary and Luftwaffe total losses on the day rose to seventy-one, the Germans could no longer pretend that they had been successful in achieving air superiority over southern England. While the weather provided a brief respite for both sides, the Luftwaffe considered its options. On 24 August, the Luftwaffe launched a concentrated, all-out assault on the fighter airfields defending the Metropolitan London area as well as aircraft factories and industrial targets along the Thames Estuary. This crucial phase would last until 6 September, and night raids in small numbers were also launched in a concerted effort to exhaust the defences. Number 1 Squadron finally tasted first blood on 26 August:

Shifted to North Weald, northeast of the capital, to relieve another squadron, the RCAF pilots completed one patrol over their new sector without incident. In mid-afternoon, while on a second patrol, they were informed by ground control that a raid was approaching across Essex. A Spitfire squadron drew off the escort of German fighters, leaving the bombers, some 25 or 30 Do 215s, for the Canadians. Maneuvering his men like a football team, S/L McNab led them in a diving attack out of the sun. He destroyed one bomber before the Dorniers' return fire forced him to land his damaged Hurricane. F/O R.L. Edwards of Cobourg, Ontario, flying next to his leader, opened fire at very close range and shot the tail off another bomber. But his aircraft was hit by the heavy cross fire from the enemy gunners and it followed the Dornier to earth. F/O Edwards was the first member of the RCAF to lose his life in combat with the enemy. F/O J.P.J. Desloges' Hurricane was also damaged in the action and he forcelanded. But another Dornier was shot down by F/L G.R. McGregor and four were damaged by F/Os H. de M. Molson, A.D. Nesbitt, T.B. Little, and F/L V.B. Corbett. In their first engagement, the RCAF pilots had destroyed three of the enemy and damaged four, with a loss to themselves of one pilot killed.[7]

From now on, 1 Squadron would be in the thick of battle. Their end-month exploits are indicative of the highly charged activity that was facing the defending fighter squadrons in the Metropolitan area at that time.

On the last day of August the Squadron was in action twice with varying success. A morning patrol over Dover was surprised by some high-flying Messerschmitts which dived out of the sun and shot down three Hurricanes. Fortunately all three pilots were able to bail out, but F/L Corbett and F/O G.G. Hyde suffered burns about the face, hands and legs. The score was evened in the afternoon when the Squadron was scrambled to meet a raid over Gravesend. Blue Section engaged the escorting Me 109s while other pilots attacked the bombers. F/Os T.B. Little and B.E. Christmas each accounted for an Me 109 and F/O R. Smither damaged another so badly that smoke streamed from it. A Do 215 that F/O J.W. Kerwin attacked dived headlong into the sea, while another shed fragments from its tail as a result of F/O B.D. Russel's bursts. The Canadians lost one aircraft when the Hurricane flown by F/O Desloges was shot down in flames; the pilot was severely burned before he could take to his parachute.[8]

Paul Pitcher recalls life in 1 (RCAF) Squadron during the battle, and the great respect the Canadians had for the sturdy, dependable Hurricane.

On arrival in the UK, the only operational type of aircraft we had ever flown was the Fairey Battle, so you can imagine the awe in which we held the Hurricane when we were first thrown into its cockpit. It turned out to be an ideal aircraft for us in the circumstances; sturdy, easy to fly, a steady gun platform capable of withstanding almost any amount of abuse and equipped with a very reliable engine. To give an example of its steadiness, one of our pilots, whose Hurricane had been damaged in combat, was unable, on returning for landing at base, to lower the port undercart. He landed on one leg and by dint of applying increasing left hand pressure on the rudder, he was able to bring the aircraft almost to a stop before the starboard wing and propeller hit the ground. By way of result, the aircraft was again serviceable in a matter of days. As a combat aircraft, its disadvantages, compared to the Me 109, were lack of speed, limited operational ceiling, and the absence of cannons in its armament. On the other hand, despite Len Deighton's assertion in his book *Fighter* that the Me 109 had a tighter turning radius, many of us survived a rear-end attack by a '109 by putting the aircraft into such a tight turn that, as a result of "G" force, your eyeballs were hanging down to your chin. The '109 appeared unable to keep on our tails . . .

None of us had the benefit of OTU training as all training, including formation flying, tactics, and air firing was carried out in the Squadron under the guidance of RAF personnel. The formation flying and tactics were taken from antediluvian Air Ministry manuals and the losses of "Tail End Charlies" were a common occurrence.

Life in the Squadron and on the Base at Northolt was chaotic, but there were a lot of laughs and we all drank too much and slept too little. Apprehension was a constant companion to the extent that at readiness, when a telephone bell rang in the dispersal hut, twelve pilots automatically drifted outside and peed against the wall of the hut. The only time at which apprehension was not present was when we were actually in combat, at which time we were far too busy to experience it. On the other hand, fatigue from the continual pressure of multiple daily operational sorties was a continuing problem, which was ultimately relieved by Hitler's decision to divert bombing attacks from fighter airfields, communications and RDF installations to the City of London . . .[9]

Until this time, the brunt of the German attacks were being borne by the fighter units of 11 Group under Air Vice-Marshal Keith Park in the southeast, and, to a certain extent, those of 10 Group in the southwest under Air Vice-Marshal Sir Christopher Quintin Brand. Air Vice-Marshal Trafford Leigh-Mallory and his 12 Group forces in the central region of the country were highly frustrated by their lack of combat to date, and were extremely eager to enter the fray. The units of 12 Group had been forced into the subordinate role of support to 11 Group; their mission during raids was to come south and cover Park's airfields from attack while the 11 Group squadrons engaged the enemy as far forward as possible. Fuelled by this sense of frustration, a great deal of animosity broke out between the two commanders, Park and Leigh-Mallory, and this animosity would prove costly to the RAF.

A 26 August request to 12 Group by Park to cover 11 Group's airfields supposedly (according to Leigh-Mallory) arrived late, resulting in an unprotected Debden being badly mauled by the Luftwaffe. A monumental clash of opinions between Leigh-Mallory and Park now became a very public matter when Leigh-Mallory initiated a direct assault on Dowding's and Park's conduct of the battle. He did so by complaining directly to Winston Churchill through Douglas Bader's distinguished Adjutant, the Honourable Peter Macdonald, MP. Leigh-Mallory and his pilots, particularly Bader, were extremely miffed at the supporting role they felt they were playing to 11 Group. They thought it ludicrous to send small, fragmented formations up against the massed Luftwaffe raids, and Bader found in Leigh-Mallory a powerful champion for his "Big Wing" tactics, which advocated the massing of at least three fighter squadrons while on the attack. The "Big Wings" took time to organize once airborne, however, and they were often unable to engage in combat until after the Germans had completed their bomb runs. Number 12 Group countered that it was far better to shoot the German raiders down in droves on target egress than it was to do minimal damage to them prior to bomb release. Bader also vehemently resented the rigid ground controlling then being practised, feeling that the Flight Leader was best qualified to assess the tactical situation and act accordingly. Naturally, these ideas were considered heresy in 11 Group when compared to Dowding's and Park's combat tactics.

During the latter days of August, four new Canadian pilots were posted to 242 Squadron. Pilot Officer Hugh N. Tamblyn from North Battleford, Saskatchewan, was tall and strikingly handsome, and possessed of a quiet yet optimistic nature. He had already had a close brush with death while flying Defiants with 141 Squadron. Next was Flying Officer John G. Cave, who was British born but had been educated in Calgary. Pilot Officer K.M. Sclanders was a Saint John native with previous service in the RAF, and Pilot Officer L.E. Cryderman was a schoolteacher from Toronto.[10] All would feature prominently in 242 Squadron's participation during the remainder of the Battle of Britain. On the morning of 30 August, 242 Squadron was told to deploy forward to Duxford airfield, nearer London. This location would assure them of much more action in the days to come. Late that afternoon, 242 made its presence felt in a big way when they were scrambled to meet an incoming raid. With Bader leading and ignoring his controller's instructions in order to gain the advantage of the sun at his back, the Squadron engaged a far superior force of bombers and fighter-bombers, destroying twelve without loss to themselves. Willie McKnight went wild that day, as witnessed by his combat report:

While patrolling with Squadron over North Weald enemy sighted on left at 1705 hrs. (approx.) Enemy a/c in vic formation stepped from 12,000–18,000 ft., attacked middle section of '110s and two enemy a/c broke off to attack. Succeeded in getting behind one enemy and opened fire at approx. 100 yds; enemy a/c burst into flames and dived towards ground. Next attacked He 111 formation and carried out beam attack on nearest one opening fire at approx. 150–200 yards. Port engine stopped and a/c rolled over on back, finally starting to smoke then burst into flames and crashed to earth. Lastly was attacked by Me 110 but succeeded in getting behind and followed him from 10,000 ft. to 1,000 ft. Enemy a/c used very steep turns for evasive action but finally straightened out. I opened fire at approx. 30 yards, enemy's starboard engine stopped and port engine burst into flames. Enemy crashed in flames alongside large reservoir. No rear fire noticed from first two enemy but last machine used large amount.[11]

While both 1 Squadron and 242 Squadron were making their presence felt, they were not by any means a full measure of Canada's contribution to the Battle of Britain. Though the forty-two Canadian pilots in these two units would destroy nearly sixty German aircraft and probably destroy or damage a further fifty, individual Canadian members of RAF fighter squadrons would at least equal this impressive record. Here are some of their stories:

Number 213 Squadron operated over the area between Portland and the Isle of Wight, in concert with 238 Squadron. Pilot Officer J. E. P. Laricheliere of Montreal flew with 238 during the battle and amassed a unique record in scoring six confirmed kills in only two days of air combat. Though his promising career as a fighter pilot was snuffed out by his death in action on 16 August, his star shone very brightly on 238 Squadron . . .

At midday on August 13th, while patrolling above the clouds over Portland, Laricheliere caught sight of a Ju 88. For fifteen minutes the two aircraft played hide and seek in the clouds until the Canadian caught his opponent in a clear patch and delivered a final burst. With its port engine on fire, the Junkers dived straight into the sea. A motor boat dashed towards the wreck. While Laricheliere was watching the rescue effort, an Me 109 made a surprise attack which he evaded by climbing steeply into the cover of the clouds. A few moments later he returned to the scene and found the Messerschmitt inspecting the wreckage of the bomber. With one good burst, Laricheliere crashed the Nazi into the sea in flames near his first victim. Three and a half hours later, on a second patrol over Portland, he saw something fall into the water below and decided to investigate what was happening above. On climbing through the thick layer of clouds, the Canadian found himself right in the middle of a "very thick" formation of Nazi fighters. It was no place for a lone British aircraft. An Me 110 was in front of his sights, so Laricheliere fired a quick burst, lingered just long enough to see the enemy disintegrate in the air, and then dived into cloud cover.

August 15th was another day of intense activity and the Luftwaffe paid heavily. In late afternoon when strong enemy forces approached Portland, No. 213 Squadron was scrambled to engage them. Within a few moments Laricheliere encountered an Me 110 that he shot down into the sea. Regaining height, he gave chase to a Ju 87 that desperately sought to escape by dodging in and out of the clouds. Laricheliere jockeyed his fighter into position for two bursts at close range. "All kinds of bits and pieces" flew about as the Junkers spun into the water. Once again the Canadian climbed to rejoin the battle and found another '110. The enemy pilot threw his aircraft about in evasive action but in vain. From very close range, Laricheliere hammered a long burst into the port engine. Half the wing seemed to explode and the Messerschmitt cartwheeled into the sea near the coast. With his guns empty — and three more victories to his credit — the Canadian pilot flew home.[12]

Working out of North Weald airfield with 249 Squadron, Flight Lieutenant R. A. Barton of Kamloops, British Columbia, ran up an impressive string of victories during and shortly after the battle. At one point, several Bf 109 fighter-bombers attacked North Weald just as 249 was scrambling for takeoff. Barton attacked six in quick succession, driving one down in flames and damaging two others. Shortly thereafter, he was awarded a richly deserved Distinguished Flying Cross.

Pilot Officer H. T. Mitchell from Port Hope, Ontario, received his baptism of fire in France with 87 Squadron, gunning down three Luftwaffe bombers alone and sharing in the destruction of a fourth. He would add three more confirmed kills and one damaged during the Battle of Britain, and three of these successes would occur during one sortie near Portland in the late afternoon of 14 August. The laconic Mitchell gets full points for brevity, as evidenced by his combat report:

Enemy aircraft sighted in large numbers at 6000–8000 feet. Climbed to 11,000 feet. Came out of the sun at Me 110 and using full deflection from vertical astern blew his tail plane off. Pulled up in steep turn with another Me 110 in sights. Gave him full deflection and saw tracers go into him, but didn't stay around to watch results. Saw Ju 87 doing nothing in particular below me. He dived away into thin layer of cloud, but I caught him in a clear patch and shot him down from dead astern.[13]

One of the most successful Canadians serving with the RAF during the war's early months was Squadron Leader M. H. Brown of Portage La Prairie, Manitoba. He served with great distinction in France, first as a Pilot Officer, then progressing through the officer ranks to command 1 (RAF) Squadron during the Battle of Britain. He scored the majority of his victories, roughly fifteen, while in France, but added at least one and a share in another over England, and was decorated with the DFC and Bar. His confirmed kill during the battle was a Bf 110, which he gunned down in flames at point-blank range. Brown's firing distance was so close that his Hurricane was heavily smeared with oil as he violently broke off his attack on the stricken Messerschmitt, narrowly avoiding a mid-air collision. He himself was shot down on 15 August but, though burned, had managed to keep his priorities straight, as witnessed by this sentiment in a letter home: "I suffered facial burns but they have healed very well and I expect to be flying in a day or two. The next time you send me anything, you might include Spanish peanuts. I was just thinking yesterday how I would like to have a chew at some . . ."[14]

"Hilly" Brown was later promoted to Wing Commander, sent to Malta, and was killed on an offensive sortie over Sicily on 12 November 1941, with a final total of at least eighteen confirmed victories to his credit.

The Luftwaffe continued its all-out assault on the RAF airfields and production facilities until 6 September, although Göring and his staff did not clearly appreciate the extent of damage that they were causing the defenders.

Around this time, Air Vice-Marshal Park pressed hard for a wholesale drain of fighter squadrons from the quiet sectors in order to fuel his daily needs in 11 Group. Dowding wisely resisted, affirming that this would be a desperate measure, to be undertaken only under extreme duress. Furthermore, Dowding felt the already overtaxed control system was incapable of handling any increased volume of friendly air traffic.[15]

Dowding could derive some comfort from the knowledge that a significant reserve of combat-ready, intact squadrons existed outside of 11 Group. Park could (and did) call upon tactical reinforcement from squadrons in Brand's and Leigh-Mallory's flanking Groups, but Brand's contributions in this regard proved more valuable and predictable than Leigh-Mallory's, whose formations — such as Bader's — hardly ever went where Park desired them, and frequently ignored instructions from the controllers, diminishing their effectiveness.

Throughout the Battle of Britain, although both sides continuously overestimated the enemy's losses, the Germans were by far the worst offenders in this respect. They were particularly horrified on 30 August, when Fighter Command was still able to mount a thousand defensive sorties and inflicted woeful losses upon the German formations. Nevertheless, the raids that day did telling damage to Biggin Hill, the Vauxhall factory at Luton, and the airfield at Detling. The following day, equally telling damage was done once more to Biggin Hill, and to Debden, Hornchurch, and Croydon. But Göring did not fathom how close he was to successfully shutting down the RAF's fighter stations. Instead, he chose to waste the next week's effort on production facilities, damage to which would not affect the RAF for a substantial period of time. The Germans had lost over 800 aircraft in the last two months, and this would soon seriously affect their sortie output rate.

During the first week of September, Fighter Command would be able to muster more sorties than both the German fighter and bomber forces combined, and just when one last concentrated, punishing blow against Fighter Command was called for, it would not be forthcoming. Thus evolved a victory for Dowding, the great pacesetter, who husbanded resources so carefully and wisely. Conversely, Göring was an absentee landlord who had little understanding of the true nature and limitations of airpower and provided little cohesion among his Air Fleet commanders to concentrate their resources until vital targets were destroyed.

Instead, he focused his planning staff on the next stage of his agenda: concentrated attacks on London as reprisals for Bomber Command's raid on Berlin on 25 August. On 7 September, Göring strutted along the clifftops at Cap Blanc Nez with two of his Air Fleet commanders, Lörzer and Kesselring, and gloated as wave after wave of Luftwaffe formations thundered overhead enroute to London. He inaugurated this new phase of his aerial assault with a savage, concentrated attack on the East London dock area. The 300 bombers and 600 short- and medium-range escort fighters that made up the attack force took so long to assemble that they provided ample warning to 11 Group Headquarters of a very large raid massing over France. By 4:30 p.m., twenty-one squadrons were airborne to greet a Luftwaffe force that covered nearly 800 square miles of sky. Though the Luftwaffe lost thirty-nine aircraft, Fighter Command also suffered heavily with thirty-one aircraft destroyed. Number 249 Squadron alone lost six Hurricanes in one engagement without scoring a kill when they met a far superior force of Bf 109s.[16] Number 1 Squadron was detained on protective cover duties over Northolt and missed the action taking part to the east.

Number 242 Squadron was in the thick of it, flying as the Duxford Wing in conjunction with an RAF Spitfire unit and a newly formed Czech squadron. They intercepted a very large force of raiders at 20,000 feet northeast of London, destroying ten of the enemy and damaging at least half as many again. Number 19, the RAF squadron, destroyed a further five raiders, as did the gallant Czechs from 310 Squadron, the sum of which gave a certain credence to the "Big Wing" theory, at least on this occasion. All this for the loss of only one Hurricane and pilot — Pilot Officer John Benzie of 242 Squadron.

In spite of the high-pitched defensive battles of the day, many of the German bombers got through and did extensive damage to the East End, and there was a great amount of rancour generated by this attack on the working class heart of the city.[17]

The ninth of September was another day of intense aerial activity in the wake of sporadic raids on the London area the day and night prior. The consistency of the German targeting, however, trumpeted the fact that they had completely changed their strategy. This time, both 242 and 1 Squadrons were heavily involved. At 5:00 p.m., 242 at Duxford, again led by Bader and again in concert with 19 and 310 Squadrons, scrambled to patrol North Weald and Hornchurch. Shortly thereafter, Bader led the two Hurricane squadrons down on a box of sixty German bombers, while the Spitfires of 19 Squadron tackled a similar box of bombers in close trail to the first. Bader's formation was in turn set upon by a large force of Bf 109s, and several of his pilots turned to engage this new threat.

McKnight was one of those who broke into the Bf 109s. A short-burst specialist, he sent one down in flames before two Messerschmitts came after him. He got between them, opened fire again, and saw one shed fragments before going down steeply. Another '109 caught him with a burst, shooting off his left aileron. McKnight dived out of control and witnessed his second victim crash. Regaining control, he flew back to base.

Pilot Officer Latta also engaged a Bf 109 from astern. At a range of 300 yards, he fired for six or eight seconds. The Messerschmitt climbed steeply to the left and turned into a torch, the fire apparently coming from the cockpit area. Latta may have hit a fuel tank. The burning wreck spun away, but the Canadian had troubles of his own. His left aileron was hit and jammed; Latta escaped by diving and was not followed. Yet another '109, attacked by Flight Lieutenant Ball, exploded in mid-air.

Meanwhile, other pilots were harrying the bombers, identified as Do 115s, but more probably the Do 17s of Luftflotte 2. Bader shot down one in flames and knocked holes in several others, weaving about among and below the Dorniers until his ammunition was exhausted. At one point he was caught amidst salvos of bombs as the Germans unloaded their deadly cargoes in their haste to get away. Powell-Sheddon, Richardson, and Lonsdale each flamed Dorniers as well. Lonsdale was caught in a crossfire by enemy gunners and his Hurricane was hit repeatedly, rendering his controls useless. With smoke, oil, and glycol pouring into his cockpit, Lonsdale bailed out at 19,000 feet. He landed in a pine tree at Caterham, slightly injuring one leg. The tree stood on the grounds of a girls' school, and the students stood about giggling for half an hour before local police retrieved Lonsdale with a ladder.

Blue Section, probably in company with some of the Czechs of No. 310 Squadron, shot down two Bf 110s. One of these was a "flamer" credited to Pilot Officer Bush. The other two fell to Pilot Officer Tamblyn . . .

No. 242 Squadron had claimed a total of eleven enemy machines, to which could be added three shot down by No. 19 Squadron and four by No. 310. Yet these victories had not been without a price. Lonsdale, of course, had bailed out safely after his Hurricane was hit. Pilot Officer Sclanders was not so fortunate. He was shot down and killed by Bf 109s. No. 310 lost three Hurricanes and one pilot in the battle.[18]

Meanwhile, 1 Squadron was also busy out of Northolt, as one of twenty-seven squadrons launched against the main bomber force of 300–350 German aircraft.

In a vicious dogfight over southeast London, the Squadron gunned down four of the German raiders. Flying Officer O.J. Peterson attacked a Dornier from such close range that exploding pieces of the bomber shattered his windscreen. His eyes full of tiny pieces of fragmented Plexiglas, the hapless pilot fell nearly two vertical miles before he was able to regain control of his Hurricane.

After three weeks of continuous hectic fighting, the pilots were bone-tired. Usually on duty by 0400 hours, many simply pulled flying clothing on over their pyjamas, thereby minimizing an expense of energy when it came time to go to bed much later in the day. By first light, Squadron pilots had reported to their dispersal hut, donned their Mae West life preservers, taken their parachutes to their Hurricanes, and settled in to wait. The dispersal hut's walls were decorated with girlie pictures and travel posters, as well as a functional centrepeice to all the decorations, the telephone. Its first ringing warned of radar contact with incoming bandits. The second ringing often constituted the scramble call, which was the order to launch. Paul Pitcher recalled that every time that telephone rang, their stomachs rolled over. At the first ringing, many of the pilots would stroll around and try to look nonchalant, and the subsequent wait for the scramble order constituted the most stressful period of all. Once the scramble order came through and twelve pilots started to dash for their aircraft, there was no time to worry. With the aircraft launched in vics of three, the most unpopular positions of all were those of the tail-end charlies, the ones detailed to weave from side to side at the rear of the formation, protecting it from stern attack. With typical gallows humour, pilots joked that they were either promoted from this duty or were buried while performing it.

As the tension built up, the pilots sought relief in various ways. Some tried to sleep the stress away; other partied hard and even travelled from Northolt to London in a 1911 Rolls Royce, complete with a sartorially impeccable chauffeur. Some tried to numb their fears with liquor, while others developed an equally strong aversion to spirits of any kind.

Wing Commander J. A. "Johnnie" Kent of Winnipeg was one of the most celebrated Canadian pilots of the Battle of Britain, with a score of thirteen German aircraft destroyed. He was a pilot of long and varied experience, having won an Air Force Cross for a series of daring experimental flights during which he deliberately flew his aircraft into balloon cables to test the strength of *both*! As a Flight Lieutenant involved in the formation of Number 1 (Polish) Squadron during the summer of 1940, "Kentski" was one of a small group of RAF officers attached to the unit as advisors and instructors. He led the Polish pilots in combat on many occasions, flying out of Northolt and frequently in the company of his fellow Canadians from 1 (RCAF) Squadron, as well as 1 (RAF) Squadron, which was also based there. While serving with the Poles, he destroyed four enemy aircraft, probably destroyed another, and damaged two more, winning both the DFC and a very high Polish decoration, the *Virtuti Militari*. After the battle was officially over, Kent was given command of 92 (Spitfire) Squadron and celebrated his promotion by shooting down three Bf 109s in two days. In 1941, while leading a Wing, he would add a further six Bf 109s to his scorecard and receive a Bar to his DFC.

The fifteenth of September has generally been regarded as the climax of the Battle of Britain, as the Luftwaffe was at its peak raiding strength on that date. After an early-morning mist, the weather cleared. Shortly after 11:00 a.m., radar reported large numbers of German aircraft massing for the first raid. Not only did radar provide ample warning of the massing attacks, but the "Ultra" code breakers at the super-secret Bletchley Park facility were able to provide direct confirmation of a forthcoming second attack prior to launch of the enemy bombers. When the first raid failed, Göring ordered a second attack via signal, and that message was passed direct to Dowding in ample time to prepare a suitable reception for the Luftwaffe. Before the second raid, however, Park's headquarters had been treated to a very high level and not-uncommon visitation in the form of Winston Churchill. As the prime minister's entourage filed into the Operations Room, Park expressed some doubt as to whether the day would bring any enemy activity.

That practised nonchalance was in ample evidence at Fighter Command airfields all over southern England, and if trouble was brewing, the RAF showed no sign of acknowledging it. Distraction was often attempted through popular music of the period. At RAF Station Hornchurch, Pilot Officer "Razz" Berry's gramophone continuously churned out "She Had to Go and Lose It at the Astor" and "Sweet Violetta," while at Duxford, 242 Squadron's loudspeaker blared out "Three Little Fishes," a comic pop tune then in vogue. Bader spent the time visiting the five squadron dispersals within his "Big Wing," bolstering the Poles under his command with his opinion that they would soon be able to go home to Warsaw.

Meanwhile, at 11 Group Headquarters, the plotters were getting every indication that the Luftwaffe was massing for a major raid. Tension and an ominous sense of foreboding hung heavy in the air. Churchill, an extinguished cigar clamped tightly in his teeth, observed that something appeared to be developing. Park assured the prime minister that someone would be there to greet the Luftwaffe upon arrival.

And indeed there *was* someone there to meet them. During this first raid, a force of nearly a hundred Dornier 17s was broken up prior to reaching the capital, and ended up bombing random targets of opportunity. Two of the Dorniers made bombing runs at Buckingham Palace, and a Canadian fighter pilot was intimately involved in the ensuing combat. Pilot Officer A.K. "Skeets" Ogilvie of 609 Squadron rolled in on one of the Dorniers and sent it crashing to earth near Victoria Station. It was later confirmed that the aircraft had been on a final target run to the Palace, and Ogilvie's attack had been instrumental in preventing this Dornier from getting through. Furthermore, the Ottawa native had a royal witness to his shooting prowess in the form of Queen Wilhelmena of the Netherlands, a Palace guest who saw the action from a balcony. Ogilvie later received a touching letter of commendation from the lady, which became one of his most treasured war souvenirs. "Skeets" would get three confirmed kills during the battle, "probably destroy" three others, and damage two more. He subsequently added several more victories to his score and was awarded a DFC prior to being shot down over France and taken prisoner the following year.

The other Dornier had completed a successful bomb run of sorts on the Palace, the net result being that one unexploded bomb ended up unceremoniously in King George's garden! Sergeant Ray Holmes, a Hurricane pilot from 504 Squadron, promptly blew the Dornier out of the air for its troubles.

In response to the first raid, at 11:25 a.m., 242 Squadron scrambled from Coltishall and assembled as a Wing overhead Duxford. The Wing was larger than ever, with five squadrons massed, led by Bader. At 12:15 p.m., this enormous formation of fighters met the German phalanx over Gravesend, with the defenders possessing all the advantages of height and sun position. Furthermore, as was the Luftwaffe's recent habit, the Bf 109 fighter escort was closely tied to the bombers and had no opportunity to take the initiative. As if the Duxford Wing did not present a formidable enough defence, four other fighter squadrons simultaneously set upon the German armada. Bader would later describe this combat as "the finest shambles" he had ever been in. "The air was thick with Spitfires and Hurricanes twisting about; Bader reported that he was seldom able to hold his sights on a target for long for fear of colliding with other fighters.

Pilot Officer Tamblyn wrote that he twice had to wait his turn for a shot at a Do 17 . . ."[19]

During the engagement, Stansfeld, Turner, and Bader all felled Dorniers, Dickie Cork, a Fleet Air Arm pilot, shot down a fourth, Pilot Officer Hugh Tamblyn shared a fifth with a companion, and Pilot Officer Norris Hart downed a Bf 109 in flames. The only British loss was Flight Lieutenant Eric Ball, who was slightly injured while crashlanding his burning Hurricane. Furthermore, the four other squadrons massed with 242 claimed twenty-three destroyed and eight probables in the fight.

Over at Northolt, 1 Squadron on its first scramble had been caught with their pants down near Biggin Hill when they were set upon by some Bf 109s, which came at them from out of the sun. Their formation was broken up, Flying Officer Smither of London, Ontario, was shot down and killed, and only two of the Squadron's Hurricanes were left in a position to engage. Flying Officer Nesbitt was quick to avenge the loss of Smither by gunning down a '109, but then was shot down himself, parachuting to safety near Tunbridge Wells with head injuries.

Around mid-afternoon the Luftwaffe tried again, but Fighter Command lay ready and waiting.

Major Adolf Galland, effectively the point man of the mighty German phalanx, was incredulous at the apparently never-ending regeneration of the RAF's fighters. For ten very long minutes, he fought for his life in the skies over Maidstone, achieving precisely nothing. Then, diving upon a Hurricane formation 2,500 feet below him, he quickly destroyed two of them, his firing range so close and attack so vicious that molten metal from the exploding British fighters beat a tattoo on his windscreen. A further 3,000 feet below him, a third Hurricane offered itself for his attentions. Galland fired a long burst into the engine cowling, drawing flames and smoke. Still the British fighter droned on, its pilot apparently unconcerned. On three more firing passes, Galland raked the Hurricane from stem to stern with gunfire. Now the Hawker aircraft entered a gentle spiral dive, and the German ace could clearly see the British pilot sitting in his cockpit, relaxed, upright, and very dead.

In effect, Fighter Command had made good use of the Luftwaffe's delay in staging the second raid, and while the Messerschmitts sparred with some of the defending fighters, the Dornier and Heinkel bombers paid a heavy price; nearly a quarter of their number were shot down.

Over London, Ernie McNab and Number 1 Squadron dove on a force of twenty Heinkels and slashed them to ribbons. Flying Officer Phil Lochman of Ottawa shot one of the Heinkels into the Thames Estuary, then belly-landed his crippled Hurricane beside it. He then committed a rather rare act for a fighter pilot by personally taking his vanquished foes prisoner and marching them off to captivity.

The afternoon's combat was replete with bizarre experiences. The fabric on Stan Turner's Hurricane tail was set ablaze by German incendiary shells. He was just contemplating the rapid evacuation of his fighter when he flew through a rain cloud, abruptly extinguishing the fire and removing the need to vacate his cozy cockpit. One of the Poles, fiercely intent on administering the coup de grâce to a crippled Dornier, got so close to his adversary that a parachuting crewmember smashed violently into his propeller, with gory and predictable results, badly damaging the prop in the process. Somehow, the Pole managed to get the obscenely decorated Hurricane safely back to earth.[20]

When the day was done, the RAF had euphorically claimed a victory of monumental proportions: 185 enemy aircraft destroyed for a loss of only twenty-nine of the defending fighters, with sixteen pilots killed. Though the British losses stuck, the RAF would eventually reassess the day's score downwards to sixty-one German aircraft destroyed, though no one bothered to inform the British public of this true state of affairs until war's end. Still, it was an impressive victory for Fighter Command.

Two days later, "Ultra" struck gold again when a signal was intercepted from the German General Staff to the officer responsible for the provisioning of troop-carrying aircraft in Holland. The signal authorized the dismantling of certain loading equipment on the Dutch airfields. Churchill asked the chief of the Air Staff for his interpretation of this signal, and what effect it could possibly have on Operation Sealion, the German invasion of the British Isles.

> Cyril Newall had been well briefed; he gave it as his considered opinion that this marked the end of Sealion, at least for this year . . . There was a very broad smile on Churchill's face now as he lit up his massive cigar and suggested that we should take a little fresh air.[21]

There would be many more raids in strength throughout the autumn, and to the naked eye this was just another in a series of postponements of Sealion. This time, however, the postponement was indefinite, and Hitler was now casting his gaze eastwards towards Russia. On 12 October, Hitler would formally defer the invasion until the following spring, and by that time he would be completely preoccupied with battles elsewhere and with planning the invasion of the Soviet Union.

To those not within the elite inner circle, there appeared to be only a slight abatement in the ferocity of the attacks for some time. In fact, the much publicized successes of the Duxford Wing, coupled with the improved tactical position, had influenced Park to henceforth commit his 11 Group squadrons to battle at least in "pairs" strength whenever possible. The practice of massing fighter resources had had some undeniable successes, particularly as a demoralizing factor to the Luftwaffe crews, and when the Wing could be committed to action on favourable terms, high scores tended to prevail. The negative effects were wild, if unintentional, exaggeration of kill claims, excessively long times to rendezvous and organize the Wing, and its cumbersome nature in combat. The Duxford Wing claimed fifty-two enemy aircraft destroyed on 15 September, while in reality it was far less successful.

The eighteenth of September was another big day for Fighter Command in general, and for the Duxford Wing in particular. With Bader leading the five squadrons on a late-afternoon patrol over London, antiaircraft fire drew their attention to a force of around fifty German bombers flying in close formation up the Thames. With no Luftwaffe fighter escorts in sight and the bombers highlighted against a background of bright white clouds, the Wing plunged ravenously upon this tempting target:

> Broken up by the first attack, the Dorniers and Junkers scattered over the sky in confusion. 242 Squadron destroyed ten and shared three more with other squadrons, as well as probably destroying or damaging three. Before the action ended, thirty of the enemy had fallen and seven more may not have reached home. Pilot Officer Campbell engaged six Junkers bombers in succession; he overshot the first, sent the second down in flames, missed the third, aided a Spitfire in shooting the fourth down all ablaze, then chased another and damaged it, and ended his action-packed sortie by setting fire

to the sixth Junkers, which a Spitfire had been attacking. Pilot Officer Hart crashed a brace of Junkers, while Pilot Officer McKnight sent a Do 17 down in flames and aided in the destruction of another '88. Finally, Pilot Officer Tamblyn shot down a Dornier well afire. In addition to these victories won by the Canadian pilots, Squadron Leader Bader scored a double and other pilots destroyed three plus a pair of probables. In his combat report. Bader commented that he had never seen so many parachutes in the air.[22]

At Northolt, 1 Squadron was scrambled many times between the sixteenth and the twenty-six of September, although only three successful combats were fought. The Squadron was also enduring battles of another nature, however, and those battles would last well into the coming year.

Red tape was a constant irritant. At the height of the Battle of Britain, RCAF Headquarters issued orders to No. 1 that sweaters and scarves were not to be worn in place of collars and ties. The diarist suggested that each pilot would have to be sartorially inspected as he leaped into his plane to go up to meet the King's enemies. Later there were regulations which forbade tucking trousers into flying boots. A 1941 diarist noted that headquarters in London could always be relied upon for volunteers for a Squadron dance, but never for a funeral. At one station, the most senior RCAF officer overseas inspected the typewriters in the orderly room and decreed one surplus. Spare parts for a type of plane the Squadron didn't fly would arrive. A draft of groundcrew would show up unannounced. There was a constant stream of niggling questions from headquarters: "It says here on Form 541 that twelve planes took off but the names of only eleven pilots are listed." Personal mail was censored. Headquarters snitched on one airman because he had told his family in a letter home that he had scrounged a pailful of coal; on another because he had won £4 gambling, officially not permitted but which went on constantly . . .[23]

By 24 September, Göring had issued orders to concentrate the bombing on aircraft factories, and the daylight raids on the capital abated substantially. That did not mean that daylight raids in strength were completely a thing of the past. Both Canadian squadrons would have a memorable day on 27 September. In fact, this would turn out to be the RCAF's finest hour during the Battle of Britain. It would also mark the Luftwaffe's last appearance as a major force in daylight over England.

September 27th was the most active and successful day in the history of the RCAF Squadrons during the Battle, a day that was not surpassed until the Battle of Dieppe on August 19th, 1942. About nine o'clock that morning, several waves of raiders crossed the Kentish coast near Dungeness, but only one group succeeded in penetrating inland beyond the Maidstone-Tunbridge line. To meet this threat, the RCAF and Polish squadrons were scrambled from Northolt. Crossing London, they soon sighted the raiders over the Kenley-Biggin Hill area and counted thirty or more Ju 88s escorted by over a score of Me 109s and '110s. Squadron Leader McNab led his two squadrons of Hurricanes in a rear attack on the bombers, while some of the Messerschmitt fighters came down in a vain attempt to protect the Junkers. After harrying the bomber formation, the Canadian and Polish pilots climbed to engage the Me 110s, which had formed their customary defensive circle 2,000 feet above. In the rapid action of the dogfights which ensued, it was difficult to assess results with accuracy, as one enemy aircraft was sometimes attacked by several in succession. The total result, however, appeared to be at least six Nazi planes destroyed (a Ju 88, an Me 109 and four Me 110s, two of which were shared with Polish pilots), a Ju 88 probably destroyed, and an Me 110 damaged. Flying Officer Russel had been particularly successful, shooting down one Me 109, whose pilot quickly bailed out, and crashing two Me 110s, one of which he shared with Polish fighters. The other victories were credited to Squadron Leader McNab, Flying Officers E. de P. Brown and B. E. Christmas who jointly brought down a Ju 88; and to McNab who subsequently crashed an Me 110. Flying Officer McGregor probably destroyed a Ju 88, which went down in a steep spiral dive, streaming smoke; forced to take evasive action, the Canadian pilot was unable to see if his opponent crashed. Finally, Flying Officer Norris shot pieces off an Me 110, which he then left to the attention of other British fighters.

Flying Officer Lochnan's combat was particularly noteworthy. When the action began he was attacked by an Me 109, whose cannon and machine-gun fire did considerable damage to the

Hurricane, shooting off half the right aileron. Lochnan headed for home, but en route, he saw a Ju 88 being attacked. He joined in, fired one burst and then held off while three other Hurricanes set the bomber on fire. After watching the Junkers crash, Lochnan again turned his battered aircraft towards base. Then, he saw another fight between a Hurricane and an Me 110. The Canadian pilot once more joined in and fired three good bursts. The machines were now down to 500 feet and after Lochnan's last burst, delivered from head-on, the enemy pilot swerved and crashed on Gatwick aerodrome. Lochnan decided to land there, left his Hurricane to be repaired, and completed his journey home in a training aircraft. In the engagement, Flying Officer W. Sprenger's plane was also shot up, forcing the pilot to land at Kenley. Flying Officer O.J. Peterson of Halifax, Nova Scotia, who had so frequently distinguished himself during the Battle, did not return from this hard-fought action. His death was the third suffered by the Canadian Squadron.

An hour after being scrambled, the pilots returned to Northolt and the groundcrews swarmed over the Hurricanes, refilling fuel tanks, reloading the guns, checking the equipment, and getting the aircraft ready for the next call for action. It soon came. At noon, another raid approached across the Channel, and again came the order to "scramble." This time the Squadron, as a result of battle casualties, could muster only eight aircraft. Flying Officer McGregor, leading the formation of Nos. 1 and 229 Squadrons, found about twenty Me 109s near Gatwick, some 2000 feet above the Hurricanes. Presently, some of the Messerschmitts dived to attack, and McGregor was able to fire damaging bursts into one. Again the Squadron returned to Northolt, and again the mechanics worked hard to get the machines refueled and rearmed.

At three o'clock, the two Squadrons were ordered up to patrol the Biggin Hill-Kenley area, south-east of London. The Canadian Squadron was now reduced to six serviceable aircraft. Soon after taking off, and while still climbing for height, the Hurricanes were vectored to an enemy raiding force which had crossed the coast between Dover and Dungeness. The German formations, numbering 150 aircraft, divided into several groups, penetrated inland as far as Maidstone; there they veered towards the London docks but were forced to sheer off westwards towards Biggin Hill where Flying Officer McGregor's group of fighters intercepted the retiring bombers. Attacking one formation of fifteen to twenty Do 215s, the Hurricanes scattered the bandits and destroyed at least five. Five of the six Canadian pilots brought their guns to bear with success; Flying Officer Brown shot one Dornier down in flames, Flying Officer McGregor damaged two and Flying Officers Pitcher, Yuile and Russel one each. Of the five damaged Dorniers, four were subsequently finished off by the pilots of No. 229 Squadron. Many Me 109 fighters were overhead during the action, but they made no concerted effort to intervene.

At four o'clock, the Canadian Squadron had landed again. Since nine o'clock that morning the Squadron, with thirteen pilots available, had made 25 sorties on three patrols; it had engaged 70 enemy aircraft in combats that resulted in the destruction of seven, the probable destruction of another, and damage to seven more. Six pilots, Flying Officers McGregor and Brown, Christmas, Pitcher, Russel and Yuile had taken part in all three patrols and between them had accounted for twelve of the fifteen successes credited to the Squadron. Flying Officer McGregor and Flying Officer Russel had each submitted four claims.[24]

Just before noon, the Duxford Wing, now reduced to four squadrons, was patrolling London. Shortly after, Bader led another perfect "bounce" on twenty Bf 109s milling in the region of Dover-Canterbury, achieving complete surprise and destroying thirteen of the Messerschmitts while probably destroying three others. John Latta got two in flames, although his Hurricane was damaged by both cannon and machine-gun rounds in his first engagement. Nevertheless, Latta persevered and finished off his second quarry. Tamblyn also did grave damage to one of the '109s, and Noel Stansfeld scored a probable on a lone Ju 88 which had wandered into the fight. Latta's double victory raised his number of confirmed kills to eight, and both he and Tamblyn were awarded DFCs shortly after this engagement.

This spirited action marked 242's sixty-sixth and last victory in the Battle of Britain. A very sad loss occurred on 17 October when three Squadron pilots engaged a Do 17 over Yarmouth and it offered stout resistance. Pilot Officer Neil Campbell, who had made a fine name for himself on the Squadron in a short period of time, did not return from this engagement. Three weeks later, on 5 November, Norris Hart was killed in a high-level encounter with some Messerschmitts over Sheerness.

Thus ended an extremely strenuous period for the members of 242 Squadron. In the preceding six months, they had fought in three separate campaigns: France, Dunkirk, and Britain. They had destroyed at least eighty-seven and a half enemy aircraft and had lost seventeen of their own number, of which all but three were Canadians:

> . . . [242] had won one Distinguished Service Order (Bader), eight Distinguished Flying Crosses and one Bar to the Distinguished Flying Cross (McKnight). In the Battle of Britain alone, No. 242 had claimed over three score confirmed victories, of which 28-1/2 were credited to eight Canadian members of the Squadron. Numbered among the six pilots killed in action during the Battle and its immediate aftermath were four from Canada: Pilot Officers J. Benzie, K. M. Sclanders, N. N. Campbell and N. Hart . . .[25]

At the end of November, the Squadron moved from Duxford back to Coltishall, but then moved again in December to Martlesham Faith. Though some flying continued, its excitement and intensity paled in comparison with what had recently occurred. The last weeks of 1940 were spent mostly on convoy and base patrols as well as the training of replacement pilots, many of whom were non-Canadians.

Over at Northolt, 1 Squadron was also seeing relatively little action, since the high-flying Messerschmitts were largely out of the reach of the Squadron's Hurricanes. The Germans usually flew their fighter sweeps between 20,000 and 30,000 feet, but the Hurricanes were sluggish and out of their element above 18,000 feet. Though the Germans almost invariably possessed an altitude advantage during this phase, they seldom elected to engage in combat.

Around this time, the three Hurricane squadrons at Northolt attempted to launch as a wing against the high-flying, massed Messerschmitts, with comedic, near-disastrous results. Hartland Molson recalls:

> #1 Squadron RCAF was on Northolt Station with #1 Polish Squadron and #1 Squadron (RAF). The Commanding Officer, Group Captain Vincent, Controllers and the three Squadron Commanders met to discuss Wing formations in response to the great numbers of German fighters which began to accompany very small bomber formations, (which really were used as bait).
>
> Up to that time, we had only been operating in Squadron formation principally because, unlike squadrons in 12 Group, there

was not sufficient time to assemble Wings to meet raids coming in over the south coast.

The decision was taken for our three Squadrons to try a Wing defence on the next German raid of size. The Squadron Commanders decided that the Poles and ourselves would line up on the west side of the field, #1 RAF would take off from the opposite end. The signal for the lead Squadron to take off was a green Very light.

The line-up for the scramble was perfect, the Very light was fired and all three Squadrons thought that they should lead so they took off. The Poles and ourselves numbered 23 Hurricanes and #1 RAF had 12. It was a magnificent sight as they all met over the field and, to everybody's astonishment, 34 took off successfully.

The other one, the 35th, was a bit too crowded so he stopped, turned and took off, going the other way. It was a magnificent spectacle and rarely, if ever, witnessed in the restricted space of one airfield. Miraculously, there were no casualties.[26]

Paul Pitcher adds his recollections of the aftereffects of this spectacular event:

By some miracle, the only casualty was the Station Commander, who had witnessed the scene and was so shaken by it that he had to be helped to his staff car and taken to the Mess for a reviving drink. Needless to say, by the time the Wing was formed up, it was too late to carry out the interception. It is interesting to note that, as a result of this event, all the RCAF Squadrons were given 400 numbers, and Number 1 (Polish) Squadron became 303 Squadron . . .[27]

On 9 October, the Squadron was relieved and headed north to Scotland and 13 Group territory for a well-deserved rest:

Since August 17th, a period of 53 days, No. 1 Squadron had been in the front line of the Battle. Its pilots had submitted combat reports for the destruction of 30 enemy aircraft, the probable destruction of 8 and damage to 35. Sixteen Hurricanes had been lost in action; three pilots had been killed (Flying Officers Edwards, Smithers, and Peterson) and ten wounded or injured (Flight Lieutenant Corbett, Flying Officers Hyde, Desloges, Kerwin, Millar, Little, Nesbitt, Yuile, Beardmore, and Molson). Several others had made successful parachute jumps from aircraft damaged in combat.

Just before the Squadron left Northolt for Scotland, His Majesty the King awarded the Distinguished Flying Cross to Squadron Leader E. A. McNab, Flying Officer G. R. McGregor and Flying Officer B. D. Russel, the three most successful pilots on No. 1, each of whom had destroyed at least four enemy aircraft with several probables and damaged for good measure. These were the first battle decorations won by members of the RCAF in the war.[28]

On 28 September, the Luftwaffe had opened the last formal phase of the battle, which they termed a "battle of attrition." This phase continued until the end of October and was forced upon Göring by the inability of his bombers to succeed on mass daylight attacks. The high-flying fighter sweeps were a clumsy attempt to further deplete Fighter Command resources, and these sweeps failed miserably. By the end of October, the pressure had definitely eased. Though the defences were hard-pressed, particularly the embryonic night fighter force, the threat of imminent invasion had passed.

The total cost to Canada during the Battle of Britain in terms of fighter pilots was three from 1 (RCAF) Squadron and seventeen on duty with RAF squadrons:

Royal Canadian Air Force
Flying Officer Robert Leslie Edwards, No. 1 Squadron
Flying Officer Otto John Peterson, No. 1 Squadron
Flying Officer Ross Smither, No. 1 Squadron

Royal Air Force
Pilot Officer Robert Wilfred Garth Beley, No. 151 Squadron
Pilot Officer John Benzie, No. 242 Squadron
Pilot Officer Camille Robespierre Bon Seigneur, No. 257 Squadron
Pilot Officer John Greer Boyle, No. 41 Squadron
Pilot Officer John Bryson, No. 92 Squadron
Pilot Officer Norman Neil Campbell, No. 242 Squadron
Pilot Officer George Henry Corbett, No. 66 Squadron
Pilot Officer Harry Davies Edwards, No. 92 Squadron
Flight Lieutenant Harry Raymond Hamilton, No. 85 Squadron
Pilot Officer Duncan Alexander Hewitt, No. 501 Squadron
Pilot Officer Richard Alexander Howley, No. 141 Squadron
Pilot Officer James Thomas Johnston, No. 151 Squadron
Pilot Officer Joseph Emile Paul Laricheliere, No. 213 Squadron

Pilot Officer Hugh William Reilley, No. 66 Squadron
Pilot Officer Kirkpatrick Maclure Sclanders, No. 242 Squadron
Flying Officer Alex Albert Gray Trueman, No. 253 Squadron
Pilot Officer Robert Roy Wilson, No. 111 Squadron

Perhaps there is none better qualified than Rolly Dibnah, who served both with 1 (RAF) Squadron and later with 242 Squadron during the battle, to close this chapter with a brief kaleidoscope of his recollections of this epic campaign. Dibnah begins where he left off, recalling his injured friends in a British hospital after his invalided return from France:

"Brochie" with a bullet through both lungs; Stewart with bullet wounds and a horribly mangled leg, the result of bailing out of a Blenheim and being hit by the leading edge of the fin; "Randy" Goodman flying up from Tangmere to visit and beating up the place in his Hurricane before leaving; deep trouble with the hospital CO; in case of invasion, was told to report to DeHaviland's at Hatfield for further orders; when mobile on sticks, did so, to find 20 Tiger Moths rigged with light series bomb carriers under the centresection, bombs released by pulling strings attached to the edge of the cockpit; rousing reunion on return to No. 1 Squadron at Northolt; "Hilly" very rude about "Gimpy" Dibnah; was equally rude to him when he bailed out of a burning Hurricane and burnt his face around the eyes and lost some hair; destroyed a Stuka off Dover, literally exploded in mid-air, strangely, both crew got away by chute; sleepless nights; at dispersal before dawn; at the ring of a phone, twelve pilots sleeping, rise from cots in a running position, only to find some orderly room wallah wants a form signed; phone moved out to a shed; the marvellous Poles with Alec Kellett, Johnny Kent and Atholl-Forbes; the green Canadians of the other No. 1 Squadron, with Ernie McNab, Gordon McGregor and Dean Nesbitt; the untried Dal Russel; the outstanding Station Commander, "Father" Vincent, so kind and concerned about his "lads"; pieces flying from a Heinkel 111; crazy swirl of '109s escorting '110s, escorting Ju 88s; the horrifying situation of being trapped into a head-on attack on a '110 and killing him before he killed me; a lone '109 pitty-patting back to France, hoping no one would see him; the careful stalk in his blind area, head turning like an owl, not believing it can be so easy, pulling up at less than 100 feet and firing; instant reaction, hood flying off, bailing out through my bullet stream, falling 17,000 feet into the Channel, chute unopened; dead tired; the enormous wrench when Flight Sergeant Berry was killed; bailing out of a burning Hurricane and his chute caught fire; "Browne with an 'e'," an irreverent, gentle, humorous, amiable English school boy, lost to a '109; Randy and I released at noon one day, to return before dawn readiness next day; to London, Punch's Club and the lovely Diana; enormous trouble keeping Randy out of trouble; dancing and drinking at the "Oak" in Ruislip, a Squadron effort to keep from not sleeping; Hawkinge and bombed on the ground; Biggin Hill in shambles; after a show and low on fuel, looking for Hornchurch, lost in misty weather, land in a field and ask a farmer where Hornchurch might be, "Over there," he says; take off and don't have time to raise the wheels before crossing the boundary of Hornchurch; London burning, seemingly forever; finally moved to Wittering for a rest; patrolled No. 11 Group stations on the 15th, lots of business in the area, but not allowed to mix; No. 1 Squadron to become night fighters with mostly new pilots; Randy posted to No. 73 Squadron in the desert, me to No. 242 Squadron at Coltishall; first time Randy and I parted since elementary school; meet Bader, "You're the man with the leg. Have it off, old boy!"; he is a better cripple than I; practice dogfighting with Corky, can't lay a gun on him; interminable kipper patrols; see a '110 attack an Anson 5000 feet below us, Anson "stopped" and '110 dived under him and pulled up, Anson killed him with one front gun; Anson crew made very rude signs at us as we came screaming by; to Duxford and the No. 12 Group Wing, incredible sight of sixty Spitfires and Hurricanes in one place at one time; one smashing victory for the Wing and never got there in time again; seventeen pilots on my two-seat and "dicky" Singer, between Norwich and Coltishall; Singer astride a hedge, all four wheels off the ground, six pilots lift it back on the road; the Bell Hotel in Norwich on an incredibly thick, foggy night, twenty pilots asleep on the floor, furniture, stairs, blankets provided by the owner, unable to move until nearly dawn; to the theatre to see the "Girl the Lord Chancellor Banned," Bader and 242 Squadron occupy a box almost on the stage, sister Squadron across the way, gorgeous creature goes through her act to background of ruderies from both Squadrons; the bar at the Bell Hotel and being told outrageously funny stories by Basil Radford and Roland Culver and being addressed as "Canada," a memorable evening; a dining-in night, rare in wartime, for Air Marshal Trafford Leigh-Mallory at Duxford, a new All New Zealand Squadron commanded by Dusky Clouston, a Czech Squadron and 242; after dinner a rugger game with chesterfield cushions; in the entrance area "Daddy" Woodhall, the Station CO, also a New Zealander, playing a Maori war chant on his accordion, Dusky doing a "Hoaka" and pulling the most amazing faces while slapping himself on knees and chest; a huge pile of pilots on the floor, Bader bent a leg and was escorted to bed; Leigh-Mallory tunic off, tie cut off immediately below the knot, saturated with beer; dawn readiness; hospital at Ely — fat graft on leg to ease the pain of cut nerve ends; the marvellous Ward Sister "Stevy"; stinking, filthy weather; down below 100 feet on kipper patrols — sorry for the fishermen; Campbell lost to a Ju 88 — his body washed up at Great Yarmouth, three weeks later; No. 257 Squadron and Stanford Tuck with us at Martlesham Heath; not one of my favourite people; Christmas at Martlesham, marvellous party; posted to Central Flying School, on rest?[29]

1   John Terraine, *The Right of the Line*, p. 171
2   Ibid., p. 178
3   Paul B. Pitcher, letter to author, July 1993
4   Sir Douglas Bader, *Airforce* magazine, September 1979
5   Len Deighton, *The Battle of Britain*, p. 127
6   Adolf Galland, *The First and the Last*, p. 27
7   RCAF Historical Branch, AFP 49, p.6
8   Ibid., p. 7
9   Paul B. Pitcher, letter to author, July 1993
10 Hugh Halliday, *242 Squadron — The Canadian Years*, p. 92
11 Ibid., p.94
12 *AFP 49*, p. 21
13 Ibid., p. 24
14 *The Canadians at War 1939/45*, p. 62
15 Basil Collier, *The Battle of Britain*, p. 115
16 Len Deighton, p. 169

17 Ibid., p. 202
18 Hugh Halliday, p. 102
19 Ibid., p. 103
20 *The Canadians at War 1939/45*, p. 75
21 John Terraine, p. 212
22 *AFP 49*, p. 18
23 Dave McIntosh, *High Blue Battle*, p. 9
24 *AFP 49*, p. 12
25 Ibid., p. 19
26 Hartland de M. Molson, letter to author, May 1993
27 Paul B. Pitcher, letter to author, July 1993
28 *AFP 49*, p. 14
29 Lloyd Hunt, *We Happy Few*, p. 42

3

THE DARKEST YEAR

1941

"Sir, I should be dead twenty times . . ."
— OMER LEVESQUE, 401 SQUADRON

Nineteen forty-one would bring new operational taskings to Fighter Command. Throughout the Battles of France and Britain, RAF fighters had been used almost exclusively in a defensive role — quite natural given the circumstances. Since then, however, life on the fighter squadrons had diametrically changed from involving intense activity to being characterized by boredom and monotony. The greyer heads with the more ardent hearts at Fighter Command Headquarters felt that the time was ripe for the Command to go on the offensive over France. The new Commander of Fighter Command, Air Marshal Sholto Douglas, had some reservations, feeling that the limited gains that might be achieved could well be cost-prohibitive.[1] At any rate, he conquered these reservations and found a zealous proponent of the offensive sweeps in the new Commander of 11 Group, Trafford Leigh-Mallory.

Thus it came about in early January that 242 Squadron and Douglas Bader would be invited to participate in the very first of these new operations.

Leigh-Mallory called Bader to Group Headquarters at Uxbridge early in the new year. In the course of their ensuing chat, the ACO suggested that things must have been quite boring for the pilots of

242 Squadron in recent weeks. Bader replied that things indeed were, to which Leigh-Mallory asked the legless ace how he felt about taking the Squadron offensively over France to give the Germans a rather rude wake-up call. Bader beamed at the prospect, and Leigh-Mallory explained that 242 Squadron's job would be to provide escort to a small bomber force tasked with striking suspected ammunition dumps near the Pas de Calais.

Though the raid was completely anticlimactic, it set the pattern for other forms of offensive operations to come, and each new type of offensive operation was given a specific code name. "Circuses," the first of which 242 Squadron had just accomplished, were fighter escort missions provided to light and medium bombers throughout the bombers' entire mission. Due to their very nature, Circuses were the sort of mission most likely to provoke a response from the German Fighter Arm. "Ramrods" were large-scale escort missions for the heavy bombers, and due to these bombers' greater range, escort was flown over only a portion of the bombers' route. Since this mission was essentially linked to the American daylight-bombing offensive, it would not come into its own until the latter part of 1942. "Rodeos" were fighter sweeps flown in either Squadron or wing strength, and were designed to lure Luftwaffe fighters into combat. "Roadsteads" were attacks on Axis shipping, particularly in the Channel, while "Rangers" were relatively large-scale, freelance intrusions into enemy territory.

Leigh-Mallory was also toying with another type of offensive mission. It entailed sending a pair of fighters at ultra low level over the Channel to shoot up targets of opportunity on the other side whenever there was a protective low cloud deck. These first "mosquito" raids, later known as "Rhubarbs," would prove disastrous for 242 Squadron — a portent of the broader-scale losses this type of mission would inflict upon Fighter Command.

Number 242 got its first chance to christen this new type of operation on 12 January, with devastating results. Stan Turner and Douglas Bader were the first out of Martlesham that fateful morning:

Taking off at 10:15 am, they flew over the English Channel at about 600 feet. Midway between Calais and Dunkirk they saw two enemy vessels — an "E" boat (motor torpedo boat) and a drifter (escort vessel, converted from or resembling a fishing boat). These were proceeding eastward. The Hurricanes turned about a mile ahead of the boats. In loose formation, Bader leading and Turner behind and to the right, they flew towards their floating targets. Bader, whose reports were invariably detailed and meticulous, describes the attack:

"Both opened fire together at a height of 50 feet and speed 200 mph. Saw bullets strike water ahead of 'E' boat and then hitting 'E' boat. Got one burst from front guns of 'E' boat — no damage. 'E' boat ceased fire. Flight Lieutenant Turner having converged slightly on me, turned away to avoid slipstream as we passed over 'E' boat. One burst from drifter before I opened fire and none of my bullets struck drifter. Passed over drifter and made for home with Flight Lieutenant Turner in formation. Did not stop to observe damage to boats but 'E' boat must have had a lot as we could see bullets from 16 guns hitting the boat; drifter probably did not receive much damage — probably killed a few of the crew."

The pilots were exhilarated by this type of operation, offering as it did both action and the thrill of low-level flying. Bader and Turner had landed at 11:35 am; at 12:15 pm four more Hurricanes took off, piloted by Flight Lieutenant Tamblyn, Flying Officers Rogers and McKnight, and Pilot Officer Brown. Twenty-five minutes later, they split up over Gravelines; Tamblyn and Rogers turned east toward Dunkirk; McKnight and Brown headed down the coast.

The first pair flew over some fishing vessels, apparently accompanied by an armed barge. Approaching the coast at 600 feet, they saw tracer fire and turned westward, machine gunning a schooner and some small armed vessels. Rogers dived on one boat, but seeing only one unarmed man on deck, he did not shoot; the sailor stood and watched as the Hurricane roared past. En route home they passed over the fishing boats viewed earlier and fired at the barge. No hits were observed but four men were seen ducking down behind the railings. On landing, Tamblyn discovered that his aircraft had been damaged slightly by a bird strike.

In the meantime, Brown and McKnight had attacked an "E" boat and registered hits on its deck. Near Gravelines they crossed the coast. About a mile inland they saw a large concentration of troops, apparently entrenching and preparing machine gun emplacements. They strafed the enemy, causing them to scatter. The Hurricanes banked around for a second pass. Brown was trailing some 800 yards behind McKnight when he spotted a Bf 109 astern, flying at 500 feet. Brown turned sharply to port, gave another gun site a "squirt," then looked around. Both the Messerschmitt and McKnight had vanished. Brown set a course for base, landing at 1:15 pm.

Flying Officer "Willie" McKnight, piloting P2961, did not return. He was dead, a victim either of flak or of the Bf 109. An original member of No. 242 Squadron, he had been its most outstanding Canadian pilot, shooting down at least sixteen (possibly eighteen) enemy aircraft and twice winning the Distinguished Flying Cross. His loss threw a pall of gloom over No. 242; it was front-page, banner headline news in Calgary two days later.

The death of McKnight was not known when the next four Hurricanes took off at 1:25 pm, flown by Cryderman, Arthur, Latta and Edmond. They picked up the French coast near Dunkirk and flew northward at 800 feet, just below the cloud base. As they did so they were subjected to anti-aircraft fire, which crept up on them. As the four Canadians were weaving to avoid it, Cryderman became separated from his companions in the murk.

The three others tried repeatedly to reach Dunkirk again; at every approach they faced tracer fire and "flaming onions" (pom-pom flak) that flashed out of the mist. Near the Dyck lightship, Arthur saw a Bf 109. The Hurricanes broke upward into cloud and lost touch with one another. Arthur and Edmond came home on their own. Flying Officer Latta, who had been flying V7203, another original member of the Squadron, failed to return. Again, it is not known whether he was killed by flak or the '109. Cryderman, proceeding on his own, had shot up some shipping, evaded flak, and seen a lone yellow-nosed Bf 109 appear and disappear in the mist. It may have been the same fighter reported by his comrades, or another.

The Squadron had taken similar losses before. Nevertheless, 12 January 1941 was one of the blackest days of its history. It had begun with high hopes for excitement; by late afternoon it had turned into shock with the double tragedy sustained in the loss of Latta and McKnight, prominent and popular members of the unit . . .[2]

Over the next two months, the once-distinctive Canadian identity of 242 Squadron was further eroded by the losses of Flying Officers Brown and Cryderman in combat, McKenna and Price on posting, and their replacement with Britons and Australians. In March, Douglas Bader was promoted to Wing Commander and posted to command the Tangmere Wing. His departure truly marked the end of the distinctively Canadian era for 242, and although some Canadians would remain with the Squadron until it was stood down on 5 October, that representation was not significantly different from the number of Canadians serving with other RAF fighter squadrons. Sir Douglas Bader recalls 242 Squadron and his Canadian friends:

When the Squadron was at Martlesham in early 1941, I received an invitation from one of the stately homes nearby, to a dinner and dance they were giving. Would I bring six of my officers? I cannot remember the six but I know it included Laurie Cryderman, Bob Grassick and Stan Turner. It was a bit dull, but there was plenty to drink. The members of 242 Squadron were getting restive and when the small locally-hired band trio "stood down" for supper, 242 took over. Laurie Cryderman, who was with a jazz band in pre-war Toronto, sat down at the piano and some other member of 242 got the drums and the party really caught fire. Nicely brought up girls from all over the country suddenly found them- selves "trucking" with Bob Grassick, who was an excellent dancer. To hell with decorum! This was it.

The majority of the girls stayed long over time. Finally I man- aged to get the members of 242 Squadron to leave. In those days it was customary to immobilize your car by removing the rotor- arm from the distributor — simple and effective. Although on this occasion the cars were parked inside the private grounds — indeed in front of the stately mansion itself — Turner elected to immobi- lize his service car (he was now Flight Lieutenant Turner replacing George Powell-Sheddon, in hospital) and placed the rotor-arm in his pocket.

When Stan finally left there were two cars in front of the stately home — Stan's and a Rolls Royce belonging to the family which was waiting to return some guests home.

Stan was intoxicated. His car wouldn't start. He peered at the engine and saw the distributor cover off and no rotor-arm. Muttering "some bugger has pinched my rotor-arm," Stan lurched over to the Rolls. He then drove back to Martlesham a few miles distant. In the morning Stan discovered a rotor-arm in his tunic pocket and through the mists of alcohol, memory awoke. Always one to grasp the nettle, Stan drove back to the stately home about 0830 on that Sunday morning after the dance. The Rolls stood there immobile, its unwanted guests presumably bedded somewhere in the great house.

A tired butler opened the door: "No, her ladyship is not awake."

Flight Lieutenant Turner, DFC, stood firm. He handed the rotor-arm to the butler saying, "Please give her ladyship Flight Lieutenant Turner's apologies and say I borrowed this last night from the Rolls."

. . . The locals round Coltishall loved 242 Squadron, to which they always referred to as "our Squadron." Every time we took off in the early morning during those long hot summer days of 1940 and returned in the evening from our forward base at Duxford, they knew what had happened. The whole Squadron — officers, NCOs and men — left an indelible impression in the neighborhood. Norwich and East Norfolk were never the same after the departure of 242. "The Samson and Charles" and "The Bull" in Norwich and that wonderful pub at Horning Ferry, near Coltishall, mourned their loss. Not so the police![3]

————————

Towards the end of 1940, the first graduates of the British Commonwealth Air Training Plan began arriving in England. Initially, a mere trickle reached British shores, but during the winter of 1940–41, that trickle turned into a torrent as Canadian aircrew were sent as replacements to every part of the globe in which the RAF was present. It became apparent that Canada must establish more RCAF squadrons overseas with great haste if Canadian aircrew were not merely to become a manpower pool for RAF units.

On January 7, 1941, the Ralston-Sinclair Agreement provided for a further twenty-five squadrons of the RCAF to be formed outside Canada. While they would be units of the RCAF, their equipment, pay and allowances would be borne by the RAF, thereby in some degree offsetting the enormous expense to Canada of the BCATP. The original plan, which called for twenty-eight squadrons, the three already in Britain and twenty-five to be formed, was subsequently increased by ten. Canadian groundcrew were added as they became available, but the demands of the training squadrons in Canada were then particularly heavy. Six additional squadrons were also posted overseas from Canada at the end of 1943.[4]

Eighteen of the new squadrons called for in the agreement would form before the end of 1941, and eleven of these would actually participate in operations before year's end. On the fighter side, Number 112 Squadron, augmented with volunteers from 110 Squadron, reformed in December 1940 at Digby as Number 2 (RCAF) Fighter Squadron. It was equipped with Hurricanes and placed in the capable hands of the recently promoted Squadron Leader Gordon McGregor, DFC, who had served with such distinction with 1 Squadron. Number 2 Squadron was declared operationally ready at the end of February, 1941. Bob Morrow, who would serve extensively in England and later in the Aleutians, recalls his early days with 112 Army Cooperation Squadron, and the unit's redesignation as Number 2 Squadron under Gordon McGregor:

We then reported to 112 Squadron on Salisbury Plain and flew out of a grass field a few miles north of Salisbury, living under canvas except for time spent in the Officers Mess, which was an old pub. Then the fall rains came, and we would put our uniforms under our sleeping bags to keep them dry. I might mention that the big deal for us in Salisbury on a Saturday night was not to get invited for dinner and a date, but dinner and a bath! George Sellers of Winnipeg persuaded Johnson (a friend) and I to form a three-Lysander unit that would hang under the scud cloud and try to pick off a passing German, of which there were quite a few. We climbed up through the overcast — 10,000 feet or so — and practically ran head-on into a squadron of Me 109s! We departed hastily — under the overcast — as it was getting dark, and we were lost. Finally, we landed in a field and stayed the night.

Around November, we were moved to Halton, a permanent Royal Air Force station a bit north of London, in order to be in better quarters. The field was tiny but OK for the Lysanders. At Halton, we could relax from the tent life and have two dry uniforms — one for work; one for Saturday night. One day, I took my "Saturday night" uniform into the local town for dry cleaning, and it came back "wet washed." Such was rural England, even though we were close to London.

While at Halton, a major reorganization took place. We were renumbered Number 2 (RCAF) Squadron and posted to Digby in Lincolnshire for Hurricane training. Unhappily, and I think unfairly, all of the old Auxiliary officers were left behind. In fact, as a Flying

Officer, I was the senior member on the move.

At Digby, Gordon McGregor became the CO; Tommy Little and Cryn Hyde, both of Montreal, became Flight Commanders. Both of them were killed and then I became a Flight Commander. Now at long last, we were in the war . . .[5]

In March, it was decided that the three RCAF squadrons presently in Britain, as well as all subsequent RCAF squadrons serving overseas, would be renumbered to prevent confusion with existing RAF units of the same numerical designation. The top half of the "400 series" of numbers (400–449) was reserved for RCAF units. 110 Squadron thus became 400 Squadron, Number 1 became 401, and the newly-formed Number 2 Squadron became 402. Number 400 Squadron traded in its ponderous Lysanders for significantly speedier Curtiss Tomahawks, but kept its Army Cooperation role, while 401 and 402 were both retained in the fighter role with their Hurricanes. Also in March, a fourth unit, 403 Squadron, was formed at Baginton as an Army Cooperation unit, with Tomahawks. In May, 403 was changed to a fighter squadron, and was then re-equipped with Spitfires and moved to Ternhill.

The first offensive sweep by an RCAF fighter unit occurred on 15 April, when 402 Squadron, led by Gordon McGregor, flew over France as part of the Wittering Wing. Not until August, however, were RCAF units routinely involved in such operations. In May, 402 was re-equipped with Hurricane IIAs, and then in August, with twelve-gun Hurricane IIBs. Number 401 Squadron, after a brief rest in Scotland, joined 402 at Digby on 23 July and was actively engaged in operations throughout the summer. In August, 403 Squadron, their training complete, moved to Hornchurch and then to Debden, exchanging their Spitfire IIAs for the latest Spitfire VBs. Thus commenced a very long period of cross-Channel operations, which for the next one and a half years would bring few notable successes to the RCAF fighter units.

Hugh Constant Godefroy was one of the flood of BCATP graduates who arrived in England in the spring of 1941. By 1944, he would be one of the RCAF's most respected wing commanders, decorated with the DSO, DFC, and Bar, and with a string of victories to his credit. In 1941, however, he was just another "rookie" Pilot Officer, destined for service with 401 Squadron at Digby.

For Godefroy, a young man many miles from home, the extremely warm welcome he and his Canadian colleagues received from the

British people at London's Café de Paris in the middle of a heavy air raid became indelibly etched in his memory:

In the taxi we heard our first London air raid siren wails. It started from a low frequency growl, then built gradually to a maddening scream, and then, just as slowly, fell back to the low pitched moan again. It was repeated so often that we felt like crying out, "We hear you, damn it! Stop!"

At first I felt as though I should be crouching down. The driver continued on as if he hadn't heard anything. At the last minute he turned the cab sharply over to the curb, almost in its own length. The door was opened by a doorman in a scarlet tunic to the knees, brass buttons, and a black silk topper.

"Good evening, sir," he said. "'He' seems to be about again. Shouldn't imagine it will be as bad as last night, though. Mind the step, sir."

A few nights later, the Café de Paris received a direct hit from a delayed action bomb. It was reported there were no survivors.

We passed through the door into the red carpeted foyer and were relieved of our coats. We were directed to a broad carpeted stairway which led to the cabaret below. From force of habit, we fell into step with one another. To the left of the stairway was a bannister, beneath which was a raised platform for the orchestra. As we started down the steps, the all-Negro orchestra in orange jackets was playing to a full dance floor. Glancing up, the conductor saw the Canada flashes on our shoulders, stopped the music he was playing and switched to "O Canada." Crimson with embarrassment, we reached the floor to a standing ovation. The smiling maitre d', large menu in hand, beckoned us to a front row table. I was instantly struck with the incongruity of the setting. Outside, the defences of London were fighting a fierce battle, the whole skyline lighted with the flash of guns and the flicker of burning buildings. The air was reverberating from the crash of bombs and the deafening defiant answer of our ack ack. Down here we were relieved of these sounds. We were listening to the music of London's social life, which drifted on unperturbed.

Being the sort of chap who slips into the last pew at church, I felt uncomfortable at a front row table. Happily, the waiter occupied our attention, and we found ourselves saying yes to all his suggestions. The standard Canadian fare we were accustomed to included soup, main course and dessert. Here we found ourselves wading through hors d'oeuvres, soup, a fish course, then pheasant under glass, washed down with a nice bottle of wine. This was followed by three more courses, the sweet, savory and the coffee. I refused the brandy and the cigars.

We were sipping our coffee with its strong chicory flavor when the band played for attention and the cabaret began. Twelve leggy, voluptuous girls burst onto the floor, and danced a sort of can can in flawless synchrony. This bobbing routine gave a dazzling emphasis to their arresting figures. Throughout, they surveyed us with such confident amusement that I found their gaze a little disconcerting.

At the end of their first number they skipped from the floor, each returning with a wooden horse. After arranging them in a line, they sat on them, and, to the music, demonstrated how they could be advanced along the floor by rocking them back and forth. While I was still wondering what the point of this was, they jumped from their horses and ran between the tables. Now, I had been particularly impressed with a tall Nordic looking blonde and my preoccupation with her had obviously not gone unnoticed. To my alarm she came straight for me. Before I could collect my wits, I found myself dragged to the floor and placed on a horse with a half a dozen other shanghaied members of the audience. The girls lined up on a designated finishing line opposite their choice, and off we went. It took a certain amount of dexterity to make any progress, but by paying attention I soon began to move. I found that if I allowed myself undue preoccupation with the cleft between the bosoms of my prize, my progress slowed. By thinking obtusely I advanced and won a bottle of champagne and a dance. Even at close range she was striking.

It was a delightful evening, and it was with considerable regret that we took our leave in time to catch the last train back to Uxbridge. When the door slammed shut behind us at the Café de Paris, we once again faced reality. We walked to the nearest tube station in "the nightly hate." On the underground platform of the tube station, a sight met our eyes that made us stop and stare. Against the wall was a row of double-decker beds, each occupied. Around the beds on the floor as far as the eye could see were men and women lying in every conceivable attitude, some on blankets, and some just on brown paper laid on the bare concrete. There was one couple asleep in each other's arms. Children slept between their parents on makeshift beds or blankets. This was just one of the underground stations, and we knew they all must be the same. These were the bombed out people of London, many having returned to their homes to find them a heap of rubble, with a pair of blankets perhaps the only thing not burnt or stolen.

There was a rush of air as the train approached through the tunnel. It built up to a roar before it appeared at the entrance of the tunnel, and with a hiss of brakes, it shuddered to a stop. Only the children stirred in their sleep. We stepped on board, the doors clanged shut, there was a jerk, and we were soon rocketing away into the inky darkness. The scene was gone, but I found it difficult to forget. I remember that instinctively I'd looked at the sleepers in search of a familiar face. How silly, I thought; the faces familiar to me were protected from this agony by a thousand miles of water.[6]

During the summer and autumn of 1941, the buildup of RCAF units in the United Kingdom was relentless. In May, 406 Squadron formed as a night fighter unit with Beaufighter IIs, while in June, 409 and 410 Squadrons also stood up as night fighter units, initially equipped with the lacklustre Boulton Paul Defiant. That same month, 411 and 412 Squadrons formed at Digby as day fighters with Spitfires, while in August, 414 Squadron was added to the battle order at Croydon as an Army Cooperation unit, flying both Lysanders and Tomahawks.

Throughout Fighter Command, tactics were rapidly evolving to emulate and improve upon those of the Luftwaffe. In May, Bader and his Tangmere airmen had introduced a variation on the German *schwarme* formation known as "finger four," which resembled the fingers of an outstretched hand. After a period of trial and error in combat, this formation evolved as the standard for the Command, since in manoeuvring, it was planned never to degenerate beyond a pair of fighters as the basic fighting unit. Not only did manoeuvring this formation in combat delineate the basic responsibilities of the fighters — that of "shooter" and of "eyeball" — but it fostered a spirit of teamwork and mutual dependency that was so much a characteristic of the fighter air war over northern Europe. By summer, it had become a backbone formation of Fighter Command, and in variations would endure for decades to follow.

During 1941 and 1942, Fighter Command frequently crossed the Channel in wing strength, often with more than one wing, either to sweep the coastal belt of occupied Europe or to provide escort to small formations of Blenheim or Stirling bombers. The intent was to lure up and destroy Luftwaffe fighters garrisoned in France, a particularly meaningful role after June, when Hitler launched his offensive against Russia. It was hoped this constant irritant would require the Luftwaffe to tie down significant fighter assets in northern Europe, thereby providing the Soviet allies with somewhat of a "poor man's second front."

In fact, the protection of the German "west wall" was left solely to two fighter wings, *Jagdgeschwader* (JG) *2 Richthofen* and *Jagdgeschwader 26 Schlageter*, based south of the Seine and in the Pas de Calais regions respectively. When the weather was sufficiently cloudy, the RAF flew in pairs or quartets on Rhubarb nuisance raids, looking for targets of opportunity to strafe. Now that Fighter Command was on the offensive, they were receiving a taste of the combat conditions encountered by the Luftwaffe during the Battle of Britain. The German defenders were largely able to engage the RAF at will, usually with the advantages of height and sun position. For a considerable time to come, Fighter Command would experience relatively high losses for minimal returns, but morale on the fighter squadrons remained high, since the pilots felt they were taking the war to the Luftwaffe and dictating the terms of combat. The success rate on the five operational RCAF fighter squadrons during 1941 was comparable to that of corresponding British units. Collectively, the Canadians scored only twenty-two confirmed kills for the entire year, and their losses far outstripped their victories.

Not only did the Germans possess the tactical advantages already mentioned, but they were also introducing new equipment, which was also giving them a technological edge. Early in 1941, a new variant of the Bf 109, the "F" model, began appearing in numbers. This excellent aircraft, often considered the best of the '109 series, boasted 1,350 horsepower, and a top speed almost 50 mph faster than the "E" model at medium combat altitudes. More manoeuvrable than its predecessor due to the addition of elliptically shaped detachable wingtips and the elimination of the wing-mounted machine guns, the Bf 109F possessed a much more streamlined engine cowling and forward fuselage. In counterbalance, the British were just beginning to field the Spitfire Mk V. Though slightly slower than the new Messerschmitt, it was still at least as manoeuvrable and now possessed comparable armament in the form of a new wing housing a 20-mm Hispano cannon as well as the Browning .303-inch machine guns.

Although the new Spitfire could hold its own against the Bf 109F, the Hurricane, which had successfully offset its inferior speed with superior manoeuvrability against the Bf 109E, was now hopelessly outclassed. It was withdrawn from front-line fighter service over northern Europe in 1941, although it would still chart an illustrious career as a fighter-bomber, particularly in the Middle East, India, and Burma. By October, 401, 411, and 412 Squadrons had all converted to Spitfire VBs. Meanwhile, 402 Squadron had withdrawn to become one of the first Hurribomber outfits, resuming operations in early November with the planes carrying a 250-lb. bomb strapped under each wing.

The Squadron's fighter-bomber role was short-lived, however, and by the following March, 402 had re-equipped with Spitfires and resumed fighter operations. Their temporary conversion to the role of fighter-bomber did not occur without some trepidation. Little information was provided to the pilots about how the bombs would affect the takeoff characteristics of the Hurricane, so they were forced to grapple with this unknown themselves. Ron Emberg, who flew with 402 that autumn, recalls both the "takeoff trial" and the first Hurribomber raid:

On 13 October 1941, 402 Squadron was stationed at Southend where the River Thames meets the sea. We were sitting in front of the Readiness/Dispersal when we saw three tractors coming through the gate of our aerodrome. Each of the tractors was towing two flatcars, each containing stacks of 250 lb. bombs. This was the biggest logistical humdinger yet. We all broke up laughing at the stupidity of the Air Force brass, sending a load of bombs to a Hurricane fighter squadron stationed on a small converted cricket field.

At that moment Squadron Leader Bob Morrow, our CO, came out, not looking too well, and informed us that the bombs were indeed to be carried by our planes. From now on we would be Hurribombers. As a leader in the best of Hollywood traditions, Morrow would not ask his men to do anything he hadn't done. So the following morning he prepared to take the first Hurricane on a trial flight armed with two 250 lb. bombs.

The plane was maneuvered into the farthest corner of the field to give him the maximum length of take-off run. They put chocks under the wheels and four airmen held the tail down. Four more held onto the wings, and two stood by to pull the chocks away at the proper time. Bob then put the flaps halfway down. White-faced and white-knuckled, he gradually opened the throttle until he had almost maximum RPM. Then on his signal everyone jumped clear and he roared down his take-off path.

It could hardly have rolled as far as you could throw your grandmother before he was airborne in a rapid climb. We soon discovered to our amazement that the bombs had no appreciable effect on the flying characteristics of the Hurricane.

. . . On the morning of 4 November 1941, Bob Morrow called in the pilots of 402 Squadron at Warmwell in Dorsetshire for a briefing. We were to carry out a low-flying raid on a German airfield at Berck-sur-Mer in France. On the wall was a large reconnaissance photograph of our target. The Squadron Leader pointed out the hangars that were to be our particular targets. Sergeant Pilot "Butch" Handley (later Group Captain/Colonel) exclaimed, "Look at that building about 200 yards off the airfield! That looks like an Officers Mess. Let's get it!"

The CO replied, "Let's have no messing around with the Officers Messes. Our job is to get those hangars."

We arrived at the target so suddenly, flying at 100 feet, that I had to turn sharply to line myself up for an attack on one of the hangars. As I dropped my bombs I saw, straight ahead of me, the building that Butch reckoned to be the Officers Mess. I fired my machine guns at it and it exploded. I was lucky not to be damaged by flying bricks.

At debriefing I told the CO that it must have been an ammunition dump to blow up on receiving my gunfire. Bob Morrow turned to Butch, however, and said, "Sergeant Handley, would you please point out the exact hangar you bombed?" Butch indicated the same one I had attacked, and added, "Of course, maybe I overshot the target a little."

Needless to say it would be next to impossible for a Hurribomber to miss a target as big as a hangar of that size by 200 yards. However I am glad that he did, because his bombs exploded when I was at 50 feet directly over the hangar he was told to hit. Had he not disobeyed orders, I would not be here to write this story.[7]

As the day fighter units made the transition from Hurricanes to Spitfires, many pilots were in a position to compare these two fine fighter aircraft. Hugh Godefroy recalls what both were like to fly:

Each time I came to the Dispersal Hut and saw the Hurricanes, I got a thrill. There was something exciting about the sputtering and crackling of a Rolls Royce Merlin engine running up. These tour-expired machines with the paint flaking off, their sturdy metal wings, the fabric stretched tightly over the ribs of the wooden tail with the patched bullet holes, made them the very epitome of the seasoned veteran of the line. I had a hundred and seventy-six hours and twenty-five minutes flying time when I took off in a Hawker Hurricane. There were no two-place Hurricanes. Therefore, there could be no dual. One was given a pre-flight briefing of what to expect and off you went.

When flying any single-engined propeller-drive fighter, if you opened the throttle fully without touching the rudder pedals, you would go around in a circle on the ground. The reason, of course, was the enormous torque produced by their powerful engines. The Hurricane was no exception. The drill, therefore, was to open the throttle slowly, while countering the torque by putting the right rudder pedal against the stop. We were warned that it was tail light, so too much forward pressure on the stick would put the plane on its nose. We had been trained on aircraft with hydraulic brakes acti-vated by toe pressure plates attached to the rudder pedals. The Hurricane, on the other hand, had compressed air brakes, activated by a single lever on the control column. Squeezing this hand brake with the rudder pedals straight across caused each of the wheels to receive equal braking. To produce more braking on one side or the other, one compressed the desired rudder pedal. At low speed, we were told, it was very light on the ailerons and had a nasty ten-dency to drop a wing. To get the flaps or wheels up or down, it was necessary to switch the control column from the right to the left hand, then reach well forward with the right to an H-shaped switch-box with a single lever. From one side of the neutral posi-tion the flaps could be put up or down, from the other, the wheels. The British would never dream of designing a fighter that was easy to fly. That wouldn't be sporting.

There was a characteristic appearance to a Hurricane taking off under the control of an inexperienced pilot on his first solo. Once airborne, it flew half-way down the field as though it were follow-ing a horizontal wavy line, then it rolled over on its side, while the pilot put the undercarriage up. The Hurricane landed almost in fly-ing position so there was a natural tendency at first to drop it on the ground tail-first. At best this would produce a hippity-hop dance before it sat down; at worst, it broke the wooden back of the airplane. All in all, a Hurricane was a bit of a challenge for an inexperienced pilot.

I distinctly remember the first time I became airborne in one. I got the wheels up without rolling over on my back, but when I slipped the coupe-top forward over my head, the thing seemed to take off at a frightening velocity. The engine sounded like a gigantic buzz-saw, and before I had a chance to even think of turning, I was miles from the airdrome in the murky haze. It was like being on a runaway horse. Gradually I got the feel of it, and after half an hour I thought I was in control. Feeling that I was ready to try a landing, I came back across the airdrome. Looking down, I counted seven Hurricanes "pranged" on the field, an eighth on final approach with flaps and wheels down. The fire truck shot a red flare arching in the air to make him go around again. I had no intention of trying to bring this juggernaut in for a landing unless I could see a nice wide long piece of grass into wind. The other Hurricane and I went round and round the field for about half and hour while they cleared away the debris. Finally, I got a green light from the watch office and with plenty of air speed on the clock, I put my flaps and wheels down. I managed to bring the brute back onto the ground, as KB used to say, "so I could walk away from it."

. . . Unlike the Hurricane, the Spitfire Mark V was all metal. After the Hurricane, everything about the Spitfire seemed small and delicate. By comparison, the wings seemed thin as razor blades, and the narrow undercarriage as sturdy looking as a couple of toothpicks. A door on the left folded down to allow access to the cockpit. With the seat in the up position, with the door locked closed, my shoulders touched each side of the cockpit, and to close the perspex top I had to lower the seat. A crowbar was provided, secured on the folding door to "jimmy" yourself out in case of emergency. To get my eyes level with the gunsight, I had to lower the seat about as far as it would go. In this position, looking through the gunsight in front and the one-inch bullet-proof windshield, one saw the seemingly endless cowling covering the long liquid-cooled engine. Two twenty-millimetre cannon protruding from the leading edge of the wings provided visible evidence of its increased firepower. The additional four machine guns in the wings were not visible from the cockpit. Each cannon contained a

Hurricanes during the French campaign, 1940. Note the mix of two- and three-bladed propellers. *PL 3055*

A Hurricane I slicing in for a rear quartering attack over rural France, spring 1940. *PL 3056*

Ernie McNab in the cockpit of his Hurricane, summer 1940. *DND Photo*

Stan Turner, leaning on the tailplane of his 242 Squadron Hurricane, 1940. *DND Photo*

Groundcrew help hold the tail of this 401 Squadron Hurricane down during an engine check, 1940. *RE 68-6298*

"Moose" Fumerton (left) and Radar Operator Pat Byng with sheet metal from the fuselage of a Junkers 88, which they shot down for the RCAF's first night kill, 1 September 1941. *PL 4658*

Smiling bravely, Squadron Leader Bob Morrow mounts up for the first Hurri-bomber raid from RAF Warmwell in Dorset, October 1941. Gun tape covers the aircraft's ten wing-mounted machine-gun ports. *Bob Morrow Photo*

Pilot Officer Omer Levesque while with 401 Squadron at RAF Biggin Hill, January 1942. *A.E. Harley Photo*

Hugh Godefroy beside his Spitfire. Note the kill markings and the indispensable silk scarf. *PL 15950*

Hartland Molson in the cockpit of his 118 Squadron Kittyhawk, circa 1942. *PL 8363*

Twin brothers Bruce Warren (left) and Douglas "Duke" Warren while serving together on 165 (RAF) Squadron, autumn 1942. The wide white bands on their sleeves were used to carry important mission information such as courses and radio frequencies. *Duke Warren Photo*

Kittyhawks of 260 (RAF) Squadron in the Western Desert, November 1942. They are about to be armed with 500-lb. bombs. *Stocky Edwards Photo*

RCAF Kittyhawk pilots of 111 Squadron in a pre-mission briefing during the Aleutian campaign, 1942. *DND Photo*

Flight Lieutenant "Stocky" Edwards while serving with 260 (RAF) Squadron at Castel Benito airfield outside Tripoli, January 1943. One week after this photograph was taken, Edwards was awarded both the DFM and the DFC. *Stocky Edwards Photo*

A youthful Flight Lieutenant Jackie Rae, DFC, while serving with 416 Squadron. *Jackie Rae Photo*

No. 111(F) Squadron, RCAF, while based at Kodiak, Alaska, winter of 1942–43. The closest Kittyhawk, "Bitsa," was reputedly the aircraft flown by Squadron Leader K. A. Boomer when he shot down a Japanese "Rufe" on 25 September 1942. *DND Photo PMR 80-197*

418 Squadron Boston (Havoc) aircraft, half of the controversial Turbinlight experiment. The aircraft equipped the Squadron from the end of 1941 until the summer of 1943. *PL 15875*

Art Sager of 416 Squadron nearly lost a lot more than his radio to flak while on a Rhubarb over Occupied Holland, 13 November 1943. *UK 6277*

Flight Lieutenant George Burroughs in his Mustang I, November 1943. Note the nose art, including the RCAF roundel, and the crude burlap protective cover on the wing. *George Burroughs Photo*

Geoff Northcott (left) and Lloyd Chadburn in front of Northcott's Spitfire. Observe the victory marks, the Squadron Leader's pennant, and the 402 Squadron logo under the cockpit. *DND Photo*

hundred and fifty rounds of ammunition, giving six seconds of fire, and the machine guns had sufficient ammunition to give an additional six seconds. All the guns were mounted outside the arc of the propeller and were synchronized to provide a cone of lethal density between two and four hundred yards ahead of the gunsight.

When the engine was properly primed and switched on ready to start, a push on the starter button fired a cartridge which turned the engine over. There were four cartridges in the starter drum, and if you failed to start with the fourth cartridge, the drum had to be reloaded by the ground crew. The small landing flaps were activated by compressed air. They had two positions, up or down. As in the Hurricane, the undercarriage lever was on the right side of the cockpit. Because of space limitations in the cockpit, the ring grip control column was hinged just above the knee to give the lateral movement needed to activate the ailerons. The Spitfire Mark II had fabric ailerons but the Mark V had metal ones that considerably improved the rate of roll at high speed. It was even more tail-light than the Hurricane on takeoff. Because of the small rudder surface, the Spitfire had a rudder trim that had to be put in the full right position on takeoff to keep it straight. To prevent the aircraft from skidding in flight, thus throwing the bullets off the line of sight, the rudder trim had to be adjusted at different speeds. Compared to those of the Hurricane, the beautiful elliptical wings looked so delicate that at first you wondered if they would snap off in a pull-out. They were stressed to withstand a sustained nine Gs, and a short snap of up to twelve. The aircraft would shudder very noticeably well in advance of a stall, useful when flying by the seat of your pants in combat. Because of the very small coolant radiator, the Spitfire was very prone to heating up when taxiing or idling on the ground. This had to be taken into account when planning formation takeoffs so as to get all the aircraft into the air before the engine temperatures went off the clock. Providing you made allowance for its peculiarities, once into the air with the wheels up, the Spitfire was superlative.[8]

The night fighter squadrons were registering limited successes in 1941. Based for many months in either the north of England or Scotland, their opportunities to score were rare. Much of the Luftwaffe's bomber assets had been moved to the eastern front, and raids of significance on the British homeland had essentially ended. The first score for the RCAF at night was a Junkers 88, which fell to the guns of Flying Officer R.C. "Moose" Fumerton and his observer, Sergeant L.P.S. Bing of 406 Squadron, during a full moon on 1 September 1941. Carl Fumerton recalls his and the RCAF's first night kill, and the circumstances leading up to it:

In June 1941, I was attached to 406 Squadron, RCAF; a newly formed night fighter unit in training for conversion to Beaufighter IIs. These aircraft were equipped with radar for air interception and based at Acklington on the East Coast of England.

I had had some previous night fighting experience on Hurricanes, which consisted mainly of flying over the target with the hood open to better scan the night sky, using flak and searchlights as indicators for height and course information. I also had had a long conversation with a very experienced Hurricane night fighter pilot, who readily imparted his experiences to me.

Beaufighter IIs (with Merlin engines) were not the easiest machines to fly. There was a tendency to swing on takeoff and landing, of which one had to be respectful. Also, and based on my own experience when on a night flight I had a piston rod fly out through the cylinder wall, I found that the aircraft, with full fuel tanks, would not maintain height on a single engine, which meant that once the wheels were down, you were committed to a landing. That required a precision approach and drill.

I sensed that by and large there was not complete confidence in the aircraft. Then one day, a Beau II (on delivery) landed and pulled up to the parking area and, with everyone watching, out came the pilot slinging a parachute not much smaller than herself. If it had been a staged performance, it couldn't have worked better. It provided quite a psychological boost. After that, everyone got down to business flying the Beaufighter.

During this period, one of the crews was aloft during a night test and accidentally left the radio transmission switch in the "on" position. The conversation went like this:

Pilot to Radar Operator (RO): "Hey Mike (not his real name), what's the colours of the day?"

Mike: "I dunno, wait a minute, I'll look in my boot — yeah! Here they are. Let's see, green and red." (Just what the Germans had been looking for.)

The conversation continued through the approach and landing.

As the aircraft pulled up to the parking pad, this pungent exclamation, "Mud, sh__ and blood — we've run over the battery." (That was the starting battery.) End of conversation.

The next morning I suggested fastening an elastic cord to all the transmission switches, so that they could not accidentally be left on. These were installed with quite a heavy cord and that process was continued in the next squadron we were on. Little did I realize that that implementation would one night prevent me from sending out a "mayday."

On the night of 1 September 1941, I took off from Acklington in Beaufighter "J", with radar operator Sgt. Pat Bing, for a night test. The flight proved to be of short duration as the radar set was malfunctioning. Back on the ground, the set was tested by the radar officer and appeared to be in working order.

Not too long after that, we were scrambled and given a height and course to steer for the interception of a bandit. On the climb up, Pat passed the word that the radar was still not working properly; that he could get only half the picture. I asked him if he could try to close, working on a partial blip. He said he could try so we continued on, and soon after made a contact with the enemy aircraft. We kept closing and I spotted the enemy aircraft drifting from port to starboard. However, there was a lot of cloud about and I lost sight of him as he flew into it. By now I had the course and height of the enemy aircraft figured out and together with the partial blip on the radar set, succeeded in following it through the cloud. I came in below the enemy aircraft, a Junkers 88, and remembering the Hurricane pilot's voice of experience, pulled up and raked the belly from one end to the other, scoring hits. An unanticipated reaction then occurred. This was not a highly maneuverable, light aircraft with .303 machine guns, but a heavy twin engine Beaufighter, complete with cannon, which tended to slow down the plane, especially when firing in that attitude. As a result, I found myself hanging on the props about 50 yards behind the Junkers 88 and I knew I was going to get it. As luck would have it, just as the gunner began the return fire, his port engine cut and everything flew to one side. That gave me the couple of seconds I needed to get back on target. I opened fire again. The Junkers 88 blew up.

The following morning, Pat Bing and I went to inspect the downed aircraft. It had landed in a brick factory north of Newcastle, scattering thousands of baking bricks and narrowly missing the manager's house. In conversation with the manager, I apologized for the damage we had caused. His reply was, "That's alright, just bring some more down."

The Intelligence Officer who was on the site informed me that the crew had been experienced veterans of the Spanish Civil War. I was taken with the sight of the large Iron Cross marking on the side of the fuselage. I obtained an axe from somewhere and cut it out, thinking that it would make a good scoreboard for the Squadron, and that subsequently was its use.

Of the crew of the Junkers 88, there were no survivors. As was the custom, a full military funeral, officered by one of our pilots, was accorded the four crew members.[9]

Fumerton, a "transplant" from day fighter operations, would later enjoy great success in the Middle East, and would eventually become Canada's highest-scoring night fighter pilot, with fourteen confirmed victories.

———◆·••·◆———

During November, engagement opportunities for both the day and the night fighters were few and far between. Just as well, for it gave two more RCAF day fighter squadrons, Numbers 416 and 417, an opportunity to form quietly at Peterhead, Scotland, and Charmy Down respectively. Both squadrons were equipped with Spitfires, though 417's stay in the United Kingdom was destined to be very brief.

On 22 November, Sergeant Omer Levesque of 401 Squadron achieved instant fame as the first pilot to shoot down one of the new German Focke Wulf 190 fighters. Hugh Godefroy recalls the event from the perspective of the post-mission Squadron debriefing session:

Jamie Rankin had led them on a perfect bounce, and they had destroyed four — one each by Ormston, Blakeslee, Morrison and Levesque. Omer Levesque was also going to be credited with one probably destroyed and four damaged. I was just in time to listen to the debriefing. Don Blakeslee was called first and with his usual offhand manner, described the details of his victory. Ormston, flushed with elation, described how his had blown up in his face. Don Morrison had chased three off Jeep Neal's tail, sending one of them down in flames into the sea.

"Has anybody else got a claim?" Jamie asked.

Bill Haggerty stood up and said, "I think Sergeant Levesque has, sir."

Everybody turned around and looked back at "Trottle." He was slumped in a chair at the back of the Briefing Room, his face bathed in sweat.

In response to the silence, he stood up like a frightened little boy and as he searched for words, his lips trembled. He took a deep breath, a long sigh, and said, "Sir, I should be dead twenty times. I could have been killed without knowing 'nutting about it.'"

There was a roar of laughter which he didn't seem to notice. Choked with emotion, he haltingly gave his report. There was no more laughter. His story had the undivided attention of every pilot in the Wing. He had been attacked by a gaggle of radial-engined aircraft faster than anything he had ever seen. He had shot two of them down and after a battle for his life, made his escape. With sweat pouring off his brow, he gave a big sigh, and slumped back on his seat. There was dead silence. Then somebody beside me said, "Boy, he's had it!"

Omer was promoted to Flight Sergeant and sent off on a forty-eight hour leave, with the full expectation that he would be sent home. After his leave, Trottle came straight to Dispersal. Habitually particular about appearance, he looked neat as a pin with his new Flight Sergeant Crowns up. He had by no means "had it." He was not a bit interested in going back to Canada. On the contrary, he planned to stay a long time. He had bought himself an MG sports car. To the delight of everyone, he was his familiar cocky self again. With a swagger, he strode over to Dean MacDonald slumped in a chair.

"Sergeant MacDonald. You see those Goddam crowns? From now on, you show respec' Chris. And smarten up."

Wreathed in smiles, Dean gave him a limp-handed salute, and Trottle retaliated by grabbing him round the neck. Before leaving, he gave the Intelligence Officer a piece of paper on which he had drawn what he remembered of the shape of the radial-engine air-craft. Copies of Levesque's drawing were circulated throughout Fighter Command and proved to be a remarkably accurate picture of the new German fighter, the Focke Wulf 190. In his absence, other pilots had reported seeing them. One had flown head-on into a formation escorting six Blenheims. He had half-rolled and gone straight down on the bombers, shooting one down at 90 degrees deflection; pulled out of the dive below the bombers and had gone straight up through them again, shooting down another. He had enough speed to climb five thousand feet for a victory roll before diving back into France. The escorting fighters couldn't get anywhere near him. As some of the aircraft had been hit by cannon fire, it was assumed that they were armed with two cannons, which only their hottest pilots could make good use of. From the point of view of speed, flying our Spitfire Mark V against Focke Wulf 190s was like flying Hurricanes against 109s. There was only one consolation. At least we could still turn inside them.[10]

The second Focke Wulf engaged by Levesque was never confirmed as a victory. Levesque would, however, soon score yet another Focke Wulf 190, along with two Bf 109s, before a '190 put an end to his wartime career. He would spend the next thirty-nine months languishing in *Stalag Luft III* POW camp. But as it turned out, his air fighting days were not over. Chosen as one of the select few pilots from the RCAF to fly a combat tour in F-86 Sabres over Korea, Omer brought down a MiG 15 in 1951, thus becoming the most recent RCAF fighter pilot to officially qualify as an ace (five kills). He was subsequently decorated with the American DFC; it is a shame that the bureaucracy did not see fit to recognize his prowess in two air wars with a Commonwealth DFC.

The Focke Wulf 190 would indeed prove to be a formidable adversary, particularly in the hands of a gifted pilot. A brilliant blend of weight consciousness, simplicity, and aerodynamic strength, its excellent flight characteristics, particularly its aileron turn capability, generated a great deal of concern at Britain's Air Ministry. *II Gruppe* of *Jagdgeschwader 26 Schlageter* was the first designated operational unit to receive the new aircraft, and the first production variants were delivered to *6 Staffel* of this unit at Moorseele, Belgium, in July 1941. On 1 September, the '190 underwent its baptism of fire, destroying three Spitfire Vs over the Dunkirk beaches without loss. Powered by a 1,600-horsepower BMW 801C radial engine, formidably armed with four 20-mm cannon and two 13-mm machine guns, the *Wuerger* (Butcherbird) displayed a marked ascendancy over the Spitfire V.[11] Furthermore, that measure of superiority enjoyed by the '190 would not be redressed until the RAF fielded the excellent Spitfire Mk IX in July 1942.

Thus, Allied air operations over northern Europe closed on a sober note in 1941. Though Fighter Command had switched roles from the defensive to the offensive, it was becoming painfully obvious that the cost of maintaining this offensive posture would be dear. Technological parity would have to be achieved early in the new year if the Command's pilots were to stand a fighting chance.

———◆·◆·◆———

Life would have been considerably easier for Fighter Command in 1941 if northern Europe had been the only combat zone. That was simply not the case, however. Since the 1920s, the RAF had maintained a significant presence in the Middle East, to protect Britain's interests there in the event of attack by another European nation. When Italy entered the war on 10 June 1940 by invading France, the RAF had over 300 front-line aircraft in the Middle East, deployed in an area comprising roughly four and a half million square miles. The primary job of the Middle East Air Force was to protect the vital sea lanes through both the Red Sea and the Mediterranean. Italy's declaration of war threatened these sea lanes by virtue of her geographical location on the Mediterranean, and also by her military interests in Cyrenaica and East Africa. Almost immediately, the Italians began an extensive mobilization and build-up in Cyrenaica, and it became patently obvious that an attack through Egypt to the Suez Canal was in the cards. In defence of the area, the RAF, under the astute command of Air Commodore Raymond Collishaw, a Canadian ace with sixty victories to his credit in the First World War, conducted a staunch though restricted air campaign based primarily on reconnaissance and ground support to friendly troops. Limited resources — particularly the fighter fleet, consisting of only three squadrons of outmoded Gladiators — dictated direct combat with the *Regia Aeronautica* (Italian air force) only when absolutely necessary. Though some offensive operations, such as the bombing of the Italian ports of Tobruk and Bardia, achieved notable success, the real Allied victory of the campaign was the creation of a defensive mentality in the Italians.

One of the forgotten heroes of these early combats in North Africa was Vernon Crompton Woodward of Victoria, British Columbia. As a Gladiator pilot with 33 Squadron in Libya, Woodward displayed a cool, calm judgement in combat that would earn him the title, "the imperturbable 'Woody.'" He became an ace in the robust little Gladiators during these early battles, and flying Hurricanes in Greece the following year would add a further sixteen kills, making him, with twenty-one confirmed victories, the leading Canadian ace of the war until the autumn of 1942.

Swift reinforcement was crucial in order to maintain the Allied strategic interests in North Africa, and Malta would assume paramount importance as a stepping stone to the air and sea reinforcement of North Africa, and also as a base for denying the enemy the capability of doing the same. In early August, 1940, twelve Hurricanes flew to the island from the carrier HMS *Argus* and were augmented by both bomber and reconnaissance aircraft routed through Gibraltar. Reinforcements, reluctantly spared from Britain, were becoming available to Collishaw's forces in North Africa as well, and by the end of November, two squadrons of air defence Hurricanes were available for operations.

The Italians under Marshal Rodolfo Graziani were extremely tentative in their advance, and General Sir Archibald Wavell, the British commander, opened his own offensive in force on 9 December. By 8 February 1941, essentially all of Cyrenaica was in British hands. The Middle East Air Force, which never had more than 200 aircraft available for operations during the campaign, destroyed or captured over 400 enemy airplanes, offset by a loss of only forty-one aircraft and seventy-six aircrew, including the wounded.

The Italians had not confined their expansionist designs to North Africa. In October 1940, anxious to make their presence felt in the Balkans, they attacked Greece from a base in Albania, in spite of an explicit warning from the Germans not to meddle there. The Middle East Air Force was ordered to assist, and accordingly Blenheims and Gladiators were deployed to help defend Athens. In spite of appalling winter weather over northern Greece, Gladiators destroyed forty Italian aircraft by year's end in the skies over the Pindus Mountains, for a loss of only six of their own. Meanwhile, staunch Wellington bomber crews from Malta kept up a series of punishing attacks on the southern Italian ports, which were attempting to supply Mussolini's invasion force.

Just when the Allies appeared triumphant on all fronts, however, the Germans, fed up with Italian military buffoonery in the region, decided to take matters into their own hands. Anxious to restore order in the area prior to launching their eastern offensive, the Germans deployed *Fliegerkorps X* from Norway to Sicily at year's end to pound Malta, the Royal Navy, and the sea lanes in the eastern Mediterranean. In January 1941, Hitler ordered his army to prepare a blocking force to assist the Italians in Libya, and deployed portions of the *Fliegerkorps* further forward to bases in Africa. One Panzer division as well as a light division were committed to this effort, under the command of a then relatively unknown German general, Erwin Rommel. The Germans regarded North Africa as a "backwater" theatre, devoting only sufficient resources to pin down as many Commonwealth forces as possible, and not to overturn British superiority there. To that end, Rommel and the Afrika Korps would be remarkably successful.

Eventually, General Wavell's commitments on other fronts, such as East Africa, ground his offensive to a halt; his Army of the Nile was seriously depleted and somewhat demoralized by conflicting priorities and "pop-up" taskings. Furthermore, Malta had become well aware of the German presence in the Mediterranean in March by virtue of heavy Luftwaffe attacks on both the island fortress and British shipping. When forward elements of *Fliegerkorps X* deployed across the Mediterranean, complete with two *Gruppen* of Bf 109 fighters hot off the Channel coast, the hard-won RAF air superiority essentially evaporated overnight.

Towards the end of March 1941, Rommel's armoured units forced the British out of El Agheila, and very soon Wavell's army was in full flight eastward. The fighter assets of the Middle East Air Force, the Hurricanes and Tomahawks that had fared so well against the *Regia Aeronautica*, found themselves seriously disadvantaged by the Bf 109Es. The Hurricane in particular, now hampered by an enormous tropical air filter, suddenly found itself with at least a 50-mph speed deficit over its old nemesis from northern Europe. In short order, the newly named Eighth Army lost all the ground it had gained. Tobruk fell in July, and Air Marshal Tedder, the Middle East Air Force Commander, now attempted to reorganize and bolster his air forces. His most important change was to make Number 204 Group the Air Headquarters, Western Desert, and responsible for all the fighter, light bomber, and reconnaissance assets in the desert, now transformed into fully mobile wings and squadrons.[12] This headquarters, under the command of Air Vice-Marshal Arthur Coningham, would shortly be renamed the Desert Air Force. Tedder's superior command was rapidly becoming a major force in its own right, expanding in time from the original twenty-nine squadrons to a powerful air army of 110 squadrons. In the fighter world, the first Spitfire Vs had arrived, and the much-improved Curtiss Kittyhawk was replacing the earlier

Tomahawk aircraft. Communications between the army and the air force greatly improved, and under Tedder's wise guidance, tactical support to the ground forces thrived as land and air forces co-located their headquarters.

Despite impatience from home, the new ground commander, General Sir Claude Auchinleck, was not prepared to initiate a counteroffensive until 18 November. On that day he launched Operation Crusader, the mandate of which was to drive all the Axis forces out of North Africa. For nights on end prior to the start of the operation, Tedder's long-range bomber forces pounded the ports of Tripoli and Benghazi, while other aircraft flew relentlessly against supply depots and troop concentrations. On Crusader's opening day, Tedder possessed 700 aircraft serving in forty-nine operational squadrons scattered from Malta to Egypt. The Axis forces could counter with 436 combat aircraft in Cyrenaica, 186 in Tripolitania, 776 scattered throughout the Mediterranean, and in excess of 600 in the Balkans and Italy. Rapid air superiority was considered essential to Auchinleck, since if the Axis forces were afforded the opportunity to call on their formidable reserves, the results would be devastating for the Allies. Though the battle raged with no significant gains on either side for the first few days, the Hurricanes, Kittyhawks, and Tomahawks of the tactical forces finally began gaining the upper hand. On 28 November, Tobruk was relieved, and by mid-December, the Axis forces had been driven back once more to El Agheila. Throughout the Eighth Army's rapid advance, the overrun Axis airfields bore witness to the ferocity of the attacks conducted by the Desert Air Force. No less than 458 German and Italian aircraft carcasses were found littered along the way. Reinforcement of the broad (1,000 mile), rapidly moving front was, however, proving difficult, and once again priorities in other theatres, such as the Japanese assault in the Far East, prevented Auchinleck from delivering a knockout punch to the Axis forces while he had them reeling.[13]

Sensing the Allied hesitancy, the Luftwaffe launched a savage onslaught of its own throughout the Mediterranean, particularly against Malta. In December alone, over 400 sorties would be flown against the tiny island, and in the first week of January, the count would increase to 500 sorties in an attempt to bomb the RAF airfields to dust. Malta was obstinate and resilient, although much greater hardship was yet to come.

Bert Houle was a longtime "flying Desert Rat" who flew over 400 operational sorties during his wartime career, and not one of them from a base in the United Kingdom. He would serve with both 213 and 145 Squadrons of the RAF before joining 417 Squadron, in due course becoming its commanding officer. He would eventually become a "double ace," decorated with the DFC and Bar. In August 1941, he boarded the aircraft carrier HMS *Furious*, not knowing for where he was bound, but in good company:

> It is impossible for most of those on board to estimate where a ship will go in wartime before arriving at its destination. Only a few people on board know the position of the ship at any time; it never stays on one course very long, and varies its course irregularly. This makes it more difficult to be waylaid or followed by enemy submarines. Our particular mission was called "Operation Scarlet" and the officer in charge of the operations called us together and warned us of the "dos" and "don'ts" to be followed. It was just as well that he did not tell us the full history of such ventures where green pilots were asked to fly off an aircraft carrier.
>
> One attempt to fly long-range Hurricanes from a carrier to Malta ended in tragedy. Only four of a total of thirteen aircraft made Malta; none of the other nine pilots were ever found. This is probably one of the mistakes of war that should not happen; the aircraft were launched too far from Malta.
>
> On 7 September, the Rock of Gibraltar loomed up ahead. All were assembled on deck as the big flat-top nosed its way into the harbour behind the break-water. The ship was saluted by each ship in harbour as it passed and the Captain returned each salute. The *Furious* nosed up to a bigger aircraft carrier, the *Ark Royal*, and immediately steps were taken to transfer twenty-four of the Hurricanes. Twenty-four pilots, including myself, were transferred with our aircraft. The *Ark* was to take the first two dozen Hurricanes out; they were to be flown off. She would then make another trip, in company with the *Furious*, and the remaining aircraft would be airborne for Malta. We had an evening ashore, met a few Canadians doing underground tunnel operations there, boarded the *Ark* and sought our quarters. When morning arrived we were well out into the Mediterranean. Groundcrews were busy assembling the aircraft on the deck and testing them to be sure they worked when they were wanted. They were familiar with their jobs and the aircraft were assembled with speed and efficiency. We

stayed pretty sober that night and went to bed early; we now knew our destination was Malta or the Middle East.

Our call came at half-past three; after a fast, silent breakfast we got busy stuffing our paraphernalia into our allotted aircraft. After we had run our aircraft up to satisfy ourselves with the engine operation, we were called in for a briefing.

Each pilot was to fly the original aircraft he had ferried in England. He was to take off according to the position of his aircraft on the deck. Two Blenheims were arriving from Malta to rendezvous with the carrier about ten minutes after dawn. The first aircraft off was to form up on the Blenheim's right, the second on its left and so on to make up a 'V' formation. The last two aircraft off were to give fighter protection in case of attack. The next twelve were to form up on the second Blenheim.

We could not use radio for fear that the enemy would pick up the signal and be alerted; we were in no condition to beat off an attack. All vectors and length of time to fly them were given in case we got separated from the formation. Due to our extra load of petrol, we carried a limited number of rounds of ammunition to save weight. With all this information safely tucked away, and with a generous supply of maps, we crawled into the cockpit. At the very last minute, Bill Swinden came over to my aircraft and asked me to sit on his raincoat. He had no room for it in his aircraft. As he was about ten inches taller than me, he could not sit on it himself; I agreed. It is alright after one gets safely home to say one wasn't scared, but I frankly admit I was — I have been scared many times since. The big carrier turned into wind and tense and fearful, those pilots near the front started their engines and waited for the dispatcher's signal for the first aircraft to take off. It was lined up, the pilot ran the engine up, held the aircraft with full brakes and waited. Finally the flag was lowered, the brakes were released and the aircraft crawled across the deck. When it hit the ramp at the bow of the ship, the aircraft was thrown in the air but it had not gained flying speed and slowly sank from sight below the ship's deck level. We breathed a sigh of relief as it staggered into view and fought for altitude. Immediately the next aircraft was off, and the next, and then it was my turn.

The memory of my fears and misgivings while watching that man with the flag are almost as clear now as if it happened this morning. I can tell you that I opened the throttle as much as I dared without putting the kite up on its nose. The only danger with this would be the sudden swing when the brakes were released. My aircraft did swing slightly but I straightened it and before I knew it, the ramp threw me in the air and I was winging out smoothly over the blue waters of the Mediterranean.

We formed up immediately and circled, waiting for the twelfth aircraft. The *Ark Royal* began to look smaller and smaller as we gained altitude on each circuit and the aircraft looked like crabs on the deck. Suddenly, one would break loose from the cluster, race across the deck and free itself from the fetters that held it to the earth.

The Blenheim straightened out and pointed her nose up the Mediterranean on the seven-hundred mile hop to Malta. With coarse pitch to run the engine as slowly as possible, and weak mixture, I relaxed a little to enjoy the trip. With the scratch pad and computer on my knee I began to check our position in case I had to make my own way to Malta. We were flying at six thousand feet, and once an enemy aircraft flew past us far below. It was allowed to go in peace as we were entirely defensive that day. At least two hours later the rocky terrain of North Africa near Bizerta could be seen on our starboard side, and a little later the Gulf of Tunis. This was our clue to change direction south and dive down, right to the deck, so that the enemy radio stations on Pantellaria would not be able to spot us.

By this time my kidneys were floating. There was no relief tube in the Hurricane and it is doubtful whether it would have been used anyway. We had heard stories of relief tubes whose outlet had been placed in a low-pressure area so that it created suction. If the private part got too close it was sucked in and one could easily believe that the extraction could be painful. Getting relief in a fighter is no easy task. The pilot sits on his packed parachute with his dinghy as a seat. A looped nylon strap came up between his legs while a strap came around each hip, passed through the loop and fastened into the lower holes in the release buckle. A back strap came over each shoulder to fasten into the upper holes in the release buckle. The buckle was on a flap which came around the left side and the parachute opening "D" ring was also attached to this flap. Over all this, one fastened the four straps of his Sutton harness, which held the pilot to his seat and which automatically locked tight if the aircraft were to decelerate. This prevented the pilot from smashing into the instrument panel during a crash. There was no way, outside of doing it in your pants, to get relief without undoing all those straps and attempting to clear all clothing. For these reasons, it was a certainty that getting relief at sea level would be dangerous. My timing was good; relief was obtained and everything was put back in place before we had to level out. Bill's raincoat had been completely forgotten; it collected a lot of salty moisture and showed a big brown stain until the end of the war.

Mile after mile of smooth surface of the sea passed beneath us as we concentrated on maintaining that four or so feet between our aircraft and the drink. Aircraft and pilots had been lost before on the same leg of the trip by hitting the water. Eventually we changed course again to east by a little south and slowly gained altitude where we maintained two thousand feet. When the island of Linosa appeared on our starboard, we knew our position and we felt a little more secure. We felt much more secure when the much bombed little limestone fortress finally appeared. We had passed the last half-hour checking gasoline gauges every few minutes, and we knew that fuel to feed the twelve hundred horsepower Merlin engine was getting short.

Everything was businesslike and warlike on Malta. We were given a cup of coffee and a few sandwiches and were told to hang around and be ready to test our aircraft in case trouble developed. On my aircraft, one long-range fuel tank pump was unserviceable and had to be repaired. I can thank my lucky stars that it had lasted until it had delivered all the fuel in that tank. After this we were driven into Musta, a small town near the airport, and were given rooms for the night. Houses, roads and fences were all made of limestone and both the aerodrome and the village showed the marks of many enemy bomber raids.

We had a pleasant evening in Musta, got feeling pretty good to celebrate our safe arrival and made up with a few girls. In the morning we did another aircraft test and flew to Luqa, which was to be our jumping-off place for Mersa Matruh in Egypt. This was an eight-hundred mile trip. A twenty-five mile an hour tail wind was required before we could make the trip with our fuel supply. Each morning we received a weather report; when it was unfavourable, we were free for the day. Valetta and Sliema were the night spots, with horse-drawn Gharis the main means of transportation. We experienced only one air raid while there and we had an opportunity to watch the famed guns and search lights in operation. One enemy bomber was brought down after a direct hit, bursting into flames immediately like a giant fireworks display.

On the evening of 13 September 1941, exactly one year after I had signed my name as a member of the Air Force, the weather brains promised favourable winds for the next hop to Mersa Matruh, Egypt. We went to bed early, our backsides still sore from the previous hop and the hard dinghy packs which formed the parachute seat.

Sure enough, the weather was OK the next morning and we were up and fed before four o'clock. By the time we had all the instructions and our luggage stowed away, dawn was just breaking. A Wellington was to lead us across this stretch of water and we all lined up behind it for takeoff. The hop was quite uneventful except for being tiresome and hard on the behind. We lost one aircraft, which developed engine trouble and force landed in the sea; the pilot was never heard of again. We flew well out to sea from the enemy-held coast of Cyrenaica and Libya, then changed course to land at Mersa Matruh.

We were getting pretty short of petrol again and it was hot in the cockpit in our blue uniforms. We had had to wear our blues and pack the tropical kit due to the shortage of space. Also, the heat from the big engine made the cockpit like the inside of a furnace; heat waves danced over the endless miles of burning sand. Some bright "Joes" had warned us of the difficulty of landing in hot climates. The thinner air had less lift than colder air. There is no stalling problem because the pilot lands at the same recommended indicated air speed, but the ground speed is higher and the landing roll will be longer. They also warned that heat waves would tend to cause mirages which would make the ground appear to shift up and down. This certainly would not make our landings any easier.

We all landed without mishap. The sand stirred up and lifted in great clouds behind the taxiing aircraft as they made for a petrol bowser standing near a small building. This turned out to be a canteen, which could only provide us with a bottle of warm beer to slake our thirst and a hot dog to stave off hunger. After that, we sat around until all our aircraft had been refueled, all the while speculating on our future in this barren-looking land. With perspiration already streaming down our backs, we climbed into cockpits which, by this time, had become too hot to touch with bare skin. The sun was a steady, unwinking ball of fire beating down on us so that we could almost feel the weight of its rays. Hot air lifted up from the sand, baking and parching anything it touched.

Soon, long V-Shaped columns of dust spread out behind each aircraft as we took off. These dust clouds were certain give-aways to any enemy aircraft flying high overhead; this had been, and would still be, the cause of a good many aircraft being shot down without any chance to fight back. We set a course for El Fayoum, which was about twenty miles south-west of Cairo. We flew over the desert waste where the battle for El Alamein was to take place just about one year later. We flew over flat desert without even a single camel or thorn bush to break the monotony. It was useless to try to map-read; we could only fly in a given direction and esti-mate position by time and speed. We were high with elation; the dangerous sea trip was over, and a forced-landing now would give us a fighting chance to live. We were also pretty sure of our chances of getting into the fight soon.[14]

Thus, 1941 closed on an extremely sober note for the Allied fighter air effort. Though primitive offensive operations had commenced over Occupied Europe, air parity, let alone air superiority, was yet a distant dream. In the outlying theatres of war, there was even less overall success in combat to provide much-needed encouragement to the beleaguered Allied air forces. Nineteen forty-two would need to be a "make or break" year for the Allies.

1 John Terraine, *The Right of the Line*, p. 284
2 Hugh Halliday, *242 Squadron: The Canadian Years*, p. 119
3 Sir Douglas Bader, *Airforce* magazine, September 1979
4 Leslie Roberts, *There Shall Be Wings*, p. 146
5 Bob Morrow, letter to author, August 1993
6 Hugh Godefroy, *Lucky Thirteen*, p. 52
7 Simpson, *We Few*, pp. 56, 103
8 Godefroy, pp. 56, 85
9 R. C. Fumerton, letter to author, July 1993
10 Godefroy, p. 110
11 Robert Grinsell, *Focke Wulf FW 190*, p. 6
12 John D. R. Rawlings, *The History of the Royal Air Force*, p. 101
13 Ibid., p. 104
14 Lloyd Hunt, *We Band of Brothers*, p. 114

4

WIN SOME,
LOSE SOME

1942

*"We seemed to have blown
right into the middle of hell . . ."*
— GEORGE FREDERICK BEURLING, 249 SQUADRON, RAF

The air war over northern Europe in 1942 would not be significantly more bountiful for the RCAF fighter squadrons than was the previous year. The losses experienced by Fighter Command in 1941, coupled with a list of ever-growing worldwide commitments, particularly in the Middle East, necessitated a temporary halt to the offensive sojourns over France. Furthermore, by the spring of 1942, the Germans had developed a magnificent air defence network consisting of a radio intercept service and a double belt of *Freya* early warning radar — one belt located along the coast and another thirty to fifty miles inland. By spring, both JG 26 and JG 2 had in large part replaced their Messerschmitt Bf 109s with Focke Wulf 190As, while Fighter Command's front-line squadrons were still making do with Spitfire VBs. And whereas much of the talent and experience within Fighter Command was being siphoned off to other war theatres, Luftwaffe counterparts in France and Belgium tended to remain in place, availing themselves of frequent opportunities to engage quality opponents. Also, finger-four tactics had not yet found universal acceptance in Fighter Command. It is therefore no great surprise that the seven RCAF fighter squadrons operational over northern Europe in 1942 only managed collectively to score thirty-five and a half confirmed victories. Nevertheless, the Canadian success rate for the period was by and large representational of the rest of Fighter Command: *nobody* scored much in 1942.

The first significant activity of the year for the Command occurred on 11 February, when the German battle cruisers *Gneisenau* and *Scharnhorst*, in concert with the cruiser *Prinz Eugen* and an escort flotilla of seven destroyers, made an audacious dash from the French port of Brest through the English Channel to German home waters at Wilhelmshaven on the Elbe River. The *General der Jagdflieger*, Adolf Galland, did all the planning for the accompanying air umbrella. Brilliantly conceived and boldly executed, the operation was completed without one British torpedo, shell, or bomb touching a German war-ship. Though both *Gneisenau* and *Scharnhorst* struck mines during the Channel dash, the damage was not disabling, and the entire German naval force was safe in home waters by midnight on 12/13 February.

The Germans considered the operation a complete success, but it was a Pyrrhic victory in that their capital ships were now bottled up in home waters for the duration of the war. The damage done to British prestige and confidence, however, was incalculable. Britain had not witnessed strong enemy naval forces in "her" Channel since Tourville's victory over the English-Dutch fleet off the Isle of Wight in 1690. Some of the RCAF fighter squadrons were active partici-pants in this Channel flight, as Hugh Godefroy recalls:

When I got back to the Mess at Biggin, I discovered I had missed "the big one." The battleships had broken out of Brest, steamed through the Channel, escaped into the North Sea and would now be able to operate from the Norwegian fjords. Group Captain Barnwell had been the first to sound the alarm. In spite of the body cast he wore because of a broken back he had sustained crash land-ing a Spitfire, Barnwell had the habit of doing his local flying over the Channel. At ten o'clock on February 11th, just off the Somme, he sighted a large destroyer force steaming along the coast towards Gris Nez. Circling in the misty rain was a swarm of Messerschmitts. He nipped into cloud and reported his discovery. Every available aircraft capable of carrying a torpedo was scrambled to the attack. The mine laying units of Bomber Command were dispatched to lay a carpet in the path of the flotilla.

A squadron of Swordfish, the pitifully obsolete torpedo launch-ing biplane of the Fleet Air Arm, landed at Manston to refuel. They attacked as a unit and every one of them was shot down. The Biggin Wing was scrambled to work in pairs on the German fighter cover. Omer Levesque and Dean McDonald had flown together. As Omer had already made a name for himself, Dean flew as Number 2. Apparently, without looking to right or left, Omer had lunged to the attack. In no time Dean discovered that he had not one Messerschmitt on his tail but three. As he turned into their attack, he warned Omer, who took no heed. Dean's last view of his friend saw him scoring hits on one '109 with two more on his tail . . .[1]

At the beginning of 1942, seven RCAF fighter squadrons existed in the British Isles, although 417 Squadron would stand down to go to the Middle East in March. In replacement, 421 Squadron would form at Digby in April, and by mid-summer, seven units were again available for action. Canadian day fighter squadrons would serve exclusively in mixed-nationality wings until the latter part of 1942, when a distinctly Canadian wing formed at Kenley. Nonetheless, other wings received a preponderance of Canadian squadrons, and such was the case at Digby, and also in the autumn at Redhill in Surrey, around twenty-five miles south of London. The only RCAF formation to achieve group status within the overall umbrella of the RAF was 6 Group in Bomber Command. Other than that, the largest RCAF formation size would be the wing. RCAF wings would eventually be represented in the fighter-bomber, army cooperation/ reconnaissance, and day fighter disciplines, while the night fighter and intruder squadrons operated as individual RCAF units within RAF wings. In keeping with RAF practice, the squadrons frequently changed locations as units moved out of the front line for a rest or for training. The squadron composition of the wings thus changed frequently, and it was common for squadrons changing places with one another on front-line, offensive operations to swap aircraft as well, the most modern equipment always going to those units most operationally engaged.

In March, the offensive sweeps were resumed, and during the next few months, fighter squadrons were able to claim several kills on bomber escort missions and fighter sweeps. One of the most promising of the BCATP graduate newcomers was Flight Sergeant Donald R. Morrison of 401 Squadron. Morrison won a Distinguished Flying Medal on 6 June when, in concert with Wing Commander Jamie Rankin, he destroyed a Focke Wulf 190 in a heated battle over

Abbeville. Morrison had destroyed two aircraft previously, had shared in the destruction of another, and had also been credited with a probable and four others damaged.

Other Canadian day fighter pilots were having their fair share of adventures in mid-1942. Bob Morrow, still CO of 402 Squadron but now flying Spitfires, recalls:

> In the 1942 fighter efforts over France and the Low Countries, things happened with blinding speed. One minute, a sky full of airplanes — the next, nothing. Left on your own, the prudent course was to head for the "deck" and home. Once during the summer of 1942, I found myself alone and took just that action. Near ground level, I found four FW 190s closing from the rear. At that point, I was near Flushing on the Dutch coast. I went down the main street at zero feet — across the harbour — over the mole, and into the North Sea, while maintaining the usual defensive mode of turning into the FW 190s. Frankly, I think that they were uncoordinated . . . Eventually they gave up and I headed for home — yes, somewhat uncoordinated myself. I crossed what I thought was the English coast and to my horror, the first thing I saw was a windmill! For one terrible moment I thought I had put "black on red"[2] and headed back into Holland. However, my "coasting" was in fact dead on and just south of the Thames Estuary where, dammit, there is a windmill . . . ![3]

Meanwhile, 400 and 414 Squadrons, the Army Cooperation units, were in the throes of equipment changes. Their Lysander and Tomahawk aircraft were certainly not considered suitable for deep offensive operations over the European continent, yet limited missions were flown with them over the Channel and the French Coast during the closing months of 1941. George Burroughs was a 414 Squadron luminary who would have a fine wartime career, winning the DFC and building a solid reputation as an able, versatile fighter pilot. He recalls his earliest days in England on Tomahawks, and the conversion to Mustangs in the spring of 1942:

> I arrived in England in January 1942, and a month later was posted from Bournemouth Holding Centre to Army Cooperation Command, #91 Operational Training Unit, at Old Sarum, Wiltshire. For the next month or so, I flew Harvards and Tomahawks out of Oatlands Hill — the satellite airfield of Old

Sarum. Having finished Service Flying Training in Canada on beautiful concrete runways, it was something of a shock to experience Oatlands Hill. It was well named — a rolling meadow on the slope of a hill — not a runway in sight. However, as they say in the song, "You get used to it."

I do not recall any serious difficulties in the conversion from Harvards to Tomahawks. They were not a difficult aircraft to fly. A quirk I do remember about the Tomahawks was that some had been destined for the French Air Force and the instrumentation was in metric. In order not to overload the brains of the intrepid pilots, some mathematician had made the conversions and had painted lines on the instruments. For instance, on final approach you could dismiss the kilometer reading from your overloaded thoughts and be guided by the mileage marks.

The main problem with Tomahawks stemmed from maintenance difficulties — engine failure accounted for most of the "pranged" Tomahawks scattered over the English countryside.

In March '42, I was posted from the OTU to 414 Squadron, flying out of Croydon. This was great news — everyone had heard of Croydon — the International Airport near London. Visions of endless, hard-surfaced runways came to mind. The reality was — another rolling, bumpy, meadow, but this time surrounded by houses and factories. Landings and takeoffs were necessarily through a gap in the barrage balloon system . . . however, we were thankful for the balloons as, after all, it was said that without them the Island would sink.

In August, a number of us watched a Hurricane enter the Croydon ciruit to land. For some reason or other he came in downwind and touched down much too late. Braking hard, the aircraft continued to slide on the wet grass. He crashed through the perimeter fence, slid over a busy road, miraculously missing traffic and other obstacles, and ended up on a residential lawn with a wingtip inches away from the front window of a house. When we saw what was going to happen, we ran over to the scene. Our Second-in-Command, with great presence of mind, grabbed a fire extinguisher and joined in the race. Unfortunately, he was holding it upside down and was trailing fluid all the way. Arriving at the resting place of the Hurricane, it was apparent that the pilot was unharmed. At the same time, our quick-thinking Second-in-Command came chugging up, rushed to the airplane, and proceeded to put out the non-existent fire. As he held up the extinguisher, it exuded its last ineffective dribbles. At the same time, the lady of the house came out and heatedly berated the hapless Hurricane pilot. "Why don't you people learn to fly properly? This is the second time this has happened and I am getting fed up with such nonsense!"

Also while at Croydon, one member of the Squadron entered hospital to have his appendix removed. This was before he had posted any "Ops" time. While [the pilot was] under anesthetic, the doctor decided that a circumcision was also in order. After the shock and pain of the loss subsided, our pilot used to say that he had lost his foreskin on his first "operation."

In June 1942, the Squadron converted to Mustang Is. Along with being heavier and having more fire power than the Tomahawk, it was equipped with a better and more reliable Allison engine, which gave it more speed. It could hold its own, or better, with Spits or Me 109s, up to about 10,000 feet. At this altitude, its effectiveness fell off. It had a roomy cockpit and was a comfortable aircraft to fly — a good reconnaissance machine, built for low level and possessed of good endurance.

Soon after we acquired Mustangs, a decision was made to test them for night operations. Three or four of us were chosen to try it out. Flare pots were set out on the longest part of the field (I have described earlier the virtues(?) of Croydon airfield). The flares were purposely of low intensity, resulting in some of them being blown out, and they were almost invisible until you got onto final approach. Anyway, takeoff was no sweat and it was quite pleasant flying in the moonlight. Coming in to land was quite different. Throttling back, a shower of flame and sparks was emitted from the engine exhausts, completely obliterating everything else. Expletives from some of the other pilots indicated quite clearly that they were having the same problems. However, we couldn't stay up all night so we experimented with different types of approaches. A low, slow, power approach through the balloons cut down on the fireworks, and brought us back to earth with no "prangs." To no-one's surprise, it was decided from the results of the trial that flame retarders were to be installed to make night operations less "hairy."[4]

Frank Hanton of Kenora, Ontario, would also have a rich, productive wartime career on fighters, completing three tours of operations and winning the DFC. He destroyed nine enemy aircraft in the air and on the ground, and with a record of fifty-four trains destroyed and many other ground targets to boot, his punishment of the enemy was exceptional and varied. During the summer of 1942, he also had the honour of scoring 400 Squadron's first air-to-air kill in the potent new Mustang Is. Frank recalls the event, which occurred on one of the Squadron's first intruder missions over the Continent:

A decision was made to start taking the fight to the enemy, by flying low level day intruder missions (Rhubarbs) against enemy airfields, rail transport locomotives, fuel storage dumps, military convoys, and particularly, Luftwaffe day and night fighter facilities. The P51's Allison engine was derated to give maximum performance at 8000 feet, and with its level speed now increased to 400 mph, plus the heaviest armament of any fighter — eight guns — the Mustang was admirably suited for this highly dangerous program. Our very intensive training in low level navigation, tree-top attacks on simulated ground targets, plus the fact that we were getting maximum performance out of our aircraft were the instigating factors for selecting our Squadron to do the job. We were delighted to get the chance to hit the enemy in his own back yard. What follows is the description of a typical day intruder mission, with our targets being the rail line from Le Havre to Paris, the Paris Marshalling Yards, the rail line from Paris to Caen, and the Caen-Carpiquet Luftwaffe fighter station.

The Marshalling Yards and the airport were hot targets! The met forecast gave us ceilings of anything from 300 to 900 feet and visibilities of one to eight miles; an ideal day for this type of operation. A check of known enemy AA batteries on the French coast brought my decision to make entry eighteen miles east of Le Havre and to cross the coast twenty miles west of Arromanche on the return to base. Takeoff time was 06:45 hours, with a mission completion time of two hours and fifteen minutes for the two aircraft.

We crossed the Channel on the deck in light misty rain, which reduced the visibility to three to five miles, crossing the French coast dead on track and missing the enemy flak batteries. Altering course south, we picked up the Le Havre/Paris rail line as well as our first target — a freight train to Paris. In order to achieve the greatest damage to the engine, our attack was started from offset astern and our 50-calibre machine guns played havoc with the boilers, splitting them open with great clouds of steam and knocking the locomotive out of commission. The one attack did the job and it was on to the next. We knocked out one more engine before we hit the Paris Marshalling Yards, where we destroyed three engines, despite the heavy flak from the AA batteries. The rail line to Caen-Carpiquet only produced one train and we stopped that in the same manner as before. Fifteen miles from Caen, course was altered to the southwest in order to attack the Luftwaffe fighter station from the south. Hopefully, with complete surprise, still flying at tree-top height, we would be onto the aerodrome before they knew it. Heading for the dispersal areas and the control tower, which were primary targets, we hit and severely damaged three Me 109s on the ground and set two more on fire in their parking bays. The flak was intense and my '51 had a few holes in each wing by the time the attack was completed. As we headed for base on the deck, it had now started to rain, coupled with some light fog. This reduced the visibility to five miles and my Number Two lost contact with me as we headed for the coast. Near Bayeux the rain stopped, and over the shoreline, two Me 109s started an attack from 45 degrees astern. I let them get to about 600 yards, then broke left into a tight turn, shoving the power through the gate. After some violent maneuvers and three or four turns, I got on the tail of the second '109. As the distance closed, I dropped ten degrees of flap on my P51 to stay inside the turn of the '109 and opened fire with all guns at 300 yards, closing to 150 yards. Strikes were made on the left wing and fuselage, plus massive hits on the fin and rudder, which disintegrated. The '109 went into a slow roll and dove into the Channel. The other '109 was now at the nine o'clock position to me and 100 feet below, so a half roll with a shallow dive to close the gap was in order. However, he immediately went into a climb at full power, disappearing into the overcast before attack distance could be reached. So it was back down on the deck to cross the Channel, and I landed at Middle Wallop at 08:10 hours — ten minutes over the computed time. After two hours and twenty-five minutes air time, the score was one enemy aircraft destroyed in the air, five enemy aircraft severely damaged on the ground, and six locomotives destroyed; plus a control tower with some badly damaged windows! There were 23 holes in my P51 from AA fire, but the combat film confirmed one Me 109 destroyed — the first air-to-air victory for 400 Squadron.[5]

The RCAF night fighter units had very few opportunities to score during 1942, due to limited German operations over the Isles. A fourth unit, however, had been added to the rosters the previous November, when 418 Squadron formed at Digby, initially equipped with Douglas Boston IIIs. Number 418 commenced operations in March, the first RCAF squadron to do so in the hazardous and highly challenging night intruder role.

Equipment changes for the night fighter forces were fast and frequent. By the beginning of 1942, 409 Squadron had exchanged its cumbersome Defiants for Beaufighter IIs, and 410 was similarly equipped in March. In June, 406 and 409 Squadrons traded in their Merlin-engined Mk IIs for new, radial-engined Mk VIs, and in October, 410 moved to Digby and converted to Mosquito IIs. The lifestyle of the squadrons was nomadic, and moves were common. The following table consolidates the location, roles, and equipment of each of the RCAF night fighter units at the end of 1942:

Squadron	Aircraft	Location	Role
406	Beaufighter VI	Scorton	night fighter
409	Beaufighter VI	Coleby Grange	night fighter
410	Mosquito II	Digby	night fighter
418	Boston III	Bradwell Bay	intruder

As 1942 drew to a close, all the night fighter units had been in existence for at least a year, but total claims to that point were only fifteen confirmed victories and another six probables. In fact, 410 Squadron would not claim its first success until 22 January 1943.

During the early years of night fighting, airborne intercept radar technology was still in its infancy. Necessity being the mother of invention, a fascinating though operationally disastrous experiment came to pass in the form of the notorious "Turbinlight" squadrons. The idea was to employ a "mixed-bag" formation of aircraft to bring down enemy raiders at night. Ken Woodhouse was one of several Canadians who would become intimately involved with this ill-fated experiment at a place called High Ercoll.

Our Squadron Commander was a jolly RAF Flight Lieutenant by the name of Fogg. Why only a Flight Lieutenant I don't recall; why he was so jolly was also lost on me as he told me that the Hurricanes flew formation at night on the twin-engined Douglas Havocs, which were loaded down with batteries that energized a powerful searchlight built into its nose. This was the "Turbinlight." The twin-engined Havoc, then, provided the searchlight and the short-range radar while the single-engine Hurricanes (one at each wingtip of the Havoc) provided the firepower of four 20mm cannons each.

Formation flying at night does present certain problems with regard to station keeping. The Havoc had what I recall as a two-inch wide, possibly eight to ten feet long, white illuminated strip along the trailing edge of each wing. On a dark night, this was all the Hurricane pilot was able to see of the Havoc. The Hurricane pilot was expected to tuck his wing behind the Havoc's wing and ahead of the Havoc's tailplane, with the propeller very close to chewing away at the Havoc's wingtip. On a dark night it was necessary to fly that close to see the illuminated strip.

From the Hurricane's cockpit, darkened so that the pilot's visibility would not be distracted by the instrument lights, the pilot flew without reference to any engine or flight instruments, since he had to give his total attention to that white strip. When the line drew away, he had to increase throttle so as not to contact the Havoc's tail. If the line appeared too close, he had to throttle back so as not to contact the Havoc's wing. Should the white strip rise above him, the Havoc was climbing, so more throttle had to be used as the stick was eased back. Similarly, should the white strip descend, throttle had to be retarded and the stick adjusted forward. If it tilted right or left, the Havoc was in a turn and this had to be followed. Should the white strip disappear, panic reigned; being tucked in so closely, there was no room for error.

Loss of the strip meant a panic turn away from where the Havoc was expected, and now the Hurricane pilot faced a new dilemma. The cockpit was dark because the lights had been turned off and these had to be turned up so the pilot could read his instruments and regain control of the aircraft. Now, because the Hurricane was on its own with no way to rejoin the Havoc, it was necessary to find a way home alone.

It can be understood why I felt that the Havoc pilots should have been awarded medals for bravery. Their lives depended on the Hurricane pilot flying perfect formation with no lapses of skill or attention; and I, this new Squadron Hurricane pilot, had less than seven hours night flying since Secondary Flying Training School!

. . . On the night of 22 December, three days before Christmas, 1942, I had my opportunity to make history. We were scrambled to intercept an unidentified enemy aircraft coming into our area of responsibility. As was the custom on any takeoff, in fact it was the only way, I took off first and circled the airfield at 1000 feet or less to await the Havoc's takeoff. Alerted by a radio signal and the flaming exhausts under full throttle, I dove at the climbing Havoc as it left the runway and tucked my port wing behind his starboard wing. With cockpit lights out, I settled down to give my undivided attention to that illuminated white strip on the trailing edge of the Havoc's wing. My hands, feet and head would have to work automatically at my newly-learned skill, and I had to have confidence that the pilot of the Havoc would make no unannounced or quick move that might result in disaster to both of us. As I've said, there was little room for error.

The night was as dark as the inside of an eight-ball. The only thing I could see, in fact the only thing I dared to look at was that illuminated white strip. We climbed and set course under the direction of the ground controller. The routine was for the ground control to maneuver the Havoc/Hurricane combination to within a short distance behind the enemy aircraft, at which point the target could now be seen on the radar screen on board the Havoc. The Havoc/Hurricane would now close in on the target to within a few hundred yards, at which point the Havoc pilot would direct the Hurricane to fly around in front of the unseen Havoc to appear on its radar screen and be guided to within a very short distance behind the enemy aircraft.

Once in position directly behind the unsuspecting enemy, the Hurricane pilot had to fly straight and level behind the invisible enemy, switch on the gun sight, have his thumb over the live firing button for the four 20mm cannon, and then inform the Havoc that he was ready to fire. The Havoc pilot would begin a short count-down and on a prearranged signal, switch on the powerful searchlight in the nose of the Havoc, illuminating the target aircraft and the Hurricane right behind it; down would go the thumb on the firing button and down would go the enemy aircraft in flames.

All these last steps were to occur in seconds, before the tail-gunner in the enemy bomber would regain his sight and his wits and reply in kind to the brilliantly illuminated Hurricane behind him. This night, history of a sort was indeed almost made, but not the history I had hoped for. When I was in position directly behind the unseen enemy, I switched on my gunsight, had my thumb on the firing button and notified the Havoc that I was ready. The count-down began. Bingo! The light came on, my thumb shot forward on the firing button. This was all routine, as it was supposed to be — but what I saw in the gunsight in that millisecond after the light came on was an RAF Whitley bomber — that unmistakable nose-down attitude of the Whitley and, of all things, the rear gunner was firing at me!

To this day I cannot remember if I fired first, last, or at all. I do know the Havoc's powerful searchlight went out, I remember pushing the Hurricane's control column into the right corner of the cockpit and I remember scrambling like mad in the darkened cockpit to read the flying instruments in order to regain control. The change, so sudden from the brilliance of the searchlight to the blackness of an eight-ball night takes a bit of getting used to. I expect I was still a bit shook up when I eventually found my lonely way back to base. I do not recall hearing what happened to the Whitley. No doubt it would at least have needed a good washing out.[6]

The Turbinlight experience, though innovative, was not cost-effective, and it posed more danger to the hunters than to the hunted. The enemy could shoot at the backlit Hurricane, or even the Havoc, before the fighter could bring its guns to bear. Turbinlight also required a complex, unwieldy procedural interdependency between the teamed aircraft. Eventually, reason prevailed and the Havocs were equipped with their own forward firing armament.

As spring became summer, the fighter squadrons received a tremendous boost to their morale in the form of new Spitfire Mk IXs. In July, 401 Squadron became the first RCAF unit to receive this excellent aircraft, and 402 Squadron exchanged their older VBs for the newer models the following month. The Mk IX was an even match for the Focke Wulf, displaying similar climb rates and top speeds at the medium and lower altitudes. The uprated Merlin 61 engine of the Spitfire boasted a two-stage supercharger, however, which gave it a decided edge above 25,000 feet. The aircraft were relative equals in terms of manoeuvring capabilities: the Spitfire bested the Focke Wulf in level turns, while the German aircraft held a slight advantage when performing aileron rolls, dives, and zoom climbs. Generally speaking, the aircraft were so evenly matched that the results of a one-on-one confrontation were determined by the relative skill of the pilots.

In August 1942, the tranquility that had temporarily characterized air operations on the Channel coast underwent a major change, namely a combined operation against the port of Dieppe. This large-scale raid would involve the most extensive use of coordinated land, sea, and air forces against the defences of enemy-occupied Europe to date. From the aerial viewpoint, it served to determine the importance of air power to an invasion force in many categories. Its overall objectives were to test the German defences while attempting to lure as much of the available Luftwaffe as possible into the skies. The raid, codenamed Operation Jubilee, was largely a Canadian operation on the ground, while the continuous air umbrella planned for the beachhead came from all available Fighter Command assets.

On 19 August, 4,961 Canadian soldiers of the 2nd Canadian Division, accompanied by 1,075 British commandos and fifty U.S. Army Rangers, stormed eight separate beaches in the Dieppe area. The raiding force had specific orders to destroy selected German defences, airfield facilities, fuel dumps, power stations, radar installations, and other priority targets. The Allies were also assigned various intelligence-gathering missions, including the capture of some German servicemen, whose specific knowledge might benefit the Allied cause.

The ill-fated attackers were unable to achieve these objectives, however. The raiding force lost the element of surprise approximately one hour before landing and never recovered. Murderous defensive fire pinned the attackers to the beaches, and when the partial withdrawal was completed nine hours later, more than 900 Canadians were dead and another 2,000 captured. Acts of valour were legion on that desperate day, resulting in the award of two Victoria Crosses and a host of lesser decorations.

The rationale for and execution of the raid are sources of bitter contention fifty years after the fact, although many valuable lessons were learned and later applied to excellent effect during the landings in North Africa, Sicily, and Italy, and ultimately at Normandy, two summers downstream. The air battle over the beaches was much less controversial. Though the aim of a continuous air umbrella was achieved, the cost was significant. When the sums were done, 106 Allied aircraft, including eighty-eight fighters, had not returned. German losses were what one might expect for a defensive battle: forty-eight aircraft overall, although ninety-six were claimed destroyed by Allied aircraft at the time. As was typical of high-pitched, large-scale engagements over enemy territory, kill claims were inadvertently exaggerated, and Allied perceptions of a modest air success were further fuelled by an erroneous intelligence report which claimed that the Germans had lost as many as 160 aircraft. There can be no doubt that the Allied aircrews were well motivated, fought bravely, and were justifiably proud of the unbroken support they provided to the raiding forces. There can also be no doubt that the day's intense aerial activities fostered a new spirit of pride and confidence within Fighter Command — a condition that would help foster much more successful performances over northern Europe in the following years. The RCAF fighter squadrons were very active over the Dieppe beaches, as were the Mustangs of the two Army Cooperation squadrons and the Intruder Bostons of 418 Squadron. In fact, of the fifty-six fighter squadrons contributing to the aerial umbrella, six were RCAF units. Canadian fighter losses on the day would total thirteen aircraft and ten pilots, but not without considerable success and pride of achievement.

Some Canadian youngsters were gaining their first combat experiences in the skies over Dieppe, and not necessarily with RCAF fighter squadrons. "Duke" and Bruce Warren were twin brothers who went overseas together and were posted to the same RAF fighter squadron in June 1942. Both would have distinguished wartime careers, and both would win DFCs over Europe. Duke Warren recalls his experiences at Dieppe and the coincidences that would follow long after 19 August 1942:

. . . On 16 August, our Squadron moved to Eastchurch, on the Isle of Sheppy, to make room for other squadrons from the north that were being flown into Gravesend. Right afterwards, on the evening of 18 August, we had a special briefing: the plan for a "raid in strength" on the French coastal town of Dieppe.

It was emphasized that it was a Canadian Army show, with great things expected of them. As the only two Canadians on 165 Squadron, Bruce and I were most interested in this news and also very proud that Canadian troops were being used. (In the nature of the friendly chaffing that went on in the flight rooms, we were often held accountable for any MT accidents or worse incidents in which the Canadian Army were involved, no matter what the circumstances.)

We were told that the troops would go ashore at daylight or earlier and begin the withdrawal around noontime. There was no suggestion that they would stay longer. As a matter of fact, we were told if we crash-landed or bailed out over the land, to make no attempt to reach Dieppe and the Canadians if it was later than 1100 hrs.

Our first takeoff was very early; shortly after first light. We patrolled over Dieppe for roughly forty minutes before being relieved. We saw no enemy aircraft, although it was possible to see a tremendous battle going on below. There were still some boats waiting off-shore it seemed, and there were many splashes around them from the German heavy guns. We returned to Eastchurch via Beachy Head, as there was a special routing that way for the fighter support. After refueling and some pilot changes, we waited for the next scramble to be sent down from Fighter Command.

Our next sortie took off at mid-morning. As there had been reports of enemy fighter and bomber aircraft over Dieppe harbour, everyone was alert as we approached Dieppe at about 18,000 feet. Our Section, Yellow, consisted of our Flight Commander, Flight Lieutenant Campbell-Colquhoun, RAF, Pilot Officer Pederson, an American in the RAF as Yellow Two, my twin as Yellow Three, and I was Number Four.

The first fifteen minutes or so were uneventful. Then a terrific air battle commenced as German fighter squadrons entered the area to provide cover for Dornier 217 and Ju 88 bombers, which were attacking Allied shipping below. Since this was really my first engagement with enemy aircraft and there were so many of both them and us, I found it too confusing to track individual aircraft. Fortunately, Flight Lieutenant Campbell-Colquhoun was an experienced fighter pilot; he kept his Section together as a fighting unit. We attacked a Do 217, which was bombing landing craft, and each of us in Yellow Section fired. The bomber was destroyed but the crew bailed out. After this episode, there was a series of small dogfights with inconclusive results on both sides. When our fuel reached minimums, we were relieved by another Spitfire squadron. Over forty RAF fighter squadrons were engaged in all, though not all at once.

Again we returned to Eastchurch to re-arm and refuel. We pilots were quite excited as we recounted our combats and this carried over to the groundcrews as they went about their work. Although some aircraft had been hit, none were lost, and Squadron morale was high. We had time for a hasty lunch at the flight line before being placed on five minute standby as soon as the aircraft were turned around.

Our next scramble came in the afternoon. We were briefed to patrol over the withdrawal which was taking place and, unless in pursuit of an enemy aircraft, we were told not to fly over land. Furthermore, we were told not to fly under 8000 feet because the Navy had been told their ships could fire on any aircraft below 7000 feet, and the RN gunners were naturally nervous about aircraft. While we were circling above the ships, a Hurricane came from the direction of Dieppe with a tell-tale stream of glycol trailing behind. We knew he was not going far. However, he made our ships and bailed out about a mile in front of one, as we had been told to do. We understood if you bailed out in front of a warship there was a good chance they would lower a boat and pick you up, but if you bailed out behind one, not only might they miss seeing you, they might be reluctant to return for pick up.

While patrolling over the area, I saw a destroyer burning. The extent of this fire rather surprised me since I believed ships made of steel and iron would be slow to burn. This was not the case, however: HMS *Berkley* was badly damaged and had to be torpedoed and sunk by HMS *Albrighton*. Although we were all keen to engage the Luftwaffe over the ships, no such event took place. This patrol finished uneventfully.

. . . If I had told my Squadron mates on that day in August, 1942, that ten years later in 1952 I would be a Squadron Commander who would lead supersonic fighters in a commemorative flight over Dieppe, they would have shouted for the men with the white coats. If I had also told them that only fifteen years from 1942 I would be the Chief Flying Instructor at a Luftwaffe Fighter OTU, they would have called for the firing squad! Yet these things did come to pass. What strange twists happen in a lifetime.

Incidentally, during my tour as CFI at Waffenshule 10 at Oldenburg, Germany, I met a German fighter pilot, Paul Schauder. Paul flew an FW 190 over Dieppe and since we became friends, we have had many interesting conversations about the raid.

Regarding Dieppe, my part, and that of my brother's, was small, in a fight that produced inconclusive results in relation to other, larger battles. Still, I remember with pride how it was to be a Canadian airman flying above Canadians involved in their first major Allied landing against Hitler.

I still say proudly, "I fought at Dieppe."[7]

War often gives rise to some truly amazing coincidences. Such was the case with Dick Reeves, a Canadian fighter pilot serving with the RAF at Dieppe.

In 1942 I was attached to the RAF and a member of 129 RAF "Mysore" Squadron, which was equipped with Spitfire 5Bs. We were briefed on the evening of 18 August 1942, and told the plan was to hold Dieppe for twenty-four hours. . . . Our Squadron was to strafe a heavy gun battery south-east of Dieppe, and then Lord Lovat's commandos were to go in and silence it.

Flying Officer Jones and I were to take off early in the dark and attack a lighthouse which was being used as a spotting position for the heavy guns. Flying Officer Jones was leading and we arrived at the coast of France, south of the lighthouse just as dawn was breaking. We made a circle to the south inland and came back out toward the coast where we were attacked by light "ack ack," and the tail of my aircraft was hit. We came out to the coast and turned north at sea level. Flying Officer Jones received a direct hit from "ack ack" on the shore and blew up beside me. I carried on to the lighthouse and gave the upper, glass portion a long burst of cannon and machine gun fire. As I swung away to the north I could see the battle raging, and some of the ships fired at me. I got out of there in a hurry and headed for home.

I was a couple of miles off Brighton, flying about half a mile from a lone Boston bomber and I relaxed for a moment. Suddenly, the Boston was attacked and blew up. Just as I was about to maneuver, I was hit by a string of bullets, a cannon shell hit my mirror and blew the canopy to pieces, shot off my oxygen mask and put small pieces of metal in my face, hands and legs. I swung the plane around and faced my attacker. I gave him a burst of cannon and machine gun fire head-on. We just missed colliding; his plane dived steeply at the sea from a low altitude and I don't think he ever pulled out. My Squadron was just leaving and they saw one of the two FW 190s. I was credited with a probable.

I landed safely at Thorney Island and the ambulance was waiting. Fortunately, my wounds were only superficial. The next day, I counted up to twenty-two holes in my plane and then gave up. I am sure the armour plating saved my hide; the Spitfire was one tough aircraft.

In Eric McGuire's book, "Dieppe August 19," he recounts how Lord Lovat was worried about blowing a hole in the barbed wire at the beach:

"By a stroke of luck, just then cannon-firing fighters came in to attack the lighthouse, which was also the battery OP, and the resulting clamour drowned out the noise of the explosions."

Just prior to takeoff, Flying Officer Jones asked to borrow my watch to time the operation because the clock in his plane was not working. It was a beautiful Gruen watch given to me by a friend before I left Canada. I had a running battle with the Air Ministry for months to recover something for my loss. They finally allowed me 2 pounds, 10 shillings.

The Squadron was called the Mysore Squadron because the Maharajah of Mysore sponsored it. If a Squadron member survived, he was presented with a medal with a two-headed Ghundabarunda bird on it. I have one.

A short while ago, I wrote to Lord Lovat, because I was curious to hear what he had to say about the attack. I enclose a copy of his reply. I believe his was one of the few successes at Dieppe! The following note was written on House of Lords stationery:

March 20th

Dear Reeves,

Many thanks for your letter of Feb. 3rd and my apologies for delay but I have been overseas in the Middle East. You certainly had a busy morning in August '42 during the Dieppe raid and all my commandos can now belatedly express their thanks for keeping the enemy's heads down — first when you shot up the light house which blacked out during the run in to the beach, and later in broad daylight when a low level attack was made on the battery of heavy guns before our final assault where we had a good scrap. Glad to hear that you are still alive and kicking.

Just in case you are interested in a full account of the Dieppe Operation where all three branches of the Services took a beating we could ill afford, I think you might be interested in this book — now in paper back. (. . . McGuire's "Dieppe August 19")

Yours,

(Signed)
Lovat[8]

———•◦••◦•———

Throughout the balance of the summer and autumn, Fighter Command continued offensive operations whenever the fickle weather over northern Europe permitted. From now on, the fighters would spend an increasing proportion of their combat time escorting a growing force of American bombers. These missions became progressively more aggressive and far-flung as the Americans attempted to prove their case for daylight precision bombing. The escort missions grew increasingly more complex and sophisticated, including the addition of diversions and feints, as the German radar controllers became more proficient. When air-to-air combats proved scarce, the Spitfires flew a plethora of strafing missions and train-busting sorties.

Commitments to other war fronts were now siphoning off many of the RAF fighter squadrons from their British bases. Many units were dispatched to North Africa for the "Torch" landings in November, and the air offensive over northwest Europe was devolving more and more to Commonwealth and other foreign-national squadrons based in the British Isles. Some combat-seasoned Canadians were now returning for second tours, and the surviving early BCATP graduates were becoming experienced enough to fill some of the more senior flying command positions. As a measure of Canadian national pride, pressure was also being brought to bear to create larger Canadian flying units. During September, 412 and 416 Squadrons flew unofficially as a Canadian wing from Redhill, while in November the first official RCAF fighter wing was created at Kenley.

Duke Warren and his twin brother Bruce spent their entire wartime careers as RCAF members of RAF units — a not-uncommon situation for Canadian airmen during the Second World War. The wide degree of variance practised by the British in accepting foreign nationals on their units is interesting, for it demonstrates both the admirable and the darker sides of wartime British society.

In many RAF squadrons, men from the UK were in a minority, the majority being made up with men from the Dominions, along with Poles, Norwegians, Free French, and others. In general terms, these "mixed" squadrons performed as well as those made up of one nationality. Indeed, I often heard it said that once on a mixed squadron, one had no wish to change to a national one.

However, I must say that in addition to the friendly chaffing and joking that went back and forth between all nationalities, it was only the English who had never left England that occasionally used the term "Colonials" in a rather mean and disparaging way. Those Englishmen who had served overseas pre-war had a rather different outlook.

At squadron level, on a one-to-one basis, one would occasionally meet an Englishman with a decidedly anti-Colonial attitude. A few possessed an unwarranted feeling of superiority, both professionally and socially, based on a perception that Colonials were of a lower order.

I recall an example of "snobbishness" or imagined superiority of class at an RAF Station where I was under training for a few weeks. There was a beautiful WAAF girl of mixed race; if I recall correctly, an English father and Burmese mother. All the English officers were terribly keen to take her out, but her boyfriend was an Australian. I remember several English officers discussing how physically attractive the young woman was. However, the situation was summed up by one officer who said, "The fool will probably marry her."

There was also an attitude among some RAF officers that Colonials were an undisciplined lot and had to be shown what soldiering was all about. The first time I personally met that attitude of superiority was when I checked into the RAF Station at Hawarden, #57 OTU, near Chester. After a few "nit-picking remarks" about Colonials, the Adjutant asked me to visit "one of your people CBd (Confined to Barracks) in Officers Quarters awaiting court-martial," and just as I was about to leave, he said, "Well, he is an American, and you are all alike from over there." His tone and manner indicated people from "over there" didn't amount to much . . .

The chap awaiting court-martial was Don Gentile, and we became good friends while chatting as I visited him while he was in confinement. He later became one of the highest scoring fighter pilots in the USAAF with 22 confirmed air-to-air and seven air-to-ground victories.

However, I must say in all fairness that I met quite a few "upper class" Englishmen, and by no means all had that air of superiority. Our Squadron Commander for part of my brother's and my first tour was a first class man whom we respected and admired, and we continued to be friends of his until the time of his death. He wrote Fighter Command Headquarters about us, asking them to send us to his Squadron for our second tours, so he obviously had confidence in our skills. Though he made a remark about us having little academic learning, this was made by a man who had attended Oxford . . . and his statement, "They represented the New World at its best," might even be considered flattering.

There was an element of RAF members who also felt that the senior Squadron Leader and Flight Commander positions should invariably go to RAF officers. Yet, my twin and I both served as Flight Commanders in an RAF Squadron, and were being looked at for Squadron CO positions, but our tours came to an end before authority could find two Squadron Leader positions for us on the same Wing . . .[9]

Carl Fumerton served extensively with RAF as well as RCAF units, and has fond recollections of the diverse cultural mosaic which was often a characteristic of the "mixed" squadrons.

It has been said that "variety is the spice of life," and in the RAF squadrons we certainly had the variety. Along with English, Scottish, Irish and Welsh members, we had Australians, New Zealanders, Americans, Canadians, South Africans, Poles and Czechs. Fighter pilots are great individualists and it was quite an insight getting to know their individual characteristics, which often tied in with their national or regional ones. For instance, take the Polish pilots when practicing dogfights . . . they were very partial to a head-on attack. What they were *not* partial to was breaking away first, regardless of the range. Knowing that propensity, I always accommodated them. They were good pilots and very brave, but their losses were understandably high. Out of about six Polish pilots in 32 Squadron, one of them later told me that he was the only survivor . . .

Without taking anything away from the Canadian squadrons, the "mixed" squadron was, by its diversity, an interesting study and a rich experience.[10]

Bad flying weather prevailed over the Continent during the latter months of 1942 and combat opportunities were scarce. Number 401 Squadron was dealt a major blow on 8 November, when Don Morrison, by now a Flight Lieutenant, failed to return from an escort mission over Lille.

Morrison was the leading RCAF scorer at the time, with six confirmed kills and a string of probables to his credit. The Fates were somewhat lenient in his case. Minus a leg, Morrison parachuted to safety and was taken prisoner. During his incarceration he garnered a tremendous amount of respect from his German captors and was eventually repatriated to Canada through Switzerland and the United Kingdom. King George VI added the DFC to his DFM at a special investiture held in his honour.

If the air war over northern Europe in 1942 was relatively benign, such was certainly not the case in the Middle East. The year there could best be characterized as one of great reversals of fortune and, in the case of Malta, uncommonly stubborn resistance and ultimate triumph.

On the eve of 1942, tiny, defiant Malta was being pummelled by combined air fleets of the *Regia Aeronautica* and the Luftwaffe. This all-out blitz continued with unabated ferocity throughout April, the worst month for the defenders. During that month, the British government awarded the island a collective George Cross, unique tribute for stout resistance in the face of near-impossible odds. Though the bombing campaign against Malta eliminated the island's offensive forces and dramatically improved the scale of supplies reaching Axis units in North Africa, this respite for the Germans and Italians would be short-lived. The losses to the defending fighter forces were significant, which made reinforcements, on the infrequent occasions when they were able to get through, a most welcome event. Noel Ogilvie, a Canadian fighter pilot who served with a number of RAF and RCAF fighter squadrons during the war, recalls his own exciting adventures in delivering much-needed Spitfires to Malta in the spring of 1942:

. . . February 1942 was a time when the most requested dance tunes at London's Hammersmith Palais and Covent Gardens were *Tangerine*, *Green Eyes* and *Frenesi* — and oh yes, *The Lambeth Walk*, *A Pair of Silver Wings*, and *I'm Going to Hang Out My Washing on the Siegfried Line*. It was also the time when nude extravaganzas at the Windmill Theatre, ("We never close" was their motto) were within the law as long as, of course, there was no square dancing. I was a member of 130 Squadron stationed at Portreath, Cornwall, in England. We had been operating out of this base for approximately eight months and were equipped with Spitfire Mark IIAs with long range tanks permanently fixed midway on the port wing. We were most often used on long range sorties, such as escorting Blenheims low level across the North Sea to Holland, or on raids on the submarine pens at Brest, France.

At this time, a signal arrived from 10 Group posting the entire Squadron overseas. Immediately, we were transported to West Kirby near Liverpool where we joined a convoy whose ships were loaded with, among other things, Spitfire Mark VCs. This Spitfire was capable of accommodating a ninety gallon belly tank.

We arrived at Gibraltar about 30 April 1942, unloaded our Spitfires, assembled and test flew them. The aircraft were then hoisted aboard the Aircraft Carrier *Eagle* and on the evening of 16 May 1942, we boarded the *Eagle*; of course, by this time the word was out that we were on our way to Malta. Before sun-up, the *Eagle* was under way and as soon as there was light enough to read the numbers on the fuselages, we wandered among the anchored Spitfires on the stern of the flight deck to claim the aircraft assigned to us. I found mine, a new Mark VC model bearing the number BR 163.

We walked around our aircraft looking for imperfections, checked inside the cockpit and double checked the fuel gauges and the tanks themselves. I was to be Number Two off the carrier, immediately behind the CO. By evening, when we were assured all was ready, we went below for a briefing by a Royal Navy carrier pilot on the basics of flying aircraft off the deck of an aircraft carrier.

Now the mood was a festive one; perhaps this was the only countermeasure the pilots could assemble before making their first takeoff at sea the following morning. This joyfulness was reinforced by:

1. an announcement that we might have to fight our way into the island, and
2. a note that was printed at the bottom of our instruction sheet. This read with typical British candor, and I quote: "If you don't make it, don't flap or WORRY."

As the *Eagle* was not a large carrier, (it had been converted from a World War I cruiser) we were promised a takeoff wind over the deck of thirty knots. For a further takeoff aid, as the Spitfire did not have adjustable flaps, a wedge of wood was inserted between the underside of the wing and the retracted flap. This was to be the icing on the confidence cake for a pilot who was about to make his first carrier takeoff with an overloaded aircraft. This confidence build-up reached its climax when we were informed that no Spitfire would be allowed to return to the *Eagle* after takeoff in the event of aircraft problems. If there was trouble, the unfortunate pilot would have a choice:

1. attempt a belly landing on the sea, or
2. bail out near one of the escort ships in the hope of being picked up, or
3. if the above options lacked appeal, then fly south into North Africa, land, destroy the aircraft and then set out for home.

Daybreak found the carrier off Algiers turning into, of all the luck — a light wind. We were all strapped in our cockpits waiting for the word to start our engines. "Twenty-two knots over the deck, sir!" The Wing Commander in charge of these operations gave the signal to start engines. Our CO, with the promise of thirty knots still ringing in his ears, and with his deep concern for the welfare of his pilots, immediately stood up in his cockpit and yelled back: "Like bloody hell!"

Well, things got a bit nervy amongst those in charge. Black smoke increased in volume from the stack, and I began to think that we were a beautiful target and were going to be torpedoed for sure in these hostile waters. Without waiting more than a minute longer, the loudspeaker announced that, by strange coincidence, there were thirty knots over the deck. Then, one by one, the Spitfires coughed into life and were sent roaring down the deck. Our CO was a heavyset chap of about 230 pounds. At the time I weighed about 170 pounds and I quietly thought, as the CO was revving up his engine with the brakes on in preparation for take-off: "If he gets off I should have no trouble."

When the CO got to the end of the carrier deck, he disappeared. "He's bought it!" I whispered to myself, while easing my aircraft into starting position. I was wrong, for suddenly, off in the distance a little Spitfire appeared, struggling for height. "He's made it! Alleluia!"

With renewed confidence, I opened the throttle, raced down the deck of the carrier and found what it was like to drop like an elevator almost to the surface of the Mediterranean. When I was at a safe height, I dropped the flaps, out flew the little wooden wedges, retracted the flaps and settled in for the long haul to Malta.

We levelled off at approximately 18,000 feet. There wasn't a cloud in the sky. Africa lay off to the right, Algeria floated behind and soon Tunisia appeared on the horizon, the air above it wavering in the torrid heat billowing off the land. Here, we banked south-east off Cap Bon for the run through the Strait of Sicily down to the Island of Pantellaria, and then east to our destination. About twenty minutes after we passed Pantellaria, we caught sight of Malta dead ahead — like a big oak leaf lying in the emerald water of the Mediterranean. As we approached the landing fields, Malta-based Spitfires protected our arrival from any enemy fighters that might have come to intercept us. Flying under this protection, we whistled in from the sea and delivered the much-needed aircraft safely.

After I had been at Halfar with 185 Squadron for two months, I was asked to return to Gibraltar and lead a new group into Malta; again, we would launch from the aircraft carrier *Eagle*. This time, we were launched with greater authority for two reasons: first, these new Spitfires had laminated wood propellers which gave much greater acceleration, and secondly, the Malta diet had reduced my weight considerably.

While preparing my course from the *Eagle* to Malta, I wasn't looking forward to the long haul around the Tunisian Cap Bon. I decided to shorten the flight by cutting across so-called neutral Tunisia from its western border on the Mediterranean to its eastern coast on the same latitude as Malta. In my mind, the gamble was that the risk of Tunisian reaction was no greater than running into Me 109s rounding Cap Bon — especially when we carried 90 gallon belly tanks.

As we left the east coast of Tunisia on our last leg, I checked my reference point and set course for Malta at approximately 105 degrees. Here we encountered a dark brown haze, where one can see straight down, but not ahead. About ten minutes off the east coast of Tunisia with only the sight of water below, I began to hunger for a little reassurance that I was on the right course. I began having visions of pulling an Amelia Earhart and missing that tiny island of ours and leading all those who were following me off into the wild blue yonder. I called fighter control at Malta, whose call-sign was Gondar, for a homing vector. At once, a national-socialist Oxford accent came on the blower that I didn't recognize: "Oh, hello Bullet Blue One, steer 040." At that moment, all hell broke loose in my cockpit. I was steering 105; and with all this being audible to the members of my following, the tail of each Spitfire twitched nervously. "My God, the winds must have changed drastically," I thought. "I must be near the coast of Libya." While I was reciting the 23rd Psalm and indicating to the Lord that I would become a monk if He got me out of this one, Gondar nearly blew the earphones out of my helmet.

"No, No. NO! Bullet One — Steer 105, steer 105, Over." There was no mistaking that voice. It was Group Captain Woodhall. He had been fighter controller at 11 Group during the Battle of Britain and had been sent out to Malta to direct air operations there. "Woody" had a voice like a Russian who had been drinking vodka all day, sitting at the bottom of an old cistern singing the *Volga Boatman*; there was no mistaking it. A German fighter controller in Sicily had been up to his old tricks again, trying to home me in to Pachino, a fighter base in Sicily. I should have identified the chicanery immediately. This controller had had some success along this line, including a Wellington with an Air Marshal on board. One can imagine their surprise on landing to find the welcoming party greeting them with: "Bonjourno, bonjourno."

With Woody's assurance, I held my course, gradually losing height, till we roared over the coast of Malta at 500 feet. We still had plenty of fuel in reserve and had knocked off considerable time from that attributable to previous flights. On 11 August, 1942, just twenty-one days after my last takeoff, the aircraft carrier *Eagle* was sunk by four torpedoes from the Nazi submarine U-73 with the loss of 230 of her crew. That "Great Lady" had made no less than ten trips into that enemy infested sea, and at each time had launched her cargo with great care, hospitality, dispatch and efficiency.[11]

Though the attacks on the island peaked in terms of sortie count during April, extremely heavy fighting occurred throughout the summer and autumn. While no RCAF fighter squadrons were deployed to Malta during the crisis period, from the summer of 1942 onwards, *at least* one in four of all fighter pilots defending the island was a Canadian in RAF service. Buck McNair was very successful prior to the peak raids, and other Canadians also forged admirable records during those days, including J. W. "Willie the Kid" Williams with ten victories. Nevertheless, the most successful Canadians did the bulk of their scoring from late spring onwards. In all, nineteen members of the RCAF died in service on Malta, and RCAF fighter pilots accounted for 160 Axis aircraft destroyed.

Rod Smith of Regina distinguished himself in Maltese skies during the second half of 1942 while serving as a fighter pilot with 126 (RAF) Squadron. He would account for six enemy aircraft destroyed during this Mediterranean tour, then add seven and a fifth more on a very successful second operational tour in northwest Europe during the final year of the war. He recollects a high-pitched action from October 1942, which marked the official beginning of what would later be referred to as the "October Blitz":

Our principal task was to intercept German and Italian aircraft attacking the island. The enemy usually made two or three fighter sweeps over us every day, but they had not come with their standard bomber, the Ju 88, since the end of July. In early October, our photographic reconnaissance over southern Sicily, some sixty miles to the north, showed that a fairly large number of '88s and a very large number of Me 109 fighters were being assembled there, so we knew something was brewing.

Early in the morning of 11 October 1942, 126 Squadron, consisting of eight Spitfires in two Sections of four, was scrambled from Luqa aerodrome to meet the first of a new series of raids that we were expecting, and which later became known as the October Blitz. As we climbed above the haze over Malta, the upper sky became more beautiful than any I had ever seen in the Mediterranean; it was bright blue and crystal clear, with a magnificent bank of cumulus cloud far off to the north-east. As we continued our climb, the cone-shaped upper part of Mount Etna, a hundred and thirty miles away, came into view as always, seeming to float on the perpetual haze which hid its lower slopes and all the rest of Sicily. It was the only part of the outside world we could see from high over Malta, so it made a superb northpoint.

Our senior Flight Commander, Rip Jones, was leading us from Red Section; I was leading Blue Section, keeping just behind and below Red. During our climb, the duty controller, constantly informed through ground radar, vectored us first to Zonqor Point at Malta's eastern tip, and then out to sea to the north-east towards the great bank of cumulus. Two or three minutes later, he told us that about ten enemy bombers, escorted by about seventy fighters were coming towards us from thirty miles away, and that we were to level out when we got to 18,000 feet, the usual approach height for German bombers attacking Malta at that time.

When we were almost up to 18,000 feet, we suddenly caught sight of the oncoming raid, ahead of us and slightly to our right. It was the most awesome sight of our lives, in large part because the background cumulus presented the whole array to a single glance. It comprised nine Ju 88s in three vics abreast, slightly above us and still quite a way off, with a close escort of about forty Me 109s rising up behind them in tiers of six abreast, like a staircase, to 24,000 feet. These were all surmounted by a top cover of about twenty '109s, stepped up from 28,000 to 32,000 feet and making vapour trails. Ranging ahead and to each side at about 22,000 feet were a few pairs of '109s, seeking to find, pounce on, and scatter formations of intercepting Spitfires, though none of them showed any signs of having spotted us.

Just as we reached the height of the '88s, the main gun panel on Rip's starboard wing blew off. He turned away and down, and in confusion, told Red Three to take over the Squadron instead of telling me, the deputy leader. This should not have made any real difference because the '88s were fast drawing abreast of us to our right, and it was obvious that all each one of us had to do was to make a 180-degree turn to the right to get in behind them, choose one, and fire at it. It caused some hesitation though, no doubt because Red Three was considering whether to bring the remainder of Red Section in behind Blue. As our closing speed with the '88s was about 500 mph, it was vital that we start turning in towards them a few seconds before they actually drew abreast, or else our attack would develop into a drawn-out chase right under the close escort, a hopeless predicament. I only saw one of Red Section's pilots begin to turn-in in time, and even he did not turn sharply enough. I began about the same time he did, but so as not to lose one more second, I turned so sharply that the other three pilots in my Section got left behind, another circumstance flowing from an armourer's failure to secure Rip's gun panel.

I decided to attack the '88 on the far side of the formation, the one on its extreme left, to avoid being embroiled in any ganging up on the nearest one or two, as had happened before. Therefore, I headed right across and behind the whole formation. I need not have worried about ganging up though, because no other pilot of the Squadron completed the inward turn, except the Red Section pilot who had turned in sufficient time, and though he opened fire at the nearest '88, he was well out of range. This was an error more the rule than the exception in the first half of the air war.

As I began my passage across, the rear gunners in the '88s began firing their machine guns at me continuously, the tracers from them looking like coils of thrown white rope. Although I kept slightly below the level of the tailplane of each '88 as I passed behind it, in order to keep out of the line of sight of its upper gunner, cross-fired tracer from the '88s on each side never let up.

Part way across, I noticed that the '109s making up the first tier of the close escort, though quite close behind the '88s, were about 400 feet above them and me. It suddenly struck me that this would be a good chance to observe the black crosses I knew were on them, but which had never actually caught my attention in the past. I therefore looked upwards to the undersides of their wings and spotted them instantly, outlined in white and as startlingly clear as recognition posters showed them to be.

For some reason, the '109s seemed to take no notice of me during my passage across, probably because I was more or less hidden under their noses. I finally arrived unscathed at a point about 250 yards behind the '88 on the far left side of the formation. I opened fire at its port engine, which almost instantly began to pour out white and black smoke, quickly followed by flames, which grew longer by the second. Cross-fired tracer was coming continuously from the two '88s to the right of the one I was firing at, though that did not worry me much because it was only rifle-calibre. After about three seconds, however, one or two streams of tracer began to pass over me from behind, telling me that the '109s were finally on to me and that from the cannon in each one of them, about a dozen non-tracing 20mm shells a second would be coming my way, along with the tracer bullets from their two machine guns. Their pilots must have been either poor shots or getting in each other's way. I was sure I wouldn't last long if I stayed there, but I hated to leave because the cannons in my Spitfire were good for twelve seconds firing, and although the flames coming from the '88's port engine were now very long, it didn't seem to be slowing down much, let alone starting down, which rather surprised me.

After about three more seconds, and with mixed feelings, I stopped firing and started violently down into an aileron turn to the right; a diving spiral a '109 could not keep up with for more than a few seconds, because its ailerons hardened up much more quickly than a Spitfire's in a dive. I had scarcely begun this, though, when I changed my mind and started back up. I desperately wanted to see the '88 finished off and it had struck me that coming back up behind it very suddenly might fox the '109s for a few seconds. I got behind it again, but this time I fired at its starboard engine, which quickly streamed smoke and caught fire, just like the port one. After about three seconds, tracer started coming at me from behind again, so after three further seconds, by which time both engines of the '88 were streaming very long flames and it had started to veer away to the left and down, I stopped firing and went down in another violent spiral to the right. I had only one round left to fire but I didn't know it at the time.

I kept in the spiral for about three or four turns, heading almost vertically downwards and feeling immune from the '109s while doing so. When my ailerons got very hard, I stopped spiralling, shallowed my dive, and aimed for Zonqor Point. I looked around for the '88 and caught sight of it going down almost vertically, streaming fire and smoke. With only two or three thousand feet to go, it suddenly exploded into two main pieces, which made great splashes in the sea.

After a very close call with two '109s, which apparently had followed me down, waiting for me to come out of my spiral, I landed safely. My '88 was the first Hun to come down in the October Blitz. The whole sequence of the interception and the engagement had been so exciting and kaleidoscopic that I felt downright exultant for an hour or so. I learned the next day that the '88's wireless operator, Gunther Grams, had been lucky enough to bail out at some stage and be picked up by one of our rescue launches. I was pleased, as I always was when aircrew got out, enemy or not.[12]

Henry Wallace McLeod of Regina, Saskatchewan, ran up an impressive scoresheet on the island and would eventually become the most successful RCAF fighter pilot of the war with twenty-one confirmed victories. During an eighteen-week shooting spree from June to October 1942, McLeod accounted for thirteen of those kills, in spite of the fact that he and his mates were often outnumbered by a factor as high as six-to-one. E.C.R. Baker remembers the Malta experiences of Wally McLeod, the "Canadian Eagle":

During his short stay in the Mediterranean, Wally was shot down twice, shot up and damaged five times, managed to shoot down a German bomber when he had only one single cannon still firing and shot down six Huns in five days. Over the same period he also lost twenty-five pounds in weight!

Henry Wallace McLeod was born in Regina, Saskatchewan, on the 17th of December, 1915. Before the war, Wally trained as a teacher at the Regina Normal School, but obtained a car and trailer and travelled from town to town in southern Saskatchewan showing movies.

Wally joined the Royal Canadian Air Force exactly one year after the start of the Second World War. He carried out his flying training at schools in Saskatchewan and Ontario. On his Wings parade in April 1941 he was commissioned, and after a brief embarkation leave was posted overseas to England, where he became a member of the famous 602 (Glasgow) Squadron. He served later with 411 (RCAF) Squadron, but during the whole of his stay in England, from May 1941 to April 1942, he saw very little action and was unable to claim any victories at all. But in May 1942 he landed in Malta and immediately things livened up. On his second day with his new unit, 603 (Edinburgh) Squadron, he was flying wingman to the Commanding Officer, Squadron Leader L.D. Hamilton, when he sighted and attacked a large formation of three-engined Italian bombers. In a combined movement Hamilton and McLeod each managed to get in several bursts at one of the bombers, which slowed down and began to smoke. Curbing his natural excitement at the prospect of his first kill, Wally concentrated his attention on the Cant 1007 to the exclusion of everything else about him — a mistake many an inexperienced fighter pilot has made before, but never made again. The inevitable happened; an unseen Italian fighter closed in behind Wally's Spitfire and the next moment, shells were pouring into the fuselage of his fighter. Breaking away sharply, Wally thanked his lucky stars that the Italian pilot was a rotten shot, and then carefully nursed his damaged aircraft back to base. As he landed, he realized that he had already learned far more in half-an-hour over Malta than he had in the previous twelve months in England. During the rest of his short stay in Malta, Wally's education in the art of aerial duelling progressed at the same rapid rate and within a few days he had destroyed his first victim, an Italian Macchi 202, which in Wally's own words "went into the drink from sheer fright." His second, a Messerschmitt 109, exploded in mid-air so close to Wally's fighter that bits of wreckage from it embedded themselves in the wing of his Spitfire.

"The pilot was thrown clear (Wally reported later) and his chute opened. After he had hit the water I circled him and he waved to me, apparently quite cheerfully. So I dropped my dinghy for him to show that I had no hard feelings either. He did not make any attempt to climb into the rubber dinghy and the reason became apparent when one of our rescue launches came out to pick him up. He had a cannon shell through his chest, and he died in the launch."

Shortly after this incident, Wally was transferred to a newly formed Spitfire unit, Number 1435 Flight, and soon became Flight Commander. During one of his first actions with his new unit, he was one of eight Spitfires who took on an armada of seventy enemy aircraft. After the initial attack in which McLeod scored hits on several bombers, the escorting fighters came down and the mainplane of Wally's aircraft was holed, his flaps were blown off and all his guns except one were put out of action. But that cannon was enough to account for one of his attackers, who carelessly overshot the Canadian and presented him with an easy target.

Awarded the Distinguished Flying Cross on 29 September 1942, Wally added a Bar to this decoration three weeks later, after shooting down six enemy aircraft in five days. Two of those he accounted for within minutes of each other after attacking a formation of six Junkers 88s. Although his Spitfire was damaged during the combat, he courageously attacked another formation of nine bombers and scored several hits before running out of ammunition. He then nursed his damaged Spitfire back to base and made a skillful landing without further trouble.

Towards the end of October 1942, Wally flew his last mission from Malta and during the course of it managed to bag his thirteenth victim. The next day he left the island, flew back to England, and before Christmas he was repatriated to Canada for a period of instructional duty at #1 Hurricane Operational Training Unit in Bagotville, Quebec.[13]

Wally McLeod's grudge against the Axis powers was far from over, however, and much more would be heard from him in later months.

Of all the Canadian names associated with the air defence of Malta, none conjures up such a host of mixed emotions as that of George Frederick Beurling. Colourful, controversial, and often downright contradictory, Beurling was a brilliant pilot and a fearless warrior. In a mere fourteen combat days over Malta, he would score an unprecedented twenty-six and a third of his eventual thirty-one and seven twelfths confirmed victories — a remarkable feat by any standards. He would become both the darling of the Canadian public and a monumental pain in the backside to the Canadian military establishment. Acquaintances would endow him with two distinctive nicknames: "Buzz," in honour of his unquenchable thirst for unauthorized low-level flying, and "Screwball," in recognition of his erratic, unpredictable behaviour.

George Beurling was born in Verdun, Quebec, in 1921. A restless, unsettled youth who rebelled against both authority and social convention, he craved high adventure wherever it might be found. Though an indifferent student and a high school dropout, he possessed a fine analytical mind and a penchant for mathematics, which would later allow him to painstakingly critique his formidable deflection shooting skills and hone them to even higher levels. After receiving his wings, he was posted as a sergeant pilot to 41 Squadron, where he managed to destroy at least two Focke Wulfs over northern France. He also acquired a reputation for lacking a team spirit and for repeatedly breaking formation to make individual attacks.

Frustrated and ostracized, he requested a transfer to Malta in the spring of 1942 — and got it. Arriving at Takali in June after a launch from the aircraft carrier *Eagle*, his own impressions of his new home are noteworthy: "We seemed to have blown right into the middle of hell. You knew you'd come to a war that was running 24 hours a day."[14] He recalls seeing fighter planes and air combat action everywhere he looked in the sky, including the occasional aircraft spinning on fire and out of control to earth. All this was accompanied by a crashing din of falling bombs and the throaty bark of antiaircraft fire. In every direction there was a beehive of human activity, created simultaneously by groundcrew vigorously filling in bomb craters, ordnance personnel detonating unexploded bombs, and schools of air-sea rescue launches charging seaward to pick up downed pilots. Being stationed on Malta during the blitzes meant to Beurling that there was never a dull moment, during either the daylight or the nighttime hours.[15]

Beurling was assigned to 242 Squadron, where his reputation had preceded him. His flight commander, RAF luminary "Laddie" Lucas, had been forewarned that Beurling might prove to be a problem child:

. . . when Lucas called him in, he took a liking to this man with the strange gentle smile and the penetrating ice-blue eyes: "I felt I was in the presence of a very unusual young man . . . champing at the bit to have a go."

Lucas warned Beurling not to repeat his lone-wolf tactics, and sent him into battle. A week later he asked the pilot assigned to fly as a two-man team with Beurling how they were getting on. "God Almighty," was the reply, "he's quick and he's got the most marvelous eyes, but he's a hell of a chap when it comes to keeping up with us."

Lucas immediately called Beurling. At the interview, the pilot began to speak candidly of how he despised sticking to formation: "I'm a loner, and I've got to play it that way." Lucas exploded: "You've got to stick to the guy you're flying with. That's why we're alive. If you let me down, you're on the next goddam airplane out of here."

Beurling sensed this was no idle threat. "Boss," he said slowly, "that's good enough for me." Within a month of this showdown, he had become a legend.[16]

To say George Beurling "rose to the occasion" in the skies over Malta would be a monumental understatement. His remarkable success was attributable to a number of factors, not least of which was that the air war over the island was ideally suited to his particular fighting style and skills. If long transit times, unpredictable weather, infrequent engagements, and rigid formation discipline characterized the air battles over northern Europe in 1942, the contrary was true over Malta. Mediterranean weather essentially guaranteed combat, and the transit times for the defending fighters were often so short that they barely had time to reach combat speeds before they were engaged. Though finger-four formations were flown from launch, the multi-bandit air environment was such that formation discipline broke down very quickly in the freewheeling engagements that followed, and a formatting wingman with the ability to clear the leader's vulnerable six-o'clock cone was often a nonexistent luxury. These combat conditions inevitably resulted in a lot of engagements, with opportunities to score abounding for both sides. The high scores resulting from this type of high-pitched, defensive combat are typical of the situation. Similar scoring streaks had also been registered by the most able fighter pilots in the Battle of France and the Battle of Britain, where target-rich environments also existed.

Though the Canadian (and other Allied) top scorers of the Second World War did not rack up nearly as many individual victories as their counterparts during the First World War, that was partly because the very nature of the European air war had changed from individualistic action to teamwork. Changing combat conditions, such as maximum speeds, service ceilings, turn radii, and shooting parameters, generated a much greater demand for team tactics. The conditions over Malta were the last great exception for the Allies, and the proportionately high scores of the "stars" were the results of individual engagements. If their scores were prorated over a longer period of time under Malta-type conditions, they would probably match those of their counterparts during the First World War. It is interesting to note that the combined score of McLeod and Beurling in less than six months of 1942 surpassed that of all RCAF fighter pilots operating on the Channel coast in that entire year!

Along with combat conditions tailored to his fighting style, Beurling also possessed superb shooting and flying skills, and used a minimum amount of energy-dissipating manoeuvres to score his victories. A master of deflection shooting, he used a combination of trigonometry and flight path prediction to visualize the impact point of his bullets on an aggressively manoeuvring bandit. During his short stay on Malta, he would be awarded the Distinguished Flying Medal and Bar, the Distinguished Flying Cross, and the Distinguished Service Order — the only Canadian airman so decorated during the war.

Combat stress, physical fatigue, and a very poor diet had combined, however, to take their toll on George Beurling. By early August, he had been hospitalized with an incapacitating case of dysentery and was ordered by London to accept an officer's commission, something he had repeatedly turned down. Fatigue and illness were making him careless, and it is somewhat ironic that on the mission for which he won his DSO, he also made a judgment error, directly attributable to his "lone-wolf" tactics, which almost cost him his life.

By September Beurling's weight was down from 175 to 125 pounds, and he was skeletal and gaunt. But he insisted on flying. He seemed to be everywhere, hair all over the place, eyes glinting, a frightening sight. By October he was talking constantly, one of the first symptoms of battle fatigue.

October 14 dawned as another apparently routine day. At 1300 hours the scramble order came. Today's show was to the east where 50 fighters and 8 bombers were headed in. In the mêlée, Beurling bagged three German planes, but made the mistake of forgetting his own tail. Suddenly his Spitfire was rocked with cannon hits, and shrapnel struck his ribs, left heel and leg. His controls shattered, the aircraft pitched into a 16,000-foot plunge, and Beurling was certain he was going to die. But at 2000 feet, with flames engulfing the cockpit, he managed to crawl out onto the wing and at 500 feet, pulled the rip cord of his parachute and floated to the sea.

When a rescue launch reached him, he was sitting in his rubber dinghy in a pool of blood. Surgeons removed as much shrapnel as they could and patched him up, but he had lost part of the heel, a wound that would plague him for the rest of his life.

His remarkable odyssey on Malta was over . . .[17]

Even the repatriation to Canada was not without incident. Near Gibraltar, the Liberator bomber carrying him home crashed into the Mediterranean and he was forced to swim approximately 160 yards to safety, an act made significantly more difficult by the fact that he was wearing a heavy leg cast.

Back home in Canada, he was fêted as a great returning war hero, something of which the nation was in desperate need at the time. Again, his rebellious, moody nature surfaced. For whatever reasons, some no doubt attributable to his youth — he was still only twenty years of age — he became a public-relations nightmare, flouting dress regulations and refusing to make speeches. He did, however, enjoy listening to tales of his combat prowess and developed a reputation as somewhat of a Lothario with the ladies. Paradoxically, his sensitive side again surfaced, on at least one occasion, as the result of an innocuous, well-meaning gesture by an adoring following. At one point on the tour, twenty-nine young ladies each gave him a red rose — one for each of his air-to-air victories at the time. All this red may well have triggered memories of a haunting experience from combat over Malta. On one mission, his eyes apparently met those of an Italian pilot just before Beurling blew his head off and subsequently saw blood streaming down the fuselage of the enemy aircraft. Though later he occasionally joked about this incident, his brother claimed that it brought on nightmares for George that made him "cry all night."[18]

In North Africa, the vicious Axis pounding of Malta was significantly assisting Rommel's Afrika Korps. On 21 January, taking advantage of bad weather, Rommel attacked the RAF airfield at Antelat. After a temporary stand by the Eighth Army at Msus, Benghazi was lost once more to the Allies and a holding action was established between Bir Hacheim and Gazala. Rommel had suffered serious ground losses during this latest offensive, though, and paused at this point prior to mustering for a final drive towards Egypt and the Nile. In May, he renewed his thrust eastward, driving the Eighth Army back to the last defendable line in front of the Suez Canal, at El Alamein. By early August, both sides were dug in on this line, and for the next two months, both desperately attempted to replenish and reprovision their beleaguered troops. By the end of October, the air assault on Malta had petered out, and with offensive operations renewed from the island fortress, Britain had begun to win the resupply race. On 23 October, under General Bernard Law Montgomery, the Eighth Army began the great offensive that in due course would drive the Axis forces back through Libya to Tunisia and ultimately off the continent.

Along with the high-pitched ground battles taking place in Africa during 1942, air activity was also intense, and Canadians were well represented during the fighting. Wing Commander James F. "Stocky" Edwards from Battleford, Saskatchewan, joined 94 (RAF) Squadron as a sergeant pilot in late January, 1942. For Edwards, this was the start of an illustrious eighteen-month desert tour that would really blossom after his transfer to 260 Squadron in May. In February, the men of 94 Squadron re-equipped from Hurricanes to Curtiss Kittyhawks and by late March, were declared operationally ready in their new aircraft. The marriage of Edwards to this American-made fighter proved to be a lethal combination. He was able to score his first air-to-air kill in a Kittyhawk on his first operational mission, and it was a Bf 109F, the most formidable opposition in North Africa at the time. Though he held the Kittyhawk in high regard, his praise was not unqualified, and indeed, the earlier versions of the aircraft were far from universally popular. Here is Edwards on the relative merits of the Kittyhawk, garnered from 195 operational sorties in three different variants:

In my estimation, the Kittyhawk Mk I was not an easy aircraft to fly properly and, as a result, we lost a good number of pilots while training. Some Hurricane pilots just flatly refused to fly it, preferring to go back to the Hurricane Squadrons. In the first few months after conversion to Kittyhawks, all the Squadrons lost heavily to the '109s. It didn't seem to matter whether they were sprogs, Sergeant Pilots, or Battle of Britain veterans. The '109s still hacked them down.

Our pilots seemed to be at a great disadvantage trying to learn how to fly the aircraft while carrying out operational sorties. I'm certain that's the reason why many of our experienced pilots were shot down. This was coupled with the rapid turnover of COs and Flight Commanders. The changes left little stability within the squadrons, and the rapid changing of faces in the Mess tent made most feel like strangers to one another. There were few exceptions. There appeared to be no shortage of Kittyhawk replacements or pilots to fill the holes. Most were Canadians from the Commonwealth Training Plan.

I found that one had to have a very strong right arm to control the Kittyhawk I during most maneuvers. In dive-bombing, the aircraft would pick up speed very quickly in the dive, but it had a great tendency to roll to the right. One could trim this out reasonably well with the left hand, but even then when one pulled up, it wanted to roll to the left quite violently. So I learned to trim out about half-way in a dive and hold the control stick central by bracing my right elbow against my right leg and the right wall of the cockpit. I found out I had more control this way and didn't have to take off so much trim when pulling out and the speed was reduced. It was also distracting to have one's left hand on the trim all the time, when it should be on the throttle.

In a dog-fight with violent changes of speed, it was all one could do to fly the aircraft. To avoid being shot down, one needed their head on a swivel — to look down into the cockpit, even for a split second, with the '109s in the air, was sure death.

The Kittyhawk Mk II (F series) with Packard-Merlin engine was a definite improvement in lateral stability over the Kitty I. While the Americans called the machine the "Warhawk," the men on 260 Squadron named it the "Goshawk." 260 Squadron flew the Kitty IIs from September 1, 1942 to December 17, 1942, when the Squadron received Kitty IIIs. There were many models and a series of improvements and we flew them to the end of the Tunisian Campaign. Eventually, with the Mk IIIs, the Kittyhawk became a good, stable fighting aircraft, although it never did have enough power or climbing ability compared to the Me 109s or Spitfires.

All Kittyhawks I flew had 6 x .50 guns, excellent for strafing or blowing up a target. However, one very annoying feature in the desert was the gun stoppages. In ground strafing one could count on firing all the ammo without problems, but when it came to dog-fighting and excessive "G" forces came into play, the guns most always packed up after a few bursts, leaving the fighter in a most perilous position. The '109s never appeared to have any problems with the nose cannon — that big gaping hole in the centre of a white spinner with black puffs of smoke emitting from it.

The cruising speed of the Kittyhawk II was reasonably fast and equal to the Spitfire V, and the Mk III was comparable to the Spitfire IX. However, the Kittyhawk didn't jump when the throttle was advanced to full power and it didn't climb worth a damn like the Spitfire. It would turn inside the '109 but not as easily as the Spitfire. When the Squadron's "Tame Me 109" flew with the Kittyhawk, we found it was necessary to throttle back to approximately seventy-two percent power to stay in formation. The Me 109s definitely flew at higher cruising speeds when operating with two or four aircraft.[19]

Jim Edwards was far from being the only Canadian Kittyhawk pilot in North Africa, and on 260 Squadron alone, eight Canadian pilots would forfeit their lives in these aircraft. He has already mentioned reasons for some of the losses, which were particularly heavy on both 94 and 260 Squadrons when they made the transition from their venerable Hurricanes to Kittyhawk Is. Not all the losses, however, could be blamed on the rapid switch to an aircraft with some limitations. German fighter forces garrisoned at that time in the desert were formidable opponents, many of whom were seasoned combat veterans from both the Channel and eastern fronts. Furthermore, in many cases RAF fighter units did themselves no favours by tenaciously clinging to outmoded tactics. Edwards's biographer, Michel Lavigne, elaborates on Stocky's frustration after transferring to 260 Squadron in May with his Canadian friend Bill Stewart:

"Since we were from 94, I'm sure we were looked upon with some suspicion," Jim remembers. "They definitely saw us as sprogs (new to operations). But, at least 260 had a commanding officer who made a point of meeting us the next day. The meeting was informal and I remember he had a jaundiced eye at the time."

Jim and Bill Stewart made new acquaintances and viewed their situation. "260 seemed the same as 94. It seemed that Flight Commanders came and went. No sooner would one be promoted and take over than he would be shot down."

Little more can describe Squadron operations than one shambles after another. "Sometimes the Squadron was lucky and sometimes it wasn't," Jim remembers. "260 still flew the stupid old Hurricane formation with six aircraft in a Flight. There were three Section Leaders and three weavers flying behind. Everyone looked after their own tails and no one coordinated anything when the '109s showed up. It seemed that everyone was for himself and the weavers had a hell of a time trying to keep up with their leader while weaving and watching behind."

The Hurricane formation was a reasonably maneuverable formation until the '109s appeared. "As a defensive formation, it was a confused glob of aircraft that could be turned into a confused shambles by a small number of '109s attacking from above, out of the sun," Jim said. "No wonder the '109s shot down so many! With their superior speed and height, the Messerschmitts had the superior initiative to engage or disengage at will."

As the men of 94 Squadron had, the pilots of 260 held a steadfast loyalty. The mission and its completion was paramount, and Jim never stopped admiring that characteristic. "On the other hand, no tactics were discussed to combat the '109s or avoid being shot down. It always seemed, particularly on bomber escort, we were easy pickings for the '109s. We were there to divert attention from the bombers, and in order not to become victim to the enemy, we were on our own. We had to turn sharply into the attacker, but to do so was to be alone, jumping from the frying pan into the fire.

"The hornets would be coming in from all directions. When it was time to head for home after bombing the target, it was every man for himself. There was also complete disregard for the attacking '109s, which usually went after the trailer first."

Jim longed for the day he might find himself in a position to improve Squadron tactics. He yearned for the time his Squadron might better defend itself and give the '109s some of their own medicine. But he was new to 260 . . .[20]

During Rommel's May offensive, which was destined to drive the Allies so precariously close to the Suez Canal, both ground and air battles were incredibly fierce. Known in the combat zone as the Gazala Battles, Rommel's first assault started on 25 May and ended four gruelling weeks later with the fall of Tobruk. Allan Simpson recalls a particularly exciting mission in a ground-attack Hurricane during that offensive, a mission which very nearly cost him his life:

In the spring of 1942 in Egypt, Wing Commander Dru-Drury arrived from England to teach us in No. 6 Squadron how to fly the Hurricane IID. It was armed with two .303 machine guns and a pair of 40mm Vickers "S" guns. These guns were slung partly exposed on the underside of the wings, with a streamlined fairing to prevent interference with the airflow. The 40mm shells could penetrate the 20 millimetre armour-plating on a German Mark III tank, and the projectile would weld itself into the metal on the far side.

We didn't have long to train, and didn't have many aircraft. But we set up two rails from a railroad, painted a lifesized tank on a piece of canvas, and secured it to two vertical rails. That was our practice target.

We listened to lectures on our new aircraft and its weapon system: tanks and their vital spots (tracks, bogey wheels, drive wheels, engine, fuel tanks, crew), the tactics tank formations used and the tactics we should use.

Our skill level was high; we had an average of more than 70% hits, firing six to ten shots per attack, not counting the machine guns. Pip Hillier and I rated about 90%.

We went to a sand strip known as Gambut East in Libya. On June 8th, the CO and two others got one enemy vehicle, but Roger's wing was damaged by the very effective German 88 mm guns, which were mounted on trucks on either flank of the tank V-formations.

Then I went out with Tony Morrison-Bell and Mike Besly. Squadron Leader Billy Drake and his "flying sharks" flew top cover to us.

Our targets were in the area of Bir Hacheim, where the Free French under General Koenig were surrounded. Our mission was to relieve the pressure on them from tanks, which were lobbing shells from a few thousand yards away. A few days later, those gallant Foreign Legionnaires made a desperate break for it by night, and escaped; also there were 1000 Jewish Palestinians, of whom about 500 survived.

As we neared the target, we dove to pick up speed and attacked level from about 1000 yards at ten feet off the deck. (Later that summer, some of the boys took off their tail-wheels by hitting tank turrets; one bent his propeller on a tank.)

When a bullet is coming straight toward you, you can see it, even though it is not tracer or incendiary.

I remember the one that hit me. I saw it coming, the way you see a snowflake coming at your windshield. Flak normally breaks away from an aircraft like snowflakes, as I had seen it in France and Belgium in 1940 from a Lysander, and as I saw it over North Korea in 1951 from an RB25. But this one kept on coming. An explosive bullet, it detonated as it entered the hull of the aircraft by my left hand. It burst a few inches in front of my chest. My goggles were cracked, and my right arm still has the blue marks after 44 years. I picked pieces out of my chest for weeks afterwards.

When I was hit and saw the blood on my shirt, I assumed I was mortally wounded. I was concerned that, even if this were not so, I might lose consciousness and be killed for that reason. I felt more than a little sorry for myself.

My initial reaction was to cost the enemy as much as possible, and so I continued my attack on the German Mark III tank, then lined up another at which I got a good run, and then a truck. I considered attacking some troops I saw on the ground, but as I came closer, I was concerned that their helmets appeared to be too light to be German. Although they might have been Italian, I was afraid they might have been French or British or other allies, so I broke it off. I was too busy with other things by this time to make a more positive identification.

I gained sufficient altitude to bail out if necessary and headed east at full throttle. After a short time (5 or 10 minutes?) something happened to the engine. It might have been a bullet, or damage due to running it at too high a rate of speed/power. In any case, hot glycol sprayed into the cockpit. It covered my goggles, cutting off my field of vision so that I had to lift the goggles to peek out, until the supply of glycol reduced and the temperature increased to an unacceptable level.

I knew I would have to land it or bail out, and there were several reasons for not landing it:

1. The engine was going to quit at any moment, and might even burn.
2. If I put the wheels down, the chances of the aircraft remaining upright were small because of the rough terrain (flat but interspersed with tufts of "camel scrub" and ridges of sand).
3. I had already undone my safety harness when I pulled away from the battle area in case I had to leave the aircraft because of further developments: feeling faint, aircraft burning, further damage, etc.
4. I had a vivid memory of meeting a New Zealand pilot who had suffered multiple injuries to his face and body from attempting to land wheels-up. His air intake had caught on the ground, making his stop very sudden and throwing his face against the reflector-sight, and the aircraft either went up on its nose or overturned. He said he ought to have bailed out.

So I made my decision. The next problem was how to do it. I started at about 1000 or 1100 feet and jettisoned the side panel. I had already let the canopy go at Bir Hacheim. Then I attempted to get out onto the wing, but the slipstream was too strong. I throttled back and trimmed the nose up. Then I got out on the starboard side, standing, facing the tail, holding on to the back corner of the cockpit with my right hand, and grasping the ripcord handle with my left. Normally the right hand is used, but my biceps had been peppered with pieces of the explosive bullet and was somehow rather numb.

By this time, I was at about 500 feet. There was probably not enough altitude to gain sufficient downward velocity to open the parachute, so I decided that I would jump sideways so as to miss the tailplane. David Bain of Pincher Creek, Alberta, had broken his arm on the tail of an Anson when he bailed out. I pulled the cord as soon as the tail passed me, and after a very short time in the air I was on the ground. I rolled over in an arc as I was supposed to do, and lay there on the sand looking up at the sky.

Not for long, as I realized I should get out of the harness in case the wind dragged me. But it was not a factor, as the noon calm was with us and the silk rested quietly on the ground. And I seemed to have the whole desert to myself.

I stood up and removed my shirt and undershirt, to see how badly I was hit. The bleeding had stopped (externally at least). I had lots of metal half-buried in my chest.

Then, while I was thus examining myself, I must have run out of adrenalin. The pain hit me. It was so severe that I could take only a very short breath. I felt that I was going to suffocate.

As long as the emergency had continued, I felt no pain. I had not been restricted in my physical movements. I had been able to breathe as much as I wanted to. Now I was an invalid. A Tomahawk flew over and I waved my shirt at him. I don't suppose he saw me.

A British army ambulance ultimately picked me up and took me to a field dressing station at El Adem and on to Tobruk. They put me on an aircraft with other horizontal casualties and flew us out to Egypt five days later, just before the Germans captured the town with 25,000 South Africans in it.[21]

As the summer rolled on with the Allied forces fighting a desperate holding action to save Egypt, air-combat tactics began to evolve to meet the threat. This was due in no small measure to the increasing influence of the new young stars such as Eddie Edwards.

All the pilots who came to the Squadron at this period had been checked out on the Kittyhawk at a conversion unit cum OTU near

Abu Suweir in the Canal Zone. They were familiar with the aircraft in circuits and formation flying. Of course, they all had to be introduced to Squadron living and combat operations.

Initially we instructed them in battle formation, the Finger Four formation, normally four aircraft to a Section and three Sections for a Squadron. A Section of four could easily break up in two Sections of two aircraft each — thus it was reasonably maneuverable. We encouraged the pilots to remain together, or at least in pairs, at all times.

Since we didn't go looking for the '109s during bomber escorts, or while we were carrying bombs, the main thing was to teach the new pilots some measure of defence against the '109 attacks. In the Kittyhawk, the only maneuver that truly thwarted a '109 attack was the steep turn. Naturally, it was important when one started the turn and how steep one should make it. Of course all conditions and circumstances are different, but the '109s had the upper hand and, as a rule, attacked from above and behind. To do this the '109s had to commit themselves to the attack, and close to firing range, approximately 350 yards or closer. It was when the '109 started its dive that the steep turn was carried out — always into the attacker.

In the Four formation, the leader would call the turnabout over the R/T or by dipping one wing two times, turning on the second dip. The leader would gauge his turn to meet the circumstances and the others would turn to maintain formation. The formation turned as a viable unit and carried out cross-over turns in the same maneuver when necessary. We taught the pilots the turns and had them carry them out in pairs and alone, right on the deck. But there were very few pilots who could do a really steep turn properly at deck level while watching behind and above.

The Finger Four formation and the turns were the basic instruction, with strict flying discipline stressed at all times to maintain the unit. The basics were very necessary during the first operational trips so they wouldn't be easy targets for the '109s. Then they were introduced to the rudiments of bomber escort, dive-bombing and strafing. They were told they had to learn to fly their aircraft to its utmost limits and capabilities. If they could do all these things properly and always saw the enemy first, had quick reflexes, some shooting ability, aggressiveness and luck, they might survive to become good fighter pilots after they had learned to lead others.

Some pilots required more training than others, but none really got enough before being committed to operations. Every flight, even on operations, was a training flight and eventually this method began to improve the Squadron combat strength. Many good pilots were lost during the following Campaign that took the Squadron through to Tunisia, but very few went down because of poor training or bad flying discipline.[22]

War and coincidence are frequent companions. Stan Turner, now a Wing Commander, was sent to Alexandria during the summer of 1942 as a tactical observer and advisor to the Royal Navy. On 14 September, he participated in an ill-fated naval raid on the port of Tobruk. The British cruiser on which he was serving, the *Coventry*, was sunk by *Hauptmann* Kurt Walter, the *Gruppenkommandeur* of III/ St.G.3, flying a Ju 87 Stuka. Turner survived the sinking and, after a brief swim, was picked up by an escorting destroyer. Six short weeks later, a Canadian avenged him when none other than Bert Houle of 213 Squadron fell upon Walter and several of his companions near Daba and El Alamein. In the ensuing engagement, Houle downed four of the Stukas, but he was only credited with two. He offers a possible explanation as to why this occurred:

> The *Stab* (staff) Headquarters Flight of *Stukageschwader 3* had *Oberleutnant* Karl Lindarfer wounded over El Alamein, but Chris Shores has received information that his Ju 87 (S7+BA) was lost. The gunner was unhurt, so the pair must have bailed out or crash landed. *III Gruppe* of the same unit lost the *Gruppenkommandeur*, *Hauptmann* Kurt Walter, who was killed when his parachute failed to open, (though) his gunner did bail out safely. Their combat was with Hurricanes over Daba. This was received in a letter from Chris Shores dated 15 February 1984. Since I was the only pilot who even got close to Daba, it is evident that they fell to my guns, and should be added to my score. The other two aircraft claimed by me must have been flown by Italians, who, I am told, did not keep a record of their losses. This was also received in a letter from Chris Shores dated 15 February 1984.[23]

During the period of the second battle of El Alamein (23 October– 4 November), air superiority was immediately established by the Desert Air Force and was never relinquished, although not without significant fighter losses. This was a tremendous morale booster to the

ground forces, and allowed bomber and fighter-bomber units to operate effectively against the Axis forces with relative impunity. During
the latter part of this battle, Air Chief Marshal Tedder gave full rein
to all his tactical support squadrons, with laudable results. In just a few
short days, over 30,000 Axis troops were taken prisoner and a great
deal of enemy equipment was either destroyed or captured. Tobruk
was captured for the last time on 13 November. Less than a week
later, British fighters operating out of Martuba in Egypt were able to
provide cover to a convoy that at long last marked an end to the siege
of Malta.[24] Bert Houle recounts the action immediately following the
end of the Battle of El Alamein:

The El Alamein line caved in on the 4th of November 1942. On
November 7th, we moved up to Landing Ground 20, on the coast
near Daba, and had a whale of a time picking up abandoned equipment. Particular care had to be taken because many articles were
booby-trapped. Although many of the boys took chances, there
were only a few casualties. Motorcycles, trucks, revolvers and rifles,
things that Jerry knew we would be interested in, were the main
items booby-trapped. The line had broken so quickly that they
hadn't much time to pack anything except essential equipment, and
not all of that. It sounded like a miniature war with machine guns,
rifles, revolvers and even a twenty-five pounder shooting out to sea.
Some of our boys uncapped Italian red-devil hand grenades and
threw them over the cliffs. I picked up a good Mauser rifle which
I kept for fifteen months. On afternoons off, I took it out to the
desert for target practice.

Our landing ground was littered with crashed and damaged
enemy planes, and LC 104 had over one hundred planes left
behind. Their maintenance system was not as good as our own, as
our aircraft were taken to maintenance units away behind the lines
for repair. Some were towed back by tying the tail-wheel to the flat
bed of a lorry.

Dead bodies lined the road. Some of them could not be
removed as the retreating Hun had even booby-trapped his own
dead. We lived pretty rough at LG 20 as it wasn't worthwhile pitch-
ing camp. The line had moved so far that we couldn't support it
from our aerodrome, and the landing grounds forward had not been
cleared of mines. We did one patrol to prevent Fieseler Storchs
(small communications aircraft used by the Jerries) from picking up

some entrapped German Generals, and two trips with long-range tanks to protect mine sweepers clearing up Mersa Matruh harbour. Roads were blocked with German and Italian soldiers making their own way to some wire encampment to get fed. They even stopped our troops on the road and wanted to be taken prisoner. They were usually told to go and ask someone else. Some of them drove themselves to wire enclosures in their own trucks and buses. Roy Marples commandeered one bus and made the Italian occupants get out and walk the rest of the way. He tried to take the shoes off a high ranking German officer because he liked them. Meeting with some resistance, he used more persuasive measures. They were a pitiful, beaten, disillusioned bunch, wandering aimlessly east for food and shelter. For our part we had tasted defeat in the summer and now we knew the elation of victory. What an uplift in morale, noticeable from the CO to the lowest erk!

Fighting, like any game or any contest, is a lot easier when things are going your way. It seems that once the breaks start working for you, they continue for some time. As the saying goes, and it is pretty true, when the going gets tough, the tough get going. I claim that is what we did in the Western Desert. We had it pretty rough and the losses were heavy. When twenty to fifty percent don't come back on a sweep it doesn't take much of a mathematician to calculate that his number must come up. Many pilots built up their courage with a philosophy that went something like this. "There is only a 25 percent chance that I'll get shot at, and if I am there is only a 25 percent chance that my aircraft will be hit. If the aircraft is hit there is only a 25 percent chance that the hit will be serious. If it hits a vulnerable spot there is only a 25 percent chance that I will be hit. If I am hit there is only a 25 percent chance that it will be fatal. With odds like that, why should I worry? However, it is better to increase all odds by preventing the enemy from getting that first shot."

Up to this period, the Axis air forces had it too much their own way. Their losses seemed to be much smaller than ours. A few squadrons of "Spits" made them a little more cautious. They were beginning to feel as if that Extra Man Above had switched sides for a change. The Axis army had not enjoyed having things all its own way, but it is a good bet that by now they were beginning to think that Montgomery had done his homework, had resisted the bad, uninspired, unreliable and misguided orders from the politicians, and now had a pretty invincible army. We had a feeling that the breakthrough at El Alamein was indeed the first yards on the invasion of Germany itself. We were right and history had proved it.[25]

Joint Anglo-American landings in Morocco and Algeria were conducted on 8 November to complement the Allied drive westward out of Egypt. Operation Torch was intended not only to hasten the end of the Axis presence in North Africa, but also to win Vichy France over to the Allied camp, secure the French fleet, and regain absolute naval supremacy in the Mediterranean. Although the giant pincers these landings created eventually worked, initial successes stagnated. The link-up with Montgomery's Eighth Army was delayed by bad weather and stiffening enemy resistance as the Germans reinforced their fighting units across the Sicilian Narrows. The Vichy French scuttled their fleet at Toulon harbour. The temporary lack of inertia on the battlefield did not, however, prevent a massive Allied buildup of forces in the area, and early the next year, victory on the African continent proved inevitable.[26]

While Allied day fighters and fighter-bombers were extremely active over North Africa and Malta during 1942, no less could be said for the night fighter force. In October 1941, "Moose" Fumerton and his observer, Pat Bing, were attached to 89 (RAF) Squadron, flying Beaufighters out of Abu Suweir, Egypt. On the night of 3 March 1942, this intrepid duo were part of a force of four Beaufighters scrambled after a radar contact over the Suez Canal Zone. High in the full moonlight, they intercepted an He 111, and the subsequent engagement won Fumerton his first of two DFCs. His squadron commander's recommendation for the award succinctly captures the event.

1. On the night of 2/3rd March, Flying Officer Fumerton was sent off to intercept a hostile raider and eventually came within sight of the enemy, a Heinkel 111. (This was) after a very skillful pursuit in the moonlight, in which the observer, Sgt. Bing, played a prominent part. Flying Officer Fumerton closed in to 100 yards and opened fire, scoring hits, whereupon the enemy aircraft opened accurate return fire, which wounded the pilot in the right leg and put the starboard motor and the reflector sight out of action.

2. In spite of this, Flying Officer Fumerton pressed home a second attack, aiming by tracer effects, and set the enemy

aircraft on fire. His own port motor then cut out also, and he was obliged to drop away.

3. He was preparing for a landing in the Delta, when one motor picked up again, the other still being out of action.

4. During the course of the next hour, Flying Officer Fumerton was able, by skillful flying and intelligent use of wireless and of signal lights, to make a homing at another aerodrome, and a safe landing with wheels up; the undercarriage mechanism having also been put out of action.

5. The enemy aircraft was afterwards forced to land in the sea, the crew being captured.

6. The offensive spirit, skill and endurance shown by Flying Officer Fumerton were of the highest order.

7. This pilot already had two previous successes to his credit.[27]

Fumerton returned to flying after a short stay in hospital and scored twice more on the night of 7 April, when he shot down two He 111s in a three-hour period.

Six crews from 89 Squadron deployed to Malta on 22 June, and the Fumerton/Bing team did not wait long to renew their grudge against the Luftwaffe. On their second night there they destroyed a Ju 87, and in the following ten-night period they accounted for a further five enemy aircraft. This torrid scoring pace was recognized by the award of the Bar to the DFC to Fumerton and the DFC to Bing.

On the night of 22 July, Fumerton accounted for yet another Ju 88, this time north of Malta, and with a stand-in radar operator, Flight Sergeant John Booth. (Usual flying companion Pat Bing was temporarily incapacitated with the "Malta Dog," the island's rough equivalent of "Montezuma's Revenge.") The charismatic and able Booth brought with him an unexpected companion on this particular mission: his pet monkey, which he frequently attired in a dapper scarlet tunic and matching pillbox hat. Fumerton swears he heard the chattering of the monkey over the chattering of his guns at the precise moment of this particular victory![28]

There is a saying, "What goes around, comes around." One night later that summer, this saying certainly applied to Fumerton. His suggestion from back in England for a method of securing the radio transmitter was about to come back in his face.

Luqa, Malta, the night of August 10/11, 1942 — we were scrambled in Beaufighter 7748 to intercept an enemy raid leaving Sicily bound for Malta.

The weather was muggy, with a stormy feel to it, and the wind was strong, out of the west. We got airborne quickly and started our climb to the north, the ground controller giving us a course and height.

A head-on contact was made while climbing, and the turn was then completed in order to close the enemy. While still about 2000 feet behind and below the enemy aircraft, there was a loud bang in the starboard engine, which cut immediately. I had no sooner tried to feather the failed engine when the same thing happened to the port engine, leaving me with limited options.

I called the controller to notify him of the situation (mayday) and he told me to transmit a continuous count. In order to do that, I had to get the elastic cord off the switch, but then found that I couldn't get it off with one hand only, as I had to keep one hand on the control column. (I made a mental note to add a quick release to that contraption [elastic cords were used to prevent one from accidentally leaving the radio switch on]).

All this started at 10,000 feet and, because of the strong west wind and the probability of high waves, which I could not land into, I told Pat (Pilot Officer Pat Bing) to bail out. The Beau didn't make a very good glider. With no power and keeping the airspeed up to 140 mph to maintain control, we were soon down to 4500 feet and dropping rapidly, so I called Pat and gave him a change of plan. "We're going to land. Buckle up tightly and release the hood as soon as I give the word."

All this time we had been gliding, dropping southerly toward Malta. This course would give us a cross-wind landing, drifting with the waves, and hopefully we could set down on a crest. As I was dropping through 500 feet, the warm air hitting the cold windshield caused it to mist over. I hurriedly reached up my arm to wipe it. I then saw the white crests and that we were drifting with them. I shouted to Pat to let the hatch go, eased back on the stick, and made a surprisingly soft landing. We got out on the wing quickly, as we knew that the Beau wouldn't stay up more than a very few minutes, but I was then flabbergasted to see Pat climbing back into the aircraft. I shouted, "Where are you going?" to which he replied, "I forgot my elephant" (a good luck charm which he wore on his helmet). He brought the elephant and the helmet out but, more importantly, there was also a miniature battery-fed light on the helmet which had been introduced for the very first time that day and which was to stand us in good stead.

By this time, the water was well over my knees as I was unravelling the K-type dinghy from the parachute attachment. In the meantime, Pat was in the sea doing the same thing, but drifting away in the wind, when he shouted, "My dinghy has split open." I shouted back, "I'm going to fill my dinghy now — keep shouting so I can reach you." I carefully spread out my dinghy, pressed the release on the CO_2 bottle and, while the dinghy was still a bit soft, turned off the CO_2 and started to swim over to Pat, who was now some distance away. As I was leaving, I looked down through the clear water and saw Beaufighter 7748 going down with the landing lights still on, just as if it knew where it was going. Together again, we got the two hand paddles out of Pat's useless dinghy which we added to mine, and we both got into my dinghy (two six-foot men in a five foot dinghy).

I was sitting upright as best I could and Pat was stretched between my legs with his legs drifting several feet behind. "Pat," I said, "I hope there are no sharks here!" His reply, a dour "I hope so too!"

Pat tested his miniature light to make sure it was working. We then strapped the paddles to our wrists and started paddling towards Malta. Polaris was just visible through the haze and the wind was still from the west. We were pretty well north and a bit east of Malta, but I figured that to make the course, we would have to cut about 45 degrees into the wind. I also calculated that if we paddled hard for six hours, we would make Malta. The alternative was drifting to the east with 1000 miles or more of open sea (excluding German-held Crete). We paddled along, flashing Pat's miniature light when we heard what we thought was one of our own aircraft overhead, and switching it off when it sounded like the enemy. We were making good time when suddenly a searchlight hit us. It was very close and quite startling. We could see that it was a boat — as it turned out, one of our rescue launches. He too was keeping count — as the chap helped us aboard, he said, "You're numbers 48 and 49."

I told him how grateful we were for being picked up so quickly and his answer was, "Would you like a drink of brandy?" I said nothing could be better and, in the semi-darkness of the cabin, he reached out to a shelf, grabbed a bottle, and poured me a hefty slug, the size of which, in the straightened state of Malta, was almost worth the trip.

I tipped the glass up, took a big gulp and very nearly swallowed it. It didn't taste like brandy and I spat it out. "Oh," he said, "I think I got the wrong bottle. That's the iodine." Iodine and brandy I thought, side by side on a shelf in the semi-darkness. That's an accident waiting to happen, but only to someone who drank brandy. In the meantime, he was pouring us brandies out of the right bottle.

Needless to say, we arrived in Malta well ahead of schedule.

I believe the boat that picked us up was a rescue launch from Kalafrana, and it had quite a score of rescues painted on the hatch. As it turned out, a Beaufighter piloted by Neville Reeves of our detachment had spotted Pat's light, and this played a big part in the pin-point pick up.

What caused the engine failures was not clear, but Pat was convinced that we had been shot down.

On a previous night engagement between Suez and the Nile Delta, we had had both engines shot out, but on that occasion, one of the engines started all on its own, a bare 100 feet above the ground. I hoped that this sort of thing wasn't becoming a habit.

You win some, you lose some, but a glass of iodine? Imagine the following on a Maltese tombstone:

> *Lost his engines*
> *Came down fine*
> *But died of a glass*
> *of iodine*
> *The chance of that*
> *being almost nil*
> *with this epitaph*
> *move over Boot Hill*[29]

———◆◆◆———

While combat in 1942 against the Germans and Italians in Europe and North Africa involved give and take, war against the Japanese in the Far East was one dismal defeat after another for the Allies. In January alone, Japanese forces entered Manila, invaded the Dutch East Indies, and occupied Malaya. The following month saw the fall of Singapore, along with the capture of 85,000 British troops. March brought the fall of Rangoon, Burma, and Bataan in the Philippines surrendered in April, followed a month later by Corregidor. By 20 May, the Japanese had occupied all of Burma and were sitting on India's doorstep.[30]

Conquest of Burma was crucial to any Japanese advance onto the vast Indian subcontinent, and, realizing this, the British had built a line of defence along the Salween River in the southeast part of the country. Seven landing grounds and one obsolete radar warning unit supported the defensive line, and at year's end in 1941 were manned by only sixteen obsolete Buffalo fighters of 67 (RAF) Squadron and twenty-one Curtiss P40s of the American Volunteer Group. Opposing this meagre force were 400 Japanese fighters and bombers. After Rangoon was bombed with great loss of life on 23 December, reinforcements were hastened to the area. A squadron of Blenheim bombers did major damage to the Japanese base at Bangkok, though at considerable cost. Simultaneously, 67 Squadron had its Buffalos augmented with thirty Hurricane Is, and in late January a second Hurricane unit (17 Squadron) arrived in the theatre. Rangoon was evacuated on 7 March and the defenders retreated north along the Irrawaddy River valley, pursued closely by the Japanese. At this juncture, most of the defending aircraft were operating out of central Burma at either Magwe or Akyab (Sittwe).

Hedley Everard of Timmins, Ontario, would have a distinguished and exceptionally well-travelled career as a Canadian fighter pilot during the Second World War, serving in North Africa, Burma, China, India, Sicily, Italy, Great Britain, and Northwest Europe. He was posted to 17 Squadron and Magwe at the end of February, 1942. Hedley recalls his impressions of the Base, the Burmese people, and a historic raid on Mingaladon:

> It was early March and the two air defence squadrons remaining in Southeast Asia have retreated to the small town in central Burma. We are on a very large, hot dry plain walled in by eroded mountains to the east and west, and to the north, behind us, the land puckers and rises gradually to become further on the mighty Himalayas of Tibet. Our airfield was on the east bank of the Irrawaddy River and was slightly elevated by reddish hand-made bricks to outline the runway during the monsoon floods. It was now the dry season and occasional pools of muddy water remained along the river bed to resemble a jade necklace carelessly tossed on

a faded orange robe. Further to the east the mighty Salween River flowed to the sea with the greenish tinge of melted snows from the top of the world. These holy waters nurse the surrounding fields of rice and vegetables, so that the total impression was again an emerald necklace on soft green velvet. Above, the sky was that pastel blue and green often seen moments after sunset. Below it was hot and silent. Sounds were magnified so that a far-off fly deceived the ears with threatening sallies.

Magwe was like any other tin-roofed town along the equator. Open air market places for local produce and the inevitable squalid Indian shops peddling cotton and tin wares. A cluster of chalky buildings here and there attested to the presence of the "British Raj" and their migratory families. The riverside pools were shared by the now-idle water buffaloes from the dry rice fields and young Burmese adults washing their bodies within the screen of their tent-like bathing sarongs. To them, war must have been as silly as the European soccer games that were practiced in the tropical evening by red-faced madmen.

The personal cleanliness of the Burmese of all ages was the striking feature of these lovable, laughing people. Whereas many of the races of the East are thought to be inscrutable, the wary brown faces of this little nation of farmers readily reflected their moods, thoughts and reactions. Perhaps their love of Buddha is reflected in their manner. Where other racial deities are strange, ethereal and frightening in some ways, the Burmese are forever following the strange stories of the Great Teacher. Pagodas are everywhere, and in the cool of the evening, they gather at these gold capped shrines, not only to hear recitations from the Teacher's life but also to tell their own amusing events of the day. It was a place of penance, prayer and picnic. At that time Burma was the second largest producer of rice in the world. That fact might explain the serenity and gaiety of the people. Thus, when we dropped out of the sky with our noisy metal birds, we were ignored with the same silent contempt they gave other airborne pests who settled seasonally on their rice paddies. We too would move on after we had eaten our fill . . .

It was almost the third week of March . . . I was still a "Sprog," unqualified by my peers to be judged a veteran — yet. Tomorrow that would change.

Our mission, as we were briefed the night before, was dangerous enough that only volunteer pilots were accepted. Eight of us took off an hour before dawn with a few kerosene lanterns along the runway to indicate the path of departure. We climbed the nine thousand feet which was above the height of the surrounding hills. Dimly and grimly I followed the blue exhaust of the Hurricane ahead of me and as we headed east into the mauve sky, I could make out the seven black blobs of my comrades. We cruised steadily and slowly eastwards to Pyu in order to conserve our fuel for the long doubtful return flight. Half an hour before sunrise we descended to the tree tops as our Squadron Leader unerringly led us to the target. The sun's first rays were almost parallel to the air-field runway as we made our first strafing attack. My task was to silence an ack-ack position on the northern approach. The glisten-ing dew on the multi-barreled weapon was clearly discernible from my position of attack. As I closed the range to 600 yards at mod-erate speed, I was able to see the half dozen members of the gun crew sitting on a low wall of sandbags sipping from bowls. They were knocked over by my initial burst from the eight machine guns. Astonishment was clearly visible on a few faces as my explo-sive-incendiary bullets crept through a gap to the gun and its ammunition boxes within. As I swept overhead, these boxes began to explode like a string of firecrackers. Jinking like mad, as taught by my AVG buddies, I attacked the second post at the far end of the field which was empty of gun and crew. Over the radio I announced calmly, I thought, "Bullseye" which meant my targets were silenced. Shorty Miller, my fellow Canadian from Cape Breton Island, gave his "Bullseye" from the other side of the field. The Squadron Leader laughingly announced "Tally-Ho chaps" over his R/T, which meant we could attack any targets of opportunity. I performed a climbing-diving 180 degree turn towards a line of fighters parked wingtip to wingtip along the runway, some of which were already smoking from the initial surprise attack by my fellow flyers. I carefully sighted my burst at the first machine in the line, but had obviously fired out of range since the bullets slammed short of the target. As I flashed overhead I looked down into the cockpit and caught the bland curious stare of the Japanese pilot who was being helped to strap in by his crewman. It was incredible. They had ignored my murderous attack. At that moment, all my fear and excitement evaporated. As I swung around for a second pass, I felt a peace and body relaxation never experienced before. It was as though I was calmly aiming at a snowshoe rabbit for my dinner stew pot on one of my many northern hunting trips. By now, the pilot had started his engine and was just beginning to move towards the runway. With deadly purpose now, my bullets riddled the engine and cockpit. The aircraft slewed up on its nose as I passed inches overhead. I glimpsed the pilot slumped in his seat as flames from the engine crept towards him. I glanced at the runway and saw my buddies picking off the fighters as they vainly attempted to take off. Without thinking, I headed to the south end of the field where I had unconsciously noticed a locomotive and cars. Khaki-clad figures with unslung rifles were stumbling out of the cars to one side of the track. In a slow deliberate pass I strafed the whole line of soldiers who threw themselves to the ground ahead of my dust-disturbing bullets. How many never moved again, I did not know or care. By then the Squadron Leader had spotted some Japanese fighters rising from other satellite airfields nearby and gave the order to "Pancake." It was our code word to return to base and land. I streaked westward and caught up to another fellow Canadian, Allan MacDougal, also at tree top height and in relative safety from the Japanese fighters searching at altitude. In my rear view mirror I caught sight of at least a dozen red and black fires from our target areas.

Since our aircraft were low on fuel, we throttled our engines back to lowest endurance power and speed. Consequently, we landed about fifteen minutes after our buddies, who had all disappeared to breakfast. After giving my battle report to the Intelligence Officer, MacDougal and I hitched a truck ride to the breakfast hut, only to find that our buddies had scattered for needed sleep.

I followed suit, pleased and relieved that my aircraft had suffered no damage. I tried to sleep, but without success. The bravery of that Japanese pilot overwhelmed my thoughts . . .[31]

In a classic example of overexuberance in combat, Everard once accidentally shot down a photo-reconnaissance Hurricane over Burma. Though the pilot survived, Hedley was understandably not exactly enthralled with this victory. He was delighted, however, with a kill confirmation from an unexpected source a short time later when he was flying from Loi-wing airfield in China.

The morning of April 8th began like any clear spring day in any temperate climate. The overnight dew on the wings of my aircraft had scarcely evaporated in the first hour of sunshine, when short blasts of sirens indicated an imminent attack on our airfield. My aircraft engine caught on the first turn of the three bladed propeller. A glance to my left revealed that my two mates had also had good starts. A further three functioning Hurricanes had been promised by the Crew Chief for mid-morning. Since I was flying the third slot for this Scramble I felt a surge of courage as three pairs of Tomahawks went snarling overhead in a battle climb. In a moment a flashing green light indicated our clearance for takeoff. Ricky and Allan were wing tip to wing tip as they roared down the runway towards the brown cocoon of dust left by the departing AVG fighters with their familiar sharks teeth emblem on their noses. The duo ahead of me created a new wall of dust through which I thundered five seconds later. Visibility ahead was almost zero, which always raised one's pulse rate to maximum, because of the danger of colliding with a balked takeoff. The green lights on the instrument panel faded and two slight lurches confirmed that my undercarriage had retracted. Easing to the left, I emerged from the dust cloud and searched overhead for my two companions. Further to my left, also at tree top level, I spied a speck of an aircraft headed towards our airfield. As I cut harder inside the turn I was astonished to identify the meatball and silhouette of a Japanese Army 01. I was in perfect position for a full deflection shot. In an instant my gun safety switch was on "FIRE" and all guns were chattering away as the range diminished. Suddenly, a mushroom of ground fire erupted between my streaking tracer salvo and the target aircraft. A hard yank on the elevator control and half roll returned my Hurricane to its original heading. Climbing into sun I soon glimpsed my two companions, but we were at least four miles high before I caught up with them. With frantic hand signals, I indicated to Ricky that the field was under a strafing attack. His hand signals were interpreted to mean that we would engage the expected bomber waves. As we patiently patrolled, I caught occasional glimpses of brief fireballs below, where I knew the Flying Tigers were having a ball. For an hour we saw nothing and returned to the field where two or three small fires still smoldered. All six Tomahawks were back on the flight line — the best indicator that it was safe to land. As I shut down my crew saw my open gun ports, clear evidence that I had fired. To their thumbs up, I gave a thumbs down, indicating our mission had been unsuccessful. A quick inspection of my aircraft revealed no holes, for which I was thankful. The brief ground fire had seemed so deadly accurate.

At debriefing I told our Intelligence Officer about my short engagement with the '01, but made no claim since no strikes had been observed. This negative report did not dampen his spirits as he dramatically described the overhead dog-fights in which the AVG rightfully claimed eleven Japanese fighters. It was stunning information and my pleasure soon matched everyone's.

Later that morning I went over to the AVG Flight Line to congratulate the overjoyed victors. I repeated the story of our unsuccessful sortie, to which Chuck Sawyer, an old friend, asked if I had been the third Hurricane off the ground. Answering in the affirmative, Sawyer turned to his flight leader and buddies. "Hey fellows, here's the guy who put the present on our door step!" Amid back slaps and excited chatter, the picture cleared. The pilots in the Ready Shack, who had not been assigned aircraft, had observed my aircraft's attack on the '01 after takeoff. The intended victim had crossed the airfield perimeter and crashed into the ground straight on, scattering debris in every direction. Other than the puff of smoke or dust on impact, his machine had simply disintegrated. At this point the pilots took me to one side of the Ready Shack where the small trunk of a human body lay naked.

. . . Still unbelieving, I stated that he must have been hit by the ack-ack post, but they had checked this out with the gunners, who admitted that in the surprise attack they had only fired at the second aircraft, which, of course, was my Hurricane.[32]

The reality of a global war in 1942 also resulted in increased operational activity on the home front. Throughout 1941, it became clear that war with Japan could not be far off. As the Battle of Britain crisis in the United Kingdom subsided, increasing attention was paid to the buildup of a viable fighter defence on the North American continent. In August, 115 Squadron formed as a fighter squadron on the West Coast, equipped with totally unsuitable Bristol Bolingbrokes. Urgent pleas to Britain for first-line fighter aircraft resulted in the release of 72 Curtiss Kittyhawk IA fighters, deliveries of which started directly from American factories in October. The next month, both 111 and 118 Squadrons formed at Rockcliffe in Ottawa with this type of fighter.

With the outbreak of hostilities against Japan in December, a new dimension of emergency was accorded the home-defence buildup, due to Canada's proximity to the Pacific war zone. Number 111 Squadron moved to Patricia Bay on Vancouver Island, under the capable leadership of seasoned veteran Squadron Leader Deane Nesbitt, and yet another Kittyhawk unit (14 Squadron) formed in January 1942. Between April and July, in response to the Pacific crisis, Canadian-produced Hurricane XIs and XIIs were commandeered from the production lines to form new fighter squadrons. The Hurricanes and additional Kittyhawks equipped eight new home-defence squadrons during this period of time, distributed as follows:

West Coast Units	Equipment
132 Squadron	Kittyhawks
133 Squadron	Kittyhawks/Hurricanes
135 Squadron	Kittyhawks/Hurricanes

East Coast Units	Equipment
125 Squadron	Hurricanes
126 Squadron	Hurricanes
127 Squadron	Hurricanes
128 Squadron	Hurricanes
130 Squadron	Kittyhawks/Hurricanes

In April, 115 Squadron's Bolingbrokes moved forward to Annette Island for use in the air defence of Alaska, and in May, the U.S. Army Commander Pacific Coast requested forward deployment of a bomber/reconnaissance squadron and an additional fighter squadron to Yakutat, Alaska, to support the limited USAAF units that were available.[33] Both 8 and 111 Squadrons, collectively known as "X" Wing, headed northward for the air defence of southern Alaska. Meanwhile, the resident Americans moved to the western and northern areas, and also to the Aleutian Chain, since the Japanese had conducted landings at both Attu and Kiska Islands on 6 June. Concurrently, both 118 and 132 Squadrons moved their Kittyhawks to Annette Island and Patricia Bay respectively, backfilling for the northern-deployed units. Number 118 Squadron in concert with 115 Squadron now became "Y" Wing, responsible for the air defence of both the Alaskan Panhandle and the British Columbia coastal region. The arrival of 118's Kittyhawks at Annette spared 115 Squadron from further humiliation in the fighter role, and they were now reassigned to much more appropriate bomber/reconnaissance duties. But national pride, in the form of a sovereignty issue, was about to surface in the Alaskan region, and this would lead to a more active role for the RCAF units deployed there, initially with tragic consequences.

During June, 8 and 111 Squadrons arrived in Alaska, 111 Squadron taking up base at Elmendorf from where it could provide cover for the Anchorage area. No long-range tanks were available at first, and all areas where the Japanese were to be found were beyond the range of the unit's aircraft. Wing commander was Wg. Cdr. G. R. McGregor, who had flown with 1 Squadron during its Battle of Britain début in England, and then commanded 2 Squadron, and who had been credited with four victories against German aircraft before his return to Canada. McGregor felt strongly that RCAF units should not be employed in action by the US commanders if any USAAF units were available, even if the latter were less experienced. Representations were made that the Canadians should play a more active role, and in July, 111 Squadron was ordered to move up to Umnak, the advanced US base in the Aleutians. The weather in Alaska was dreadful, with much cloud and fog which could ground units for days. 111 had already lost one aircraft due to a fire following technical trouble, when on 16 July, seven Kittyhawks and three US C47 transports took off for the last leg of the flight from Cold Bay to Umnak. A sudden fog developed with disastrous consequences; one fighter pilot became lost and wandered out over the sea, not being seen again, while four more and one of the transports flew into a mountainside. In three days the Squadron had lost seven aircraft and five pilots, including their new commanding officer, Squadron Leader Kerwin.

Meanwhile, the first major success for Western Air Command units had occurred on 7 July. On this date F/Sgt. P. M. G. Thomas of 115 Squadron, while on an antisubmarine patrol in his Bolingbroke, saw and attacked the Japanese submarine Ro-32. Sufficiently severe damage was inflicted to immobilize the vessel, and Thomas directed US destroyers to the area, these administering the "coup de grace."

At Umnak, the depleted 111 Squadron discovered that the USAAF had plenty of P40E aircraft but were short of pilots. Ten

Canadians were therefore attached to the US 11th Fighter Squadron as F Flight until late August, when nine new P40Ks were provided for the Squadron by the Americans. During September 1942 a new base at Adak was completed, from which raids by fighters could be made on the Japanese base at Kiska, from where the enemy was operating Nakajima A6M2-N "Rufe" floatplane fighters. The new commanding officer of 111 Squadron, Squadron Leader K. A. Boomer, requested that RCAF representation be included in one of the early raids there, and on 26 September he led four Canadian-manned P40Ks to undertake flak suppression duties during such an attack. He was able to engage and shoot down an intercepting "Rufe" — the only aerial victory of the war for the home-based RCAF. Shortly after this success, however, the Squadron was ordered back to Anchorage, moving then to Umnak again to provide defence for the US naval base at Kodiak Island.[34]

The Campaign in the Aleutians was dull, dreary and dangerous, yet the threat had to be met immediately and in force. That the RCAF took the threat seriously is shown by the calibre of the leaders it sent into the field. Squadron Leaders Deane Nesbitt, E. M. Reyno and A. M. Yuile all were veterans of the Battle of Britain and original members of No. 1 Fighter Squadron. Brad Walker had fought over the English Channel on 12 February 1942, when the German warships *Scharnhorst*, *Gneisenau* and *Prinz Eugen*, after escaping from Brest, passed through the Strait of Dover under fog cover. Wing Commander Morrow, who commanded the RCAF at Anchorage, was another veteran combat officer. It was a team which could have held its own anywhere in the world.[35]

Though the RCAF fighter units deployed to Alaska would continue to see action well into the following year, they were by no means the only RCAF fighter squadrons tasked with the air defence of North America. This commitment had snowballed during 1942 and at year's end had grown to a force of formidable proportions:

EASTERN AIR COMMAND
HQ Halifax, Nova Scotia

Unit	Equipment
126 (F) Squadron	Hurricane I
128 (F) Squadron	Hurricane I

| 129 (F) Squadron | Hurricane I |
| 130 (F) Squadron | Hurricane I |

1 Group; HQ St. John's, Newfoundland

Unit	Equipment
125 (F) Squadron	Hurricane I
127 (F) Squadron	Hurricane I

WESTERN AIR COMMAND
2 Group; HQ Victoria, British Columbia

Unit	Equipment
14 (F) Squadron	Kittyhawk IA
132 (F) Squadron	Kittyhawk IA
133 (F) Squadron	Hurricane XII
135 (F) Squadron	Hurricane XII

RCAF DETACHED OPERATIONS - ALASKA
X Wing, Anchorage

Unit	Equipment
111 (F) Squadron	Kittyhawk IA and P40K

Y Wing, Annette Island

Unit	Equipment
118 (F) Squadron	Kittyhawk IA

This sizeable fighter buildup on the North American continent would be relatively short-lived, though. As the drive to victory in Europe intensified and the threat to homeland diminished, many of these squadrons would be renumbered and sent overseas for the massive invasion of the Continent that was soon to come.

---

1 Hugh Godefroy, *Lucky Thirteen*, p. 124
2 A checking device on the magnetic compass to ensure flying a proper heading and not a reciprocal course — DB
3 Bob Morrow, letter to author, August 1993
4 George Burroughs, letter to author, September 1993
5 F. E. Hanton, letter to author, August 1993
6 Lloyd Hunt, *We Band of Brothers*, p. 260
7 Lloyd Hunt, *We Happy Few*, p. 141

8   Lloyd Hunt, *We Band of Brothers*, p. 215
9   Duke Warren, letter to author, September 1993
10 R. C. Fumerton, letter to author, July 1993
11 Lloyd Hunt, *We Band of Brothers*, p. 189
12 R. I. A. Smith, letter to author, October 1993
13 E. C. R. Baker, *Fighter Aces of the RAF*, p. 140
14 George Beurling, *Malta Spitfire*, p. 116
15 Ibid.
16 Brian Nolan, *Hero: The "Buzz" Beurling Story*, p. 50
17 Ibid., p. 74
18 *The Canadians at War 1939/45*, p. 153
19 Michel Lavigne and J. F. Edwards, *Kittyhawk Pilot*, p. 51, and J. F. Edwards, letter to author, September 1995
20 Ibid., p. 57
21 Lloyd Hunt, *We Happy Few*, p. 129
22 Edwards and Lavigne, p. 143
23 Bert Houle, letter to author, April 1993
24 John D. R. Rawlings, *The History of the Royal Air Force*, p. 106
25 Allan Simpson, *We Few*, p. 66
26 John D. R. Rawlings, p. 108
27 R. C. Fumerton, letter to author, July 1993
28 Tom Coughlin, *The Dangerous Sky*, p. 41, and R. C. Fumerton, conversation with author, February 1995
29 R. C. Fumerton, letter to author, July 1993
30 John Terraine, *The Right of the Line*, p. 363
31 Hedley Everard, *A Mouse in My Pocket*, pp. 149, 159
32 Ibid., p. 182
33 Christopher Shores, *The History of the Royal Canadian Air Force*, p. 35
34 Ibid., p. 36
35 Leslie Roberts, There Shall Be Wings, p. 153

5

TURNING
POINT

1943

"That ain't flak, that's only salt and pepper . . ."
— FREDDIE GREEN, 402 SQUADRON

The world at the threshold of 1943 seemed a great deal brighter for the Allied cause than it had been in recent years. There were many signs that the Axis forces were being held at bay or were starting to lose ground. In North Africa, Rommel's Afrika Korps and his Italian allies were in full retreat, caught in inexorable Allied pincers which would close upon them in Tunisia. On the high seas, the Battle of the Atlantic was in full stride, and the U-boat war would reach its zenith in May. After that, improving weather, longer-range patrol planes, better escort vessels with sophisticated new detection equipment, and improved radar and weaponry would sound the death knell for the German submarine arm. There would also be an abrupt reduction in Allied shipping losses.

On the *Ostfront*, the *Wehrmacht*'s Sixth Army was slowly being squeezed to death at Stalingrad. When *Generalfeldmarschall* von Paulus surrendered to the Russians with 91,000 soldiers on 2 February, it marked the end of a siege that had cost the Germans at least 600,000 men. Irrevocably weakened, they would never again be able to gain the offensive on the eastern front, and the Russians would not pause in their relentless thrust westward until they had occupied Berlin two years later.

On the home front in 1943, industry and commerce were running around the clock at an unprecedented breakneck pace to sustain the war effort. Rationing had been introduced in Canada the year prior, although compared to the hardships of life in wartime Britain, Occupied Europe, and the Third Reich, it was more of a nuisance than anything else. New songs were released every week, and folks danced to the big band sounds of Glen Miller and Tommy Dorsey. Warner Brother's *Casablanca* dominated the movie theatres that year, as audiences empathized with Humphrey Bogart and Ingrid Bergman over their impossible wartime love affair.

A number of factors combined to greatly increase the success rate of the RCAF fighter squadrons serving in the United Kingdom in 1943. In the immediate wake of the Dieppe fiasco, a great number of RAF fighter units were sent to the Middle East, and the fighter air offensive over northwest Europe was predominately relegated to Commonwealth and foreign-national squadrons. Also, the excellent stopgap Spitfire Mk IX, which was basically a modified Mk V airframe housing an uprated Merlin engine, was now in near-universal service with the front-line, U.K.-based squadrons. Tactics were now evolving in both the Allied and Axis camps to bring air combat back down to lower altitudes, and this was having a decided effect on fighter aircraft design. Jeffrey Quill, celebrated Spitfire test pilot, comments on this evolution of tactics, its effect on aircraft and engine design, and the development of the Spitfire Mk VIII, which followed the Mk IX into production. The Mk VIII saw widespread service in the Middle and Far East theatres and was considered by some to be the best variant of the aircraft.

The fighter-to-fighter combats in the Battle of Britain and subsequently the offensive sweeps across the Channel had set the opposing fighters clawing for more and more height, and the development of both the Spitfire and the Me 109 had responded to this increasing search for altitude.

Then at some indefinite time in 1942, there seemed to be a change of tactical philosophy on both sides. It was rather as if, by some sort of tacit mutual consent between enemies, it was realized that the band between 30,000 and 40,000 feet was a silly place in which to have an air battle, and the fighting tended to drop down into the more practical regions, roughly between 15,000 feet and 25,000 feet. I remember how, at the time, this trend interested me very much indeed. It was clearly reflected in the LF Mk IX (Merlin 66) with the engine performance adjusted to the reduced height band. It was also reflected in the fact that, by removing the wing tips of the Spitfire, an improvement in lateral control could be achieved, but because it thereby increased the wing loading and the span loading of the wing, an aerodynamic penalty was incurred at high altitude. Such a proposition would have been unthinkable in 1940/1 but in 1942/3, the idea was enthusiastically adopted by some squadrons in No. 11 Group, and the "clipped-wing" Spitfire became a common sight in the sky.

When the decision was taken to go ahead with the two-speed two-stage supercharged engine in an unpressurized Spitfire, there were other improvements required in the fighter apart from simply increased altitude performance. Foremost amongst these were increased range and endurance, implying more internal fuel capacity as well as external jettisonable tanks (the latter had just been developed) and also increased fire power, which clearly meant at least four cannon. Although the Mk Vc (with the "universal" wing) had provision for four cannon, it was normally possible to fit only two, because heating for the outboard cannon was inadequate. Only some squadrons operating overseas in low-level roles ever operated the Mk Vc with four cannon fitted, so a fully operational four-cannon installation was now required. The increasing importance of the Middle East and, later, other overseas theatres also demanded the modification of future fighters to suit them for tropical conditions.

So the aeroplane which Supermarine designed to take the two-stage engine, the Mk VIII, embodied extra internal fuel tanks in the wing roots, bringing the internal fuel capacity up to 124 gallons, a four-cannon wing, full tropicalisation and a retractable tail wheel. It also embodied ailerons on which the long overhang outboard of the outer hinge was shortened in order to increase the stiffness of the aileron structure. Because the emphasis was, at the time the aircraft was ordered, still firmly on improved performance at altitude, the Mk VIII was originally designed with extended wing tips similar to those designed for the Mk VI and Mk VII pressure cabin aeroplanes. These changes to the Mk VIII obviously took time to get into production, and the Merlin 61 engines were available ahead of the aeroplanes so the Mk IX, essentially conceived as an interim type, came into service well ahead of the Mk VIII. Paradoxically, the "interim" Mk IX was produced in greater quantities than any other mark of Spitfire.

. . . The Mk VIII, however, was by far the better aeroplane and because of its tropicalisation, improved range and other refinements, it was allocated to the overseas commands while Fighter Command soldiered on with the Mk IX in the temperate conditions at home.

. . . I considered the extended wing tips on the early Mk VIIIs entirely unnecessary.

The airplane was not, in my view, a specialized high-altitude machine — it was an air combat fighter of excellent all-round performance and destined for theatres of war where it would have to operate in a wide variety of circumstances. The extended wing tips did nothing for it except increase the lateral damping and spoil the aileron control. I complained incessantly to Joe Smith about them and did my best to get rid of them. Eventually, God be praised, when the Merlin 66 engine was brought in on the Mk VIII, we reverted to the standard wing tip configuration. We then had an excellent aeroplane, very pleasant to handle and of performance as good as the Mk IX, with many other advantages added on.[1]

In 1943, the U.K.-based RCAF fighter squadrons received a boost to national pride by the rise in seniority of selected Canadian fighter pilots to Wing Commander rank. Combat-experienced Canadians were now available for second tours of operations and were ready to don the mantle of leadership which had thus far largely been placed on the shoulders of British Wing Commanders. Additionally, the American Eighth Air Force had just begun its daylight bomber offensive in strength. Since both Bomber Command and the USAAF now possessed many medium and heavy day bombers, increased opportunities were presented to the RCAF Spitfire squadrons to escort raids of a more damaging, sustained nature. Naturally, this new and evolving Allied bomber threat required increased reinforcement by the Germans of the western front. With the war demands on so many fronts spreading the ranks of the experienced *experten* (aces) so thin, the Spitfire pilots would from now on frequently encounter enemy fighters that were obviously being flown by novices. Finally, the universal acceptance of finger-four tactics, which had met stubborn resistance on some units, would be a decisive contribution towards air combat success for RCAF fighter pilots in 1943. To this point, some of the Canadian fighter squadrons were still inexplicably clinging tenaciously to the obsolete "pairs line astern" formation on operations.

While some highly competent and charismatic Canadian fighter wing leaders were emerging in 1943, several Britons were providing leadership to the Canadians that was nothing short of inspirational, and none more so than a young civil engineer from Leicestershire named James Edgar Johnson.

"Johnnie" Johnson was destined to become the highest-scoring Commonwealth ace of the Second World War, with 38 confirmed victories. When he was given command of the Kenley Wing in the spring of 1943, however, he was a relative unknown with only eight confirmed kills to his credit, though his scoresheet was representative of a highly skilled combat pilot on the Channel Coast at that stage of the war. Very few Allied pilots in the United Kingdom who had missed the high-pitched defensive Battles of France and Britain had been presented with opportunities to run up impressive scores. This was not the case in Malta and North Africa, where the opportunities to score abounded. The balance of Johnson's impressive victory count would be accumulated while leading various RCAF fighter units throughout the rest of the war in Europe, and thus his wartime success is inextricably linked to the Canadians. While he would be revered by the Canadians with whom he served so gallantly and effectively, his welcome to Kenley in 1943 was somewhat conditional. Johnnie recalls his first impressions of his new command:

I drove to the Mess and parked the small Morris outside, much to the amusement of a party of husky Canadian pilots who were obviously comparing its size to the glittering monsters they used at home. A smart, broad-shouldered Squadron Leader walked out of the Mess and gave me a snappy salute.

"Wing Commander Johnson?"

"That's right," I replied.

"I'm Bud Malloy. Wing Commander Hodson, whose job you are taking, is off for the day and so is the Group Captain. Shall we have a can of beer, then some food, and I'll take you round and introduce you to your wild Canadians."

After lunch I inspected my room. The Mess seemed to be hermetically sealed and the central heating was going full blast. This, I was to learn, was a feature of the North American way of life, but I had been brought up the hard way and soon changed to a room in one of the wings which did not have the benefit of steam heat.

It was a day of low cloud and drizzle, so Malloy and I made a leisurely tour of the airfield and met the two Squadron Commanders and upwards of seventy pilots. The lean, slightly balding Syd Ford of 403 Squadron came from Nova Scotia, already held the DFC and Bar, and had established his reputation as a sound leader and an aggressive pilot. Foss Bolton of 416 Squadron hailed from Alberta and was an open-faced, friendly character who was a relative newcomer to the game, having spent the greater part of his flying career in Canada.

I was surprised to learn that they still flew in the old-fashioned line-astern formation. We had a long talk about this. I pointed out the benefits of the abreast, finger-four style. A more aggressive, offensive formation and so on. Syd Ford, who had flown the Spitfire 9 quite a lot, favoured the line astern despite my arguments. Bolton seemed to waver between the two types and perhaps could not assess a new Wing Leader who wanted to change things within a few minutes of arriving. I felt it was time for a decision:

"For the first few Wing shows I'll lead Foss's Squadron and we'll fly in finger-fours. You, Syd, will hold your position down-sun, 3000 feet higher, and you can fly in what formation you like providing you do your job. We'll see how it goes for the first few times and then decide one way or the other for the whole Wing."

I met the tall, good-looking Keith Hodson, himself a Canadian, on the following day and he gave me a sketch of the Wing's recent activities. The two Squadrons had received their Spitfire 9s some months previously and during January they had lost a Wing Leader over France and Keith was promoted into the vacancy.

"This weather of yours has been against us. We've not had a real chance to get together. But it should improve any time now, and a good thing — the boys are getting a bit restless. They've got a fine aeroplane and I think they fly well. What they want is a few good scraps with the '190s. If you can pull that off during your first few shows they'll be right with you."

"What you mean is that I'm on approval at present?" I suggested.

"I guess that's about the size of it," grinned Keith.[2]

After several weeks of indifferent flying weather failed to provide any conclusive engagements with enemy fighters, Johnson was afforded the opportunity in early April for that "good scrap" which would ultimately weld the Wing together.

We were having lunch when the Tannoy announced that the Wing would come to readiness in one hour's time. I walked over to the ops. block to study the details so that I could brief the Wing. It was only a small show, but far better than idling away the afternoon on the ground. Crow was to lead his Squadron of Typhoons across the Channel at low level, dive-bomb the Abbeville airfield and then withdraw at a high rate of knots. Our job was to climb over France as the Typhoons came out and knock down any Messerschmitts or Focke Wulfs flushed by the bombing.

It was a simple little operation, just Crow's Squadron and my Wing. What really appealed to me was that we were operating in a free-lance role and were not confined to any particular area. The weather was perfect and we were to operate under the control of a new radar station in Kent which was rapidly acquiring a reputation for excellent long-distance controlling. It was a week-end, and there always seemed to be a stronger enemy reaction on Saturdays and Sundays than any other day.

I telephoned Squadron Leader Hunter, the senior controller of the new radar station, outlined my tactics and agreed that he would not break radio silence unless he had an enemy plot on his scopes.

Crossing the French coast just south of Le Touquet, I caught a glimpse of Crow's Typhoons well below and heading back towards England. Our superchargers cut in at 19,000 feet with an unpleasant thump and the engines surged and we eased back our throttles. At 24,000 feet I levelled out and Bolton's Squadron drew abreast of me in the finger-four formation. Ford's Squadron were just beginning to make condensation trails and these could be seen from a great distance and would betray our position. But before I could call him he dropped his Squadron a few hundred feet and the twelve conspicuous thin white banners creased.

Hunter broke the silence:

"Greycap from Grass-seed. Twenty plus bandits climbing up inland. Steer 140."

"OK, Grass-seed," I acknowledged. "Any height on the bandits?"

"Well below you, Greycap. They are approaching the coast and I'll try and bring you out of the sun. Continue on 140."

This was perfect teamwork between controller and Wing Leader. It was the first time we had worked with Hunter; he seemed to have something of Woodhall's ability to put his information across in a quiet, reassuring manner. The whole intricate mechanics of long-range radar interception seemed to be working perfectly. Suddenly I was brimming with confidence, for I knew that Hunter and I would pull this one off.

"Greycap. Bandits have crossed below you at 15,000 feet. Port on to 310. Buster."

"OK Grass-seed. Port on to 310," I replied.

"Greycap. Bandits now seven miles ahead. 5000 feet below. Gate."

I put the Spitfires into a shallow dive and scanned the area ahead. The sky seemed empty.

"Greycap. Another strong formation of bandits behind you. About five to eight miles. Exercise caution."

Here were the makings of a perfect shambles! We were almost on top of the first enemy formation with another gaggle not far behind. How far? Hunter had said between five and eight miles, but the radar was scanning at its maximum range and five miles could be one mile — or ten. Should I call the whole thing off and set course for Dungeness now? The decision was mine. For a moment it seemed as if we were suspended and motionless in the high sky, with the Canadians clustered around me waiting for an order.

Then I saw our quarry. One bunch of twelve '190s just below us and a mile ahead, and a further ten '190s well out on the starboard side. It was too golden an opportunity to miss. Height, sun and surprise in our favour and I had to take a chance on how far behind the other enemy formation was.

"Greycap to Wing. Twenty-plus Huns below from twelve to three o'clock. Syd, I'm taking the left-hand bunch. Come down and take the right-hand gaggle. Get in!"

I turned slightly to get directly behind the '190s and remembered to make the turn slow and easy so that our wingmen could keep well up. I put the nose down and had to fight back an instinct to slam the throttle wide open. We had to hit these brutes together.

My own '190 was flying on the extreme port side of the enemy formation. We came down on their tails in a long, slanting dive. Before I opened fire, I looked to the starboard, saw Bolton's boys fanning out alongside and Ford's arrowhead of Spitfires falling down on their prey about three miles away. The attack was coordinated, and my task of leading the Wing was temporarily suspended. Now it was up to the individual pilots to select their opponents and smack them down.

I missed the '190 with my first short burst and steadied the gun platform with coarse stick and rudder. I fired again and hit him on the wing root and just behind the cockpit. The spot harmonization paid off and the cannon shells thudded into him in a deadly concentration of winking explosions. He started to burn, but before he fell on to his back I gave him another long burst. Then I broke away in a steep climbing turn and searched the sky behind. Still nothing there. Below me another '190 was falling in flames, and on the starboard a parachute had opened into full bloom. Hunter was still concerned for our safety:

"Greycap. Withdraw. Strong force of bandits approaching. Almost on top of you."

I spoke to the Wing:

"All Greycap aircraft. Get out now! We won't reform. And keep a sharp look-out behind!"

The pilots didn't need telling twice; we poured across the Channel at high speed in pairs and fours. My Section was the first to land and when I climbed out of the cockpit I was met by a small posse of officers, for the good word that we had bounced the '190s soon spread. I lit a cigarette and counted the Spits as they joined the circuit over Kenley. Sixteen down, four on the circuit — twenty. A singleton — twenty-one. A long pause and a pair — twenty-three. One to come. It seemed very important that he should swing in over Caterham and land. But we had waited too long; he was either missing or at some other airfield.

The pilots walked into the briefing room still excited and full of the flight. We totted up the score with the Spies listening silently and ever ready to reduce a claim from a destroyed to a damaged or, if they had the chance, to nothing at all! The total came to six '190s destroyed for the loss of one of our pilots, who, we could only surmise, must have been clobbered by a '190 after our first attack.

I was delighted with our effort. The controlling had been superb and the Canadians had flown really well. I made out my report, called the radar station and thanked Hunter, and checked with our operations room for any news of our missing pilot. They had no information.

The next morning Syd Ford walked into my office. He laid a pair of blue Canada shoulder-flashes on my desk and said:

"The boys would like you to wear these. After all, we're a Canadian Wing and we've got to convert you. Better start this way."

"Thanks Syd," I replied. "I'll get them sewn on today."

A simple gesture, but for me it had a deep significance. The flashes were sewn on and two years were to elapse before it was time to take them down.[3]

Johnnie Johnson firmly believed that fighter leadership was not embodied in running up a personal scoresheet, but by fostering the overall success of the Wing in battle. To that end, he could be extremely generous in sharing the spoils of war with his subordinates. He was also acutely attuned to the psychology of men in battle and had a knack for bringing out the best in others while helping them over the rougher moments. Karl Linton of Plaster Rock, New Brunswick, who went on to win a well-deserved DFC with 421 Squadron in 1944, recalls the steep learning curve he climbed during early combat days as a Sergeant Pilot with the Kenley Wing. He also recalls the help Johnson provided him in both scoring and later dealing with his first combat victory:

> Real early on, during my 21st trip, I was flying "tail-end Charlie" and supposed to be protecting my Number One, when a '109 clobbered me, blew my coupe top off, put two or three bullet holes through my Sergeant's hooks, several in the armour plating at my back, and some in the engine block, but I didn't get a scratch. After that, no Jerry ever got on my tail, and if he tried, I turned swiftly, usually into a sharp port turn and up, up and away! We couldn't out-dive them but we laughed at them in a turn and climb.
>
> . . . On my 48th sortie, I was flying Number Two to Johnnie over Amsterdam. I reported a bogey at 10 o'clock below. He said, "OK Red Two, you saw him, go get him!" I did, and it was a "flamer." Johnnie got one that day too. After I got that one over Amsterdam, I followed custom and bought the usual round of drinks that night in the Mess. The guys were cheering, "Cheers, Karl!," etcetera, and after a few drinks of "mild and bitters" it progressed to "Killer Karl," and "Cheers, Killer!" I didn't like that as a nickname so I left the Mess for my room a little bit misty-eyed. I was twenty, had never killed before, and with the excitement and fun in the Mess, I guess it kinda got to me. But in the lobby I met Johnnie, and he shook my hand, then congratulated me on spotting

the enemy aircraft and on my good shooting. However, he must have seen a tear in my eye so he called me aside, talked with me a few minutes, cheered me up a bit and said, "Come back in the Mess in a half-hour and join the crowd. You won't be called that again." Guess he must have lectured a bit; it didn't happen again. You know, we really had some wonderful leaders . . .[4]

--- ❖ ---

Of all the fine young RCAF fighter wing commanders who would rise to prominence during the Second World War, perhaps none fostered more admiration, respect, and affection from his peers than Lloyd Chadburn of Aurora, Ontario. Commissioned a Pilot Officer in October 1940, he took part in the first RCAF sweep over enemy territory on 15 April 1941. A year later, he was in command of 416 Squadron, and led it with great distinction over the beaches of Dieppe, winning the DFC. Jackie Rae, a DFC winner on 416 Squadron, describes the social life at Redhill at the time with his boss, Lloyd Chadburn, and the effect that the Canadians had upon their generally more staid British hosts:

Canadians had developed a reputation with the British for being somewhat unconventional when our Squadron was newly posted to the RAF Redhill base. When we had settled into our bunks, we went to the Mess to get acquainted. After we had introduced ourselves to the British officers and their wives, we went to one end of the room and they went to the other. The atmosphere was very stodgy and dry and it was obvious that we didn't live up to their expectations of what an officer should be.

At that time my Squadron Commander was Lloyd Chadburn, who later went on to earn two DSOs and a DFC. He felt that we should do something to change the atmosphere. Chadburn called me outside and told me to take three or four other guys and a truck and go to the Chequers Hotel, where they were having a dance and pick up a sufficient number of young women and bring them back to the Mess. He said to promise them all the stockings, chocolates and perfume they wanted.

The oldest guy in our Squadron was 23 and we were well supplied by our mothers and friends with items that were hard to get. They weren't standard Air Force issue, but were part of a young man's survival kit.

When we arrived at the hotel, it was in the middle of a black-out. The lights of the hotel were dimmed for the dance, but despite the low light levels, we were able to entice a truck load of young women to return with us to the Mess.

When we stepped foot inside the Mess with our newly found companions, the British officers and their ladies beat a hasty retreat in disgust. At the time we thought that it was pretty big of them, as it left the Mess free to us to stage quite a memorable party.

The next morning, Chadburn was called on the carpet to explain what was described by the CO as our outrageous and disgusting behavior. He agreed with the CO that it was indeed disgusting behavior, that it was all my fault and he would see I was punished. Shortly thereafter, I reminded him that it was his idea, something he chose to forget. I was never disciplined but it certainly was a night to remember.[5]

"Chad" was never a particularly high scorer, though he was a distinguished ace in his own right, known above all for fostering team spirit among his men. To that end, he was very generous in sharing victories with his peers and subordinates. Jackie Rae recalls Lloyd Chadburn's fine leadership qualities, which were apparent from 416 Squadron's earliest days in Scotland, and which were present "in spades" in the skies over the beaches at Dieppe:

When 416 Squadron was forming at Peterhead, we were very much in awe of Chad, who had already served in 11 Group. His discipline on the ground was relaxed, and in the air the complete opposite. He flew us day and night; tight formation, battle climbs, low flying, etc., and molded a bunch of totally inexperienced and not-too-talented pilots into a Squadron ready to get into the thick of it in 11 Group. I remember him flying to London to lobby on our behalf, having told us that somehow he was going to get us South . . . and he did it. It was from Redhill in 1942 that we first started to take part in fighter sweeps over enemy territory, and soon 416 Squadron became truly operational. My first real contact with enemy fighters came on August 19, 1942, when the Squadron took part in the ill-fated landing at Dieppe. On that day we flew four missions, but our most exciting one was during the withdrawal of the ground forces, when our formation was very heavily engaged and Lloyd Chadburn fought a brilliant action without loss. As our

Spitfires approached the battered convoy of ships to commence our protective patrol formation, fifteen Focke Wulf 190s dived on us from astern. Chadburn brought the Squadron round in a very tight turn and reversed the tables so effectively that three of the '190s were destroyed. Hurriedly reforming, we resumed our cover over the ships when seven Ju 88s appeared. Chad attacked head-on and we damaged six enemy bombers before they withdrew. In my view, he was not out to build a score, as was the case with others. Rather, he would do his job as a leader who had taught his people how to thrive as a group. Then, he would get us home. We loved him, and will never forget him as the man who developed good pilots and whose character, I hope, rubbed off on us.[6]

In November 1942, the Digby Wing, which Chadburn had commanded since June, was declared the highest scoring in all of Fighter Command, due in no small measure to his courageous example and excellent leadership. It was thus highly fitting that he became the first RCAF officer to be awarded a Bar to the Distinguished Service Order. His modest, laconic reaction to the award was typical of the man: "It's a funny thing that when the boys put on a good show, the Wing Commander gets the DSO. They put on another, and he gets the Bar."[7]

Art Sager, an ace and DFC winner who would lead 443 Squadron during the final drive into Germany, fondly recollects Lloyd Chadburn's leadership style, and how lucky Sager felt to be part of the Digby Wing in 1943:

The Mess is not as well-equipped as at Kenley but the atmosphere in the lounge and dining room is lively, buoyant, exhilarating. Good spirits reign and there are no cliques. Morale is obviously high and the ésprit de corps you sense animates everyone, ground and flying personnel.

The Station Commander is Group Captain Ernie McNab, DFC. Short and stocky, in his late thirties, Ernie was a peacetime member of the RCAF who won his DFC with #1 Squadron, the first all-Canadian fighter squadron to be formed. He's modest, quiet-spoken with no side to him, and he chats with everyone, using their first names. Clearly all the pilots like him, feeling he is one of them. Our personal friendship, started here, continues after the war. Digby is a happy station and to Ernie goes much of the credit.

But it's the vibrant personality of the Wing Commander that makes Digby unique. It is felt by everyone — pilots, groundcrew, support staff — and when the youthful, blond Wingco visits dispersals and hangars, faces light up and work is done with a will. Chad has all the qualities of a natural born leader, on the ground and in the air. The adjective "inspired" is more than apt, for his leadership is effortless, stemming from character rather than conscious act.

Chadburn was born in Oshawa twenty-four years earlier on what he says was the wrong side of the tracks. He went to vocational school and, after leaving before the outbreak of war, volunteered for service but was turned down by the Army, Navy and Air Force. Finally, on a second try, he was accepted by the Air Force for training as an air gunner. After passing the course, and undoubtedly using his personal charm, he was able to remuster as a pilot. He was overseas in 1940 and in November 1941, on a Roadstead, he attacked and destroyed a German "E" boat, the first fighter pilot to do so. His progress upwards was rapid: from Pilot Officer to Flight Lieutenant to Squadron Leader, and then, in the summer of 1943, to Wing Commander, the youngest in the RCAF. He has a DFC and, when three weeks after my arrival at Digby he is awarded the DSO, everyone celebrates. His citation reads in part, ". . . has displayed exceptional leadership and great skill, while his fine fighting spirit has set a most inspired example."

Chad is worshipped by his pilots and the verb is not too strong. I sense this as they crowd around him in the Mess, beer in hand, "shooting the shit" as he would say, or in the Unicorn pub, the Wing's favourite, where he is always at the centre of festivities. In his company, jokes, laughter, and high spirits abound. His two Squadron Leaders, S/L Geoff Northcott, DFC, and later S/L Kelly Walker, are his converts and I can see that they model themselves on the master. When Freddy Green returns in October for a second tour and takes over 416, I'm delighted and convinced that no Wing anywhere could have a better triumvirate of leaders than that of Chad, Freddy and Geoff.

Chad instills confidence in all who fly with him. He's an excellent pilot and marksman and a superb Wing leader. In the air he's steady and cool, giving his orders clearly but nearly always with some quip that makes one smile and relax. "Don't panic, chaps," he says when "forty plus" bandits are reported. "We'll just about make it, I figure." Or, going too close to Dunkirk, "Get into that flak, chaps!" Attacked by a large gaggle of Huns, he says, "Okay, chaps, we'll go through them like shit through a goose." He's an astute and generous tactician, seeking always to get the Squadrons into position so that all Sections can bring their guns to bear on the target. It's always line abreast with Chad. For him the objective is not to increase one's personal score but to do maximum damage to the enemy, everyone participating. There are only two Squadrons in his Wing — 402 and 416 — but by 1 December 1943, four months after its formation, the Wing has destroyed 42 enemy aircraft, probably destroyed several and damaged a dozen with the loss of only one fighter. In this period the Wing earns one DFM, six DFCs, and Chad's DSO. In forty-five operations escorting Marauders they lose one bomber, and the Hun who shot it down paid with his life.

In pre-mission briefings, Chad is a showman. He deliberately puts on an act to relieve tension and the result is always hilarious. He laughs and jokes as if planning a picnic. Essential information on course, height, speed and tactics are given in colourful slang of his own coinage, some of it bawdy. "We'll go thataway," he says, pointing to North Foreland, "and we'll meet up with the big boys at North Foreskin." You start engines on "tit-pressing time" and on takeoff you "give her the goose." I have a lexicon of Chadburn and Green expressions, all graphic and most unprintable. Chad's fame as an entertainer spreads and his briefings attract many unauthorized personnel, including WAAFs. His enthusiasm is contagious and pilots leave his briefings and head for their kites in high spirits.[8]

Nineteen forty-three brought a great decline in the number of sergeant pilots serving in RCAF squadrons, due to a decision that had been reached on the issue the previous year. The divisive policy of using the sergeant pilot rank, rooted as it was in the anachronistic British class system, created a lot of ill-will on the operational units, for it often meant that men who could fight and frequently die on equal terms could not socialize on the same terms in the same Mess. Furthermore, British policy was biased against the use of sergeant pilots for leadership roles in the air, regardless of ability, although lower-level RAF leaders would often turn a blind eye to this silly operating procedure whenever it was expedient to do so. The Canadian solution had been to commission the sergeant pilots on their first operational squadron as quickly as possible. Leslie Roberts comments on the decline and fall of this unpopular policy:

> One tempest in a teapot arose over the commissioning of Canadian Air Plan graduates serving overseas with RAF units, as almost sixty percent of Canadian aircrew did. The RAF commissioned only twenty-five percent of its flyers. Canada tended to give officer status to all who merited it by Canadian standards. A verbal compromise was reached as the first Air Plan graduates moved overseas.
>
> Despite this agreement, Canadians flying with RAF units did not receive their commissions as promised, but remained in the Sergeants Mess. Complaints reached Canada. Members of Parliament received letters from irate parents, and took the matter to the Air Minister. Finally Power decided on drastic action. Thirty-five Sergeants flying in RAF units were gazetted by the RCAF, of which they were members. Their British commanding officers replied by refusing to recognize their new status, a united action which was certainly not a coincidence.
>
> After bringing the issue to a head, Power brought about settlement in his own forthright manner. "I gave these young fellows my word," he told the British, "but only after you agreed. I realize that Canadian and British ideas on commissions are not identical and that we may upset your Officer/NCO balance in RAF squadrons. Nevertheless I hope to live in Canada after the war, but you fellows will still be in England."
>
> In the revised BCATP Agreement of 5 June 1942, which extended the life of the Plan from 1943 to 1945, it was stated that all pilots, observers, navigators and air bombers who were considered suitable according to the standards of the Canadian government, and who were recommended for commissions, would be commissioned. Thereafter Canada established its own quotas . . .[9]

Hugh Godefroy, who had been commissioned a Pilot Officer when he received his wings, notes that discrimination against sergeant pilots started long before they reached an operational squadron:

> At the wings parade everybody had been promoted but quite a few of my friends were not officers. They were Sergeant Pilots. As we recounted to each other the events of our embarkation leave, it was obvious that something had happened to the "Esprit de Corps."

The windscreen of Karl Linton's Spitfire after its direct hit by flak while crossing the French coast at very low level, January 1944. *Karl Linton Photo*

Bert Houle, DFC and Bar, the able and charismatic leader of 417 Squadron from late 1943 to early 1944. *RE 74-216*

George "Buzz" Beurling, Canada's highest-scoring fighter ace, while on a 1943 public relations tour of Canada. *PL 14940*

Al "The Chief" Corston and feathered friends, while serving with 67 (RAF) Squadron at Calcutta, India, early 1944. *Al Corston Photo*

Dick Reeves as a Sergeant Pilot with his Spitfire. Note the "Saint" emblem under the canopy. *Dick Reeves Photo*

Gib Coons in appropriate fighter-pilot attire for the air war over Burma, 607 (RAF) Squadron, March 1944. *Gib Coons Photo*

Gord Ockenden as a mere twenty-year-old with 443 Squadron at RAF Station Westhampnett, just prior to the Normandy invasion, May 1944. *Gord Ockenden Photo*

Rod Smith, who "won his spurs" over Malta with the RAF, later led 401 Squadron on what would be the first destruction of a German jet aircraft by a Commonwealth unit (5 October 1944). *PL 29398*

RCAF groundcrew hand-painting invasion stripes on a 411 Squadron Spitfire just prior to "The Big Show," June 1944. *DND Photo*

Flying Officer Bill Burgess, Flight Lieutenant Bill Pendelton, and Pilot Officer Jack Doyle of 417 Squadron "debriefing" the Squadron cook, Italy, 1944. *PL 18786*

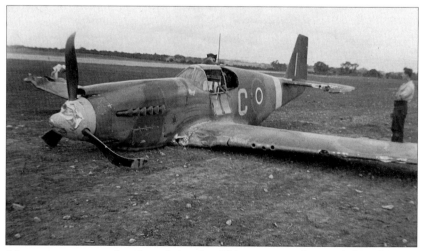

Mustangs were rugged and needed to be. This one, severely crippled by flak, was brought back in April 1944 by Flying Officer Davidson, using lots of trim and a heavy foot. *George Burroughs Photo*

". . . to fight another day;" — August 1944. This 403 Squadron Spitfire may well do so, thanks to the tireless efforts of the salvage crews. *PL 31115*

Flying Officer Sandy McRoberts of Calgary, shortly after scoring a double victory over Normandy. Observe the 421 Squadron Red Indian logo and McRoberts's "fifty mission crush" hat. *DND Photo PL 30719*

Much loved by the infantry, Typhoons in Normandy, 1944. *DND Photo*

Fighter-pilot cunning and proper alignment of priorities gets fine British ale to the boys at the front in Normandy, 1944. *Johnnie Johnson Photo*

An RCAF Spitfire Mark IX in Normandy, 1944. Note the "liberated" German motorcycle and helmet draped over the wing cannon. The pilot is Flying Officer "Bud" Bowker of Granby, Quebec. *PL 30259*

Typhoons armed and ready to go. Not exactly the last word on streamlining, those rocket rails! Observe the mix of four- and three-bladed propellers. *DND Photo PL 42759*

Squadron Leader Howie Cleveland of 418 Squadron posing beside "Li'l Abner." The former advertising executive's Mosquito displays seven confirmed kills and a "damaged," although Cleveland would eventually get another confirmed victory. *DND Photo PL 29159*

Those who were Sergeants treated the rest of us with a suspicion of reserve. No matter what we said, it just didn't seem to be the same. "From now on I'm going to have to salute you, Hughie," said Sandy Morrison. "It just can never be the same. You're going to be in your Mess, and I'm going to be in mine. That's two different worlds, boy, two different worlds."

There was a long silence. Finally Sandy raised his head and said: "I'll tell you what, Hughie, on this bloody trip there is no way they can divide us. Let's enjoy our last days together and forget it!"[10]

The discriminatory regulations applying to officers and NCOs would not even allow fast friends to remain together on trips, however, and nowhere was the class separation more apparent than on the treacherous North Atlantic crossing. Gordon Wilson, who would serve as a pilot with 134, 213, and 92 Squadrons of the RAF, describes his experiences of "crossing the pond" as a Sergeant Pilot:

I think many, including myself, cried "dirty pool" when we went overseas as Sergeant Pilots, and our buddies, for some unknown reasons were commissioned Pilot Officers. But I guess that was the luck of the game.

The trip by ship to England had its moments. There was the usual buzz at our Halifax barracks. Then the news was out — we would be boarding ship at Halifax on Friday. Sure enough, at 10 am we were lined up and given our deck and berth number on the *Empress of Asia* — a large ship, especially to the prairie airmen who had seen nothing larger than a sailing boat. The *Empress* had brought Italian prisoners of war to Canada, and with no time to refit was ordered immediately to join a convoy. The ship was not just dirty, but filthy. There were about 100 officer pilots, 700 Canadian Sergeant Pilots, and several hundreds of Australian pilots.

The officers went up to the upper decks, while the Sergeant Pilots went down and down to the lower decks. Finally when the Australian Sergeant Pilots found their deck and their berths consisted of hammocks swinging from the ceiling of a low storage room — ours was similar — in their customary Australian language (and I won't repeat the wording but it went something like this — possibly stronger) "Chaps, let's get off this so and so tub. If they think we are going to ride in this, they're crazy." So they found a stairway up to the main deck and down the gang plank onto the dock, with Canadian Sergeant Pilots following them. It must have been quite a sight to see hundreds of Sergeant Pilots boarding the *Empress of Asia* on one side, and an equal number coming off the *Empress* from another gang plank.

What do you do when you have created a scene similar to *Mutiny on the Bounty* — 1941 version? Well, it was cold on the dock and the ever resourceful Sergeant Pilots knew just what to do about it. Packing our kits before boarding, we were told by those who knew, to go light on the air force clothing issue, but heavy on all the Canadian Club rye whisky and nylon stockings we could find. So out came the Canadian Club, and we had a very happy band of warriors on the dock until the Canadian Club ran out. An army contingent in their correct discipline marched on board and found their proper deck. As the night wore on and the flood lights came on, army individuals would open a porthole and yell at us, "Come on board, you yellowbellies!" Just by coincidence there were about forty cases of apples on the dock. So when a porthole would open and a head appear, the head became the target of forty well aimed apples. Then the rumors started . . . the Air Vice-Marshal was inspecting the ship and if it was not in good shape it would not leave port — but please clear the dock and come on board for the night. Many of us went on board only to find the Military police prepared to see that we did not leave the *Empress* the next morning. An Inquiry stated that airmen would not be subjected to these conditions in the future.

Food on the *Empress* was also a problem for the Sergeants. It was poorly prepared and handled. Again we thought we should do something about it. So with Canadian ingenuity, our little group did. On all ships there are a great number of pipes and human pipelines. We found a particularly good pipeline down to the officer's galley — the ship's catering Sergeant. Our dinner hour was not exactly to our choosing — 2:30 in the morning, after lights out, and our eating quarters consisted of a narrow dark hallway. But the night cooks made up for the inconvenience by bringing out their finest food.[11]

As denigrating as the sergeant pilot policy was on the ground, it could reach the limits of absurdity in the air. Such a travesty happened to Stocky Edwards in the Western Desert just prior to his commissioning and accelerated promotion to Flight Lieutenant. At the time, Edwards was one of the highest scoring aces in the theatre.

The next day, Eddie was in the air again, heading the Squadron. This time there was more excitement. The boy from Battleford shot down a Messerschmitt for which he was never credited.

At 12.20 hours, fifteen '109s of JG 27 had taken off from their home base to escort Ju 87 Stukas on a raid in the Alamein area. At 12.35 hours, 5 SAAF Tomahawks and seven Kittyhawk IIs from 260 Squadron were scrambled to intercept the Stuka party. 260 was flying top cover to the South African Squadron. Just as the unit got into position and was still climbing, '109s were spotted approaching from the west. At least twelve Messerschmitts, spread over a wide area, flew in pairs. Four of them turned and attacked the top Section while four others dove head-on through Eddie's Section. The remaining four went for the South Africans below. Staying together, Eddie's Section was making a controlled turn when a '109 was seen coming from below in a steep climbing turn. Banking his FL223, Eddie fired a burst from about 200 yards at 30 degrees deflection and watched as the enemy aircraft exploded from the back of the engine and above the starboard wing root. He saw it turn over on its back and spin out of control before the Squadron reformed. 260 returned to base together, with no losses, but 5 SAAF was not as lucky. After they had been split up, they lost many aircraft to the '109s. Leutnant Werner Schroer of III Gruppe claimed three victories within fifteen minutes of combat.

By 13.20 hours, exactly one hour and five minutes after take-off, Eddie and his Kittys were back at LG97 where the AOC, AVM Coningham was making his visit. Filing their reports, Eddie claimed an Me 109 destroyed. The hit had been witnessed by both his No. 2 and 3. Both had seen the enemy aircraft spinning to earth completely out of control. As the AOC talked with the men, he learned that Eddie had just come home from leading the Squadron in action. He discovered F/Sgt. Cundy was also taking the Squadron up. In fact, Cundy had led the entire Wing on operations the same day.

"This sort of thing isn't done, Old Boy! Sergeant Pilots just don't lead RAF squadrons," Coningham told them. Although it might not have been in the rule book, there were many unorthodox practices carried out in the desert; they were necessary in order to get the job done.

In his diary, Sgt. Cartwright wrote, "Eddie got a '109. 'Cobber' Cundy his PO. We all go to celebrate it." But it wasn't long before

Eddie learned his '109 was not confirmed and in his log-book he noted, "Led Squadron. Ran into Me 109s and I claim an Me 109 destroyed." No one will ever know if the young Sergeant Pilot's leadership of the Squadron into battle that day had anything to do with the re-evaluation of Eddie's claim.

It wasn't long after Coningham's visit to the unit, Eddie was interviewed for his commission by Wing Commander Haysom. F/Sgt. Cundy was commissioned and promoted to Flight Lieutenant. He replaced F/L Strawson whose tour had expired as "A" Flight Commander. Although it would be back-dated, Eddie would have to wait until December to hear officially that his commission had gone through.

Three days after Eddie's interview, 18 September, 1942, 260 Squadron saw a new Flight Commander arrive to take over "B" Flight. It was a short appointment that ended when the new commander refused to fly on a Friday the 13th. Only weeks after he had joined the unit, the fateful day was upon them. On a past Friday the 13th, the new arrival to the desert had been shot down over the English Channel. He had no intention of repeating the experience. "This sort of thing isn't done, Old Boy!" S/L Hanbury said. The new officer was ordered into the air but refused to obey the command. Although a good leader and officer, he soon left the Squadron and Eddie continued to lead "B" Flight into action. Although still an NCO who couldn't officially be given the responsibility, Eddie continued to fill the position until he was commissioned several weeks later. All the while, everyone knew, "This sort of thing isn't done."[12]

And so, a Dominion nation, speaking with the authority of a major contributor to the war effort, was able to exercise its independence from Britain in yet another case, tailoring its commissioning policy to suit its own needs. Noel Ogilvie comments on his own experiences as a Sergeant Pilot, and on the observations already documented by Stocky Edwards and Hugh Godefroy:

Both Stocky and Hugh, two of the best, were right on regarding the bitterness created by the Sergeant Pilot designation. Doing the same job as the officers for less pay and less accommodation, etc., was not very popular with those who experienced this situation.

I went overseas as a Sergeant Pilot, although after obtaining my RCAF file sometime after World War Two under the Freedom of Information provision, it became apparent that I was awarded a commission upon graduation as a pilot; but through some foul-up this never followed me overseas.

Having said all that, I must confess that my experience as a Sergeant Pilot was different than most. For the early part of my first tour (June '41), I was with an RAF squadron (130) where I eventually received my commission (February '42). Here, one Squadron Commander was a bit of a twit but our Flight Commanders were superb; Stevenson and Doe, who both had large scores in the Battle of Britain. Stevenson had 21 destroyed. They both treated us according to our ability as pilots — rank was secondary. A number of Sergeant Pilots were made Section Leaders with officers as wingmen, and on one raid I had a visiting Squadron Leader as a Number Two. I really enjoyed my tenure as a Sergeant Pilot in 130 Squadron because of the atmosphere created by our two Flight Commanders. This, I would have to admit, was not par for the course. Stocky is right about Sergeants leading large formations, regardless of their experience. To my knowledge this never happened. Having experienced the Sergeant position, this enabled me, as I rose in rank, to have a good understanding of Sergeant's feelings. Later on when I became President of the Special Cases Committee in Britain, because of this background, I went out of my way to ensure the Sergeant Pilots got a fair shake. In summation, I would have to say that the Sergeant Pilot designation was stupid and was just a carry-over from the RAF where before WWII, the RAF make-up was influenced by the class system that existed in Britain at that time. The fact that some of the finest fighter pilots in the Battle of Britain and in the Battle of Malta were Sergeant Pilots confirms how idiotic the Sergeant Pilot selection was . . .[13]

Flying combat over Occupied Europe was tough enough, and replete with all sorts of hazards, without freak occurrences entering into the equation. "Mac" MacLeod recalls one such event that happened while he was flying with the Digby Wing in 1943:

The biggest fright in my Air Force career occurred on 3 November 1943 — and it was caused by looking at maps! I was a careful pilot and kept a full set of maps of Western Europe in the little tin map case that was located in the cockpit of the Spit, just about level with the left knee.

Chad was leading the Wing that day and I was flying Red 4 behind him. Red 3 had to turn back so I had moved up a notch. We were escorting Marauders on a bombing run on Schiphol (Amsterdam) aerodrome. The bombers had just completed their task when we tangled with about fifteen Me 109s. My orders were clear — as I had no Number 2, I was to stick with my Flight. Chad was having a picnic; in a flash he nailed a '109, then he spotted another '109 on the tail of a Spit, and that's when my trouble began!

The pilot of the '109 wanted out in a hurry. He pushed everything forward and headed for the deck. Chad did the same thing and so did Red 2. I jammed the stick forward to follow. We were playing "crack the whip" and I was the last aircraft in the game. To my horror, negative "G" set in; my maps rose out of their holder in a neat package and, as they reached eye-level, an invisible hand opened each one and plastered it neatly against my coupe top!

Imagine what it's like when you poke a stick into a wasps nest. That's what it was like outside. There were aircraft criss-crossing in front of me, above me and below me, all just a few feet away. All I could see was a map of Holland in front of me. I clawed the maps away with my left hand and pulled back with all my might. Miraculously, there was Chad in front of me finishing off the '109 and I was still in position.

Chad got two that day; Geoff Northcott got one, and Mitchener got two. 416 Squadron got four destroyed for the loss of one aircraft. I got a lesson in map reading I never want to repeat![14]

———————

During the autumn of 1943, a major organizational change took place in the United Kingdom as the fighter and support squadrons prepared for the upcoming invasion of the Continent. In October, in advance of the official formation of the Second Tactical Air Force, 410, 411, and 412 Squadrons moved to Biggin Hill under the official designation of 126 Airfield, while 403 and 421 Squadrons at Kenley were redesignated 127 Airfield. During the following months, the new formations operated from under canvas in preparation for the nomadic trek across Europe that was soon to follow.

FAMILIAR NAMES — RCAF UNITS

Day Fighters	Familiar Name
401 Squadron	Rams
402 Squadron	Winnipeg Bears
403 Squadron	Wolves
411 Squadron	Grizzly Bears
412 Squadron	Falcons
416 Squadron	City of Oshawa
417 Squadron	City of Windsor
421 Squadron	Red Indians
441 Squadron	Silver Fox
442 Squadron	Caribous
443 Squadron	Hornets

Night Fighters	Familiar Name
406 Squadron	Lynx
409 Squadron	Night Hawks
410 Squadron	Cougars
418 Squadron	City of Edmonton

Army Cooperation/ Reconnaissance	Familiar Name
400 Squadron	City of Toronto
414 Squadron	Imperials
430 Squadron	City of Sudbury

Fighter-Bombers	Familiar Name
438 Squadron	Wildcats
439 Squadron	City of Westmount
440 Squadron	City of Ottawa, Beavers

In 1943, RCAF day fighter units claimed more than 135 air combat victories; 403 Squadron led the way with fifty confirmed kills, while 421 Squadron posted a highly respectable thirty-five victories. The most successful individual scorer was Johnnie Johnson, who claimed thirteen individual kills plus five shared during his six-month tenure as head of the Kenley Wing. By the end of the year, at least ten RCAF pilots had claimed five or more victories over the Continent since offensive operations had commenced in 1941. Most successful was Buck

McNair, who had scored once in 1941, then added a further eight confirmed over Malta, and would augment his victory tally with eight more kills during his second tour in the United Kingdom. McNair was a fearless, dynamic commander who led by example and was a true inspiration to his peers and subordinates. After leading 421 Squadron on his return from Malta, McNair was given command of 126 Airfield in October 1943. Totally focused and uncompromising, he was characteristically blunt with superiors and subordinates alike, as recalled on separate occasions by Hugh Godefroy, during McNair's tenure as a Squadron Commander, and later as a Wing Commander under Harry Broadhurst during the build-up phase to the Normandy invasion.

Buck McNair, who had completed a very successful tour in Malta, was in command of 421 Squadron. He was a handsome blond Westerner renowned for his outspoken criticism of Headquarters personnel. His fearless aggressiveness as a fighter pilot and his natural ability to lead forced the higher-ups to tolerate him. His Squadron was the most important thing in his life. He insisted on implicit obedience to his flying orders which included following his example of bulldog aggressiveness in battle. Anyone he found hesitating, he turfed. Those who stood behind him he would defend even though he was threatened with Court Martial. He believed in the merit system, and he had no use for promotion based on seniority. On one occasion when he was away on a forty-eight hour pass, a signal arrived promoting one of his pilots to Flight Commander. Buck had not authorized this change in leadership. With his face white with rage, he picked up the telephone and called Air Chief Marshal Leigh-Mallory at Fighter Command Headquarters. He was put straight through.

"Leigh-Mallory here."

"McNair here. If you want to run this Squadron, you come down here and lead it. As long as I'm in command, I'm gonna decide who gets promoted. Do you understand?"

Without listening for an answer, he slammed down the receiver. The Air Marshal spent the next half hour trying to find out who had called him. Fortunately, he was unsuccessful. Buck made his own choice for the Flight Commander vacancy and the appointment was changed quietly at a local level.

When day gave way to night, he became a different person. He absolutely refused to talk shop. He mixed with everyone on an equal basis. If anything, alcohol seemed to increase his tolerance, and he drank just enough to enjoy such carefree moments to the full. He was generous with women, claiming that he was incapable of watching them suffer. For a while, a striking-looking plotter in the Ops Room received most of his attention but not with serious intent. Unbeknownst to anyone, the continuous bombing in Malta had opened a chink in his armour. A raw nerve had been bared. One evening in the bar a pilot touched that nerve. This lad was a new replacement in Buck's outfit and was fascinated by his Commanding Officer. He hung on Buck's every word. While standing beside him, during a lull in the conversation, he began to whistle imitating the sound of a falling bomb. Buck's smile evaporated. With a lightning right to the jaw, he knocked the lad to the floor. Then slowly and emphatically he said:

"I don't find that a bit funny — never do that again."

. . . As soon as his Field Headquarters was established, Broadhurst started weekly conferences for all the Wing Leaders under his command. Broady, as he was referred to, had led a Wing in the Battle of Britain and subsequently made a name for himself as an efficient Staff Officer and a hard-nosed Field Commander. He openly admitted at first that he had little use for Canadians and Buck McNair in particular. Buck had flown under him at Hornchurch before he had left for Malta. As far as Buck was concerned, the feeling was mutual. I distinctly remember the first Wing Commanders' conference that Broady called in his Headquarters. In desert tradition, the meeting was held in a long rectangular field-tent furnished with a mobile conference table, field maps and collapsible chairs. Broady chaired the meeting from one end of the table, and by chance Buck McNair occupied the chair at the other end. Through the meeting Buck sat with his chair pushed back, his arms folded, with a disgruntled frown on his face. The meeting had no particular purpose, except to give the Air Vice-Marshal an opportunity to tell us exactly what he expected of us. His remarks required no comment, and instead of asking if there were any questions, the Air Vice-Marshal hunched forward in his chair and, glaring at Buck, said:

"McNair, I'm disappointed in you. This is the first time I have seen you sit there without opening your big mouth. Are you ill?"

There was a long silence as Buck measured his gaze without blinking an eye. Finally he said with a smile:

"These meetings of yours are interfering with my social life, Sir."
For a second Broady's jaw stiffened, and he glowered down the table at Buck. Just when the tension was getting unbearable, Broady suddenly threw his head back and laughed uncontrollably. Nervously the Company followed his example.[15]

By war's end, McNair wore a DSO and three DFCs, and with seventeen confirmed victories and a string of probables, his place in Canadian military history as a great fighter pilot and combat leader was assured. Many of his young charges owed their lives to his uncompromising behaviour, and Karl Linton was no exception. McNair was rarely neutral on any subject, and since he had personally experienced unpleasant forced excursions into the Channel, he was bound and determined to prevent it from happening unnecessarily to his pilots. Karl Linton recalls:

One time during 1943, we were in a dogfight 5–10 miles inside France, buzzing around like bees with 60+ '109s and '190s. Suddenly I noticed a plane on my tail, guns and cannons blazing, but I knew it was a Spit. However, I also thought that the pilot did not have enough deflection and that he must have been on the tail of a Jerry behind me. Anyway, the Spit hit my aircraft, Buck McNair and others saw it, and Buck radioed for us to head towards England, and for the rest to "cover me." We figured later that I was about six miles inside France. My engine was sputtering but I managed to climb to 36,000 feet and put the old Spit in its best gliding attitude. Buck took off after the Spit that had hit me, but lost him in the haze around London and could not get his serial number. Buck then came back and took over the lead of the Squadron. I then radioed twice that I was going to bail out into the Channel. Buck came back on both occasions over the radio with an adamant "No!", stressing that I could glide to British soil. So I did, and after I had picked out a fairly nice field for a belly landing and positioned myself into the wind, I did NOT see the concrete columns (camouflaged to keep enemy gliders from landing en masse) until I was 100'–150' above ground and heading straight into the mess! But I was lucky . . . I swept between several, tearing up a bit of the wing tips and tail and finally ground to a halt, fuselage and myself intact . . .[16]

While Buck McNair, Wally McLeod, and other returning Malta veterans would provide distinguished, inspired leadership to the RCAF
fighter units operating out of the United Kingdom, the assimilation
of these heroes of Malta into the northwest European theatre and its
particular style of disciplined air combat was not universally successful. Hugh Godefroy remembers the arrival of George Beurling,
recently transferred to the RCAF and fresh from a public relations
tour of Canada, where he had encountered unfettered adulation for
his exploits in the Mediterranean:

Early in the month of July, Johnnie Johnson called me up.

"Hughie, I've just had a call from RCAF Headquarters asking
me if I would take George Beurling. You've heard all the stories
about how difficult he is to manage. Are you interested in taking a
shot at him?"

"I've never met the fellow, Johnnie, but he must be a hell of a
good fighter pilot. He's got 29 destroyed, hasn't he? I never judge
a man on second-hand information alone. If he is willing to come
and fly like any other pilot in the Squadron, I'll be pleased to take
him. However, I would want to hear him agree to these terms
without reservation."

"Okay, Hughie, I'll tell them to send him down, and we'll have
a chat with him."

We had been concerned with the inaccuracy in shooting displayed by some of the combat films. We had set up a ground
training device in the briefing room in the hope of improving it. It
consisted of a chair with a ring and bead sight in front of it.
Accurate models of enemy aircraft were impaled on a support
attached to a ball joint. This was mounted on a tripod to be moved
along a track in the line of sight. Marks on the floor that were
shielded from the pilots' view were scaled with every range from
150 to 600 yards. When the tripod was placed opposite these marks,
the model would look the size of a real aircraft at that range. The
model could be turned to any position, and the exact angle of
attack could be read off on a circular scale by a pointer. Beurling
would be the ideal man to be put in charge of this programme, we
thought. Beurling was a tallish slim fellow with a dishevelled crop
of blond hair, sharp features and deep creases down each cheek. He
was given to chewing gum slowly and deliberately with his mouth
open. He had large ice-blue eyes that rarely blinked. With George

there was no place for preambles. I went straight to the point. I outlined the conditions under which I would accept him into my Squadron. He listened in silence, his face an expressionless mask. Johnnie then pointed out that we needed experienced leaders with his capability and that he wanted him to take charge of the Ground Gunner Programme. There was a long pause while we both waited. Finally he said:

"Yep, I'll do it!"

"Okay," I said, "go on down to the Dispersal Hut and meet your Squadron mates and familiarize yourself with the Spitfire IX. You'll find it a lot different from the V's that you flew before."

Without a change of expression he turned on his heel and strode out.

"Friendly chap, isn't he?" Johnnie chuckled.[17]

Though he would destroy a further two Focke Wulfs over northwest Europe, Beurling's lone-wolf tactics and undisciplined, unconventional behaviour would incur the hostility of not only his superiors but also his peers. Hugh Godefroy explains:

Bob Buckham, one of the pilots in 403, had had an unusual upbringing. He had been raised near the Japanese Community in Vancouver. They had trained him like one of their own and taught him Judo. He was a black belt. To those who were interested, he was happy to demonstrate the art. At about five feet eight and a hundred and thirty-five pounds, he was more than a match for the biggest man in the outfit. Although cool and aggressive in battle, he maintained an Oriental placidity in outlook back on the field. He loved children and all wild creatures. One day we were sitting together on the patio of the Estates House enjoying a cigarette after lunch. In front of us, two steps led down to a formal garden with floral borders and a central pond edged with lilies. A wood duck had taken up residence in the pond and become tame enough to be hand-fed. Buck never left the dining table without taking him some scraps. "Buzz" Beurling strolled out of the dining-room and stood for a moment in front of us on the top step surveying the scene. To our utter amazement, he pulled his Webley revolver from his holster, took aim at the duck and proceeded to shoot feathers out of its tail. Before he could fire the third shot, Buckham was beside him and with a lightning chop, knocked the revolver from his hand. With his eyes burning like two coals of fire, he said very slowly:

"Beurling, if you ever shoot at that duck again, I'll kill you with my bare hands!"

Beurling just looked at him with those cold blue eyes, then slowly his face broke into a grin as he said:

"Okay, Buck, I wasn't going to hurt it."[18]

While George Beurling had been fêted with unprecedented adulation and enthusiasm during his homecoming victory tour of Canada, he was something less than a household word in England. Padre Don Carlson recalls a hunting experience with the great ace of Malta in 1943 that drives the point home:

When there was a lull we often shot skeet with 28 gauge shotguns provided by the Service. This exercise was intended to sharpen the eye of the pilot and develop his reactions. A day or two after his arrival I met Beurling on the skeet range. We decided to hunt rabbits, for which permission was granted by the local farmer.

We went hunting on several occasions. A rabbit or two or a pheasant could be delivered to the Mess cook with a gift of a package or two of Canadian cigarettes. He would cook the game and provide a tasty snack for three or four of the boys in a tent before we retired or after we had returned from an evening session at the local pub. With a National Loaf and a cup of coffee brewed on the primus stove, it was a welcome addition to the Mess meals where meat was relatively scarce.

On one occasion, a rather amusing and illuminating incident occurred. I had shot a rabbit at a range of seventy-five yards and was quite proud of my marksmanship. As I stepped forward to retrieve my game, two figures emerged from among the trees between me and the rabbit. One was obviously a gentleman-farmer, and the other his game keeper, a big man, stripped to the waist, carrying a long club. Apparently we had strayed from the farm into his property. He was terribly angry and dressed us down in no uncertain terms for poaching. My rabbit was snatched up by the keeper and put in his bag. We soon learned that poaching was not a venial sin. As one of the pilots quipped after hearing the story: "You can seduce his daughter with impunity, but do not shoot his game."

In the midst of this tirade, Beurling nudged me and said, "Tell him who I am." Which I proceeded to do. "Sir," I said, "my companion is Flight Lieutenant George Beurling, DSO, DFC, DFM and Bar, our leading Canadian fighter pilot." "Never heard of him," the gentleman farmer retorted, "and what is more I wish you Colonials would go home. We can manage this war quite well without you." And we were summarily dismissed.[19]

In September, Hugh Godefroy replaced Johnnie Johnson at the helm of the Kenley Wing. Beurling's insubordination and defiance became openly blatant. With a court martial looming, he was transferred to 412 Squadron. That didn't work either. Again openly defiant of command and completely unpredictable both in the air and on the ground, Beurling was unceremoniously returned to Canada. Lloyd Hunt recollects this undeniably great warrior's last days in the RCAF:

Back in Canada, George was groomed to be a ferry pilot on the local scene. This was something that George simply could not accept, and he sought interview after interview to try to be sent back to an operational squadron. His fortunes were fading rather rapidly now as he could no longer be used for political gain. It may have been a petulant move on his part, but George sent in a letter of resignation. It was accepted with almost indecent haste. Where it had taken months for the RCAF to bring George into the ranks, it took days for their acceptance of his departure . . .[20]

By late 1943, bomber escort was one of the most productive and satisfying missions for the RCAF fighter squadrons based in the United Kingdom. Due to their very nature, these missions were highly likely to provoke a response from defending Luftwaffe fighters, and therefore air combat was highly probable. Art Sager describes a typical Ramrod of the period, and candidly relates the psychological effect that losing men in battle had upon him as a Flight Leader:

On 26 November, the Wing flies to Manston to escort thirty-six Marauders on Ramrod 339, a bombing raid on the air base at Cambrai.

Off Dungeness we rendezvous with the bombers who climb and cross the French coast at 13,000 feet. Chad is leading 402 on the starboard of the first box of eighteen while 416 covers the second on the port, 2,000 feet above. I am Green 1, Dubnick my Number 2.

There is a little flak south of Le Touquet but it's not very accurate and not enough to bother the bombers. Cloud is two-tenths at six thousand and should not obscure the target.

As I switch on the reflector sight, I realize how every action has now become routine: Gun button at English coast, reflector sight at French coast. The whole thing has become a habit, not quite but almost. And how familiar the French countryside has become! There's the Somme estuary to the right, the Forest of Crecy almost below, and off to the right Abbeville, its aerodrome a nest of Huns. We're following the valley up from Berck towards Douellens, peaceful farming country and so green.

We're thirty miles in when Chad breaks radio silence. "Hello Boxer, Buckle Leader here, what's the situation now please?"

"Hello Buckle Leader. Sorry, nothing to report." Operations Control always seems so casual.

"Thanks Boxer. Keep your eyes skinned below, fellas," Chad says. "That's where they'll be, the little rascals!" He's chuckling as always.

We cross the railway line going north from Albert, still keeping the same course. There's an aerodrome below now but deserted. A small amount of scrappy flak bursts beneath our box of Marauders, from the aerodrome perhaps.

I waggle my wings, look behind to see that the Section is well in the clear, and drop the extra fuel tanks.

When the bombers start to turn port for their run-up on the target, Chad calls again, this time to Freddy, "Okay, Lastex Leader, cross over now and we'll have a little looksee further in. And watch out for that flak, Chum!"

"Okay, Buckle Leader," Freddy replies with his drawl. "But that ain't flak, that's only salt and pepper!" The two of them always joke about flak.

There is quite a bit now, showing up between the two bomber boxes. But they keep serenely on, sticking close together. Their bombs seem to be well on target.

416 keeps above 402 as the Wing continues southeast, turning starboard first and then making a long swing to port to rejoin the bombers on their way out. Twenty-four sets of eyes scour the sky, above and below. There's smoke from a railway engine over to the

east but apart from that the land seems lifeless. Except for heavier smoke I can now also see coming from buildings around the aerodrome on my port.

Chad calls again. "Hello Boxer, Buckle Leader here. Anything for us?"

"Hello Buckle Leader. No, sorry, nothing at all."

"Thanks Boxer. Okay, Lastex Leader, we'll get back to the big boys now."

He completes the turn and I can see 402 moving in closer to the leading box. Freddy speeds up to get back into position behind the second box.

On Freddy's starboard, I straggle a bit to have another good look behind and below, tipping my wings to right and left. There's an aerodrome a bit behind on the starboard, a grass field with a few buildings on one side. The grass is a lighter colour than the fields around it and I can just make out some markings near what must be the control tower. My eyesight is pretty sharp now, no problems there. The small town nearby is Croiselles, I think. But there's no life on the field. All the Huns must have taken off and screamed south or they're well camouflaged.

I start to turn away. Then, suddenly, I look back. A speck of light grey catches my eye. There it is again, brown-grey, moving across the aerodrome. An aircraft taking off! And another one, no two, three more, taking off together!

I start talking before switching on to transmit. Then, keeping the excitement out of my voice, I call. "Hello, Buckle Leader, Green 1 here, there are four aircraft taking off from an aerodrome at about five o'clock to you now."

"Okay. Can you see them, Lastex Leader?"

"No," Freddy replies. "Can't see them yet. Where are they, Art?"

"Below me on the starboard, Freddy, going northwest on the deck."

There's a pause.

Then Freddy again. "Still can't see them, Art. Go after them if you want. We'll cover you."

"Okay, Lastex Leader." Then, after taking another look at the Huns — they're still there! — I call, "Green Section turning starboard and diving."

I do a half-roll and dive straight down, in an orbit to starboard to keep the Huns in sight. Straightening out, I glance to right and left and see that my Section is with me.

I push the throttle through the gate and the stick fully forward. The Huns — I see all four of them now — disappear under a small cloud but I catch sight of them again, straight ahead, still on the deck, going northwest.

The speed builds up quickly. My ears become plugged but I can hear the thundering engine and the whistling of the wind through the joints in the perspex.

I lower the seat, tighten the harness straps, start to trim. Look right and left again. Good boys, they're still there, Dubnick on my port, the other two on the starboard, all a bit behind but keeping up.

I've a sickening feeling that I've lost the Huns. But no, there they are, three in loose formation, one lagging behind. I'm at 8,000 feet now.

A great calmness comes over me.

"Take it easy, take it easy, make sure of everything!" I say to myself. "Pitch, revs, rad temperature okay but open it a notch so it won't overheat. Now get the damn trim better, can't shoot if I'm skidding." Everything I'd done wrong before.

Don't look behind, no Huns there anyway, and the boys will cover my tail. Keep my eyes on those Huns ahead. Make sure, get right up their bottoms.

Take a quick look at the airspeed indicator. 460 and going up! 4,000 feet now, better ease out. Take it slowly, keep hand on trim. Hope the kite will take it, look at those ailerons!

Pull back on the stick. It's heavy as lead. I'm being pushed into the seat, everything turning green, blacking out! Push head forward, close eyes, that's better. Keep pulling stick back.

On the deck now, tearing over fields and trees. One Hun is half a mile away, the other three further ahead, in loose formation. And they're not '109s, they're Focke Wulf 190s!

Go for the straggler. He's 200 feet up, flying straight and level, hasn't seen me!

Both hands on the stick. Trim, trim, I'm skidding! Thumb on the gun button, Hun squarely in the sights, he's getting bigger. 800 yards, no, more, take it easy! Keep below him.

600 yards and he hasn't seen me, flying like a turkey! High tension line, over it, down again. 400 yards. Hold my fire, hold it, hold it! 300 yards. Get the bead right on, he's big now! 200 yards. Wait! Wait! Now — fire!

There's an explosion and the Hun breaks into pieces. The fuselage slides to the right, flames streaming from it. It hits the ground and bounces, once, twice, and slithers across a field. Still going on, a ball of fire, it hits a railway embankment, parts of it continuing across the line.

Just as the Hun explodes, my Number 2, Dubnick, flashes by on my port. He's too close and too fast! Must have caught up when I throttled back. I turn right to avoid the muck ahead but Dubnick goes straight ahead, right through the spattering metal. I swing back and see him, straight and level, on the deck.

Then he calls, calmly, "Green 2 here, Art. Engine's packed up . . . lost my prop I think." He's been hit by the debris. I shout, "Get altitude and bail out!" He comes back, "No, I'll try to put her down."

I follow him. There's a small forest ahead. Presumably seeing he won't get over it, he noses down into a field. But he's still going too fast. The Spit crashes in a cloud of earth, loses a wing and skids, coming to a stop just short of the trees, tail in the air. I circle around but Dubnick does not get out.

Freddy, above and seeing all this, calls, "Lastex Leader here. Reform with us at 10,000, Green Leader, and we'll get back to the big boys." The Squadron joins up with the Marauders as the last box is crossing the French coast.

I agonize about Dubnick, hoping he's wounded only and will be hospitalized quickly by the Germans. This hope is dashed when later the Wing learns through the Resistance that he was killed on crash-landing.

My victory is a bitter one. Again I've lost a Number 2! I tell myself it wasn't my fault but that doesn't help much. Dubnick was a good pilot and a courageous one, a loner, fanatically keen.

I get a bit drunk that night and the night following, at Digby. I record it all in my diary, ending the account with reflections on my state of mind:

I've changed in the past months, I know it. Have become hard, callous, insensitive. Poor Dubnick and that poor German. I try not to think of them — and do so far too easily. What's going on inside? I've no fear now, none whatever, and I don't seem to give a damn about anything anymore. Just get up and into them as often as I can. Oh yes, I think about the Flight, the boys, and want to lead them as well as I can, but I no longer worry about them or think about them as individuals. Just laugh and fly and drink with them, and Hell take tomorrow. And I'm drinking too much, I know . . .[21]

Luckily for fighter pilots, not all crash landings are fatal. "Mac" MacLeod recalls a spectacular crash with amusing side effects that he endured while flying Spitfires in England during 1943:

We were up at daybreak on 1 December 1943, taking off for Bradwell Bay to rendezvous with other squadrons. Just as we were about to start engines, nature called and I made a rush trip to the luxurious outside privy beside our flight shack at Digby. There wasn't time to fasten six buttons on my braces and four on my fly, so I just hauled everything up and tied the straps on my mae west to keep my pants from falling.

It was a beautiful day for flying and we arrived at Bradwell Bay just as the sun rose over the horizon. I touched down "wheels first" and, as I did, my left tire blew. The aircraft flipped on its back. I have a vague memory of being surrounded by feet and then I took a long nap.

They had an emergency medical post on the edge of the airfield and I was taken there. The Medical Officer on duty evidently believed it of first importance to guard against shock and he had me placed in a "heat tent." This was somewhat like a pup tent lined with heat lamps.

I returned to consciousness and knew immediately that I had been in an accident but wasn't hurt. But when I opened my eyes I was surrounded by a bright orange glow. The thought flashed through my mind: "My God, I've died and gone to hell." And then I DID go into shock!

I went ice-cold and shivered and shook. They poured hot tea into me and in a few minutes I was back to normal but with a firm resolve to lead a more saintly life. I was lucky; the usual fate in an accident of this type was a broken back. I was flying again after a few days rest.

I suspect though, that today there are some elderly erks who tell their grandchildren about the time they hauled a pilot out of a Spitfire that had crashed so hard that the buttons on his pants were undone.[22]

Life for a Canadian fighter pilot in wartime Britain was not all work. There was an excellent leave organization, headquartered in London and headed by Lady Ryder, that would organize any kind of holiday in the British Isles for RCAF aircrew who had a week or so of leave coming. That holiday might consist of hunting or fishing in Scotland, sightseeing in Wales, or placement with British families, which often included the aristocracy. Karl Linton is among the many Canadian aircrew who have fond memories of the kindnesses afforded them by a caring British public.

. . . When we first arrived at Bournemouth, there were more aircrew than training bases, so Ken Grant and I, both Sergeants, were offered a trip of one week to some place, city or country in the British Isles. We chose a visit to Scotland and we were told to report to the Lady Frances Ryder Organization on Princes Street in Edinburgh. They then told us that we were scheduled to spend a week with the Duke and Duchess of Brceleugh at Brumlanrig Castle in Dumphrieshire. I said, "Gee, Ken, I won't know how to act with Royalty for a full week." Ken said, "Chance of a lifetime . . . let's go!" I agreed.

It was like a movie setting . . . a chauffeur met these two Canadian Sergeants at the station, took us ten miles to the huge castle through high arches, and there the Duchess, a daughter about our age, a son about sixteen, and a ten-year-old daughter met us at the bottom of the entrance. At the time, her husband was attending Parliament.

For the first dinner there, after Her Grace had shown us to our room (the same one Bonnie Prince Charlie had used), she led us through what I had dreaded: a dining room half the size of our house, with much cutlery and a small garden in the middle of the room! Back home we were lucky to have enough silverware to go around once! Fortunately though, she led us off into a small kitchenette with a four foot by six foot table, told us what was cooking in each of a half-dozen pots, and told us to just help ourselves. She was a very gentle lady and made us feel at ease immediately.

Well, it was a perfect week. We tramped with the son, John, in the hills, burned some heather, packed a lunch, and I had my first alcoholic drink, a beer, in the highlands. We spent a lot of time in the pool and on the lake fishing; wild fowl and game abounding everywhere on the estate.

One day at lunch, we were talking about the fish and fowl as viewed from a wharf and boathouse on the lake. Her Grace asked me which wharf and boathouse I was referring to and I said, "The one that's whitewashed." They all looked at me, seriously for a second or so, and then laughter broke out all around. Turns out that it was pigeon and bird droppings that made the boathouse and wharf look so white. My face was red for hours, it seemed![23]

Leave could produce its own ironic situations. Cec Brown, an RCAF Spitfire pilot with 403 Squadron, remembers one such event:

. . . Regarding the Lady Ryder leave scheme for Allied officers, you applied, stated a preference of locality and, presto, you were confirmed in a private home as guests of the residents. On one such leave, Jim McKelvie and I asked to go to a country location and it was arranged that we go to Dorset to stay a week at a Manor House as guests of Mr. and Mrs. Pass. Jim and I had learned that even if one bought a first-class ticket you could never be sure of a first-class seat. Better to buy a third-class and if a first-class became available, then pay the difference. Jim and I therefore bought third-class.

In the first-class compartment where we found seats, was a solitary lady who, unlike most Britishers, had learned to strike up a conversation without formal introduction. The "Canada" on our shoulders prompted her to say she had visited Canada, and where were we from, etc. Then she asked where we were going and when we told her our destination and the name of our hosts she said, "Isn't that interesting? I'm Mrs. Pass."

With that the conversation became very friendly but then we were embarrassed to have the trainman ask for our tickets. Jim and I could have crawled under the seat when we had to show third-class tickets. Mrs. Pass was a great sport and fully supported our reasoning.

We spent a delightful week at their home and enjoyed the company of their niece Anne and her husband George Davies. George was a Flight Lieutenant in the RAF but wore no wings, and since he did not volunteer what his job was, protocol prevented us from asking. Much later, in 1976, I had lunch with George in London. The conversation flowed so that I found an opening to ask, "What was your job in the RAF?" He replied, "If you had asked me six months ago I could not have told you."

A news release flashed in my mind. "Were you working on the Ultra Secret (code breaking) operation?" I asked. George admitted that indeed that was what he had been doing and the existence of this highly secret operation had recently been made public.[24]

———◦•◦•◦———

Towards the end of 1943, Rhubarb missions were becoming more and more frequent. The extremely hostile low-level environment would eventually prove very costly for the ill-suited Spitfire, although the inherent dangers were not well known at the time. In mid-November, 416 Squadron's Art Sager led Flight Sergeant Harry Dubnick and two others on an innovative, well-planned Rhubarb to the Netherlands. Little did Sager know that the mission would almost cost him his life, and that the highly enthusiastic Dubnick had only two weeks to live.

On 13 November, I lead a Section of four on a Rhubarb into Holland, a mission that is almost my last. The Dutch Underground reports that the German torpedo bombers that have been harassing Allied shipping in the North Sea are doing training over the Zuider Zee, the "artificial" sea in the centre of Holland. I think it might be possible, in the right kind of weather, to sneak across the eighteen-mile stretch of land to this practicing area and have a go at the bombers before the Huns realize what is happening. Both Freddy Green and Chad are lukewarm about the idea, but when the Intelligence Officer concedes there's a fifty percent chance of success, they agree reluctantly to let me go. But Chad insists that I take two Sections of four to Coltishall, the jump-off base, in the event that support is needed on the way out.

I wait for the best weather — cloud cover in Holland low enough to nip into if attacked in force by Hun fighters, but high enough so as not to prohibit practice flying by the bombers. I study Intelligence reports and supporting maps on gun positions on the coast and inland — and I get a profile map of the coastline show-ing church steeples, towers, buildings and other structures in the area between Haarlem and Den Helder. Finally, I settle on entry at a point north of Ijmuiden and south of Egmond. This should take us over the coast at a reportedly lightly-defended area, and the two towns will serve as markers en route to the Zuider Zee, passing just north of Edam. The torpedo bomber bases are near Hoorn and on the east side of the Zuider Zee.

Good navigation is essential, for if we hit the coast too far south or too far north, we'll be greeted by hot metal from anti-aircraft batteries. But it's difficult to be precise when flying over the 130 miles of the North Sea in winter. To avoid being picked up by German radar, we'll fly at wave-top level where the winds can be variable, and the direction and force of the wind are major factors in establishing a course. I work out several based on winds of varying force from the north-west, west and south-west; their usual direction at this time of year.

On 12 November, the Wing is grounded by bad weather and Intelligence reports that it should be ideal for the mission on the following day — cloud covering all of northern Europe, its base at about 3000 feet over Holland.

The pilots in my Flight know what I've been planning and all want to go. I pick eight with the most experience: for my Section, keen-as-mustard Dubnick as my Number 2, Danny Noonan as Number 3 and second-in-command, Gould with him as Number 4. The reserve Section is led by Dave Prentice. I work out courses, in and out, based on the Met's wind estimation and I ask all pilots to jot them down.

After breakfast on the 13th, I lead the two Sections to Coltishall for refueling and a final briefing in the Intelligence office. Met provides a new estimate on the wind: it's now 20 mph from the northwest, gusting over Holland. I alter the courses accordingly and give the new ones to all pilots. Danny has a copy of the coast profile as well in case he has to take over.

My Section takes off at 10:00 hours. The other Section will follow twenty minutes later, fly to within first sight of the coast but no further, orbit and wait for my call if I'm attacked on the way out. Absolute radio silence is to be maintained by both Sections throughout except by myself in attacks on bombers, or by others if Huns appear and a break is called for.

I fly at cruising speed and in wide line abreast formation, myself slightly ahead of the other three. Coast profile and map strapped to my knee, I concentrate on the compass and airspeed indicator, vital elements in maintaining a steady course.

After about thirty minutes of flying, the Dutch coastline appears on the horizon, some fifteen to twenty miles away. The weather seems clearer and the cloud base higher than Met had forecast, but I decide to continue.

I can just make out higher land or buildings slightly to the right of my line of flight, nothing to the left; a flat grey line on the horizon. In a minute or so, the silhouette becomes clearer. There's a higher building on the right, no, a tower or steeple, and there are two of them. I glance several times at the profile on my knee, look again ahead, and I'm sure: yes, it's Ijmuiden. I'm much too close, the wind must have been stronger than forecast, pushed us south. I dip my wings twice and then turn port thirty degrees. The others turn with me. After two minutes I signal again, return to the original course, allowing five degrees for the stronger wind from the north-west.

The coast is five miles away now. I drop the extra fuel tank and the others follow suit. This is also the signal to add on the power and I push the throttle through to the "gate."

There's nothing ahead but a long white beach and fields beyond, flat land with a few trees. I'm at fifty feet when I cross the beach. Pull up a bit to go over some trees, weave and skid as planned. All is going well; I'm over the coast and on the way!

Suddenly there's an explosion, a huge boom! and I'm thrown over the stick. Knocked out momentarily, I straighten up, pull the stick back. When I open my eyes, I can see nothing — the cockpit is full of smoke! Thinking immediately of fire, I pull the hood back. Too low to bail out but I'll crash land if I have to. Immediately the smoke clears. I close the hood. Apart from a pain in the back of the head, I seem to be intact, everything working, no blood.

And the engine is still going — bless the solid Merlin! — and the kite is still flying. I look at the instrument panel. RPM and oil pressure gauges working, all engine instruments OK, but airspeed indicator at zero, turn and bank wonky, altimeter doubtful. Compass seems to be alright. Flying controls respond. But there's a whizzing sound, air blowing into the cockpit.

I switch on the RT and call Danny. He's closer now, on my starboard. There's a dull sound in my ears but no reply. Try again. No sound. The radio is dead.

I can't go on, certainly can't lead without radio. And I've no idea where the kite had been hit, how badly damaged. Best get back if I can, don't want to become a POW . . .

Danny is almost in formation now and my Number 2 has come up close on the port. I point at Danny and point ahead, several times, to tell him to lead and go on with the show. He shakes his head back and forth and points at my kite.

I waggle my wings slightly and start a turn to starboard, slowly as I'm not sure how stable the Spitfire is. Keeping as low as possible, I get onto the reverse course, the homebound course, and straighten out. Danny, Dubnick and Gould turn too, and when I look behind they're still with me. Obviously they have seen something and are not leaving.

Danny speeds ahead and I take up position behind and on his port. I catch a glimpse of flashing guns below. As I lose sight of the coast, Danny starts a slow climb to about 2000 feet and I stick with him. He probably suspects, and rightly, that my instruments aren't working. Later I learn that he has ordered the reserve Section to return to base.

I'm mightily glad to see the coast of England. Bailing out in the North Sea in winter is not a cheerful prospect. Nearing Coltishall, I move into close formation with Danny and land with him

It is only when I get out of the plane that I realize how lucky I am. A 20mm shell has blown a big hole in the fuselage behind the cockpit on the left, exploded inside and come out in a hundred or more pieces of shrapnel on the other side, shattering the perspex behind my head. Had it hit a fraction of a second earlier, I'd have been full of metal, but as it is thank God for the armour plating! It protected me from the shrapnel and bits of metal lying on the cockpit floor.

My picture is taken, standing and grinning foolishly from both sides of the Spit. I hope it doesn't appear in Vancouver papers (it does). It's 13 November, my second wedding anniversary, and my "lucky thirteenth."

In retrospect, I realize that Freddy and Chad had been right — it was a nigh-on suicidal operation. Intelligence had been wrong on the strength of coastal batteries. I'd been hit by a fluke, but clearly even the unsettled areas of the Dutch coast were heavily defended. I'd seen other guns flashing as the Section turned back and splashes on the water as I crossed the coast. That had been the most dangerous phase. The effort proved one thing: Rhubarbs over Holland were risky, not very profitable. It was one of the last attempted by the Wing.

Freddy Green was never an enthusiast about Rhubarbs, considering the odds against success too great. Operations Headquarters did not propose them; they were always voluntary missions. Squadron Leaders and Wing Commanders gave the green light only when pilots were restless from inaction due to bad weather and obviously needed release, a chance to use their guns. They were morale boosters only. The amount of damage done by them to military and semi-military targets — locomotives, marshalling yards, and the odd lorry — was minimal compared to the risks involved. There were many losses. Ten days after this Holland do, Dubnick led Carpenter on a Rhubarb to the Oosterschelde Estuary, shot up a couple of trains, but Carpenter is downed, wounded, and taken prisoner . . .[25]

During the Second World War, the RAF invented a fictional cartoon character, Pilot Officer Prune, who was meant to serve as an example to aircrew and groundcrew alike of how not to get things done. Prune was an affable chap who, in spite of circumstances, often managed to land on his feet. That he did so was most frequently due to blind luck rather than good judgement. Don Laubman of 412 Squadron committed classic "Prunery" during his first encounter with the enemy, but sometimes "Lady Luck" intervened.

On 30 December 1943, 126 Wing was ordered to conduct a fighter sweep over northwest France in Wing strength of thirty-six aircraft. I was designated to fly Blue Four with 412 Squadron. We launched thirteen aircraft, including one spare, whose mission was to fill in if one of the twelve had a problem and was forced to abort. The spare would return to base after a few minutes if he was not required.

In this case, Blue Three had trouble and was forced to return. Accordingly, I moved up to his position as Section Leader and the spare (Bill Bliss) became my Number Two as Blue Four.

The Wing, under the leadership of Buck McNair, proceeded as ordered at an altitude of 15,000 feet. The weather was good, although there were masses of cumulus cloud below us. In the vicinity of Rouen, I spotted two Me 109s below us and reported that fact to the Wing Leader. He then directed me to go after them. So Bill and I set off on our first trip down the path to glory . . .

The '109s were eight or nine thousand feet below us and, during the descent, we picked up a great deal of speed. I picked one of the aircraft and was concerned about overshooting him. However, I managed to get my speed down, and as I was closing from his right rear quarter, he seemed unaware of my presence. As

I closed, I turned on the gun firing button and the gun sight, and seemed to have everything under control. At about 200 yards, with the '109 squarely in my gun sight, I pressed the button to give him a lethal burst. Silence. I tried again with the same result. As I was now very close to him and in danger of overshooting, I broke off, flew into one of the nearby clouds and away, all the while cursing guns, armourers, and my bad luck.

As I was crossing the Channel on the way home, a horrible thought struck me. To check again, I turned on the gun button and pressed it. The aircraft shuddered as all guns fired in unison. In the excitement, I had pressed the camera button instead of the gun button. I decided that I would say nothing of the incident in an attempt to hide my embarrassment.

The gun ports were covered with patches to keep out dust and to reduce drag. When the guns were fired, these patches were blown away, and when that happened on an operational trip, the armourers automatically took out the camera film and sent it to Fighter Command for assessment. I was not aware of this procedure at the time.

Periodically, the Wing would receive a film from Command which contained various combat films and a statement of the Fighter Command assessment in each case. When one of these arrived, all available pilots were called to the Wing briefing room to watch the film and, hopefully, to learn.

One morning, we were duly summoned to view a film. As we watched, several combat films were displayed, together with the assessed results. Suddenly the next film stated that we were about to see Flying Officer D. C. Laubman of 412 Squadron in combat with an Me 109. Then there appeared the most beautiful picture of a '109 that I have ever seen. Mercifully, it was only on screen for a couple of seconds. We were then privileged to read the assessment which said, in effect, that range and deflection were correct, strikes could be observed on the '109, and that I had been awarded one damaged. (The strikes referred to were actually the sun glinting off the wings of the '109.)

I felt about six inches tall, but Pilot Officer Prune would have been pleased . . .[26]

After that experience, Don Laubman never looked back. Within fifteen months he would be a Squadron Leader with the DFC and Bar, and the ranking ace of the Second Tactical Air Force with fifteen confirmed air-to-air kills.

The Army Cooperation squadrons were also very busy during 1943. After Dieppe, 400 and 414 Squadrons became fully operational on the Mustang, flying a variety of intruder missions thereafter, both day and night. On New Year's Day, 1943, 400 and 414 were joined by a third Canadian Mustang squadron, Number 430. The Mustang squadrons were versatile, and Frank Hanton recalls the evolution of yet another type of mission for them in 1943:

When we started to bomb Italy from England, we were losing air-craft to night fighters over the Brest Peninsula and Normandy on their return, because the crews were dead tired from the long trip and their aircraft were generally low on fuel. We did not have enough night fighters to cover the Luftwaffe stations in France so a few of us were picked, after night vision tests, etc., to join 418 Squadron at Ford on the south coast to perform night intruder operations. What follows is an example of a mission I flew during that time period.

Duty time was worked on an eight-day system — five nights on and three nights off. My targets were four enemy aerodromes; Evreux, St. André, Argentan, and Rennes in France . . . all heav-ily defended by AA guns. To coincide with the bombers' return, takeoff time was 00:45 hours; crossing the French coast west of Fecamp to avoid the AA batteries and altering course for Evreux and St. André, with all flying at tree-top height to avoid the radar until I reached the target.

At Evreux there was no activity, and after circling for ten min-utes, I continued on to St. André which was also quiet, as was Argentan. After circling Argentan several times and preparing to leave the area, AA guns opened up with a heavy barrage that was counteracted by going down to tree-top height to avoid the flak. Arriving at Rennes, the aerodrome was active with lights on, so I joined the circuit as planned and was not detected. In one circuit, a silhouette of an aircraft was picked up and, on closing in behind, I recognized it as a Ju 88. I started my attack from dead astern at 300 yards with all guns, closing to 200 yards, and got strikes on the wing and engine, which caught fire. I followed his evasive action to the starboard with a further attack, and registered strikes on the fuselage as the aircraft went into a spiral dive towards the ground.

Breaking left, I lined my aircraft up with the runway in use and an Me 110 on final, 500 yards in front. I quickly closed the gap to 250 yards, and my P51's eight guns registered hits all over the Messerschmitt, with the incendiary shells starting a fire. A further short burst from 150 yards caused an explosion in the '110's starboard wing, and it dove into the ground. All lights were immediately extinguished, with searchlight batteries trying to pick up my Mustang, and AA bursts were all over the sky. So it was down on the deck once again, plus some violent dipsy-doodling to get out of the searchlights with their predicted AA fire. More batteries of searchlights came on as I set course for the coast, and my P51 was coned twice as I gained altitude to avoid obstacles. Each time, the only alternative was to go down amongst the trees and, after the second session with the lights and flak, I had to forget caution over hitting ground obstacles in order to get back. I completed the remainder of the Intruder trip without further incident, and landed at Ford at 03:35 hours. My credits were two enemy aircraft destroyed against eighteen holes in the stabilizer, fin, and rear fuselage of my Mustang . . . plus one shaky pilot. On the good side, those holes had to be repaired and it got me forty-eight hours leave in London to visit the girl to whom I am still married, my wife Joyce.[27]

Although, as the preceding narrative amply demonstrates, spectacular successes were possible for the Canadian Mustangs in 1943, misfortunes were unfortunately more often the norm. George Burroughs recollects:

In June '43 the Squadron was temporarily deployed to Cornwall, where our job was to protect friendly shipping in and around the Bay of Biscay (Me 110s were apparently trying to do the opposite). The longer missions lasted 2-1/2 to 3-1/2 hours. It was uncomfortable flying — low (50'-60'), to escape detection, throttled well back, coarse pitch, lean mixture — not much margin for error if that single engine gave trouble. These sorties were very unproductive and costly. In a period of two weeks, the Squadron lost three good pilots — one pilot got too low and just flew into the sea; another on a two-ship patrol, was shot down by FW 190s; and the third pilot was shot down by a Spitfire, who thought he had an Me 109 in his sights. No enemy aircraft were destroyed in this two week period . . .[28]

Manned aerial reconnaissance has often been described as an art. It is a combat flying discipline that involves incredible precision, concentration, and attention to detail. George Burroughs describes learning the reconnaissance business in 1943:

> How one got to be a recce pilot instead of a fighter or bomber jock is not clear to me, although I note that my assessment from Service Flying Training School showed "high average" as a pilot-navigator. Perhaps it was that or, as happened many times during the war, one became what was most needed at the time. In any case, being able to fly at tree-top height at some 250–300 mph and navigate via map references to a precise target was mandatory. Practice, practice, practice was the only way to go. The prime objective of the recce pilot was to bring back information required by other operational groups from visual sightings or photos. Targets included radar installations, bridges, road and rail junctions, "Noball" sites (flying bombs), coastal installations, etc. Such targets were usually protected by "flak" emplacements. Flying straight and level in broad daylight to get information or take photos while being targeted by flak guns was to be expected.
>
> Although designated as "fighter reconnaissance," the "fighter" part of the role was a lesser one. Most missions were performed by a flight of two aircraft. Number One's job was to get the information or photos as required. Number Two's job was to cover Number One, and he usually flew line abreast and slightly to the rear of his leader. Occasionally, four aircraft would be tasked. It should be evident that with such numbers, it was not our role to do the sweeps used by Fighter Command. However, we did have gunnery practice sessions and some training on fighter tactics. It was, of course, inevitable that some enemy aircraft were encountered while doing operations. It was then that the "fighter" training came in handy, and some of the boys had a respectable number of scores.[29]

The night fighter and multi-engined intruder force was also extremely active during 1943. In March, 406 Squadron moved to Middle Wallop under the control of 10 Group, while 409 Squadron moved to Acklington in the north, 410 Squadron taking 409's place at Coleby Grange. Meanwhile, 418 Squadron moved up to Ford.

Though all four units claimed kills in March, in spite of the atrocious weather attempting to conspire against them, "pickings" were lean in 1943 due to the minimal number of offensive operations launched by the Luftwaffe.

One of the talented young crews emerging on 410 Squadron during the summer of 1942 consisted of Flying Officer R.D. "Joe" Schultz and his navigator, Flying Officer Vernon Williams. Their first air-to-air victory is a classic example of how air combat during the Second World War could occur at the most unlikely and unexpected moments.

On 15 August 1943, I was on an intruder hop over France. To put it simply, we got lost taking some evasive action over the coast and we never really did find ourselves after that until we got back to England. It was while we were crossing the Channel, pretty close to Beachy Head, that this particular action occurred. We had turned off all the armament switches after getting rid of our bombs over the target somewhat earlier. I turned my head to speak to my navigator on my right and, lo and behold, over top of him I saw this aircraft in tight formation. I simultaneously realized that it had German markings! Believe me, confusion reigned supreme as I attempted to get the guns armed in a hurry. About the same time I saw him, he saw me, and made a break turn, which was when he probably made his biggest mistake since he turned away from me. Had he broken down and into me, he probably would have gotten away with it. After that, it only took a few seconds to destroy him . . . I topped that off with probably the second-worst landing of my life when we returned to Ford. I stalled in from about 15–20 feet up and landed with quite a crump.

I was met at the aircraft by Group Captain Paul Davoud, one of my personal heroes of the war. He said, "Well, that was a fine effort out there over the Channel. We saw the thing explode from here (20–30 miles away), but that was also quite a landing!" We had a good chuckle about that as we went in for the debriefing . . .[30]

The intruder squadrons were posting considerable successes as they took their fight to the enemy on the Continent. Furthermore, some of the RCAF crews were scoring their kills in a spectacular if somewhat unconventional manner, as remembered by Jim Johnson of 418 Squadron.

On the night of 23 September 1943, we were on a patrol of fighter bases in northern France in the area of Evreux and Dreux airstrips when an aircraft with lights on passed in front of us. I increased speed, and the enemy aircraft made a turn which allowed me to overtake him. When I had closed in to where I thought I could get a visual on him, I looked through the reflector sight. Simultaneously, the enemy aircraft turned off all lights. I pressed on not seeing anything nor feeling any slipstream. Suddenly, my navigator — who is not a swearing man — said, "For Christ sake, shoot!" So I did, and the aircraft blew up right in front of me; it fell away to the right. I never did get a visual on the target, but my navigator did and he said it was a FW 190. My camera recorded the explosion.

On 12 December 1943, I was leading a day intruder trip and we had gotten as far as Bourges Avard in France when I saw a He 111 ahead. I closed the range and prepared to line up with the sight and fire. The only trouble was that the rheostat on the sight shorted out just as I fired and I was without a gunsight. I kept lining up the old Mosquito, firing short bursts and seeing strikes at times. Shortly after, I could see bits and pieces fly off the enemy aircraft. After using up ten of my thirteen seconds of ammunition, I was able to start a fire in the starboard engine and one in the fuselage of the He 111. I sheared off and my Number Two finished off the job to an interested audience of Frenchmen leaning on their bicycles on a nearby road.

Immediately after this I met another He 111 flying at right angles to me. I fired the remaining three seconds of ammo and — wonder of wonders — saw numerous strikes on the fuselage. My Number Two followed this aircraft with inconclusive results. Later on in my tour I was able to show that I could do much better when I used a serviceable gunsight. A funny thing happened at the end of my tour — I was sent to gunnery school to learn how to shoot![31]

Unusual circumstances with respect to his combat experiences pursued Jim Johnson until well after the war. What follows is a combat report with attached note sent to Lloyd Hunt and the Canadian Fighter Pilots Association in the early 1980s. In his own words, Jim considers the report interesting for a number of reasons:

1. It was the first long range low level daylight intruder mission attempted by 418 Squadron;

2. I've never been more frightened in my life; and

3. The results that came to light thirty-five years later are as follows:

A frogman club was investigating the area (a lake in France near the Bay of Biscay coast about 100 km north of the Spanish border) in about 1978 — give or take a year, and they found aircraft wreckage exactly where my navigator had said it was in 1943. So they checked back through the records and identified my sortie as being responsible. I was contacted, and sent them a copy of my ops report. This was done through an interested English newspaperman who was bilingual.

I was invited over for the eventful day when they raised the seaplane, but not being bilingual, I didn't go. Anyway, the airplane was brought to the surface — my aircraft recognition never was very good — it was a Dornier of some kind. They sent me additional word which was, "and tell him the other one is down there, too."

Who else has been credited with two additional enemy aircraft destroyed one third of a century after the occurrence?

Pilot: - F/O J.R. Johnson, (R.C.A.F.)
Nav.: - F/O N.J. Gibbons, (R.C.A.F.)

INTELLIGENCE FORM 'F'
FINAL RANGER/INTRUDER REPORT
AND
PILOT'S PERSONAL COMBAT REPORT
NO. 418 (RCAF) SQDN, R.A.F., FORD, SUSSEX

From: - R.A.F. Station Ford, Sussex.   Serial No. 4666, 18 Nov.

To: - H.Q. ADGB (2 copies), H.Q. 11 Group,
   Officer Commanding Ford
   S.I.O. Tangmere, S.I.O. Bradwell Bay, S.I.O. Manston,
   S.I.O. Honiley, S.I.O. Castle Camps, S.I.O. Hunsdon,
   S.I.O. Middle Wallop, S.I.O. West Malling, S.I.O. Sculthorpe,
   G.I.O. H.Q. No. 2 Group, I.O. 418 sqdn., and File

STATISTICAL

Date	(A) 28 November, 1943
Unit, Flight, Squadron	(B) 418 (RCAF) Sqdn, 'B' Flight

Type and mark of our aircraft (C) 2 Mosquito VIs

Time attack was delivered (D) 1800 hrs

Place of attack (E) Biscarrosse/Egang Seaplane base

Weather (F) from English Coast to 46°40'N rain and 10/10 cloud from 200 - 800 feet.

In Bay of Biscay layer cloud above 1000 feet.

In Bordeaux area cloud to 200 feet.

Our casualties, aircraft (G) Nil

Our casualties, personnel (H) Nil

Emeny casualties in air combat (J) Nil

Enemy casualties - ground or sea targets (K) Two Arado 196s damaged by F/O Johnson and F/O Gibbons

GENERAL

Two Mosquitos, piloted by F/O Johnson (RCAF), (Observer F/O Gibbons RCAF) and F/O Scherf (RCAF), (Observer F/O Brown RCAF), took off from Ford at 1545 hrs, for a Daylight-Dark Patrol to the Bordeaux - Biscarosse area. Both A/C flew together at 0 feet, making landfall at St. Marcauf, to Avranches. Thence to Laval, Angers, Les Sables, where they left the coast, climbing to 4000 feet as the cloud base was higher over the sea. They turned south at 4605N, 0150W, and flew parallel to the coast until they were opposite Biscarosse, where they dived to 0 feet crossing in at the south end of the lake.

F/O Scherf flying up the W. bank of the lake saw a sailing boat and opened fire; immediately afterwards seeing a large flying boat, in such a position that there was only time for a short burst to be fired. Pilot believes this to be a BV 222. Camouflage was pale blue. This aircraft was on a slipway cut in from the beach and surrounded on three sides by trees 1/2 mile S. of hangars. F/O Scherf saw no strikes, and had to do a violent left bank, as intense L/F from about eight positions opened up from whole shore S. of hangars as far as a point 1/2 mile to the South East. Mosquito suffered severe jolt and red flash was seen below port engine. This was later discovered to be caused by cannon shells having hit port propeller. F/O Scherf then circled, flew to S. of Lake, then to Bordeaux and Cognac but no activity was seen at these AFs.

F/O Johnson flew N. up centre of Lake Biscarosse and as he turned towards the seaplane base he saw about 6 Arado 196s anchored about 1/2 mile E. of the main slipway. He fired a short burst of cannon and machine gun, closing from about 500 to 300 yards, height 400 feet, and F/O Gibbons saw many strikes on the nearest a/c in the neighbourhood of the cockpit, while the last part of the burst hit the second a/c. Immediately after the pilot opened fire, light flak with red tracer came up from about 8 gun positions extending from the slipway northwards near the shore for about 1/4 mile. Evasive action was taken by a violent climbing turn to starboard and no damage was sustained. This crew continued N. past Gazaux A/F. By this time it was pretty dark, but F/O Johnson got the impression that there were 2 runways or prepared strips of a light colour crossing on the landing ground.

The rest of this patrol which continued past Hourtin/Contau seaplane base and later Cognac A/F which was completely uneventful.

Both Mosquitos flew independently on a fairly direct course back to St. Marcouf and base where they landed at 2000 hrs.

Both pilots agree that the formation adopted during daylight — namely loose echelon to starboard — is ideal for this type of operation, as the leading navigator can give the whole of his attention to navigation while the observer in the second aircraft can look behind for hostile aircraft in addition to keeping a check on the navigation.

OTHER OBSERVATIONS

On leaving Biscarosse F/O Scherf and F/O Brown saw a rectangular formation of lights parallel to the W. side of the main N/S railway line at Bourvuques (grid ref. (A) O.3733) and a long hutted camp running E and W between this railway and LIPOSTHEY (Approx. (A) O.4030).

On crossing in at St. Marcouf F/O Johnson and F/O Gibbons flew over a long gun (?) emplacement, containing numerous sandbag compartments, running along the shore near Les Dunes de Varreville (approx. 0.4300).

(J.R.F. Johnson)	(O.H. Hopgood)
Flying Officer (Pilot)	Flight Lieutenant
418 (RCAF) Squadron	Intelligence Officer
R.A.F. Station FORD	R.A.F. Station FORD

(N.J. Gibbons)
Flying Officer (Observer)
418 (RCAF) Squadron
R.A.F. Station FORD[32]

One of the most spectacular Allied night fighter combats of the war occurred near the end of the year, fought by 410 Squadron's Joe Schultz and Vern Williams. Schultz recalls this historic engagement, which was almost stillborn due to a question of conflicting fighter-pilot priorities. He was also developing a rather disturbing tendency of making unceremonious arrivals back at base after feats of great aerial prowess. The action on 10 December 1943 was no exception.

I was fortunate enough to get a "triple kill" of Dornier 217s on the night of 10 December 1943 . . . Actually, I had no intention of flying that night, even though I was on the Duty Roster for readiness. We were well down the list, with four or five crews to go before us, but a lot of the aircraft had been having trouble with the flame traps on the engine nacelles, and modifications had to be performed. As it turned out, though very few Mosquitos were fit to fly that particular night, mine was one that was. My ground-crew were very devoted and special. At any rate, I was told to take the patrol. It was a brilliant, moonlit night, so the likelihood of there being any "trade" for us was small. Also, I had been in a poker game and had made around £10–£15, which was exceptional at the time, so I really didn't want to leave the game. Anyway, the boss, Wing Commander George Elms, said that I had better get going . . .

We took off, and quite frankly, I was "bitching" about it for the next fifty minutes, when Vern Williams, my navigator, noticed a flashing marker beacon on the coast at Westkapelle on Walcheren Island. He then said, "Oh, I've been reading in the Intelligence summaries that that could signify a raid in progress now, because that is part of the new system they use." A few seconds later, our GCI told us that they were painting bandits on their radar and directed us to investigate. We were vectored after one and got in pretty close. It was crossing our flight path fairly rapidly when we picked it up in the moonlight against scattered clouds. My navigator had it on radar so we whipped around and closed in for the kill. It was a Do 217m, and a few short bursts put him in very bad trouble. As he tried to get down towards the sea, I hit him again and he broke into many flaming pieces on the water.

I took pictures of the results, but while I was doing this our controller was calling that he had more trade, and told us to get back up to 15,000 feet as quickly as possible, which we did. Vern picked up the next contact and we were closing at a very high rate and, in fact, were unquestionably going to overshoot our target. However, I was able to recognize it as another Do 217, so I fired a very short burst . . . just a very few rounds. It exploded immediately — probably the bomb load went up. It was so violent that it really viciously threw our aircraft around the sky.

While I was trying to figure out if our Mosquito was still in one piece, Vern said, "I've got another contact." He gave me a turn instruction and, sure enough, we closed in on this third aircraft, another Dornier 217m. As we closed from behind and I was trying to confirm what it was visually and get into firing range, he spotted us or had seen the explosion from the previous one, and knew there was trouble. He started a very violent porpoising up and down, and believe me, he was much better at this than I. I just couldn't get in synchronization with his movements, and I wasted a lot of ammunition trying to hit him between the "peaks and the hollows." This went on for what I thought was an eternity, but it was probably only a very short period of time, since the whole combat took place in something less than fifteen minutes. However, I guess he could only do this for so long. The Mosquito was still by far the most capable airplane, much more manoeuvrable, and he broke off to the left and started to turn for home, losing altitude at the same time. It was in this turn that I was able to make my first hits . . .

After this Dornier crashed into the sea, I started to examine my engine instruments, of which there weren't any working anymore, and I then noticed that the port engine wasn't in very good shape. So we started for home, and I declared the equivalent of a "Mayday" in rather rough language. A female controller called back and said that they would do all they could to get me home, but there was no need for language of that sort, thank you very much.

That cooled me down somewhat, but after that fifteen minutes of combat, my system was still pretty full of adrenalin and my imagination was running wild. On the way back to base at Bradwell Bay, I started to think, "My goodness, I'm hit," because my left foot felt as though it was soaking wet. I called base and said I thought I had a boot full of blood and that I was also bleeding from somewhere on my left side. When we landed on one engine at Bradwell, we were met by the "meat wagon" (ambulance) and the doctor wrestled me to the ground, since I wouldn't do what he asked me to do. He whipped off my left boot and with measured sarcasm said, "Must just be sweat — no blood here!" and promptly took off in his vehicle and left me there in the soaking wet, damp infield . . .[33]

Commonwealth aircrew had made great progress in the skies over northwest Europe during 1943. Widespread service use of the Spitfire Mk IX had given the day fighter pilots technological parity with the members of the Luftwaffe, who were now struggling on multiple fronts. The night fighter and intruder forces had also experienced considerable success during the year, and all the operational elements were now comfortable with the predominantly offensive nature of their missions, although the gains had not come without cost. The stage was being set for the massive invasion of the Continent soon to follow in 1944.

1   Jeffrey Quill, *Spitfire*, p. 205
2   Johnnie Johnson, *Wing Leader*, p. 159
3   Ibid., p. 164
4   Karl Linton, letter to author, March 1993
5   Jackie Rae, *Airforce* magazine, Spring 1989, p. 8
6   Jackie Rae, letter to author, July 1993
7   Tom Coughlin, *The Dangerous Sky*, p. 28
8   Art Sager, letter to author, May 1993
9   Leslie Roberts, *There Shall Be Wings*, p. 156
10 Hugh Godefroy, *Lucky Thirteen*, p. 39
11 Gordon A. Wilson, letter to author, June 1993
12 Lavigne and Edwards, *Kittyhawk Pilot*, p. 163
13 Noel Ogilvie, letter to author, May 1993
14 Lloyd Hunt, *We Band of Brothers*, p. 181

15 Hugh Godefroy, p. 202
16 Karl Linton, letter to author, April 1993
17 Hugh Godefroy, p. 201
18 Ibid., p. 213
19 Don Carlson, *RCAF Padre with Spitfire Squadrons*, p. 23
20 Lloyd Hunt, *We Band of Brothers*, p. 120
21 Art Sager, letter to author, April 1993
22 Lloyd Hunt, *We Band of Brothers*, p. 180
23 Karl Linton, letter to author, May 1993
24 Cec Brown, letter to author, March 1993
25 Art Sager, letter to author, April 1993
26 D. C. Laubman, letter to author, August 1993
27 F. E. Hanton, letter to author, August 1993
28 George Burroughs, letter to author, September 1993
29 Ibid.
30 R. D. Schultz, tape to author, September 1993
31 Lloyd Hunt, *We Band of Brothers*, p. 169
32 Lloyd Hunt, *We Happy Few*, p. 49
33 R. D. Schultz, tape to author, September 1993

6

REGAINING LOST GROUND

"How could I miss?"
— AL CORSTON, 67 (RAF) SQUADRON

While 1943 was a watershed year in which the air war over north-west Europe took a decided upturn for the Allies, it was also a year marked by resounding successes in the Mediterranean theatre, mixed results in the Far East, and a final resolution of that miserable war in the Far North, the Aleutians campaign. In Algeria and Tunisia, massive buildups of Allied aircraft took place throughout December 1942 and January 1943. The final phase of the Tunisian campaign occurred in late March, when Montgomery's Eighth Army carried out a brilliant flanking manoeuvre near Mareth, and was equally brilliantly supported by units of the Desert Air Force under Air Vice-Marshal Harry Broadhurst. By 8 April, units of the Eighth Army and the U.S. II Corps were able to link up near Gafsa in southern Tunisia. For the next five weeks, a host of enemy airfields were overrun, and soon all remaining Axis forces in Africa were totally encircled in a 160-kilometre by 80-kilometre pocket located in the extreme northern part of the country.[1] In desperation, the Germans now tried to evacuate their beleaguered forces by any means possible, including the enormous but highly vulnerable Messerschmitt Me 323 transports. On 22 April 1943, Stocky Edwards scored the last of his fifteen and a half confirmed air-to-air victories of the North African campaign over one of these behemoths, although he would later augment his impressive scoresheet with air-to-air kills over Italy and northwest Europe.

At 07.10 hours on the morning of 22 April 1943, Kittyhawks from 7 SAAF Wing took off with other escorting squadrons. They set their course for the Gulf of Tunisia. Fifteen minutes later, Eddie and his comrades left for the same area. Because of the last minute serviceability of Wing Commander Burton's aircraft, Eddie had been called upon to lead the four Squadrons of 239 Wing as Wing Commander.

Sometime earlier in Sicily, *Gruppen* of transport aircraft, Ju 52s and Me 323s had set off for Tunis, escorted by MC 202s and II/JG 27 Me 109s. By the time Eddie was on his way to the area, the Junkers had reached Tunis safely. But the huge six-engined Messerschmitt 323s had taken a different course and were intercepted by South Africans as they passed Zembra Island on their approach to Tunis. The Kittyhawk pilots reported seeing twenty 323s, with the escort fighters stepped up to 8000 feet. Representing the entire strength of a new unit, Transport *Geschwader* 5, the Me 323s had joined the remains of another unit, KGzb.V.323.

The South African pilots dived for the kill and within minutes it was over. At the head of 239 Wing, Eddie arrived over the battle area just in time to witness the results: "When 239 Wing reached the Bay of Tunis," he wrote, "the Bay seemed to be on fire with burning aircraft on the water."

As they approached, a few enemy fighters dived on the Kittys but, within minutes, 250 Squadron, flying top cover, had taken care of them. In the meantime, Eddie looked at the scene below and watched his surroundings. "Flying through the smoke at approximately 500 feet," Eddie said, "I saw a large aircraft directly in front. At approximately 250 yards, I fired a long burst and the Me 323 folded up like a stack of cards and fell into the sea. The SAAF Wing ahead of our formation had shot down twenty-three of the transports. Twenty-plus Me 109s were patrolling high above but did not attack — it looked like they lost heart."

Back at the Intelligence Officer's headquarters at Kairouan, the pilots made their reports. During his attack on the Me 323, Eddie had been flanked by both his No. 2 and No. 3, F/O Flury and Sgt. Lorry. Although recorded that they had assisted in the destruction of the enemy aircraft, it is likely they never fired their guns. As usual the Intelligence Officer, Johnny Walker, proposed the victory be shared between three. Eddie agreed. It would be good for the morale of the young pilots.

Transport *Geschwader* 5 had been wiped out as a unit that day. It was the last great slaughter of enemy transports. Since the beginning of "Operation Flax," more than four hundred transport planes had been claimed by the Allied pilots for a loss of about thirty-five fighters. F/L Edwards claimed the last of the enemy transports and recorded the last confirmed victory for 260 Squadron in North Africa. Now the enemy was being forced to airlift by night.[2]

By 5 May, the enemy's defensive line had been completely torn apart, and on a day which witnessed no less than 2,154 sorties by the Northwest African Air Forces, the Allied armies were steamrolling towards Tunis. The city would fall to the British 7th Armoured Division two days later.

Bill Olmsted of Hamilton, Ontario, would eventually rise to command 442 Squadron in a very distinguished manner during the drive across northwest Europe, winning a DSO, DFC, and Bar along the way. At the end of the Tunisian campaign, however, he was still a relatively inexperienced fighter pilot with 81 (RAF) Squadron, attempting to learn the tricks of the trade from a wealth of experienced desert aces, including New Zealand's Colin Gray, South Africa's "Dutch" Hugo, and England's "Razz" Berry, a distinguished Battle of Britain veteran. Olmsted describes life in Tunisia after the withdrawal and surrender of the Axis forces:

On May 13, the day the African Campaign officially ended, we moved to Le Sebala airdrome, some seven miles north and west of Tunis. It was from here, only five days before, while flying at 15,000 feet I had watched twenty Me 109s take off to fight us. It was an excellent airdrome, wide and flat, completely grass-covered with no litter or useless material left lying around. Unlike the British, the Germans seemed to be tidy and orderly.

To observe the victory we decided to celebrate with a drinking party. A number of pilots were dispatched in various directions with four-gallon tins in hand and orders to return only when each container was filled with wine. Several hours later we assembled to drink and revel. The hours passed, and we drank and drank, but nothing happened. It was as though the date wine we'd found was water. Eventually, thoroughly disgusted, we retired to our canvas beds, quite sober. By morning we were all roaring drunk — the slow-acting wine finally revealed its potency — and drunk we stayed all day. Despite considerable tippling experience since that time, I have yet to find another drink as slow-acting yet as potent as that Tunisian date wine.

Some ten burned-out Ju 52 transports lay broken and crippled at the edges of the field and several '109s stood intact and untouched in their bays, hidden in the orange groves at the south edge of the 'drome. But we dared not touch any wire, tool, gun, or anything else which struck our fancy, since most were rigged with explosives set to go off at the slightest touch of any unwary scrounger. Often the most innocent-appearing object would be wired with explosives which successfully blasted an unsuspecting souvenir hunter to bits. The enemy could be extremely cunning and diabolical and proved his ingenuity in innumerable gruesome ways.

During the next three weeks we were to move to Utique airfield, then to Prottville, and finally to La Marsa. All had been well-established enemy operational fields, which minimized the amount of work we had to do to make them suitable for our own operations. This gave us sufficient free time to enjoy the aftermath of victory, and individually and in groups we took off in every direction to explore, to enjoy, and in particular, to acquire souvenirs and mementos.

We found seventeen broken and battered '109s on one 'drome, full of bullet holes acquired in combat. We rejoiced to see the once-proud Ace of Spades crest laying shattered in the Tunisian dust. Later on I was to meet this top-scoring German fighter group again in France.

As we wandered about the country, we saw many strange sights, including German and Italian prisoners driving themselves in their own military trucks to our prison compounds. Sometimes a truckload would be guarded by one lonely Tommy sitting in the rear, rubbing shoulders with the prisoners in the overloaded vehicle. Generally, however, there were no guards. I watched Italian prisoners proceeding by truck or on foot to our hastily constructed prison camps. Their uniforms appeared to be neat and clean, and the Italians smiled pleasantly at us whenever we stared. They were a happy bunch! The German prisoners — the pride of the Afrika Korps — seemed to be young, tall, fair-haired and powerfully built.

They laughed and joked amongst themselves, while with us they were arrogant or sullen. We were to understand that they regarded their defeat as only a passing misfortune and that they would somehow soon be rescued by Adolf to fight again. From a physical standpoint these men were marvelous specimens. Little wonder they were able to put up such a long, desperate struggle.

We roamed from Tunis to Bizerte and back again. On every hand lay devastated and hastily abandoned German equipment. We examined half-tracks, Tiger tanks, and the deadly 88 millimeter gun. We searched supply dumps, army stores, and discarded equipment. In a few days we were well stocked with souvenirs and trivial loot. The more fancied possessions included Mauser rifles, cap badges, flags, Luger pistols, and German manuscripts. A few managed to get hold of cars or motorcycles and particularly prized was the Volkswagen, a superb little machine not unlike our Jeep. With wheels we were able to roam much further afield, far more quickly.

I visited Grombalia, formerly a supply and storage depot and a last center of German resistance, some thirty-five miles south of Tunis. The approach to the town was littered with the carcasses of horses and German soldiers, and surrounded by hordes of flies, and in the intense heat, the stench of decaying flesh was overwhelming. The distinctive smell of German equipment, created by the paint or preservative used to color the various objects, added to the unpleasantness. By following this distinctive stink, however, we were able to locate souvenirs which we might otherwise have missed.[3]

Number 417 (City of Windsor) Squadron had formed at Charmy Down near Bath in November 1941. The unit was first equipped with clapped-out, war-weary Spitfire IIs, very difficult to keep serviceable. Fortunately, these aircraft did not follow them to Tain in northern Scotland in February. There, foul weather, substandard food, and poor accommodation took a morale toll. Furthermore, and in direct contrast to the normal Fighter Command policy of integrating a healthy mix of many different foreign nationals and Commonwealth pilots into a Squadron, 417 was initially staffed with twenty Canadian pilots, of whom sixteen were Sergeants, and very few had any previous combat time. The CO was a remote New Zealander and the Flight Commanders had virtually no combat experience. But 417 Squadron was soon to round a corner and never look back. Its success in the upcoming Sicilian and Italian campaigns would be due in no small measure to an infusion of inspired, battle-hardened leadership. Stan Turner was about to drop rank in order to command the Squadron, and Bert Houle, who had already distinguished himself in North Africa with RAF squadrons, had requested a transfer there as a Flight Commander. He recalls the sorry state of affairs on 417 Squadron upon his arrival, and the problems which had plagued it to that point in time:

> My information was that the RCAF higher-ups in England, and probably in Canada, wanted to have some part in the successes that were being accomplished in the Western Desert. They selected officers who could be spared, not those who had proved themselves. In the last days of driving the enemy out of North Africa, while the RAF squadrons were shooting down four enemy aircraft for every one they lost themselves, 417 had the reverse . . . one down for every four that it lost. I was off on rest after my first tour and had a letter from Lefty Steele, who had been in my Flight on 213 Squadron and had been transferred to 417, giving details of how poorly they were organized and led in the air. I went to see Wing Commander Patterson, the head of the RCAF in the Middle East, and requested that my rest tour be cut down and that I be posted to 417. It came through. When I landed at Ben Gardone, I could not believe the mess the Canadian area was in; they certainly lacked leadership and desire.
>
> The morning we were to move to Malta, I went down to check my aircraft and found a big bulge in the left tire. The Wing took off and I was forced to fly over alone after it was fixed. When I got to Malta, only the left wheel came down; I could not get the right wheel down. I even tried flying on my back and pulling on acceleration forces. I then decided that it might cause less damage by landing with both wheels up, but discovered that I could not raise the left wheel. Anyway, I did a one-wheel landing and miraculously did little damage. Stan Turner arrived a few days later and that was all the Squadron needed. From then on, it was as good as any in the invasion of Sicily and Italy. I got seven enemy fighters destroyed over Italy before I was wounded over the Anzio beachhead. I firmly believe that 417 was the top fighter squadron in Italy, at least until it was assigned to bombing and strafing later on in the Campaign . . .[4]

With the move to Malta complete, Hedley Everard, another seasoned veteran who had recently joined the unit, witnessed the differences in Squadron performance and attitude brought about by the leadership of Stan Turner ("The Bull") and Bert Houle.

The Squadron's arrival in Malta coincided with the arrival of a new commanding officer and his deputy. Both were veteran leaders from RAF units. The new Squadron Leader wore battle honours earned during the Fall of France and the now famous Battle of Britain. He was both fearfully and affectionately called "The Bull."

The Bull was a slightly-built city-bred Canadian with tight curly red hair above watery blue eyes. He had enlisted in the Royal Air Force in the mid-thirties. His Canadian twang permeated his lexicon of proper British phraseology and RAF slang. Cryptic radio communications between fighters had altered our everyday language usage. Immediate compliance to his orders was now essential for survival in his Unit. Failure to obey properly and promptly meant instant dismissal. Many of 417's mouthy pilots found themselves airborne to Cairo on a transport the same day. His deputy was also completely intolerant of breaches of air discipline. Within two days, challenging air drills, lead by "The Bull and Bert" had eliminated all the "bad apples." Replacement pilots were treated less harshly and coached in the ability of the pilots of twelve Spitfires to act as a team in battle tactics. Individual "tail-chases" were practiced. Basically these were dog-fights between two Spitfires where the aim of the target aircraft was to lose his "tail" by any maneuver or combination of tricks. All guns were made safe before flight and only the camera gun operated, so results could be accurately analyzed. My evident enjoyment of these mock fights, and my previous experiences against the Japanese resulted in my Spitfire becoming the target on many of these training fights. I became most adept at evasive actions which perhaps accounted for my survival in the years ahead. To my delight, I was made a Section Leader in the first fighter sweep of Sicily within a week of our arrival in Malta. In those last days of June we made a number of fighter sweeps over enemy territory, but few Axis fighters rose to the challenge of two dozen Spitfires. Limited engagements did occur but without positive results. On these occasions I would exercise my cannon on fleeting Me 109s that were invariably out of range. It was taboo to break formation and chase decoy bandits, since other bandits could be perched high above ready to pounce. Every preflight briefing carried the words: "Beware the Hun in the Sun." These wise words were ignored one morning by another Spitfire squadron and a fierce dog-fight occurred in which three Spits and two '109s were downed. We were scrambled to give assistance but when our twelve Spits with overheated engines reached the battle ground fifty miles north of Malta, the sky was empty. Below five dinghies bobbed in the water where friend and foe would be distinguished by the color of their one man rubber rafts. Both Axis and Allied fighter pilots had cursed the folded hard rubber bundles that replaced the foam rubber cushions of their parachute packs. Every fighter pilot at some time had been required to practice an emergency dinghy-opening drill with full flying gear in some frigid pool. The sight of five successfully inflated rafts below somehow eased our posterior pain as we flew above the downed airmen. After an hour we were replaced by another protecting squadron and returned to base. As we refueled another squadron was scrambled. From the nearby radio repair truck I heard the leader's "Tally-Ho" and knew that another dog-fight was in progress. Rapidly we were all refueled and strapped into our cockpits ready to take off. A third Spitfire squadron was hurled into the Mediterranean sky prior to the return of the second wave. Only ten aircraft of the second wave landed, so we knew that two more Spitfires had been lost. The third wave returned intact at which time we were ordered aloft. On arrival at the battle area, I peered unbelievingly at nine dinghies bobbing in the water — four of ours and five of theirs. Whether by instinct or orders, "The Bull" placed us on a low patrol line west of the rubber flotilla. In a moment, I spied and reported a dozen bandits flying at our level two miles east. The Bull's voice barked: "Shut up Blue One!" I knew then he had already spotted the '109s. In complete silence and in almost parade formation, we patrolled our sentinel line to the west whilst the enemy repeated our maneuver to the east. I concluded our cross-over turns and aircraft separations were much smoother and smarter than our opponents. This cat-and-mouse drama produced a river of sweat down my spine. This was my first opportunity to examine the enemy's principal fighter at relatively close range. I memorized the silhouette of the Me 109 from every angle, much like a camera-bug on a photo spree. The formation they flew was different than ours, and this was an enemy recognition feature which assisted me greatly in the years ahead. The frontal view of an attacking fighter is so small that it is extremely difficult to determine if it is hostile or a dangerous error in aircraft recognition. Since the Battle of Britain, the nose cones of Spitfire propellers had been painted a dull red. The Germans adopted a white spiral on a black background which appeared a dull grey in flight. American fighters displayed nothing distinctive and fired at everything.

After some time, a rescue boat from Sicily and another from Malta arrived and began to fish out their respective downed airmen. When the task was completed, we escorted our rescue craft back to Malta and I could see the '109s were providing the same cover to their boat. I smiled in my oxygen mask as I recalled a boyhood picture of stretcher bearers removing the wounded in the trench warfare of the First World War. As the news of our sortie spread, the airmen adopted the big grin on our leader's face. From that moment on, even through the difficult winter months that lay ahead, the morale of 417 Squadron members improved. This was the stimulant that was needed to erase the slump in spirits of the Unit's previous year in the Desert. From then on I never heard another Canadian grumble, whether pilot or airman. The Bull and Bert were truly king and crown prince of Four Seventeen.[5]

<hr />

The invasion of Sicily, code-named Operation Husky, was about to begin. Since preparations for a cross-Channel invasion of northwest Europe would not be complete until the following year, the Allied hierarchy reasoned that an attack on the Continent's "soft underbelly" was now possible. Not only would such an invasion take some heat off the Russian army's drive towards the Third Reich in the East, it would also provide invaluable experience for the landings to come the following year in northern France, and with luck force the capitulation of Italy, part of the Axis triumvirate of power.

Mediterranean Air Command under Sir Arthur Tedder possessed 306 operational squadrons totalling over 2,500 first-line aircraft. Opposing them would be over 1,800 German and Italian aircraft, based on the islands of Sicily and Sardinia as well as the Italian mainland. Although at least 1,000 of these aircraft could be considered combat ready, many of the most able veterans of both the Luftwaffe and the *Regia Aeronautica* had been killed or captured in North Africa, and the quality of the replacements was generally not that high.

Furthermore, the lack of availability of spare equipment and support facilities was beginning to be a real problem in the Axis camp.[6]

After a massive round of preliminary bombardments of the Axis landing grounds and airfields, the initial landings on 10 July went virtually unopposed. That same day, an RAF Servicing Commando unit hacked out an emergency airstrip at Pachino, and a Ground Controlled Interception (GCI) unit was installed there during the night to service the night-fighting Beaufighters from Malta as well as intruder Mosquitos operating in the area. Gordon Wilson, now commissioned and flying Spitfires with 92 (RAF) Squadron, arrived at Pachino shortly thereafter. Getting out of the small field where he made an emergency landing near the main Pachino strip later that same day would be of far greater concern than his unscheduled arrival there.

[No.] 92 Squadron with Spit IXs and stationed in Malta was assigned air cover responsibility to the Allied troops landing in Sicily. We did our early morning 13 July 1943 patrol, flying out from Luqa Airport in Malta, and with our usual 1:45 flying time, landed later at Pachino, Sicily. The first Squadron and the first Wing to do this on D-Day-plus-three. The air force had arrived in Sicily. I was typically dressed for the invasion times, hadn't shaved for two days, had my pajama top under my khaki tunic and the usual white scarf . . . the trademark of a fighter pilot . . . in fact I looked quite rough. Later that day the Squadron took off for a second patrol of code-name "Acid," the Mount Etna area. Returning to Pachino base, I noticed I was completely out of fuel. Calling up my leader to explain my predicament brought no response. I made the decision that I must force land.

The field I picked looked fair, although it had irrigation ditches on two sides and a ploughed field at the end. It looked good enough. My confidence soared, so I put the wheels down and dropped to a perfect landing over the irrigation ditch and let it roll and roll and roll. Just before it came to a stop, I hit the ploughed field — just enough to put the Spitfire on its nose — only a damaged prop. However, there I was hanging in my safety harness and cockpit, about seven feet in the air, and waiting for the tail to drop. Finally I climbed out, down the side, and to my horror saw about thirty people running towards me. I had landed a short distance from a Sicilian villa. Naturally you think the worst. However, one man came up to me and offered me a drink of wine. I was suspicious and thought the wine could be poisoned, but he laughed, took a drink and handed it over to me to drink, which I did. He said: "Mussolini bad — King of Italy good." I was on show all day.

It turned out they were Sicilians who had lived in the USA before the war, but at Mussolini's request came back to Sicily and were farming in this malaria-infected part of the country. They spoke fair English and were friendly and helpful. Naturally I wanted to guard the Spitfire so I asked a young man to get help from the British Army. The thought of retreating Italian or German soldiers never entered my mind. The young Sicilian was away for several hours, then came back — shrugged his shoulders and said he couldn't find any help. My situation suddenly became serious, so I had him lead and show me the way to the Allies. After an hour's walk we came upon the Calgary Tanks coming forward, but not prepared to stop for a mere airman. Finally I was able to stop an army jeep which took me to the Tank headquarters. I was given an MP escort and we made our way back to the Spitfire, still up on its nose. It was agreed with the MPs we would take turns guarding the plane during the night. They cheated on me by letting me sleep all night and, as I was exhausted, I needed and appreciated their token of friendship. I also gained a new respect for MPs.

The next morning a jeep took me and my parachute to a road junction and I was told to hitch a ride to Pachino. There was an American GI at this junction who was going back with a "set of nerves." His talk almost had me windy. He was sure the Allied Forces could never stay in Sicily. Finally a truck came along and I found my way back to Pachino.

I was in for a real shock. I had been absent for over eighteen hours with a Spit IX aeroplane and no one had missed me, including my groundcrew and the other pilots. My ego hit a new low. However, the newspaper people thought this forced landing incident important, because I was the first pilot to force land in Sicily and walk back. It was a good omen that pilots could expect good treatment from the Sicilian citizens.

Ten days later, my Flight Commander and I decided to have a look at the Spitfire IX. The groundcrew had put on a new propeller. It was now good as new. After checking the aircraft, the Flight Commander asked me if I felt the field was long enough to fly it off. It looked short to me — and that irrigation ditch at the end could create problems. However, with all the confidence in the world, I said, "no problem," thinking an experienced pilot like the Flight Commander could fly it out. However he shook me to my sock feet by saying, "Okay, you fly it out tomorrow." You can be sure I wasted no time having the groundcrew remove the guns and ammo and all other surplus weight to lighten the load.

Next morning, with full brakes on, groundcrew hanging onto the tail, I revved the engine, started across the field, and just before reaching the irrigation ditch, lifted the Spitfire neatly off the ground. Confidence in myself soared, but not nearly as much as my confidence in the Spitfire. What a pleasure and a treat to fly the best aeroplane in the world without the weight of guns and other extra equipment. Every pilot should have this experience, and in the words of "High Flight" by P/O Magee, "I've chased the shouting wind along, and flung my eager craft through footless halls of air." Yes, this is the experience I had bringing this aircraft safely back to base. My confidence and admiration for the Spitfire IX will remain with me forever.[7]

As the occupation of Sicily progressed, more airfields became available for use by Allied aircraft, dramatically reducing the transit time for the air war and also providing a measure of relief for tiny Malta, whose facilities were extremely overburdened. Bill Olmsted recalls the move to Sicily:

July 22 was the day we had been eagerly awaiting — our move to Sicily. We packed in haste with my groundcrew stuffing a parachute bag of belongings into the machine gun trays and somehow storing my bedroll behind the seat. After a hasty lunch we said goodbye to the staff in the Mess, and took a last look at the comforts we had enjoyed for over two months, knowing that it would be a long time before we lived in such style again.

Our destination was Lentini East, a new field bulldozed out of a swamp bordering another swamp called Lake Lentini, the largest lake in Sicily. We were in the midst of the hot dry season when lakes and rivers dried up and the ground baked into a hardpan surface heavily cracked with wide fissures. We were eight miles inland from the Gulf of Catania, some ten miles from the site of my Catania airdrome experience and five miles from the German front lines. It took us fifteen minutes of stooging around to locate our new base, a testimony to its primitive condition. I suppose a bulldozer had appeared one day, cleared a strip 1000 yards long by seventy feet wide through the fields of vegetables, with a few side swipes to make largely imaginary parking spots for aircraft. And then it was called an airdrome!

In effect, we were operating from dried dirt and clay, surrounded by fields of fruit and vegetables. Clouds of dust and debris flew up when an aircraft engine was tested or when we taxied. Strict smoking controls were established because, since we were parked so close together, a carelessly started fire could wipe out our Squadron quite easily. Worst of all there were no Allied troops between ourselves and the Germans — we were the front line! Behind us were bags of troops and tanks ready to rush to our rescue should we be attacked, but we were not particularly impressed with that arrangement.

When a squadron moved to a new location hacked out of the local terrain, the priorities were to first look after the aircraft and then to improvise a camp for living comfort. The camp should be a mile or so from the 'drome so that during night bombings and daytime attacks, the personnel are relatively safe when resting. The "spy" and the Adjutant had been in charge of our advance party, arriving three days before the aircraft flew in. They had B Flight groundcrew to help service all of our aircraft until A Flight crews arrived some days later. It was a sort of leap-frog process.

They had chosen a camp site on high ground a half mile north of the field, well dispersed in a grove of large olive trees. Below us was a huge irrigation ditch, carrying water to nurture the surrounding orange and lemon groves. The ditch had high banks and a couple of feet of moving water and became an instant hit as a giant bathtub. We had no tents — just canvas flysheets stretched between trees and poles, enclosed at the sides with completely pervious, useless, mosquito netting. It was all improvised on the spot and certainly not rainproof. Pep was my "tent" partner, however, and I knew he could dream up something if foul weather arrived.

Our Mess was just a much larger version of our sleeping covers. But by clever and assiduous scrounging we were able to find chairs, good carpets to lay on the bare ground, tables, radios, gramophones, china, crystal, decanters, and other comforts, including a large variety of wines. It was completely open but for captured German drogue netting — in red, white, and blue themes, very patriotic — acting as walls. It also failed to keep out the ever-present mosquitoes. We enjoyed our outdoor living, except that at night, we could not smoke or display lights which might attract German artillery fire. Howard MacMinniman, a Canadian from Fredericton, was duly elected bar officer and Jim Woodhill, a Canadian from Halifax, was made messing officer. Obviously we Canadians had certain attributes or qualifications admired by the other nationalities.

It was weeks later when we complained about the lack of regular food supplies that we discovered we were supposed to exist on hardtack, cheese, and what we could obtain locally. Our invasion planners had made an important gamble in providing a bare subsistence level of rations, and we considered ourselves extremely fortunate to be surrounded by plentiful, and free, fresh fruit and vegetables. We had fields of tomatoes, ripening successively, with musk melons, watermelons, oranges, lemons, lettuce, onions, and other garden vegetables close at hand. Plentiful food, wine, and beautiful weather were great aids in promoting a sense of well-being among the pilots and groundcrews.[8]

Mosquitoes were, however, by no means the only nuisance from the animal kingdom encountered on Sicily. Rex Probert of Calgary, who won a DFC while flying Spitfires with 92 (RAF) Squadron, remembers a friend's penchant for collecting unusual creatures, a hobby that very nearly had serious operational ramifications:

Like all squadrons, 92 Spitfire Squadron had its share of characters; one of whom was an English chap by the name of Tony Bruce.

Tony loved all animals, large or small, and it did not matter to him whether they crawled or walked. One day in Sicily, where the Squadron was camped in a cotton field, we found that friend Tony was the proud owner of three very large snakes; all, I was told, poisonous. It wasn't unusual for Tony to arrive in the Mess tent with at least one of these snakes draped around his neck as he presented himself for an evening beer or two. Naturally, this was much to the chagrin of the other Mess members who, as a rule and of course under protest, quickly evacuated the Mess.

On investigation, we discovered that these snakes, when not being carried around by Tony, were kept in a cardboard box, and not too big a box at that. One afternoon Tony arrived in the Mess in a rage, demanding to know who had let his snakes out. Of course no one knew as everyone stayed as far away from the snake box as possible. Now there were three big snakes loose in the area, and nobody knew where they were. I can assure you that when we went to bed at night we all checked our sleeping bags with a flashlight before retiring — drunk or sober!

About two days later while on a sweep over Italy, one of the Spitfires in the formation began to act strangely. It was dipsy-doodling all over the sky; nipping in and out of the formation, while at the same time neglecting to answer our calls. We thought at first he was being attacked by someone we couldn't see, but after some time he returned to the formation and we all completed the sweep.

Naturally, when we landed we all went over to Jocko, an Aussie, and quizzed him about his strange behavior. It was then that we discovered where one of Tony's snakes was — in Jocko's cockpit, stabbed through the head. It had emerged from under the instrument panel when Jocko had gone through 10,000 feet during the climb. Apparently the snake was beginning to suffer from lack of oxygen. Unhappily, someone on the ground had left the coupe-top open during the night and, I suppose, the snake crept into the cockpit to get warm. When it emerged, there was a fight between Jocko and the snake. Fortunately Jocko won; had it been some other pilot on the Squadron, the Allies might have lost a Spitfire. Many of us under those circumstances would have bailed out, preferring to take our chances with the Italians. Such was life with Tony Bruce on the Squadron![9]

A great deal of bitter fighting characterized the latter part of the Sicilian campaign, as the Allies encountered stiffened German resistance on the northeastern part of the island. One by one, however, the remaining towns and ports fell into Allied hands, and the day after Messina capitulated on 16 August, all enemy resistance on the island ceased. Nonetheless, the German retreat across the Straits of Messina was so well organized that they managed to evacuate a substantial number of assets, both human and material. Nevertheless, the campaign had cost the Axis forces dearly, including over 32,000 men killed or wounded and a further 162,000 captured. Furthermore, at least 1,800 aircraft had been lost, against Allied losses of 400 aircraft, excluding assault gliders.[10] The thirty-eight-day conquest of the island was over, and the invasion of the European mainland was about to begin.

In the early-morning hours of 3 September, Canadian troops of the 1st Division and those of the British 5th Division crossed the Straits of Messina and attacked German fortifications on the toe of Italy at

Reggio, San Giovanni, and Bognora, averaging an advance of nearly twenty miles a day for the next week. Italian resistance had all but crumbled and on 8 September, Italy, now under Marshal Badoglio, surrendered unconditionally. There was, however, still the problem of a host of very unwelcome German tenants in the country, and the next day, an extremely large invasion force from British X Corps and the U.S. VI Corps stormed the beaches at Salerno, forty miles south-east of Naples. Number 417 Squadron, under the able leadership of Stan Turner, was heavily involved in covering the landing beaches while operating out of their Sicilian base at Lentini during the first half of September.

Although the fighters were originally operating at extreme range from Sicilian bases over the beachhead, by mid-September facilities became available on the mainland to garrison the Spitfire squadrons closer to the action. Allied progress was initially rapid and by the end of September Naples had been occupied, though the U.S. Fifth Army would soon become bogged down a few miles north of the city at the Volturno River. On the west side of the Italian peninsula, the Germans had created formidable defences in the northern half of the country. Bill Olmsted's 232 Squadron had moved along the coast from Asa near the Sorrento Peninsula to nearby Serretelle, and by mid-October to Gioia del Colle, thirty miles north of Taranto on the heel of Italy. Bill recalls life at Gioia del Colle during the waning days of this particular Allied advance:

Gioia del Colle airdrome was an enormous, all-weather grass plot, 2000 yards in diameter. It was so big that our entire Squadron could take off at one time, in almost any direction. It had been a training base for Italian bomber pilots and their training continued on Savoias and Cants while we shared the 'drome. They were not very good pilots, and they crashed their planes regularly.

The Base Commander, an Italian Colonel, thought he saw an opportunity to extend his authority when our Wing of four Spitfire squadrons started sharing his facilities. Within a day of our arrival, he issued instructions that we were to stand at attention and salute when the Italian flag was raised and lowered at dusk, that all RAF non-commissioned ranks were to salute all Italian officers, and that Allied officers were to salute the Italian senior ranks. Within hours of the issuance of these ridiculous orders, Group Captain Hugo had them rescinded and reversed.

The Italian winter was fast approaching, heralded by frequent rainy days and bitterly cold, damp nights. We pilots and groundcrew were only prepared for warm weather operations, our main dress being summer khaki. Our blue uniforms and warm clothing had been packed and left in Africa and were supposed to follow when we settled in one spot long enough for our baggage to catch up.

Our ground personnel were billeted far from the 'drome in a cold, damp, and poorly constructed barracks, with no beds and only two blankets per man. We urgently required beds, stoves, additional blankets, and warm clothing. On the other hand, the Italian ground personnel were billeted in warm, modern barracks, furnished with beds and ample blankets.

We had been campaigning for nearly a year, with our shabby, mismatched clothes being positive proof of the dirt and hard living we had experienced. The Italians were neatly, even smartly, dressed, and they seemed to relish the contrast between them and us, not acknowledging that we portrayed victory while they stood for something quite different.

Our men began to wonder if we had won or lost the war to the Italians. We met this superior attitude in cities and rural areas, but it was particularly noticeable in the streets — the natives rarely gave us any room when we passed on foot. They ignored us completely. Prices in stores were immediately raised when we entered. And, although not openly hostile, the locals refused to assist us in any way, which was exactly opposite to the cooperation we had found on the west coast.

This eastern half of the country had little contact with the Germans throughout the war and suffered little or no damage as the enemy had hastily retreated, allowing the Eighth Army to advance with minimum opposition. Indeed, there was little resistance until our troops neared Foggia and the thirteen important airfields in the area, which formed the principal German Air Force maintenance base in Italy. Perhaps the strange and hostile attitude of these Italians resulted from being sheltered from much of the war's destruction, and this stimulated resentment at being overrun again, this time by us, even though we were now supposed to be "Allies."

The pilots lived in a modern farmhouse that Cam and I had commandeered, located a mile down the road from our crews. The house was stone, very large, and equipped with all normal conveniences. A magnificent stone and wood barn was located almost beside the house, and our practiced eyes told us it would convert easily into a superb Mess and lounge. Further away was a large two-storey stone building divided into separate dwellings to house the farm families. We found that we were on a large farm owned by an absentee landlord who lived in Bari. We had blundered into the feudal system at work, for the tenant farmers were little more than serfs, owning nothing and working hard for just a small share of the crops harvested.

The farmers and their large families treated us in a friendly and generous manner, quite unassuming and yet helpful in many respects, pointing out ripe vegetables or small lambs ready for slaughter or chickens which could be spared. We watched as they washed their gnarled feet to stamp grapes piled in huge vats, and we delighted in the sweet nectar released from a bunghole at the bottom. We returned their friendship with generous donations of canned M and V, Spam, plum pudding, cigarettes, and chocolate. The owner would have been apoplectic had he suspected that his tenants were gleefully sabotaging him behind his back.

When we first found the farmhouse, Cam and I had stood guard while Duke used his van to round up the rest of the pilots. Possession was our strong point, and we did not want anyone else, Allied or Italian, to take it away from us. Before our reinforcements arrived, however, the owner drove up with two fully armed Carabiniari, obviously intent on forcing us to vacate his property. We drew our pistols, looking as menacing and determined as possible; we both had had enough of being pushed around by our "Allies." The would-be evictors sensed this and after much shouting and gesturing they left, promising to return.

As it happened, the owner did return daily, bringing us food, chickens, and farm produce while he inspected the buildings. We pretended that he was being helpful and generous, not just trying to protect his property.

We built a huge bar in the barn, stocking it with champagne, whiskey, gin and a variety of wines and liqueurs. The straw originally stored in the barn had been thrown out and the barn interior had been thoroughly scrubbed, leaving little barn or animal odor. A tiny forty-four-year-old Italian pianist named Vincenzo de Lisio had fastened himself to us a few weeks earlier, and in return for food, attention, and security, he provided us with innumerable hours of delight. Before the war, he had played at Grosvenor House in London, a high point in his musical career. Once hostilities started, he entertained Italian and German troops on all fronts until meeting up with us. We scrounged an old piano so that Vince could entertain us with renditions of Bach, Beethoven, or Chopin or contemporary Italian and German music. Our relaxing evenings in a warm barn under soft lights dispelled our thoughts of war and our frustration over our work being made even more difficult by horrid weather. We drank to excess, sang until our voices became hoarse, and felt a peace and happiness we had not known for many months. To his musical talents, Vince added the skills of a gourmet cook and an expert scrounger. This little skinny man, barely five feet tall, repaid us many times over for being allowed to live with us. Sadly, his end was brutal, for in December he was accidentally run over by a truck in the blackout, dying instantly.

On October 23 Jim Woodhill, while on a Bari-Brindisi patrol, came across an Me 210, which he chased and damaged before his cannon packed up. We were delighted to think that we might encounter the odd enemy aircraft to relieve the boredom of uneventful patrols.

That afternoon I was doing a similar patrol at 22,000 feet with Bowring as my Number 2. For a change I was flying a Spit IX, fitted with a thirty-gallon long-range tank. After about thirty minutes' stooging around, our ground control interceptor "Blackbeer" called, "Tampax Leader, I have two bogies for you. To converge steer zero-three-zero degrees and climb." "Roger, Blackbeer," I replied as I opened my throttle wide and started to climb.

At 27,000 feet I suddenly saw them coming from the east. At our altitude and on our course we would have met or converged at some point ahead. They were Me 109G6s with long-range tanks suspended under their bellies.

We saw each other almost simultaneously. The '109s immediately turned hard starboard as they dropped their long-range fuel tanks, and we dropped our tanks as we dove after the fleeing enemy. I got in one short burst of cannon fire before the Messerschmitts drew out of range. They maintained a steady dive to 14,000 feet, still staying ahead of us, but the gap was small enough to leave us some hope of combat. We were screaming across the Adriatic Sea toward Albania, which is less than one hundred miles from the Italian mainland.

As their dive became shallower, I kept my dive a little steeper, so that I pulled abreast of them, but at a considerably lower altitude. Then I pulled up the nose of my Spit to climb to their altitude. The Messerschmitts, seeing my intention, also started to climb, with the port machine lagging a bit behind the other. "Yellow 2," I called, "hold your fire. We'll catch these guys as soon as our blowers kick in."

Sure enough, at 19,500 feet my supercharger engaged with a roar and a jolt, causing my aircraft to leap ahead. Within seconds I had closed the gap to one hundred yards and opened fire with all my guns. As my bullets struck, my target jinked slightly to port, running into my massed fire and taking numerous strikes on his port wing root, engine, and cockpit. There was a small explosion, pieces flew off the '109, and a reddish brown smoke poured out, which enveloped both his aircraft and mine. He slowly rolled onto his back and headed straight down, with more pieces flying off the machine. I then turned my attention to the starboard '109. After a short burst my cannon jammed. I called to Bowring, who was now very close, to go in and finish him off. Bowring did just that and with a smart bit of accurate shooting, hit the '109 so hard that it exploded in front of our eyes.

It had been a long chase and the coast of Albania was appearing below us. It was time to retreat before fuel or enemy fighters became a problem.

Blackbeer congratulated us, and I thanked him for his excellent controlling, which brought about our interception. He phoned our success to the Wing, and everyone there was on the field waiting to greet us. For the only time in my operational career, I made a high speed dive over the 'drome and did a victory roll on the deck.[11]

Meanwhile, 417 Squadron had commenced operations from within Italy at Grottaglie in the heel, then moved north to Gioia del Colle, through Foggia on the Adriatic, and on to Triolo, directly east of Rome, by 18 October. From then on, "General Winter" played a major role in slowing the Allied advance, coupled with the fact that the Germans had dug in along the Sangro River and were not prepared to give up any more Italian real estate without stiff resistance. The havoc wrought on the Allied motorized division in the area by the entrenched elite German units was enormous. For the next five weeks, 417 flew convoy patrols, bomber escort missions, and standing patrols over Foggia, and also kept a watchful eye on German activities along the Sangro. However, the incessant rains and accompanying mud soon drove the Squadron to drier ground at Canne near Termoli, still on the Adriatic coast.

At this time, Stan Turner took command of the Wing (244), while the scrappy Bert Houle was promoted to Squadron Leader and command of 417 Squadron. Early in December, Stocky Edwards was posted to the Squadron for a short tour as a supernumerary prior to getting command of 92 (RAF) Squadron. Edwards describes his short stay with the Windsors, and the opportunity for him to fly a fine new variant of a proven aircraft:

> I flew ten sorties with 417 Squadron. The squadrons of the Wing operated off a strip or single runway made of perforated steel planking (PSP) that was interlocked in sections. The base was referred to as Canne, near Termoli, approximately eighty miles north of Foggia, on the east side of Italy on the Adriatic coast. This was a complete change from the desert. It was the winter season and weather conditions were normal for the area — wet and damp with mud everywhere.
>
> Over green fields and trees and surrounded by high mountains in the central regions, the Squadron flew Spitfire VIIIs. They were all brand new, and what a beautiful aircraft to fly. Normal cruising speed wasn't much faster than the Kittyhawk IIIs, but you could open the throttle and feel an immediate and positive response. The Spitfire was as fast as the '109 and it could catch the enemy in a climb or dive. My experience flying the '109F was that, as the speed increased, the stick forces increased, indicating very heavy wing loading. The Spitfire was light on the elevators at all speeds. Indeed, it was fast and smooth, making it a real joy to fly. In order to fully appreciate the outstanding qualities of a Spitfire, pilots should have first been required to do a tour of ops on Kittyhawks.[12]

Nineteen forty-three would also be characterized by distinct Allied reversals of fortune in the Far East. In fact, as exemplified by the Battles of Midway and the Coral Sea the year before, Allied naval power was already dominant in the Central Pacific. Control of the Solomon Islands was fiercely contested, although Guadacanal ultimately fell to the Americans in early February. During the same month, the southeastern end of New Guinea was also wrested from the Japanese by a joint force of Australians and Americans. By June, the Japanese were completely on the defensive throughout the Pacific. MacArthur was progressing steadily westward along the northern coast of New Guinea and Admiral Halsey was doggedly island-hopping through the Solomons towards Rabaul.

Burma, however, was another matter. When the monsoons arrived in 1942, all of the country except a particularly slender belt in the extreme north had been conquered by the Japanese. The danger to India, specifically the city of Calcutta and the province of Bengal, was patently obvious. But with an extensive infusion of air resources into the theatre, coupled with the construction of an unprecedented number of new airfields, Lord Wavell was able to turn a tenuous defensive position into a series of limited offensive operations. The First Arakan campaign, fought between the end of 1942 and May 1943, was intended to recapture the key airfield at Akyab and oust the Japanese from the Burmese coast on the Mayu Peninsula. although this land campaign ended in failure for the Allies, excellent air support was provided by the RAF throughout.

Simultaneously with this coastal action, a fascinating engagement was being fought in the Burmese interior. Seven columns of Chindits, jungle-trained specialist troops under the able command of a British Brigadier named Orde Wingate, created a great deal of confusion and mayhem behind enemy lines. Entirely sustained by extremely hazardous air drops, most frequently conducted in the dead of night, these brave troops left an impressive 1,000-mile swath of destroyed lines of communication and bridges in their wake. Then the 1943 iteration of monsoons, which arrived in June, temporarily hampered all further progress.

By this time there were fifty-three combatant squadrons in the region, seventeen of which were fighter units equipped with the ubiquitous Hurricane, although by October Spitfires were beginning to arrive in the theatre. As the year wore on, South East Asia Command was formed under Lord Mountbatten, and a number of "softening-up" limited offensive operations were launched, prior to a second attempt to retake the airfield at Akyab. Calcutta harbour was attacked heavily at this time, but now both the Japanese raiders and, to a lesser extent, the defenders suffered substantial losses. Both sides fielded improved equipment, but by year's end the excellent Spitfire VIII, now arriving in substantial numbers, was proving to be more than a match for the Nakajima Ki 44 "Tojo" fighter favoured by the

Japanese.[13] Al Corston, a full-blooded Cree Indian, relates some of his adventures from the period while serving with 67 (RAF) Squadron, starting with his arrival in India:

It was necessary for us to get some refresher flying, so thirty-two of us were sent to Poona where they had a few Harvards. Later, I ended up at Risalpur on the Northwest Frontier Khyber Pass flying some beat-up old Hurricanes that had seen better days. I thought: "What the hell am I doing here?" I had read about this place in my history books and I had read Rudyard Kipling: "Me, a Cree from Northern Ontario!" I made the best of it and after a few hours on Hurricanes I was on the move again. This time I went across the breadth of India to join 67 Squadron on the Arakan Burma front. My social life had so deteriorated by this time that everything was looking good to me — especially the girls. I didn't care if they had rings in their noses and ears and bangles on their feet, they were beautiful!

When I joined 67 Squadron I found one other Canadian there — Aubrey Bond, who was later killed in action. There was one American whose name was Jackson, an English CO, and five more RAF, two Australians, and all the rest were New Zealanders who had come through the British retreat from Malaya and Burma. They were a grand bunch!

The Squadron carried out every conceivable type of duty sent down by 224 Group Operations and Army Intelligence; Upper Air Observations (Met. Flights — it was primitive out there), escorts of all types (supply drops, dive bombers), long range strikes (we carried long range tanks and four 20mm cannon — poor Hurricane), scrambles and convoy patrols. One squadron even started chemical warfare by spraying the jungle with DDT. The irony of this was that it also benefitted the enemy. We also did a type of napalm bombing by dropping our long range tanks on target and in turn, strafing these with cannon that carried incendiary ammunition which fired the dropped fuel.

We carried on these duties during the late summer and on 1 December 1943 we were withdrawn to Alipure, Calcutta for rest and the rumour of new equipment. We had done our jobs dutifully, although our poor Hurricanes were out-classed by the Jap Oscar which would come over at their best height of 10,000– 14,000 feet on escorts and sweeps. I never saw one blow up in front of me, but I don't know how I missed. One time we were scrambled after "thirty-plus" and we all became separated and there it was. A most beautiful coloured Jap Oscar fighter: bright pale green, dark green and light brown, and the biggest meatball on its side. It was a beauty! It was so close as he passed in front of me that I could see the pilot; I was in a shallow dive looking for the bombers which had been in and out of the cloud and it seemed a shame to shoot such a beautiful thing. I let go with all guns as he pulled around in front of me — how could I miss? I never claimed because in a short time there was one up my ass and I dived for the ground hanging on my straps. When I straightened out near treetop level I was alone — whew! When I arrived back there were a couple of holes in the tailplane. The rest of my tour on Hurricanes was the same: scrambles, rhubarbs, convoy patrols, army cooperations, long range escorts and just before we left the front I had qualified for night intruder duties. This happened after three nights of sector reconnaissance and circuits. It promised to be a lonely job, but all the senior pilots had done them. Night Intruder sorties consisted of patrols along the rivers and coast until near the point of no return. We shot up river traffic which the Japs used at night and we only went out on clear moonlit nights, when we could see below — especially the wake of the boats in the water. A trip lasted three to four hours (with long range tanks) and when tired, our eyes played tricks on us. There were some funny tales of what we saw . . . for instance, one Hurri pilot came back one night and reported that he had shot up a large boat and had set it on fire. The next day he was summoned before the CO and he arrived anticipating a recommendation for a gong. He was told with good humour that the boat he had set on fire and had presumably sunk was in reality a small island in the middle of the river. The swift current made wake-like waves off the island. He slunk out of the office amid great laughter — no DFC, only Pilot Officer Prune's fabled Most Highly Derogatory Order of the Irremovable Finger . . .

[No.] 67 Squadron was finally pulled out of the front line on 1 December 1943 and took up residence at Alipore aerodrome in Calcutta for rest, but the Japanese Air Force were still harassing the Squadron. On 5 December 1943 they carried out a devastating punch at Calcutta harbour to slow up the flow of supplies to the offensive on the Imphal Kohima area where they had penetrated into India. They came over at mid-morning in two waves of 36 bombers with a mixed escort of 100-plus Oscar and Zero fighters. I scrambled with the lead Section, unaware that my radio was unserviceable — I thought it was a practice; Japs wouldn't raid Calcutta in daylight — too far from their bases, and especially we wouldn't expect to meet their fighters. It was a well-planned raid and their intelligence was aware of the fact that the *lone* Spitfire squadron (136) had just departed the day before.

Four of us climbed line astern and soon I saw my Section spread out left and right in battle formation. I was on the extreme right of the Section and still didn't know what was going on — I had no radio. I should have returned to base, but kept on as I didn't realize it was a true scramble. I kept checking all knobs and connections with my head in the cockpit *for only a few seconds* and when I looked up I was all alone. I had not heard the "Tally Ho." I spotted my Section away below and gave chase — looked around, and in disbelief saw two grey radial-engined fighters on my tail getting ready to clobber me — Jap Zeros? Once again I rolled on my back and dived inverted, hanging on my straps, as the engine coughed and the aircraft shuddered. On roll out, I looked behind and was alone again but the engine was very rough now. Crossing my path was another Hurricane crash landing in a paddy field and above me was a body coming down in a parachute — ours or theirs?

I pranged in a paddy field in a cloud of dust and as I jumped out, the cockpit filled with fumes. I thought there was a fire, but it turned out to be the hot glycol. As I stood there, trying to piece together what the hell had happened, some natives came up and took me to their village and put me in one of their bashas. After a while, I was summoned outside. "Good show," I thought, "now I'll get a lift back." Instead, I was confronted by two Indian Army officers and a few soldiers. As soon as they saw me, the officers drew their pistols and the soldiers came to readiness. "Damn," I thought, "they think I'm Japanese because of my likeness." I had no ID except my dog-tags which I kept waving at them as I jabbered at them that I was a Canadian — RAF! They were very apprehensive, but I finally convinced them when I told them where my Hurricane was. It was getting late in the evening and I guessed that I was reported missing. Finally, they got through to someone and I was given a lift back to the Squadron. I had been gone ten hours by this time. We had lost three Hurricanes out of that Section with one pilot, Aubrey Bond, RCAF, killed in action, and my Number

1 and myself pranged but OK. The Squadron immediately had two cannon removed from each aircraft until we got our Spitfire VIIIs. I suppose they thought that would improve performance?

Those were the highlights of my Hurricane tour, and I stayed on to do some more operations on Spitfires, which is another story. My social life, however, was improving. A madam of a swank social club fell in love with me — I had promised her a fur coat. Why do they think Canadians all own fur coats? I hope she didn't get too cold because it could get cold after dark during their winter. When I wasn't flying I spent many hours relaxing and she treated me royally — I guess I was young and dashing — and a fighter pilot! We got along marvellously and I had many fond memories to dwell on when I returned to operations and that Godforsaken jungle.[14]

Back in North America, 1943 would see an end to the backwater Aleutians campaign. During the spring, 111 Squadron's Kittyhawk pilots started converting to the fighter-bomber role, a task for which their aircraft were much more admirably suited. In March, 15 Squadron replaced 8 Squadron and moved forward to Amchitka, working in concert with the USAAF, where a pool of 24 P40Ks were available for operations. The Americans began their offensive to recapture Kiska on 18 April, and during the following month 14 Squadron flew eighty-eight ground-attack sorties in support of this effort. In mid-May, 111 Squadron took 14 Squadron's place on the front line, flying a similar one-month tour. Each Squadron then flew another thirty-day tour on a rotational basis. In July, 111 Squadron gave its remaining aircraft to 14 Squadron and returned to Canada; 14 Squadron completed one last round of operations in August, then returned to Canada in September at the end of the campaign.[15]

Bob Morrow, who as a Wing Commander headed the RCAF's efforts in the Aleutians from Anchorage, reflects on the campaign in terms of weather, cooperation from the American allies, and a frigid dip he experienced in Alaskan waters one day in May 1943:

The weather in the Aleutians was pretty bad, no doubt due to the Japanese Current meeting the Bering Sea in the region. Interestingly enough, the Aleutians were never hot, but neither were they cold. Snow was a rarity and never seemed to last on the ground.

In thinking of the Campaign, I would like to stress the

extremely good relations that we had with the Americans. Anything that they had was ours for the asking, or even taking. Perhaps this was to some degree a reflection of the Commanding General, Simon Bolivar Buckner, one of the finest men I ever met. He had retired and made his home on Kodiak Island. At the outbreak of war, he was recalled to service and given command of Alaska and the Islands. Later on, he was in command of U.S. forces on Okinawa. Unfortunately, in the closing phase of that action, he was killed by a stray shell. A great loss . . .

General Butler was the senior USAAF officer, and he later commanded all of the U.S. fighter forces in Europe. These senior U.S. officers were a terrific bunch, and they also played host to many of the visiting VIPs that I had to contend with.

Major Chennault was a USAAF friend, and his father was famous for his activities in China. Colonel Jim Walt was also a good friend, who had been at Pearl Harbour on 7 December 1941. When the U.S. recaptured Attu from the Japs, Jim led a flypast of P38s to beat off a bomber attack, and he was credited with shooting three down.

It's a good question as to what the Japanese were even *doing* in the Aleutians . . . First, the attack on Dutch Harbour, but then their establishment of two bases on Kiska and Attu . . . Yes, it was an effort to divert U.S. forces, but perhaps there was more to it than that. Anyone stupid enough to attack Pearl and start a war with the U.S. could not have been too bright, and therefore could have been capable of such outlandish activity . . .

Regarding my crash at Amchitka where I came to grief . . . no excuses here, just plain carelessness. The original strip on the island, which was later replaced by a major runway, was made by dyking off part of a bay. The strip was gravel and backed up against a hill, making it one way — regardless of wind. You landed in from the sea and took off towards the sea. On this day, 6 May 1943, I set off in a Curtiss P40 with a fairly stiff tailwind, and had carelessly not locked the hood closed. On takeoff, the hood rolled open and the cockpit filled with dust. I took my hand off the throttle to close the hood, then realized that I was running out of runway. I jammed it into War Emergency Boost and tried to heave the aeroplane over the dyke. I struck heavily — the port oleo came right through the wing and the prop diameter was decreased by about a foot. Fortunately, I managed to stagger into the air. My intent was to fly over the island and then to bail out, but the aeroplane was in bad shape and shaking apart. The engine cowl came off and finally I had an engine fire. With about 150 gallons of high octane practically in my lap, I left hurriedly at an altitude of about 1200 feet or so. I could not roll the aeroplane to fall out, so I went over the port side, striking the tailplane and fracturing some bones in my back. The chute deployed, and when I came to it was open. There was no sign of my P40.

I discarded my flying boots and dropped into a very heavy sea. I had a one-man dinghy which opened and inflated, just like the book said, but I had a big struggle getting into it. My next problem was that I was being blown out towards a very rocky reef, so I got out the paddles and set to work to miss it. Fortunately for me, there was a U.S. Army detachment nearby. Several soldiers got a rope and came out on the reef in heavy surf and grabbed the dinghy. Small wonder I am pro-American!

Years later, a man stopped me on the street in Montreal. "Is your name Morrow?" He was one of those soldiers . . .[16]

In Canada, new units were still forming, although the fighter element remained relatively static. Like so many other aspiring fighter pilots "champing at the bit" to get into the shooting war, Bill Gould of Fredericton, New Brunswick, was frustrated by seemingly endless months of instructional duties in Canada. Though he would eventually fulfill his wish to fly combat operations on Spitfires in Europe, he first had to learn the fighter trade on one of the east-coast Home Defence squadrons. Bill explains:

In November 1942, after instructing at Summerside, Prince Edward Island, Moncton, New Brunswick, and Centralia, Ontario, I was finally posted to No. 1 Operational Training Unit, Bagotville, Quebec, on Hurricanes. I thought, "This time I'll get overseas for sure. No more instruction for me!" Well, I was partially right. I was transferred to No. 128 Fighter Squadron at Sydney, Nova Scotia, on Hurricanes. At least it had nothing to do with instructing . . .

Life on an east coast Squadron was certainly different than instructing. There were no more of those boring, repetitious pre-flight and post-flight briefings, no more responsibility for the many errors a student can make while training. Flying was now more relaxing, a real pleasure to be enjoyed for the flying itself. Many of the exercises we carried out, such as practice formations, scrambles, cine gun attacks, Rhubarbs, and night flying, were similar to those at the OTU in Bagotville. They were almost completely unrelated to operational flying, but they did hone up our skills in these facets of flying that make up the fighter pilot's trade.

On 24 June 1943, the Squadron was posted to Torbay, Newfoundland. I travelled over in a Douglas Digby, the predecessor of the DC3 or Dakota. This was the largest aircraft I had flown in at that time. Torbay was situated a few miles from St. John's, and the Station was well equipped with hangars, Messes, and everything needed to handle three squadrons. The other two Squadrons were 5 BR (Bomber Reconnaissance) and 10 BR, equipped with Canso and Lockheed Ventura aircraft respectively.

The atmosphere was completely different than Sydney. Wartime conditions were in effect. The Station was completely blacked out at night, and the food was similar to the menus we saw in England and Europe later in the war. Almost all vegetables came in powdered form, even powdered eggs for breakfast and powdered ice cream for dessert. The main protein seemed to be whale meat. Some whale cuts were not too bad, but mostly the meat was tough with a fishy, smoky taste. It didn't take long for the officer pilots to find the Crows Nest, an upstairs club on Water Street in St. John's, where cod tongues, steak, and other good food could be obtained. We also found a couple of pretty good clubs, the Buena Vista and the Old Colony Club, near St. John's, and they provided reasonably good entertainment.

Flying at Torbay took on an operational atmosphere. The Cansos and Venturas were almost constantly on patrol, and they occasionally returned to base after encountering a German submarine. These attacks bolstered everyone's morale.

Shortly after we reached Torbay, someone in our armament section devised a way to make bomb racks out of the angle iron used in the double bunks so familiar to all service personnel. The racks were okayed by Eastern Air Command Headquarters in Halifax, and for the rest of the time at Torbay we were able to carry a depth charge under each wing. Four of our Hurricanes were fitted with these racks, and two aircraft were kept on constant readiness. Also, with twelve machine guns on each aircraft, the Hurricanes constituted a very formidable weapon against an enemy submarine.

A British Major, an armament expert, arrived about this time from London. The purpose of his visit was to discuss with aircrew the latest tactics of German submarines. Instead of diving immediately on seeing a patrol aircraft, the subs were now armed with deck guns and were shooting back. Several patrol aircraft had been shot down. All available crew from the three Torbay squadrons were called together for a talk by the Major, who spent most of his time raving about the Hurricanes armed with depth charges that he had seen on the flight line. "In all my travels to squadrons around the world," he said, "I have never seen such a deadly combination. The Number One aircraft could clear the deck of all living things with one burst from his twelve machine guns, and Number Two could drop his depth charges at leisure. It's marvellous!" After his talks, the Major visited our Squadron and talked with the pilots. He left an Air Ministry address with Squadron Leader Cannon, the CO, and made him promise to forward to him the results of any encounters a Hurricane might have with a German submarine. "No matter where I am in the world, I'll get the message." There was no message to pass on to the Major for two reasons. Firstly, we never did get to attack a German sub, and secondly, the same day as his visit, a Canso carrying the Major to Botwood, Newfoundland, crashed while landing on glassy water, killing everyone on board, including the Major.

It was only natural that our pilots, after acquiring the depth charges, were looking for some suitable targets on which to practice. No land target would do it, since the depth charges had to sink to a pre-set depth before exploding. Ingenuity apparently knows no limits. After a few weeks, a message arrived from Eastern Air Command Headquarters stating that information had been obtained to the effect that aircraft were known to be dumping depth charges on whales off eastern Newfoundland. The same message relegated to the fires of hell any pilot caught performing such a dastardly deed. They probably never even considered that the pilots were only retaliating against their monotonous diet of whale meat. Someone then mentioned that he had dropped some depth charges on an iceberg, so icebergs became the new targets. Since depth charges were in unlimited supply, we spent many happy days trying to make ice cubes out of icebergs.

Navigation posed the biggest problem for 128 Squadron pilots. Our radios permitted us to receive takeoff and landing instructions from the control tower, and we could talk to the other aircraft in our Squadron, but that was it. We had no approach aids of any kind, no radio range, no ADF homings, nothing. Navigation was simply a matter of map reading and dead reckoning. Since many of our trips were scrambles to the sites of reported submarine activity, a primitive but effective system was devised to aid our navigation. On a table in our flight room we had a large map of our flying area, including a large area of the ocean off the coast of Newfoundland's Avalon Peninsula. Superimposed on the map, centered at the Torbay airport, was a large plastic square subdivided into many smaller squares like a checkerboard. Each smaller square was again divided into four parts. EACHQ had the same setup. EACHQ in Halifax would call in a message reporting submarine activity in area P4. This meant the submarine was in the lower right hand section of P square. After that it was simply a matter of drawing a track line to the area, measuring the distance, applying variation, wind and time to target, followed by a scramble.

In good weather, these trips could be quite interesting. Occasionally we would find ships burning in the target area, a positive indication of submarine activity, but we were never able to sight a periscope. We would have given anything for the opportunity to attack a submarine with our enormous striking power, but we were never able to spot that tell-tale periscope.

I recall one morning being awakened at five o'clock on a miserable day and being told that there was submarine activity off St. John's and that we were to get airborne immediately. I awakened a grumpy Number Two and we proceeded out into one of those cold, damp, dark winter mornings which one encountered quite often in Newfoundland. We took off in the darkness for a point about forty miles east of St. John's. This time we did see burning ships, several in fact. I wondered then, as I do now, what we were doing out over the Atlantic at that hour of the morning looking for submarines in the dark. By the time it became light enough to see properly, we had used up so much fuel that it was time to return to base. Even that provided a bit of a problem on submarine patrols, particularly if the weather was not so good. After patrolling over the water for forty minutes or so, the chances of flying directly to St. John's, after a bit of mental dead reckoning, were virtually nil. The coastline of Newfoundland was so featureless that a map was of little use. We simply figured out a mental course for home, and then added on about thirty degrees. It was intended that this course would enable us to make a landfall north of St. John's. It was then just a matter of turning left and flying along the coast until St. John's harbour came into sight. And it worked. No one ever got lost on a patrol.

Along with submarine patrols, 128 Squadron carried out a fair number of exercises with the Army and Navy in addition to our normal Squadron exercises. On 6 July 1943, the USS *Wasp*, an American aircraft carrier, arrived in St. John's harbour after completing a tour of duty against the Japanese in the Pacific Theater. The *Wasp* carried a full complement of Grumman Wildcat fighters. That evening, many of the Wildcat pilots arrived at our Mess in Torbay. We heard some pretty hairy stories of events that some of them had experienced in the Pacific. After a few rounds from the bar, a discussion developed regarding the merits of the Wildcat versus the Hurricane. It continued until the Americans issued a challenge. They would have four Wildcats at Torbay the following morning. The tactics were simple. Four pairs, each consisting of a Wildcat and a Hurricane, would meet at an agreed upon altitude, in each of the four quadrants of the sky, north, west, south and east of the airport. They would meet, fly in formation for a minute or two, then break up and approach each other head on. From then on it was a straight dogfight, with each pilot trying to get on the other fellow's tail. Flight Commanders were not allowed to fly on either side. We were part of the large audience assembled on the ground to see the show. Everything went according to plan. The aircraft met, flew in formation for a minute or two, and then began dogfighting. In a couple of minutes there were four Hurricanes on the tails of four Wildcats, and they stayed there, to great applause and shouts from the audience below.

After landing, everyone adjourned to the hangar to hash over the situation. The Americans seemed completely nonplused by the turn of events. They could not understand how things could have turned out the way they had. It must have been some kind of aberration that could never happen again, so they issued another challenge for the following afternoon. This time, they announced, Flight Commanders could fly, so I decided to get in on the fun in Hurricane 5485. That afternoon the two readiness aircraft, equipped with depth charges, were sitting on the tarmac. "Butch" Washburn and "Gibby" Gibbs were the readiness pilots that day and Butch said to me, "You know Bill, I think we can take on these buggers with those readiness aircraft." "Why not?" I replied . . . "Have a go." We lined up a fourth pilot and the exercise was carried out all over again with four Hurricanes on the tails of four Wildcats once again. Butch Washburn was so keen that he stayed on the Wildcat's tail until it landed on the runway. The Americans were forced to admit that the Hurricane was the better aircraft, even when it was ladened with depth charges. We had a party in the Mess that night with the Americans becoming more generous and more lavish with their praise as the evening wore on. According to some of them, if 128 Squadron, complete with aircraft and personnel, could suddenly be transported to the Pacific Theater, we would make short work of the Japanese Air Force. Yes, it was a great party . . .[17]

With the U.S. firmly in control of the Japanese in the Pacific, however, the direct threat to North America had substantially abated. A full-scale invasion of the European continent was imminent, and all surplus fighter resources were required for that effort. During the final quarter of 1943, six of the home-based fighter squadrons were selected for overseas service, which would involve re-equipping and renumbering to "400 series" designations. Three of the squadrons would go to war as a fighter-bomber Wing flying Typhoons, while the other three would re-equip with Spitfires in the day fighter role:

OLD DESIGNATION	NEW DESIGNATION	AIRCRAFT
118 Squadron (Kittyhawks)	438 Squadron	Typhoons
123 Squadron (Hurricanes)	439 Squadron	Typhoons
111 Squadron (Kittyhawks)	440 Squadron	Typhoons
125 Squadron (Hurricanes)	441 Squadron	Spitfires
14 Squadron (Kittyhawks)	442 Squadron	Spitfires
127 Squadron (Hurricanes)	443 Squadron	Spitfires

Gord Ockenden flew Hurricanes with 127 Squadron at Gander, Newfoundland, and Dartmouth, Nova Scotia, as a nineteen-year-old in 1943. He then went to war with the unit in its new guise as 443 Squadron, distinguishing himself in combat over the Continent and winning the DFC in the process. Gord recalls life at Gander on 127 during 1943:

The Squadron was housed in the old Trans Canada Airlines (TCA) hangar next to the control tower. When we were in a controlled sequence, we would take off from one of the prepared runways, but since the confluence of all the runways was directly in front of the TCA tarmac, it was possible to do "scramble" takeoffs straight ahead, inclined into the wind. Practice scrambles of the two alert Hurricane 2Bs (now designated Hurricane XXIIs) on actual scrambles were initiated from the control tower by Klaxon horn. When I joined the Squadron, there was terrific competition with respect to the fastest scramble time. My first four such "run, jump in an aircraft already started, and go" scrambles took only 25–35 seconds. We didn't put the 'chute straps, harness, headset, etc. on until after we were airborne . . . a disaster waiting to happen. This procedure was changed after a Hurricane ended up on its nose with a broken prop during takeoff.

The Squadron role was coastal defence against a threatening German naval force that, in fact, never came near our colony of Newfoundland, considered at the time to be overseas service for Canadians. We also did dawn, day and dusk patrols on the alert for submarines or fishing vessels which were assisting submarines. Patrols out to sea — 50 to 100 miles — meant loss of radio contact after coastal passage. If you saw anything or had an emergency, then you headed for shore to establish radio contact! Real efficient?

Social life on the huge U.S./Canadian overseas refueling stop for ferry operations to Europe was limited. Our "Queen Bee" for the WDs was Flight Officer Bea, and she was dead against rank fraternization. We officer pilots used to sneak down the Newfie railroad track area with very agreeable girlfriends for picnics, parties, etc. One of E.P. Taylor's daughters, a WD, met the man she subsequently married (Flight Lieutenant Fred Ward) that way. He was killed in France on Spitfires shortly after D-Day . . .

The USAAF hospital on the far side of the field from the RCAF detachment had a Sergeant who would sell us five gallon jugs of embalming alcohol for about $4.00. When mixed in a large garbage pail with eight tins of grapefruit juice, it provided about four bedroom areas in Bachelor Officer's Quarters with a hell of a cheap party.

After our move from Gander to Dartmouth we continued training, high altitude tests (34,000 feet in a non-pressurized Hurricane where the roof of your mouth dropped onto your lower teeth) and much formation and low level flying. We also kept two-plane detachments at Penfield Ridge in New Brunswick doing fighter attack training against Hudsons and Venturas, and at Yarmouth, Nova Scotia, working against six and nine plane formations of

Swordfish. We got so that we could fly fighter formation by instinct, and it sure helped later in Europe.

Several of us had Halifax/Dartmouth girlfriends who kept tuned in on our antiquated HF radio frequencies, and we often set-up and finalized dates as we returned from dusk patrols over those frequencies.

We also did many low level shipping patrols and on weekends, when the ambitious sailing amateurs got out of Halifax harbour, we were known on occasion to "jump skim" over a small sailboat and in the process, cause considerable sail difficulty. The Navy troops later got even in the war theatre by shooting at us in our Hurricanes and Spitfires, and anything else that flew near them.

One of our more ambitious birdmen, Syd Bregman, overshot on landing a Hurricane at Dartmouth and went through the tarmac vehicle control barrier and down the access road. He nosed up just in front of the Station Headquarters. The walk to the CO's office was only a few yards to meet a very irate Station Commander . . .

We were also the test squadron for a relief bag device similar to that used by the streetcar motormen of the period. A suitable tube mounted over the penis drained into a flexible bag tied to one's leg. Unfortunately, they didn't modify the motorman's model and sloppy flying or negative "G" returned the contents to the owner's crotch! Needless to say, unsatisfactory reports ensued and the test was terminated. We went back to using a straight tube with the contents vented overboard into the aircraft's slipstream.[18]

Canadian fighter pilots serving in home defence duties had certainly "made their own fun" during 1943. But with the Japanese no longer a threat to North America, the U-boat menace largely contained, and the Allied invasion of northwest Europe imminent, Gord Ockenden and his friends were eagerly awaiting their deployment to England and the opportunity to test their mettle in a real shooting war.

---

1   John D. R. Rawlings, *The History of the Royal Air Force*, p. 109
2   Lavigne and Edwards, *Kittyhawk Pilot*, p. 263, and J. F. Edwards, letter to author, September 1995
3   Bill Olmsted, *Blue Skies*, p. 90
4   Bert Houle, letter to author, April 1993
5   Hedley Everard, *A Mouse in My Pocket*, p. 266

6 John D. R. Rawlings, p. 138
7 Gordon Wilson, letter to author, May 1993
8 Bill Olmsted, p. 119
9 Lloyd Hunt, *We Happy Few*, p. 117
10 John D. R. Rawlings, p. 139
11 Bill Olmsted, p. 146
12 Lavigne and Edwards, p. 272
13 John D. R. Rawlings, p. 170
14 Lloyd Hunt, *We Band of Brothers*, p. 58
15 Christopher Shores, *The History of the Royal Canadian Air Force*, p. 37
16 Bob Morrow, letter to author, August 1993
17 Bill Gould, letter to author, August 1993
18 Gord Ockenden, letter to author, July 1993

7

RELENTLESS
ADVANCE
1944

"The Mosquito was screaming in every joint."
— DAVE MCINTOSH, 418 SQUADRON

With the dawn of 1944, Axis forces were in full retreat on all fronts and on the high seas. Though many bloody battles lay ahead, Allied confidence in an ultimate triumph was pervasive. In the East, the Soviets had retaken most of the Ukraine. In the central region, Somolensk had been liberated, and in the process, the Soviets had soundly thrashed three separate German armies and destroyed highly fortified belts of German defences.[1] By mid-January, the Russians were attacking on a 120-mile front in the north from Lake Ilmen to Leningrad, a city long under siege. Soon, onslaughts west of Kiev would push the Germans back to the old Polish border, and in the extreme south, back across the Dniestr River and the Carpathian Mountains into Romania and Poland. In the Pacific, MacArthur's island-hopping campaign was doggedly driving the Japanese back towards the Home Islands, while Allied control of the oceans was near absolute. In Italy, although the rains and mud of winter would temporarily slow the Allied advance, great gains were in the offing. In England, preparations continued at a frenzied pitch for the cross-Channel invasion that was soon to come. At home, the fear of a Japanese invasion on the Pacific Coast and in Alaska had been completely eliminated. *Going My Way* would dominate the box offices that year and would win Bing Crosby a Best Actor Oscar. Ingrid Bergman would win for the ladies in *Gaslight*. "Sentimental Journey," "Swinging on a Star," and "Don't Fence Me In" would dominate the pop charts, the Saint Louis Cardinals would win the World Series, and the Montreal Canadiens would triumph in hockey to capture the Stanley Cup.

Back in the British Isles, the Spitfire Wings, though still scoring, were not being presented with nearly as many air-to-air kill opportunities as their American counterparts. U.S. fighter pilots in their long-range Mustangs were able to provide continuous, round-trip escort to the "Big Friends" of the Eighth Air Force, now fully immersed in their campaign to bomb the Third Reich into oblivion. In order to take the fight to the enemy, Rhubarbs and Rangers were still popular ways of letting off steam and contributing to the war effort. If the Germans were suffering grave shortages in other areas, they never seemed to run out of flak, however. Karl Linton's experience early in the new year, when he took a direct hit on the windscreen from flak, underscores just how devastating air-to-ground operations could be for Spitfires over northwest Europe.

On January 3rd 1944, I was leading a group of four on a Ranger . . . just 50'–100' above the waves . . . to the Bernay area of France. We climbed to clear the cliffs, houses, telephone lines, even farmers' fences, shooting at anything the enemy showed, when I saw a bright flash 1/8 to 1/4 mile ahead, dead level, and coming from a haystack. I ducked my head and put all the "Gs" I could on that old Spit . . . I came out of my "grey-out" in the clouds, "X" thousands of feet up . . . no radio, no team mates, no artificial horizon, no altimeter, no compass, and no clues. I then went into a spin, pulled out of it after I got out of the clouds, then headed back to England using the old sun. I finally recognized Beachy Head and landed at Biggin Hill. I guess that Wing Commander Buck McNair must have seen me land, because he came out to meet me in a jeep. I was white all over with powdered glass, so Buck took me to the hospital and they pulled small pieces of glass out of the back of my head and my eyes. Fortunately, I didn't have any *really* bad cuts, but Buck thought it would be best if I spent the night with him before returning to my home base. I did, and we managed to down quite a few beers that night . . .[2]

Two months after Karl Linton's narrow escape, another Canadian fighter pilot was not so lucky on a low-level mission, although he and Karl would live to serve together on 417 Squadron later during the war. Dave Goldberg recalls:

. . . During my initial tour with 403 Squadron at Kenley starting on 19 July 1943, we were involved in the main with routine fighter sweeps and bomber escort operations, which were somewhat unproductive and did not result in significant fighter opposition. There were times when our only function seemed to be providing target practice for enemy anti-aircraft personnel. Personal experience has shown me that the anti-aircraft fire on low level operations proved to be rather telling. On 8 March 1944, I was shot down over Occupied France, due to extremely effective flak while I was engaged in a low-level Ranger mission. On the same mission, another Spitfire crashed and blew up, killing the pilot, and yet another aircraft was damaged, but managed to get back to England. I crash landed in France but with the help of the French Resistance and considerable good fortune, I evaded capture and eventually reached England in May, after a memorable journey through France and Spain to Gibraltar.[3]

In early 1944, the RCAF day fighter force in the United Kingdom consisted of 401, 411, and 412 Squadrons, known as 126 Airfield, at Biggin Hill under Buck McNair, and 403, 416, and 421 Squadrons, known as 127 Airfield, at Kenley under Hugh Godefroy. Both of these units were considered formations of 83 Group of the embryonic Second Tactical Air Force, and although 402 Squadron was not initially allocated to 2TAF, that would change in the fullness of time. 2TAF had officially formed the previous November, and divided its fighter and fighter-bomber assets into two Groups. Number 83 Group was tasked to support the British Second Army, while 84 Group's mandate was to support the Canadian First Army. As fate would have it, since the Canadian army advanced along the coast and the British army's thrust took it through central Belgium and Holland, 83 Group's area became the focal point of the majority of air combat operations on the Continent. The initial nomenclature of "Airfield" was only temporary, and the new units soon became "Wings."

In February, the number of Canadian day fighter squadrons garrisoned in the British Isles was increased to ten, when 441, 442, and

443 Squadrons collectively formed at Digby as 144 Wing on Spitfire IXs under the able leadership of an old British friend, Johnnie Johnson. The legendary Leicestershireman was glad to be back commanding Canadians and remembers his first impressions of his three new Squadron Commanders:

. . . George Hill, a wiry, tousle-headed veteran of twenty-six, from Pictou in Nova Scotia, commanded 441 Squadron. He was one of the few recipients of the DFC and two Bars and he had shot down his first Hun during the Dieppe raid. Later, in North Africa, George led the famous "treble one" (111) Squadron and piled up a score of fourteen victories. He was a man of strong character who knew his own mind and stated his opinions with forthright candor. He would be a good man in a tight spot, and I couldn't have a better or more experienced Squadron Commander.

The quiet, well-built "Brad" Walker commanded 442 Squadron, and also held the DFC. He had already completed one tour of fighter operations from England and had led his Squadron when it was based in the Aleutians before coming to Digby.

The third Squadron Commander, Wally McLeod, was a tall, alert, cool-eyed man of almost thirty from Regina in Saskatchewan. He was credited with thirteen victories, most of which he scored over Malta, where he was a contemporary of Buck McNair and Screwball Beurling. He moved about the room with a restlessness which I came to know well during the following months. Wally had the reputation of being a deadly shot and very fast on the draw.

"A killer, if ever there was one," I thought. "I'm pleased he's with me and not on the other side. He might be inclined to stick his neck out too far, so I'll watch him."[4]

A rapid build-up of air forces was occurring in more than just the day fighter community. Early in the new year, 438, 439, and 440 Squadrons formed in the fighter-bomber role on Hurricane IVs as 143 Airfield. In February, the new unit traded in their elderly Hurricanes for robust, powerful Typhoon IBs, a mount which would carry the Wing to great distinction in the forthcoming months of bitter battles on the European continent. Desmond Scott, a distinguished New Zealander, describes what it was like to fly this enormous beast from the Hawker Aircraft Company:

At 1600 hours I was back at "A" Flight and surveying the cockpit of a Typhoon, which was like looking up at a second-storey window. The small glasshouse, streamlined into the fuselage and directly behind the large engine of this seven-ton monster, was nine feet above ground. You climbed up to it by placing the toes of your shoes into small covered recesses in the metal skin. These almost invisible steps had spring-loaded covers, which snapped back into position as soon as you extracted your toes. A rigger had already placed a parachute in the cockpit's metal bucket-type seat, and I lowered myself down onto it, linked up my harness, and strapped myself in securely.

I was already well familiar with the Typhoon's operating manual, and Murphy had positioned himself on the wing alongside the cockpit to give me detailed instructions on the starting-up procedure. He also reminded me of some of the Typhoon's less admirable characteristics. When I felt ready I waved Murphy away, donned my helmet and oxygen mask, and plugged in my earphones. Turning the petrol cock on to the gravity position, in case of pump failure during take-off, I actuated the two toggle pumps which would shoot a mixture of oil and petrol into the cylinders and alcohol and ether into the carburetors.

The 24 cylinders of the Napier Sabre engine were forced into life by what was known as a Koffman starter, which was itself motivated by a large shotgun-type cartridge. When fired, the expansion of this charge turned over the huge motor and acted like a one-shot self-starter. If the engine did not come to life with the first explosion you could guarantee to have a fire in the air intake, which was a large aperture in the centre of the radiator scoop situated directly under the engine housing. This scoop also contained the oil and glycol radiators. A short burst from a fire extinguisher into this flaming tunnel was normally sufficient to douse the flames.

I gave the thumbs up sign to the two riggers standing by with their fire extinguishers, switched on and pressed the starter button. There was a loud noise, a cross between a hiss and bang. The engine snarled, spat, and rumbled into life. The huge propeller began to rotate, and as I eased the throttle forward, the engine immediately settled into a more even and less rebellious rhythm. The two riggers put down their extinguishers and positioned themselves at either wing tip.

I rechecked the instrument panel, made sure the canopy was locked in position, and wound up my side window. Then I slowly pushed the throttle to give maximum revolutions and tested both magnetos. The Typhoon tugged, shook and roared, but there was barely a waver in the rev counter between one magneto and the other; so I eased back to less than quarter throttle, waved "chocks away," released the brakes, and began rolling out of the bay and on to the taxiway.

The first thing I noticed was the Typhoon's poor forward visibility. Although my seat was hoisted to its maximum height, I had to crab along in zigzag fashion. In a Hurricane or Spitfire, you could slide your canopy back and stand up if necessary, but this was not possible in the early Typhoons. Later they were to be fitted with a bubble-type hood which not only overcame the vision problem but also gave a tremendous all-round view — the best of any aircraft I ever flew.

I called the control tower for permission to take off. The morning's wind had died away and the indicator sock by the tower was hanging like a limp rag. I braced myself and taxied straight on to the runway and applied full brake. With the control column hard back in my lap, I opened up the motor to 3000 rpm to ensure that all the plugs were cleaned off after the slow revs. The aircraft strained at the leash until I eased back to about quarter boost. After lowering my seat and tightening my straps again, I carried out a final check of the instrument panel: oxygen five pounds — hydraulic pressure OK — flaps down 15 degrees — radiator flap open — pitch control in the "fine" position — throttle lever screwed tight.

I let go the brakes and slowly pushed the boost lever until it reached the fully-open position. She bounded forward at a great rate and tried to swing slightly to starboard. This tendency was easily corrected by applying a little left rudder. Then we thundered down the runway as straight as an arrow before rocketing into the sky in the direction of Chichester. I flicked up the lever operating the undercarriage hydraulics and felt the wheels thud into their wing bays. She sank a little as I raised the flaps, but soon recovered when I reduced the boost and eased her propeller into a coarser pitch. Before I could check out my instrument panel again we were already over Chichester, heading fast in the direction of Selsey Bill.

My Typhoon and I began our airborne association by climbing up to 15,000 feet, where I pulled her up straight onto her tail. After reaching her zenith, she spun off quickly, and I was agreeably surprised when she recovered almost as soon as I had applied corrective action. To make sure she was not fooling me I again put her into a spin, and once more she recovered beautifully. We then headed earthwards in a vertical power dive. As the speedo needle was winding up towards the 450 mph mark, I pulled her up into a loop and rolled off the top. We did ever-increasing tight turns until she blacked me out. We slow-rolled and barrel-rolled as I thrashed her about the sky for a full half-hour.

She roared, screamed, groaned and whined, but apart from being rather heavy on the controls at high speeds, she came through her tests with flying colours. She rocked a bit as the landing wheels were forced down into their locked positions, and she also gave a final high-pitched whine as I moved her propeller into fine pitch. Applying a few degrees of flap, we swung on down into the airfield approach, levelled out above the runway, and softly eased down onto her two wheels, leaving her tail up until she dropped it of her own accord.

We were soon back in her bay by the dispersal hut, where I turned off the petrol supply cock. After a few moments she ran herself out, and with a spit, sob and weary sigh, her great three-bladed propeller came to a stop. So that was it: I was drenched in perspiration and tired out. Clambering out of the hothouse, I slid down the wing and onto the ground, thanked my fitter and rigger, and drove straight off to the Officers Mess.[5]

While many RAF Typhoon units used air-to-ground rockets as their primary weapon, the Canadian Typhoon Wing specialized in dive bombing. A normal war load consisted of two 500-lb. bombs per aircraft, although 1,000-lb. bombs were also used, along with a full load of 20-mm cannon shells. Early targets included railway marshalling yards and V1 flying bomb launch sites. Number 438 Squadron flew the first RCAF Typhoon operations of the war on 28 March, and the whole Wing became operational a few days later under the able guidance of Wing Commander R.T.P. Davidson. Bob Davidson was an outstanding Canadian fighter pilot. He had also flown in both the Middle East and Ceylon, and was unique as a Canadian in scoring confirmed air-to-air kills against the Japanese, the Germans, and the Italians.

Number 143 Wing would serve with great distinction within 83 Group, despite suffering grave losses. These were due to the very nature of the work, with constant exposure to enemy flak and groundfire. If risks imposed by the enemy were not enough, there was also the temperamental nature of the massive 2,400-horsepower Napier Sabre engine and frequent ground-proximity judgement errors by pilots in combat. Initially, the Canadians of 143 Wing flew general interdiction missions, but the Typhoon's real heyday occurred after the commencement of the invasion, when close air support to the army became the Wing's *raison d'être*. These support missions included bombing bridges, rail junctions, supply columns, command posts and headquarters, artillery positions, and reinforced bunkers. Throughout the course of later hostilities, Canadian Typhoon pilots would also score a significant number of air-to-air kills.

While it was unquestionably the aircrews who carried the war from England to the enemy, there are a legion of stories concerning mission-oriented support personnel who, in their own way, did all that they could to help win the war. Hugh Godefroy recalls two such types, the first being the world's most understanding supply officer, and the second, a batman of considerable courage and fortitude:

. . . After bailing out over the Channel, I was saved from abject penury by a British equipment officer. I was applying for an RAF issue wristwatch to replace the one I had lost in the Channel. He had my equipment record, and before listing the watch he became absorbed in reading it.

"Sir," he said, "May I make a useful suggestion?"

"Please do," I replied.

"Do you by any chance have any of these articles in your possession: Airmen's boots black — airmen's flying boots, brown, fur — brass shield, buttons — navigator computer Mark III — gauntlets, leather brown — gauntlets, leather heated electric . . ."

"Stop," I said. "No, I don't have that stuff. I don't remember where or when I lost it, and I don't particularly care at this point."

"But sir, they are charged against you. May I remind you that your most recent unfortunate adventure affords us a unique opportunity?"

"What's that?" I asked.

"May I, on your behalf, list all this equipment down to 'watches, Mark II, aircrew, for the use of,' as having been lost at sea?"

"My God, I would have to have been flying a Lancaster."

"Sir," he replied, "for your information I am not required by KR and ACI (King's Regulations and Air Crew Instructions) to list the mode of transport, and hopefully another occasion like this may never arise."

Equipment officers as a group may have been guilty as charged with centuries of undetected crime, but they were one of us and God bless them, every one!![6]

. . . If it hadn't been for LeBoeuf, our French Canadian batman, we would never have made it. LeBoeuf was a dark-haired determined little fellow who never smiled. He was stuck with the job of getting us out of bed. He was up to all our *"maudit naisiere."* If the first warning didn't work, LeBoeuf resorted to brute force. When it was discovered that he was consistently managing to get John Weir and me on readiness on time, he was given the additional task of handling Bud Connell. The other batman had given up on Bud. Connell had had a longer exposure to military life than the rest of us; he was a graduate of RMC. He was not the usual swashbuckling RMC type. He liked to live well and relax. He always enjoyed a few good snorts when he came off readiness at night, and as soon as he finished his dinner, he would fall asleep. By 3.00 in the morning the only sign that suggested that he was living was shallow respiration. LeBoeuf took on his new task with a vengeance. Each morning, he started by getting John Weir and me on our feet in the damp grass; then he would brace himself and stride into Connell's tent. Immediately there would be the sounds of a furious struggle.

"Get up, Goddamn hit!" LeBoeuf would be heard to shout as he burst through the flaps of the tent breathing hard, carrying Connell's sleeping bag. He would dive back in muttering to himself, and would come out dragging Connell by the feet. After he had rolled him two or three times in the dew, Bud would begin to move. When he finally got him sitting up, he would invariably exclaim with satisfaction: *"Tiens!* Nobody beats LeBoeuf, not even Goddamn Connell."[7]

In anticipation of the impending invasion, the day fighter squadrons were being forced to embrace some new tactical concepts and changing conditions. Long-range warning radars would no longer be effective for the Allies in the fluid fighting expected on the Continent. The time required to mass large formations of fighters would be inappropriate and dangerous. Therefore, the days of the "Big Wing" leaders were all but over, and units would fly most frequently in either Squadron, or even Flight, strength. Numerical superiority over the Axis forces in northwest Europe was now such that few large gaggles of German aircraft were expected to be encountered. Since airborne targets were expected to be relatively scarce, many of the Spitfire Wings would play a dual role, in both the air-to-air and air-to-ground disciplines. Johnnie Johnson recollects coming to grips with the role changes in 144 Wing:

I had to remember that, apart from our air fighting role, we were now classified as a fighter-bomber Wing: when the time came we would be required to strafe enemy troops and vehicles and carry out dive-bombing operations. In France, our first and most important task would be to clear the skies of enemy aircraft and so let our ground forces get on with their job without being harassed by the Luftwaffe. Once air superiority was established, we should have to get on with the more mundane tasks of a fighter-bomber unit.

To assist us in our ground-strafing activities, a system of "contact cars" had been devised. These cars advanced with our own troops and reported the positions of any serious enemy opposition, such as tanks, armoured vehicles and heavy artillery. In a fluid situation, they were also of the greatest value in keeping the various headquarters informed of the exact positions of our spearheads. The RAF member of the contact car was usually a very experienced Squadron Leader, on a well-earned "rest" from flying duties, who had a radio and told us, in pilot's language, of the position, type and size of enemy targets. These contact cars simplified our identification problems, especially as our ground troops would often mark an enemy target with coloured smoke.

Our dive-bombing missions would be to assist our bombers in their efforts to isolate the battle area. Operations carried out in support of a carefully planned isolation campaign would aim at the destruction of essential road and rail bridges, viaducts and centres of communication on the perimeter of the battle area, so that the Germans could not easily move their ground forces and armour into any particular sector. Dive-bombing was an important part of our training, especially as the "boffins" had recently discovered that fighter-bombers could knock out a bridge with far less weight of high explosive than the light or medium bombers.

For this dive-bombing, our Spitfires were fitted with racks under each wing and the aeroplane was stressed to carry two 500-pound bombs. The theory of dive-bombing was to put your aeroplane into a steep dive, aim it at the target and release your bombs about the same time as you pulled out of the dive. Unfortunately, the bombs did not possess the same line of flight as our Spitfires and if you aimed directly at the target, then the bombs fell short. You also had to make the necessary allowance for the prevailing wind on any particular day. Our latest gyroscopic gunsights automatically computed the amount of deflection you should allow when attacking an enemy aircraft, but we had no such assistance to determine the distance or time you should allow before releasing your bombs. Some leaders counted "one, two, three," and then released their bombs. Others counted to "four," and some devised a system whereby the bombs were released when the target passed through a certain portion of the gunsight.

The first time I saw my lean Spitfire with two bombs hanging on its slender wings, I decided that I was never going to be crazy about this phase of our work. The Spitfire seemed to be intolerably burdened with her load, and the ugly, blunt bombs were a basic contradiction of all the beauty and symmetry of the aeroplane. Perhaps I was unduly sensitive after flying Spitfires for a long time. It was one thing to dive-bomb with a heavier type of fighter-bomber strapped to your back, which weighed almost seven tons and literally descended like a bomb, but it was quite another matter to force this relatively light, sensitive aircraft into a screaming dive against a ground target.

"What do you think of it, Wally?" I said to McLeod as we stood together inspecting a bombed-up Spitfire.

"Not much, sir," replied the veteran from Malta. "If we'd got two decent long-range tanks to hang under the wings, instead of those things," — pointing to the bombs — "we could go to Berlin with the Yanks and get stuck into some real fighting."[8]

Between November 1943 and June 1944, German aircraft were not often seen within the Spitfire's operating radius. Only fifty-six victories were claimed by the Canadian Wings, of which fourteen fell to the guns of 401 Squadron's pilots. Leadership changes were also in the cards. George Keefer, a distinguished North African campaigner, replaced Buck McNair of 126 Wing in April, and Lloyd Chadburn succeeded tour-expired Hugh Godefroy at the helm of 127 Wing. Also in April, both 126 and 127 Wings moved to Tangmere on the Sussex coast in preparation for the upcoming assault on Hitler's Atlantic Wall. Simultaneously, 144 Wing moved to Ford, the unit's stepping-off point to France. All three Wings now began living under canvas in order to acclimatize themselves for the nomadic existence soon to come on the Continent.

Although Canadian fighter pilots in the wartime United Kingdom forged an enduring reputation with their British hosts for their ebullient, open personalities and their feisty, fighting spirits, they also acquired a reputation for colourful use of the vernacular. Arthur Jewett, a wartime pilot with 441 Squadron, explains:

> When we were operating out of our base just behind Folkestone on the English Channel, I formed an alliance with one of the ladies of the RAF Women's Auxiliary Air Force (WAAF). She was stationed at the radar station near Sandwich and her duties there included plotting bearings, plotting the location of airborne aircraft (both friendly and enemy), and recording radio conversations between all the aircraft on her frequency.
>
> Anyhow, we had a date one night to meet in Folkestone and I was to take her to the local cinema. That particular day, we were doing something out over the Channel near the French coast and the language got a bit rough. She had been on duty that day and had been required to record all the various comments and snippets of conversation, verbatim if possible. We met and on our way to the cinema, she looked at me and very seriously said, "I say, Arthur; could I ask you a question?" I said, "Certainly Norah, what is it?" — and she replied, "When you Canadians are in the air in your bloody Spitfires, do you know any words that *don't* start with the letter 'F'?" To this day, I don't remember my answer.[9]

RCAF night fighter and intruder units were very active during 1944, and 418 Squadron, stationed at Bradwell Bay, was exceptionally successful. To the end of 1943, the Squadron had claimed only twenty air-to-air victories. During the first five months of 1944, the unit claimed a further fifty-seven air-to-air kills and also accounted for forty-six enemy aircraft destroyed on the ground, making 418 the most successful RCAF fighter unit of the period. Led by Wing Commander Paul Davoud, other Squadron luminaries included Flying Officer J. T. Caine, Squadron Leader R. A. Kipp, Squadron Leader C. C. Scherf (an Australian), Squadron Leader H. D. Cleveland, and Flight Lieutenant D. A. MacFadyen.[10]

In March, 406 Squadron moved south to Exeter, and during the next three months, its pilots racked up twelve more confirmed air-to-air victories under the outstanding leadership of Wing Commander "Moose" Fumerton. In fact, one of the twelve victories claimed by 406 during the period fell to the guns of Fumerton himself, who claimed both the first and the last of his fourteen night victories while flying with this unit. Now flying Mosquito XIIs instead of Beaufighters, Fumerton was able to measure the relative merits of both these fine aircraft.

There was quite a difference between the Beaufighter II with 1250 HP Merlin engines and the Beau I and VI with air-cooled Hercules 1400 and 1700 HP engines.

The Hercules engines seemed to provide a better feel and performance, although some of the early Is also had their problems, one of these being that the engine had no feathering device.

Most models of the Mosquito were a pleasure to fly — light on the controls, fast and fully aerobatic, even on one engine. The handling characteristics reminded me somewhat of a Spitfire, but heavier, of course. One of the later models, however, had the nose section enlarged to accommodate the latest radar and that altered the flying characteristics to the extent that it didn't feel like the same aircraft.

To compare the two for military use is difficult. A lot would depend on what they were to be used for. The Beau, especially the Beau VI, was good on the controls — not as fast as the Mosquito, but equal to the Hurricane. It was a bit heavier on maneuvers than the Mosquito, but was a much tougher aircraft, and a stable firing platform. It gave the feeling that it could take the punishment and bring you home, whereas the Mosquito was more maneuverable, but also more vulnerable.

There were reports of the odd Mosquito breaking up in the air as late as 1944–45. Regrettably that fate overtook one of my own students, but I believe the defect was eventually rectified by a modification to the main spar.[11]

In January 1944, 410 Squadron, stationed at Hunsdon in southeast England, was re-equipped with the potent Mosquito Mk XIII. Shortly thereafter, 410 moved to Castle Camps and scored an additional eight victories during the first five months of the year. In fact, it was 410 Squadron that boasted the first use of the new Mk VIII AI centimetric radar over enemy territory, when the novel technology was employed on an intruder sortie on 18 May. Senior RAF staff had been reluctant to fly the sophisticated new equipment in enemy airspace until that time, for fear of technological compromise in the event of a combat loss.

The men of 409 Squadron saw no action during this period, having been moved north for a well-deserved rest from operations. They also converted to Mosquito XIIIs during their respite from action, and in the spring, briefly joined 410 Squadron at Hunsdon before moving on to West Malling. On the eve of the Normandy invasion, 409 Squadron became part of 148 Wing, which included 29 (Mosquito) Squadron of the RAF and one of the first of the Griffon-engined Spit XIV units. Number 410 Squadron rounded out 141 Wing at Hartford Bridge, in concert with 264 (Mosquito) Squadron of the RAF and another Spit XIV squadron. All this to underscore the fact that RCAF night fighter squadrons fully assimilated into RAF Wings, instead of forming indigenous RCAF Wings as was the practice with the day fighters.

The former RCAF Army Cooperation Squadrons were productive during 1944, although the winter months had been rather slow-paced following their transfer from Fighter Command to 2TAF in November. In January, 400 Squadron assumed a pure reconnaissance role by converting its "A" Flight to Spitfire XIs, while "B" Flight re-equipped with Mosquito XVIs — both of which were unarmed photo reconnaissance specialty aircraft. By June, "B" Flight had traded in its Mosquitos for Spit XIs, and was employed exclusively on high-altitude reconnaissance missions, for which the aircraft was admirably suited. By now, 400, 414, and 430 Squadrons had joined forces to become collectively known as 39 (Reconnaissance) Wing within 83 Group of the 2TAF. Although 414 and 430 remained Mustang Squadrons for the time being, their day-to-day taskings were divided between low-level intruder missions and low-level reconnaissance of a variety of enemy holdings.

In Italy, the wet winter of 1943–44 had turned the country into a quagmire, restricting movement of friend and foe alike on the battlefield and transforming many acres of forward airfields into vast seas of mud. Hedley Everard describes the living conditions during that dismal winter in 417 Squadron's new home near Naples:

By mid-January, the Wing was moved to a sea of mud called Marcianise, about 12 miles north of Naples. The pierced steel planking of the runway and taxi tracks was almost hidden by a top layer of oozing clay. After our initial landing, two Spitfires went up on their noses, which served as a salutary reminder to pilots to remain between the fluttering red markers. This was to be "home" for the next three months of winter, which was described by locals as the worst in decades.

Although tents were to continue as shelters and to provide workshops on the airfield, 417 Squadron personnel were housed in a large three storey stone building nearby. For most of us, this provided the first semi-permanent roof over our heads since leaving England in 1941 and 1942. The cold grey-black building was centuries old and had been converted from a monastery into a home for the aged sometime in the early Thirties. Due to the usual misconception that senility was a handmaiden to insanity, the state had seen fit to saturate the services of this institution with the discards of a fascist society. The understaffed Nuns were barely able to feed the patients, let alone attend to their mental and physical disorders. Thus it occurred that the members of a Canadian fighter unit occupied one wing of the haven and the deprived were left in the other. In short order, the young compassionate kids from prairie and coastal towns were assisting the Nuns with their daily burdens and problems of surviving. The bedridden now rejoiced in the warmth of real woolen blankets, and aged shufflers were clad in battle jackets, trousers, shoes and socks, which the airmen firmly insisted were surplus to their needs. Our Squadron doctor, when required, could usually be found tending the elderly sick. Not to be outdone, the Squadron cooks, with volunteer help from off-duty officers and airmen, now kept a huge oil-heated vat of beef stew at the simmering state on a 24 hour basis. A hot meal was now available anytime, and everyone was blind to the Matron Sister and her assistants filling their crock pots for the patients or themselves. The Adjutant made his contribution by drawing rations for personnel who had long departed the Unit. Extra foodstuffs were purchased from monies carelessly thrown into a five gallon can near the steaming vat. The shared stew pot contributed greatly to the manifest increase in morale . . .[12]

Throughout the long Italian winter, the front stabilized with the combatants deadlocked in the southern third of the country. Hoping to break this impasse, the Allies put a sizeable amphibious landing force ashore at Anzio behind enemy lines on 22 January 1944. Although the force was of significant proportions, the number of troops available for the operation was vastly depleted due to a siphoning off of resources for the impending invasion of the Continent from England. Therefore, the weight of effort committed to Anzio was woefully inadequate for the task at hand. This attempt to force the Germans into a retreat mode backfired, and the net result was an expensive, bloody containment of the 50,000-man landing force.

After this abortive deadlock-breaking attempt by the Allies at Anzio, the Germans evacuated Corsica and Sardinia, which bolstered by two fresh divisions their already-formidable Gothic Line of fortifications north of Rome. Before the roads to the capital would lie open, an ancient mountain-top monastery at Cassino had to be suppressed. In concert with the grim assault on the heights of Cassino, in a further effort to isolate and contain the battlefield, the Mediterranean Air Forces launched Operation Strangle, an all-out attempt to smash Axis supply lines in Italy. Although the mission was somewhat successful, bad weather hampered the operation's overall impact, and the Germans were able to continue providing at least the essentials of life and battle to their front-line troops. As the spring weather improved, however, so did the momentum of the Allied drive northward, and on 4 June, just two days before D-Day at Normandy, U.S. forces under General Mark Clark drove into the outskirts of Rome.

In Burma, the second Arakan campaign had been initiated in November 1943, and on 9 January 1944, Maungdaw on the Mayu Peninsula fell to troops of XV Corps. At that time, a second thrust was launched towards Kyauktaw by the 81st West African Division, an operation which was wholly dependent upon resupply through air drops. The Japanese reacted with customary zeal, and the advance stalled at Sinzweya on the coast, resulting in the encirclement of the

7th Indian Division. For a month, the situation remained desperately critical, as over 2,600 tons of food and ammunition was air-dropped to the beleaguered Indians. Only one Dakota was lost during this remarkable operation, due in no small measure to the stalwart protection provided to the transports by Spitfires and Hurricanes of the Far East Air Force.

Just when it seemed as though the Japanese would prevail, their theatre commander, Lieutenant General Hanaya, made a tactical blunder. He chose that moment to launch a major offensive in the north, designed to split the British front by capturing Chittagong to the west, isolating the forces in the Arakan, then capturing the bases at Imphal and Dimapur, and, in the process, rupturing the Allied lines of communication through Assam. With Hanaya redirecting his forces elsewhere, XV Corps was able to consolidate its hold on Maungdaw, and a victory of survival was registered at Sinzweya. Furthermore, Hanaya had completely disregarded the fact that the Allies now had firm control of the air over Burma. In a tactically bold stroke, Lord Mountbatten airlifted the entire 5th Indian Division from Arakan to Imphal in early March, an event which undoubtedly saved the day for Imphal. Now the gateway to India was firmly guarded by four separate Indian divisions, and another massive and constant aerial resupply operation prevailed.

It is worthy of note that at least 150,000 Allied troops were in close contact with the Japanese in this region, and 400 tons of supplies had to be air-dropped daily to sustain them. Without air superiority, this task would have been utterly hopeless.[13] Gib Coons, who flew the excellent Spitfire Mk VIII with 607 (RAF) Squadron in Burma, recalls typical Allied fighter activity in the area prior to and during the Siege of Imphal in the spring of 1944:

The newly equipped (607) Squadron was moved from an airdrome outside Calcutta to a remote strip called Ramu in December 1943. Ramu was situated almost midway between Chittagong and Akyab (held by the Japanese, and situated just off the coast of the Bay of Bengal). Air activity can best be described as spotty and inconsistent, since the Japanese Air Force would move their squadrons around from one temporary strip to another. What intelligence reports we did receive always seemed to be 24 or 48 hours after the fact, so it was difficult to come to grips with the enemy. To compound the problem, our radar was often unreliable. In fairness, it should be noted that the jungle topography did not lend itself to setting up proper radar installations. On several occasions, their Oscars strafed our strip without our knowledge that they were even in the vicinity. On two occasions, we were bounced just after take-off on a scramble. Fortunately, a combination of Lady Luck, Japanese lack of persistence, and our new Spitfires kept the damage to minimal proportions. With typical dark humour, we suggested the radar boys would be better off using smoke signals. It became obvious the tactics of the Japanese were "hit and run" and, as it turned out, not that successful.

On 5 February 1944, radar managed to pick up a small raid of Dinah 100s off the coast that seemed to be returning south to their base. My Number Two, W/O Joe Neville, and I spotted a straggler as they headed south along the coast. My first two bursts must have been a direct hit as the Dinah burst into flames, falling into the water. Intelligence, to the best of my knowledge, were never able to determine their prime target nor their reason for turning back.

During the four or five months we were stationed at Ramu, the Squadron escorted B25s, Wellingtons and Vengeances on various bombing missions inside Burma territory and on only one occasion did we encounter enemy air activity. On that day, several Oscars made a couple of half-hearted passes at the bombers and then took off. Pursuit of their fighters, however, was not the order of the day. Our instructions were most explicit: "You stick with the bombers, period." Strafing sorties carried out on the Japanese airstrips accounted for assorted motor transport, petrol bowsers, etc., but never any of their aircraft, although our intelligence would report their presence. On 19 April 1944, 607 Squadron moved to Imphal Valley.

The Burma Campaign has often been dubbed "the forgotten war," or as Churchill once said, "the forgotten front." This is understandable when one considers the magnitude of the European and Pacific theatres of operations.

War historian Norman Franks, in his book, "The Air Battle of Imphal," sets the background at that time:

> The battles of Imphal and Kohima in 1944, on the very borders of India, were fought under siege conditions. Attacked and surrounded by three Japanese Army Divisions, the Imphal Valley with its vital airstrips, and Kohima had to be held at all costs. Failure to do so would surrender not just the one and

only road from Burma into India, but would also give the Japanese a secure air base for their conquest of India.

While under siege, General Bill Slim's 14th Army held on to its position, supplied and defended by the airmen and aircraft of the Royal Air Force. They played a vital part in these battles. Without the daily supply missions into Imphal and over Kohima, both would certainly have fallen. Without the Spitfires and Hurricanes of 221 Fighter Group defending the valley from Japanese aircraft or attacking enemy positions and their lines of supply, the Japanese would not have been stopped.

On 4 May 1944, Churchill, fully realizing the seriousness of the situation, sent the following dispatch to Mountbatten, the recently appointed Chief of Combined Operations, South East Asia Command, and I quote from his memoirs:

"Let nothing go from the battle that you need for victory. I will not accept denial of this from any quarter, and will back you to the full."

Sir Winston did have a way with words! Translation of this directive as it filtered down to the Army and Air Force in Imphal Valley literally meant that monsoon conditions, mud, dysentery, etc. notwithstanding, we were to stick it to the Japanese with all the resources available. Mountbatten, never one to ignore the gauntlet, would respond to the challenge in typical fashion. The following excerpts from Norman Franks' book provide a glimpse of events that took place at that time and, of course, tell only part of the story:

April 26, 1944, three Spitfires were scrambled, 81 was kept too high by the Group Controller and failed to make contact. 607 were sent racing to their Spitfires at 9:05 am for 6+ bandits, but once airborne another plot of 3+ was also seen, both coming in from the south. At 9:15, the plot changed to 55+ from the east, flying north-east. They joined with 81 Squadron but when the raiders were reported bombing Tulihal and were on their way out, 607 were vectored back to Wangjing, the ground operator there, F/O Benson, calling that the Japs were right overhead. F/L L.G. Coons, leading 607 (Call-sign Ping Pong Leader) led them towards Sapam, then spotted an Oscar right above him. P/O M.B. Hole saw AA fire bursting to the right, and then saw three Jap bombers. Coons pulled up to attack the Oscars as Hole turned after the bombers.

Although my log book records this particular attack on an Oscar, the details are sketchy. I was able to get off a burst before being forced to turn. I observed strikes along the fuselage; however, in the mêlée that followed, I could not determine the extent of damage. My log book reads "NO JOY" and probably that tells it all. Consequently, I did not make a claim on landing back at base.

More of the Squadron's encounter follows, but thinking back to the screw-up in operations that day, we did reasonably well, claiming two Japanese destroyed and three damaged.

Again, from "The Air Battle of Imphal":

On Saturday, 16th May, the Japanese were over the Valley again. 25 Oscars from the 64th and 204th Sentais swept over Imphal in the early morning. 607 Squadron had sent the usual dawn patrol off and had just landed without incident.

No sooner had these aircraft got down than a scramble call came. It was just 7:30 am. Twelve Spitfires, led by Flight Lieutenant Coons, roared into the sky where they were vectored towards Bishempur where bandits were reported bombing the road from 8000 feet. Coons saw two Oscars at this height, flying south-east towards Tulihal. One was in line-abreast going away from the Spitfires. Coons turned after it, opening fire at 200 yards. The Oscar turned onto its back and as it fell, Coons saw a ball of flame from its engine, but then broke away. He discovered his radio was U/S and with other fighters about, thought he'd better get back to base. Coon's Number 2, Warrant Officer Neville, saw the Oscar go down, saw flame coming from the engine, and what appeared to be petrol gushing from its belly. Meanwhile, Pilot Officer D.L. Stuart (RAAF) attacked the second Oscar, firing as he closed to 100 yards, which produced strikes before it burst into flames and went down near Tulihal.

At the end of this official Squadron report, Franks notes that the Japanese records claim that at least two Spitfires were shot down by their pilots from the 64th Sentai. Since our Squadron, 607, was the only one involved in this encounter and we all returned to base, I

War is not always hell . . .
Don Walz with the fetching
Hervé sisters in front of the
Hotel Boule d'Or in
Malicarne, France. Gord
Ockenden couldn't under-
stand why Walz returned to
the Squadron once liberated!
Gord Ockenden Photo

400 Squadron photo reconnaissance pilots while away the hours at their disper-
sal in England. Clockwise around the table from the left are Flight Lieutenant
P. G. Wigle, Flight Lieutenant H. E. Walters, Flight Lieutenant G. H. E. Maloney,
Flight Lieutenant J. A. Morton, Flying Officer J. G. Greenwood, and Flight
Lieutenant E. E. Tummon. *DND Photo PL 30208*

Jim Prendergast and the "Lazy Lady," his deadly Spitfire Mark FR XIVE.
Jim Prendergast photo

"Judy" Garland's outstanding Tempest V, photographed while he was serving with 80 (RAF) Squadron in Holland, 1944. *John Garland Photo*

416 Squadron dispersal at B.82 Grave in Holland, October 1944, shortly after the Me 262 jet fighter-bomber attack to which Gord Ockenden referred. *DND Photo*

Dal Russel, a very distinguished fighter leader, served operationally from 1940 until 1945 and completed an extremely rare third tour of operations. *PL 29373*

Flak damage in Holland, 1944. The Spitfire could often absorb an incredible amount of damage and still bring its pilot back. *DND Photo PL 33414*

Two 418 Squadron pilots update the unit's impressive scoreboard. *DND Photo PL 33953*

Russ Bannock and his Radar Operator, Bob Bruce, in front of their Mosquito. Note the scoresheet on the fuselage. *PL 31295*

Squadron Leader Don Laubman, DFC and Bar, ranking ace of the 2nd Tactical Air Force. *PMR 78-306*

Karl Linton with 417 Squadron at Bellaria, Italy, February 1945. Note the coarse material of his battledress jacket and shirt. *Karl Linton Photo*

Pilot Officer Richard Watson climbs into his 440 Squadron Typhoon at Eindhoven, Holland, 22 December 1944. *DND Photo*

Wing Commander "Johnnie" Johnson (left), the ranking Commonwealth ace of the war with thirty-eight confirmed victories, during a lighter moment with Group Captain Stan Turner, early 1945. *PL 43239*

A 409 Squadron Mosquito Mark NF XIII in a picturesque French wartime setting, early 1945. Note the potent centimetric radar in the nose. *PL 41735*

A superb 414 Squadron Spitfire Mark FR XIVE at Wunstorf, Germany, April 1945. The bomb-damaged hangar in the background provides an interesting contrast. *Jim Prendergast Photo*

can only assume that the boys from the 64th Sentai had been into the *Sake* and got a little carried away with their claims.

The malaria bug finally caught up to me and also two or three other pilots on the Squadron. As a result, we were out of action for several weeks. During the Imphal siege (March–June 1944), eight RAF squadrons had destroyed 33 enemy aircraft, plus an additional 22 probably destroyed. 61 damaged were also claimed. 607 Squadron had tallied 10 destroyed, 8 probably destroyed, with 23 damaged. Our Squadron's loss was one Spitfire VIII and one pilot.[14]

At the same time, a second Chindit (British Special Forces) expedition was staged in northern Burma, in an attempt to sever the supply routes of Japanese forces opposing Lieutenant General "Vinegar Joe" Stilwell's joint American-Chinese columns advancing southward from Ledo. During 5–11 March, four brigades comprising over 9,000 men were airlifted in Dakotas and gliders many miles behind Japanese lines. As if flying fighters in wartime Burma was not challenging enough for a young Canadian, Dave Bockus, who won the DFC in the theatre, volunteered for duty with the Chindits. To say that Bockus had a very exciting time of it while attached to that organization would be a massive understatement. He explains:

I joined the British Special Forces (Chindits) to operate on the ground behind the Jap lines, with the objective of destroying their troops, supplies, roads, and so on. On 5 March 1944, while flying in the jump seat of a 1st Air Commando Waco glider with Dick Kuoensler as first pilot, we made a night landing(!?!) 185 miles behind Jap lines on an unlit, unmarked jungle paddy, codenamed "Broadway," writing off the Waco in the process. Casualties were high but by the following midnight, we had a flare-path and strip ready and DC3s began landing. They unloaded troops, barbed wire, machine guns, AA, and a small USAAF radar unit from 31 Air Commando Group, then evacuated the casualties. A few days later, Flight Lieutenant Bob Day of Vancouver, an RCAF officer in the RAF, landed with six Spitfires. As the estimated number of Japs in the area was in the tens of thousands, the Yanks predicted that this would trigger heavy Jap air strikes . . . and it did. Although greatly outnumbered, the Spits put up a terrific battle, shooting down at least four. Bob got two and ground fire got one or two more, but the radar and AA were destroyed. The surviving Spits were withdrawn and another flight of Spits was flown in, but the operating situation was almost impossible. There was no warning system, and protective cover was out with the nearest airport an hour's flying time away. The Spit pilots were greatly outnumbered . . . two of the pilots were killed immediately, and others were wounded. The cost in pilots and Spits was too high, and no further attempts to land Spits were made, but it left the Japs with the uneasy feeling that Spits could operate deep inside their territory.

However, Broadway was by now heavily defended, and I set out with the Chindits on our jungle objectives. After a few weeks though, we were ordered back to Broadway, which was in danger of being overrun. Eric Loken, also RCAF but serving with the RAF, a "Wimpy" (Vickers Wellington) pilot from B.C., had replaced Bob Lasser, also RCAF in the RAF and from B.C., who had been killed the first night. A small U.S. light plane group had escaped, leaving behind two damaged L5s. Eric and I got them flyable and began picking up wounded and dropping supplies to the Chindits. At one point I flew into China, accompanied by two 1st Air Commando L1s, in order to pick up three Special Forces members. However, on departing China I crashed on takeoff, though the two L1s escaped with my injured passenger. The attacking Japs burned my plane and Eric, flying alone, hunted for me, attracting a lot of ground fire in the bargain. The Chinese led me to another Chindit named Kennedy, who was also hiding out. We even spent one night in an opium *basha*, where all but one of the lodgers passed out. When the remaining individual left, we knew we were being betrayed and we slipped out into the jungle. We dodged Jap patrols ranging in size from 12 to 200 men and even stole the food from the rear guard of one patrol! We joined up with the American OSS operative Pete Joost and his band of Chinese guerillas, and when one was wounded in the upper leg, Pete and I removed the bullet. 1st Air eventually picked me up and returned me to Broadway, where the Yanks loaned me another plane. Though Eric and I returned to China to pick up more wounded on May 15th, the decision was made that Broadway could not be held any longer. My first attempt to fly out with Eric, by now seriously ill, failed due to weather problems. On the second attempt, we met two Jap fighters! Now, after 2-1/2 months in enemy territory and being only one flying hour from safety, I was immediately hit with deep despair. However, as I prepared for a rapidly approaching death, my despair turned into utter hatred and anger regarding my fate. Flying below tree level and doing 180° breaks into the sides of the surrounding high hills and also into a dead end chaung, we managed to escape. Eric later said that he believed we were dead ducks. He was hospitalized and then sent home while I flew more trips, picking up U.S. casualties before returning to fighter operations on Spitfires. When the Chindit era was over, Eric and I had flown, between the two of us, more than 200 unofficial flights inside occupied Burma. Though I did my share of fighter operations, my short period as a Chindit behind Jap lines stands out as a real highlight of my wartime career.[15]

<hr />

Back in Europe, first light of 6 June 1944 was somewhat anticlimatic and straightforward. The pessimistic forecasts of operationally impossible weather conditions did not materialize. A sullen, pewter overcast at around 2,000 feet, coupled with choppy seas, would characterize the day. So would prevailing visibilities of at least five miles, more than adequate to provide reasonable cover to the 5,000-ship invasion force choking the Channel from Dover to Normandy. For all three Services, the years of waiting and training, the legacy of Dieppe, was over. The big push towards Berlin was about to begin.

Shortly after daybreak at Ford airfield, the gloved hands of Johnnie Johnson and thirty-five of his contemporaries from 144 (RCAF) Wing went through the following drill to fire up their Spitfire Mk IXs for war:

Fuel Cock — ON
Ignition Switches — OFF
Throttle — 1/2 in.–1 in. OPEN
Propeller Speed
Control Lever — FULLY FORWARD
Supercharger Switch — AUTO NORMAL POSITION
Carburetor Air Intake
Filter Control — CLOSED or FILTER IN OPERATION
Ki-gass Priming Pump — AS REQUIRED FOR
     TEMPERATURE
Ignition Switches — ON
Starter and Booster Coil Buttons — PRESS SIMULTANEOUSLY

Soon, blue smoke was belching from the exhaust stacks of three dozen Spitfires, and minutes later, Johnson was leading the Wing to their designated patrol line over Sword, Juno, and Gold Beaches, situated between Bayeux and the mouth of the Orne River. Below them, British and Canadian troops were stumbling ashore, cold, wet, and nauseated, but nevertheless in France for the first time in four years.

In direct contrast to the high-pitched action taking place on the beaches below, almost all the RCAF day fighter squadrons flew four separate patrols on the sixth and only one unit managed even to *see* any enemy aircraft — a pair of FW 190s which high-tailed it for sanctuary before the Canadians could close to gun range. George Keefer's 126 Wing would have a field day over the battlefield on the seventh, destroying twelve Ju 88s caught strafing the beaches near St. Aubin. Other isolated victories would occur against the German fighter arm that day, but opportunities for engagement would be few and far between for the eager day fighter pilots during the landings.

In air-to-air combat, the German aggressiveness experienced on D+1 was short-lived. The daily routine of dawn-to-dusk patrols continued unabated, but nearly three weeks would elapse before the day fighter Wings would once more encounter the Luftwaffe in significant numbers. While the opportunities to score were scarce, and the day fighters suffered some losses in the immediate aftermath of the invasion, most of those losses were sustained during ground-attack sorties. The casualties were nowhere near what had been anticipated, or, for that matter, what had been determined acceptable for the period. Art Jewett remembers an incident prior to the invasion, at the end of his Operational Training Unit course, which helped him put higher authority's perception of his relative worth into perspective:

At the end of our operational training, we had a special visit from an RAF Air Commodore from Fighter Command, who gave us the gen on what was to be expected of us when D-Day arrived, and thereafter until the end of the war — or our end, whichever came first. He mentioned that during the first few days, Fighter Command was prepared to handle casualties of up to 28%, at which time I did some mental arithmetic and concluded that the future was a bit chancy. At the conclusion of his talk, the Air Commodore asked if we had any questions. Like an idiot, I stood up and said, "Sir, I read quite recently in *The Aeroplane* magazine that successful preliminary work has been done on creating an 'automatic pilot' for unmanned, drone aircraft, and if this is so, why couldn't our combat aircraft be equipped with these things, thereby saving many lives?" He looked at me and said, "You are quite young, aren't you?" I replied, "Yes Sir, I am." He then said, "Automatic pilots, if successful, would be very expensive and would cost a lot of pounds — and do you know that people, mostly men and women, get together every night and create pilots for us and enjoy doing it — and they don't cost us a damn penny. Does that answer your question?" I said, "Yes Sir, it does," and sat down . . .[16]

Number 39 Reconnaissance Wing was very active during D-Day and also in its aftermath, 400 Squadron doing the high-level work in its Spitfire XIs while 414 and 430 Squadrons slugged it out at low level in their aging Mustangs. During the landings, these last two units were used primarily for spotting and directing the offshore guns of the navy on German coastal defences from Le Havre to Cherbourg. George Burroughs recalls 39 Wing's activities during the landing, viewed from the cockpit of his Mustang:

My most memorable day was D-Day, 6 June 1944. The Squadron had a different mission that day and to prepare for it, we did considerable training in Scotland with the Royal Navy. Our job was to bring naval guns to bear on specific targets, and this involved the use of a relatively simple procedure. Having agreed upon the target, the pilot positioned himself to report the location of the landing of the shells from the ship. A check reference was used to inform the ship how close the shots were to the target. For example, the pilot would report 12 o'clock 500, meaning the shot had landed at 12 o'clock on a clock face superimposed on the map, and 500 yards from the target. Corrections were made until the shots were "bang on." The ship would then open up and receive hit reports from the pilot, who then ascertained whether or not the target had been destroyed. (While this was going on, of course, the ship was going full speed, a number of miles out to sea.)

I made two trips that day, and worked with HMS *Ajax*. Takeoff for the first trip was in the dark in order to arrive at the beachhead at the break of dawn. The sight was staggering — ships everywhere — lots of aircraft — the pyrotechnics were spectacular — incendiaries hosing the sky — red-hot shells from the naval guns streaking towards the beach and causing turbulence if they were close — no words can truly describe such a massive effort.

After contacting HMS *Ajax*, we got down to business. The first target was a coastal battery. *Ajax* got into it pretty quickly, and after a few salvos I could report that the battery was out of action. After returning to base to refuel, I flew back to the beach. It was now much lighter, and one could see that progress was being made. The army was doing its job and there was a lot of ground activity on the beach and beyond. I reported to HMS *Ajax* that our second target had already been destroyed. They were anxious to get at anything and therefore asked me to seek out another target. I flew a few miles inland and received fire from an ack-ack battery. *Ajax* picked up the reference quickly and silenced it. They next asked me to find more in the small sector to which we had been assigned. I reported that the only movement seen was a herd of cows. They promptly advised me that livestock was not a suitable target, since our "boys" might make use of them later! So ended my experiences on D-Day.[17]

After the invasion, the Wing shifted roles to tactical reconnaissance in support of the army, watching enemy road and rail movements. Needless to say, free-ranging missions at low level over a very dynamic battlefield constituted a high risk, and ten Mustangs were lost in June alone, prior to the move to French soil at the end of the month. At that time, 39 Wing moved to Sommervieu (B.8), but 414 Squadron stayed at Odiham, from where the unit continued to operate, although it also frequently utilized an advanced landing strip on the beachhead in Normandy during July. In August, 414 converted to Spitfire IXs and caught up with the rest of 39 Wing at St. Honorine (B.21), just in time to participate in the holocaust at Falaise.

———————

D-Day also ushered in the most successful period in the scoring history of the RCAF night fighter and intruder units. To the end of May 1944, 406, 409, and 410 Squadrons had collectively destroyed only fifty-three and a quarter enemy aircraft (plus thirty-eight probables) during a period of operations spanning thirty-three months. By the end of August, their kill totals would be 117 1/4 confirmed and fifty-six probables, while 418 Squadron would add a further eighteen confirmed kills and twelve probables.[18] Once the invasion got underway, the night fighter squadrons were largely released from their defensive duties over the United Kingdom, assuming more and more of the intruder role being flown with such distinction by 418 Squadron. While the three dedicated night fighter squadrons patrolled from dawn to dusk over the great invasion task forces, the Edmontonians (418 Squadron) were having great success further inland, destroying five German aircraft over Chateaudun and Orleans airfields within twenty minutes on the night of 6 June. Although there was initially a dearth of enemy air activity at night over the invasion fleets, that calm ended on the ninth, when 409 and 410 Squadrons each scored kills over Ju 188s, the first in a string of eleven claims for each of the units that month. The 409 Nighthawks had a particularly good night on the tenth, when they downed three more '188s, and they followed those successes with a further two kills the next night. Not to be outdone, 410 Squadron's Cougars downed six in three nights between the twelfth and the fourteenth.

By mid-month, however, 409 and 418 Squadrons were temporarily diverted from manned targets to wage all-out war against the sinister V1 "buzz-bombs." Russ Bannock teamed with Flying Officer Bob Bruce to become Canada's most successful bomb-destroying team, with nineteen of 418 Squadron's sixty-eight confirmed missiles. He describes some of the innovative tactics required to down this slippery, high-performance prey:

V1s were initially launched from fixed launching sites located on the north coast of France (Pas de Calais), commencing in mid-June 1944. They were aimed at London and carried enough fuel to fly to the heart of the Metropolis, cruising at approximately 380 mph and at an altitude of approximately 300 feet above sea level. 418 Squadron, where I was a Flight Commander at the time, was assigned along with three other night fighter/intruder squadrons to patrol the English Channel from dusk until dawn. Each squadron had a sector to patrol with two aircraft each on two hour shifts. The first couple of nights, while we were on patrol at around 2,000 feet, we had no success because we were unable to obtain enough speed to close on the V1. We then worked out a plan whereby we would patrol at 10,000 feet, wait until we saw a V1 launched on the French coast, and then fly a course to intercept it around mid-Channel. We would then wait for the V1 to arrive directly underneath. By diving from 10,000 feet, we could attain a speed of 430 mph, which gave us about forty seconds to close. On a clear night the actual launch from France was visible, producing a large flash, and then the V1 trailed a long flame from the pulse-jet engine.

We usually fired a deflection shot from a 30 degree angle to avoid getting directly behind and picking up debris from the explosion. The Mosquito was particularly vulnerable to debris because of the two leading-edge radiators. The fuel tanks usually exploded with a vivid flash (hydrogen peroxide and kerosene) which could cause temporary disorientation, while the warhead usually exploded when the V1 hit the water. A simple autopilot kept the V1 level and on course. On one occasion, I hit a V1 with a short burst of machine gun fire (out of cannon) and it then proceeded to do a 180 degree turn. At that point, the autopilot righted it, so I let it continue back into France — it went down as it reached the coast.

There were two hazards . . . firstly, German coastal radar were vectoring night fighters on our Mosquitos; secondly, there was a distinct danger of collision when two aircraft were diving on the same bomb. After some near misses, we all agreed to turn on our navigation lights once we entered the dive. We lost at least two aircraft in our Squadron during these sorties, due in all likelihood to enemy night fighters.

On June 19th, I scored the first-ever V1 destroyed, followed by three on July 3rd, four on July 6th and others later in the month. On July 6th, at least forty were launched during my two hour patrol, but I ran out of ammo after downing the fourth bomb . . .[19]

Sometimes range estimation and closure rate were very difficult to judge when going up against the bombs, and crews had to be very careful not to "frag" themselves in secondary explosions from their targets. Dave McIntosh, a Quebec native, paired with an American pilot and had a distinguished tour on 418 Squadron as a navigator, winning the DFC in the process. During one wild chase after a bomb over the Channel, however, he undoubtedly wondered if he was even going to survive the war, let alone return home with distinction.

Down, down, down. We were gaining some because the fire coming out of the ass end of the V1 was getting bigger. The Mosquito was screaming in every joint. Sid had both big hairy hands on the stick. When he began to pull back, I thought the wings would never stand it. But we began to level out and the clock said 400 mph. Sid pulled and pulled and she kept coming out of the dive. I tore my eyes away from the shaking wing and looked ahead. It was just like looking into a blast furnace. "We're too close," I screamed. I shut my eyes as the cannons began banging away. I was thrown hard against my straps because cannons going off cut down the speed suddenly.

When the explosion came I thought I was going to be dead. The goddam thing went off right in our faces. I opened my eyes and caught a glimpse of things whirling around outside the window. Black things and blobs of smoke.

"I can't see," Sid said.

"OK boy," I said. "Just keep her like that. You can cut your speed though." He throttled back. After those hours of darkness, he had been blinded for a few seconds by the flash. Why we hadn't been smashed up by all that flying debris, I don't know. We had flown right through it.

"I got too close," Sid said.

"I noticed," I said. Now that I found myself in one piece and the props still going around, I wanted to laugh and natter and be Jesus H. (for Hannah) Christ in a blue bottle sitting on the mantelpiece. "Boy, I bet we saved the life of some limey in London reading his paper about how all the doddlebugs are being shot down by the ack-ack guns," I babbled. "Yes, you're quite a little savior," Sid said. But he didn't fool me. He was pleased he had finally made a score, no matter how small, in his Jewish war against the Germans. "Well, we got one," was all he said. "I hope it's the last," . . . that to myself . . .[20]

Anti-V1 patrols were not the only missions that 418 Squadron was tasked with during June 1944. Russ Bannock recalls an eventful night intruder sortie, flown in support of bomber operations:

A typical intruder mission took place on June 14th 1944 when I was assigned to patrol two German night fighter airfields near Bourges, 100 miles south of Paris, from 10 pm to midnight. That evening, our bombers were attacking railway yards to the south of Paris and the runway lights at Bourges airfield were lit, indicating some flying activity. I commenced right hand circuits at 500 feet, hoping to spot engine exhausts passing overhead, because at this stage of the war the Germans no longer illuminated their nav lights around their airfields. After one complete circuit and halfway up the downwind leg, we spotted some exhausts, then turned and headed for the point where the aircraft would be turning final. We again spotted the exhausts and started to follow the aircraft on final approach. However, we were immediately "coned" in searchlights and subjected to AA fire. We broke off to the side of the airfield, evading the searchlights, and soon noticed that the aircraft had turned on its landing lights, meaning that it was just about to touch down. We attacked in a shallow dive and hit the aircraft on the runway (Me 110), which exploded and caught fire. We were again coned in searchlights and subjected to intense AA fire, but by staying at treetop height, we were not hit.

Most airfield intruder successes took place as the German night fighters were returning after attacking the bomber stream. In 418 Squadron we were equipped with the Mk VI Mosquito which had no forward looking radar, so it was not possible to intercept aircraft taking off. However, as was the case with earlier technologies, after November 1944, the Air Ministry permitted Mosquitos equipped with the Mk X AI radar to roam over enemy territory, so it was then possible to pick up aircraft on the upwind side of the airfield and try to catch them before they climbed up to the bomber stream. We would later have considerable success when operating Mk 30 Mosquitos in 406 Squadron, which were equipped with the superb Mk X radar.

By way of note, the most outstanding personality that I met in the night fighting business was Group Captain John Cunningham, who was the leading Allied scorer at night with twenty confirmed victories. He commanded 85 Squadron when I was converting 406 Squadron to night intruding with Mk 30 Mosquitos. His Squadron was having great success doing high level intruding with this aircraft (equipped with the Mk X radar) at known German night fighter orbiting beacons, usually at 20,000 feet. At that height, the Mk X had an effective range of about ten miles. As we were doing low level intruding with this AI radar, he was very helpful in sharing information with us.[21]

By 1944, the ubiquitous Mosquito was in many ways to the night fighter force what the Spitfire was to the day fighters. Many technological improvements had been made to this fine aircraft throughout the course of the war, but the improvements did not always coincide with better handling characteristics. Joe Schultz compares the relative virtues and drawbacks of the numerous Marks of Mosquitos with which he had experience:

The Mosquito, in my opinion, was one of the nicest airplanes to fly that I ever touched. The reassuring sound of the Rolls Royce engines had a definite psychological effect. A lot of people have spoken about the aircraft as being tricky, particularly difficult on one engine, and with a tendency to swing on the ground, but I personally couldn't disagree *more*. I found that any of its idiosyncrasies would only really come to the fore if you couldn't handle the airplane properly, or if you mistreated it or attempted to do things with it for which it wasn't designed. I flew over 1,000 hours in it on all Marks from the Mk II to the Mk 30 series. The earlier models, particularly the II and the III (which was a trainer), as well as the VI (which was a fighter-bomber and used for intruder operations), were by far the nicest to fly. They were quite a bit lighter than the later models, and they hadn't had a lot of "nonsense" added on to their airframes. They were good at low level, as well as in the medium-to-high levels. Later on, they put 60–70 Series Merlin engines with the two-stage "blowers" in the aircraft for high-level operations. Since we used them operationally only below 10,000 feet, this feature wasn't really required! In fact, relatively speaking, they were very rough running and I didn't like them one little bit. These airplanes were heavy and fairly cumbersome. As far as I'm concerned, they were nowhere near the fighting machines that the earlier Marks were. Having said that, this assessment is all relative, and I really liked the airplane overall through the whole series of Marks I experienced during three years of war, and later in peacetime. What I liked most about it was its steadiness and its manoeuvrability, within the limitations of an aircraft of its size and the fact that it had twin engines. Its firepower was also impressive. On the Mk VI, we had four 20-mm cannon and these were augmented by four machine guns. We also carried bombs, and had we wished, we could have carried rockets as well. It was also a very fine instrument flying machine. It even had ultraviolet lighting for the instruments — very innovative at the time. The ergonomic layout of the instruments was also first-rate, with only minor lapses in engineering, and these were perfectly understandable for an aircraft which was conceived and produced in such a short period of time.

Overall, I think it was a very fine machine, and it was universally accepted as being able to do just about any job whatsoever. The only other aircraft that I think even came close to matching the Mosquito for versatility was the Junkers 88 in its various Marks . . .[22]

The Mk X centimetric radar was an American/Canadian-developed AI system, which incorporated some of the features of the Mk VIII, but was lighter and more resistant to jamming. It would soldier on as the RAF's primary night fighter radar until 1958.

Moose Fumerton's Lynx Squadron (406) had little to share in the summer successes being enjoyed by the other night fighter squadrons. Their routine but essential patrols of the home ports were sheer drudgery, punctuated only by an occasional freelance thrust into enemy territory. But by 10 July, 406 Squadron was finally relieved of the odious Channel patrols and given new orders to guard Allied destroyers on coastal operations at Ushant and Brest. The very first day at this new assignment brought success to the Squadron, as the Germans obviously found the destroyers too tempting a target to ignore. "Blackie" Williams, a distinguished night-fighter ace flying with 406 at the time, describes what happened as two Do 217s attempted to make a torpedo run on the ships:

I closed to 1000 yards and noticed what appeared to be torpedoes slung beneath the fuselages of both enemy aircraft. I opened fire at this distance to distract their attention. They were flying in echelon starboard and both opened fire on me. I closed on the starboard one and attacked, striking his port engine, which caught fire and exploded. The Dornier turned on its back and crashed into the sea. Just then, we noticed our starboard engine streaming white smoke, and the radiator temperature went off the clock. The starboard engine was immediately feathered and we found one Dornier still ahead of us. As we were going home anyway, I closed on my one engine and opened fire. His port engine also exploded and he started diving steeply to starboard. As my starboard engine was u/s, I was unable to follow, but noticed one of the crew bail out and the rest starting to climb out on the wings. Just before the Dornier crashed and when it was at about 100 feet, another Mosquito attacked, causing the enemy aircraft to disintegrate and hit the sea in flames.[23]

This engagement made aces of Williams and navigator Kirkpatrick. It also raised Lynx Squadron's total number of kills to thirty. Shortly after, Blackie Williams took command of the Squadron from Fumerton, whose sterling leadership qualities had helped the unit destroy seventeen German aircraft during his tenure as Commander. The Squadron was then stood down to convert to the potent Mosquito Mk 30, as did 410 Squadron. Meanwhile, 409 became the first RCAF night fighter squadron to deploy to France when it moved to Carpiquet (B.17) on 25 August.

If one RCAF night fighter/intruder team stood out above all others during invasion summer, it was unquestionably 418 Squadron's Russ Bannock and Bob Bruce. Along with their record-setting nineteen confirmed flying bombs, they would eventually rack up nine air-to-air kills, destroy a host of ground targets, and be handsomely decorated in the process. Their night Ranger mission to Germany on 17 July is typical of their freewheeling successes during that period.

Pilots were permitted to plan night Rangers to airfields where Intelligence indicated that there was training activity. On July 17th 1944, I therefore planned one to Altenburg airfield, some 100 miles south of Berlin, where Intelligence reports stated that pilots were training on FW 190s for night fighting. In company with Bob Bruce, I took off from Manston in Kent, made landfall on the Belgian coast, established pinpoints on the Meuse River, the Rhine River, a reservoir north of Nürnberg, and then on to Altenburg. We cruised at around 1,000 feet above sea level, and on arrival found the airfield lit up, with two aircraft burning their navigation lights and practising interceptions with searchlights. We attacked the nearest aircraft and saw it crash, then hit the second with a good burst of cannon. We were then, not surprisingly, subjected to searchlights and AA fire, and were forced to break off the attack. As we did not see this second aircraft crash, it could only be claimed as damaged.[24]

Later the next month, this same crew, flying in formation with Sid Seid and Dave McIntosh, would have a productive day in the Copenhagen area.

Starting in early 1944, 418 Squadron crews were very successful in doing day Ranger sorties by flying in pairs at treetop height to avoid enemy radar detection. These missions were usually done on low overcast days so that we could seek cloud cover if jumped by a squadron of enemy fighters. If we did not encounter aircraft in the air, we would plan to attack an airfield and set grounded aircraft on fire. You could usually get away with one pass before the airfield defences could start reacting.

Typical of this type of mission was a trip I made to Copenhagen's Vaerlose airfield on August 30th, 1944. I was in the lead aircraft with my navigator, Flight Lieutenant Bob Bruce, followed in a second Mosquito piloted by Flying Officer Sid Seid and navigated by Flying Officer Dave McIntosh. We refueled at RAF Coltishall and flew out low across the North Sea, crossing the Danish coast at "zero feet." We then continued in the treetops, on a zig-zag course to make it more difficult for the Germans to vector in fighters, based on information from ground observers. We cruised at 275 mph but considering that both the Me 109 and FW 190 only had a top speed of about 340 at sea level, they would have had difficulty making an interception. We appeared to arrive at Vaerlose undetected and made one pass from east to west. I spotted a Ju 88 and an Me 110 at the end of the main runway and got a good burst in on each. Both were burning as we exited the airfield boundary. Sid Seid fired a good burst at some aircraft parked on the side of the airfield, but since they probably had no fuel in them, they failed to catch fire. Since we were being fired upon as we left the field, we did not attempt a second pass. I did, however, have a little difficulty in refraining Sid from doing one, since I'm positive he would not have made it across the field without being clobbered by the AA . . . .[25]

Dave McIntosh's accounting from the starboard seat of the second Mosquito provides an amusing counterpoint to Russ Bannock's recollections of the day.

Twentieth minute: coast again, those beautiful cottages, small boats bobbing at anchor, but nobody in sight, look far to starboard in direction of Kastrup, Copenhagen's main airfield — no planes in air, thank heaven — a highway and secondary field, again nothing in sight. Twenty-first minute: double railway, highway, railway, road, Russ and Sid swinging hard to port. Twenty-second minute: a grove, a pond, Vaerlose.

We had to pull up to be able to see anything on the ground at

Vaerlose. There were some planes parked on the far side of the field near the hangars.

Russ, in the lead, began firing first, at the planes to the left. I got a glimpse of an explosion. Sid opened up on the planes parked to the right. My feet began jumping because of the banging of the cannons under the floorboards.

Sid made some strikes on one or two planes. My attention was diverted by a strange sight to starboard. A man in overalls was on top of a ladder painting the front part of a hangar, the section over the big doors. He was a good twenty feet in the air. He had tried to get down the ladder too quickly when he heard us and had pushed the ladder out from the wall. He teetered at the top of the ladder, his arms flailing like some hilarious clown circus act. The ladder slowly went over and the man fell backwards in a ninety-degree arc. Before he hit the pavement in front of the hangar, we were gone.

"Goddam it," said Sid. "They wouldn't burn."

I looked back and saw what he meant. Russ had hit two planes and both were on fire. Sid had hit two, and nothing had happened except that some pieces had flown off.

A squirt of flak came up just as Sid put the Mosquito into a deep turn. "We'll try again," Sid said.

He was turning so steeply the blood started to drain out of my head. There was a crackle in the earphones. "Don't go back, Sid," Russ said.

God bless you, Russ Bannock, I thought.

Sid mumbled something but he didn't question the order, which had broken the silence since takeoff between our two planes. He pushed the stick the other way and we began to level out and, more important, put distance between us and the field. There were a couple more rounds of flak but apparently it didn't come anywhere near us. As long as it missed, I didn't care how narrow or wide the miss was.

"Goddam it," Sid said.

He was burned up that he had only damaged two planes, while Russ had destroyed two. How in hell was he going to whip Hitler single-handedly if he couldn't shoot straighter than that? I could practically hear the words going through his head.

"Well, at least we saw some Jerries," I said.

It didn't appease him. "What in hell is the point of seeing Jerries if we can't knock them off?"

"Maybe we got a real one," I said.

"What?"

I told him about the guy falling off the ladder.

"Is that what you were watching?" Sid asked.

"It took my mind off the shooting," I said.

"Jesus."

I began to take in the beauty of the Danish countryside again.[26]

——◆◆◆——

With the approach of autumn, the weather took a turn for the worse, and, coupled with the dynamics of the German retreat on the Continent, that meant fewer targets for the night fighter/intruder squadrons. On 10 September, 409 Squadron moved forward to Saint André, while 410 Squadron deployed to France on 22 September, initially to Amiens-Glisy.[27] Although victories were elusive during most of the remainder of the year for the Mosquito squadrons, Russ Bannock had another memorable day in late September. This time, his astonishing good luck nearly ran out.

On September 27th, I planned a day/night Ranger to Parrow airfield on the Baltic coast, north of Berlin. While the Eighth Air Force was conducting daylight bombing attacks, their escorting fighters were beating up airfields on the way home, forcing the German Air Force to conduct their training early in the morning and late in the evenings when there were no fighters around. I took off at around 0400 hours, planning to arrive at Parrow at first light. Once we had crossed Holland, we stayed as low to the tree tops as lighting conditions would permit and arrived at Parrow undetected. The circuit was already full of training aircraft. We destroyed two Me 108s in quick succession and started to attack a third, but the instructor saw us and managed to out-turn us. We were then attacked by an older Me 109 (strutted tailplane), who managed a couple of strikes on our wing. Realizing that it would be unwise to stay and dogfight, we opened up to full power and headed for the tree tops. We quickly pulled away from the Me 109 but had only flown about ten miles from Parrow when our port engine caught fire. We quickly feathered the engine and activated the fire extinguisher, which put out the fire — then stayed in the tree tops. We really hugged the ground as we crossed Denmark and managed to reach the North Sea undetected. On one engine, the Mosquito

Mk VI still cruised at 190 mph and although we saw some Ju 52 transports in the distance, we saw no fighters.[28]

By 12 October, 409 Squadron had moved to Lille-Vendeville, as did the Cougars of 410 Squadron on 3 November. Later still in the year, particularly during the December Ardennes offensive, the RCAF night fighter squadrons encountered intensified enemy air activity, and an additional sixteen victories were claimed by both the Nighthawks and the Cougars, bringing their respective air-to-air scores in the wake of the invasion to thirty-eight for 409 Squadron and forty-one for 410 Squadron. Even better was the fact that these victories had cost the units only half a dozen aircraft. By 1 November, 418 Squadron was posted to Hartford Bridge as part of 136 Wing in 2 Group of 2TAF, and became tasked solely with operations against ground targets on the Continent for the duration of the war. Meanwhile, 406 Squadron, under newly promoted Russ Bannock, took 418's place on intruder operations in their formidable Mk 30 Mosquitos, and from December 1944 until the end of the war, scored a further twenty-three aerial victories, plus nine more on the ground. Russ Bannock and Don MacFadyen each accounted for four more in the air, usually during nocturnal prowlings over the German night fighter fields.[29] Thus, the Canadian night fighters and intruders closed the books on a very productive calendar year, but their work was far from over, and they would continue to make very productive contributions to the war effort right up until the final collapse of the Third Reich the following spring.

1   S. L. Mayer, *The Russian War Machine 1917–1945*, p. 204
2   Karl Linton, letter to author, May 1993
3   David Goldberg, letter to author, May 1993
4   Johnnie Johnson, *Wing Leader*, p. 202
5   Desmond Scott, *Typhoon Pilot*, p. 18
6   Hugh Godefroy, *Lucky Thirteen*, p. 19
7   Ibid., p. 80
8   Johnnie Johnson, p. 205
9   Arthur Jewett, letter to author, August 1993
10 Christopher Shores, *The History of the Royal Canadian Air Force*, p. 53
11 R. C. Fumerton, letter to author, July 1993
12 Hedley Everard, *A Mouse in My Pocket*, p. 300
13 John D. R. Rawlings, *The History of the Royal Air Force*, p. 171
14 Lloyd Hunt, *We Band of Brothers*, p. 52
15 Dave Bockus, letter to author, June 1993

16 Arthur Jewett, letter to author, August 1993
17 George Burroughs, letter to author, September 1993
18 *RCAF Overseas: The Fifth Year*, p. 274
19 Russell Bannock, letter to author, April 1993
20 Dave McIntosh, *Terror in the Starboard Seat*, p. 67
21 Russell Bannock, letter to author, April 1993
22 R. D. Schultz, tape to author, September 1993
23 *RCAF Overseas: The Fifth Year*, p. 282
24 Russell Bannock, letter to author, April 1993
25 Ibid.
26 Dave McIntosh, *Terror in the Starboard Seat*, p. 133
27 Christopher Shores, p. 55
28 Russell Bannock, letter to author, April 1993
29 Christopher Shores, p. 55

8

THE
HOME STRETCH

"I'm hit. I'm going home . . ."
— BILL BROWN, 441 SQUADRON

If there was one predominant characteristic which typified the lifestyle of the Allied Tactical Air Forces in the wake of the Normandy invasion, it was their extreme mobility. The months of practice under canvas in southern England were about to reap dividends, since the nomadic lifestyle demanded by rapidly moving front lines would last for nearly a year. It would also require a considerable amount of flexibility, dogged determination, and innovation, particularly from the field engineers, the maintainers, and the provisioners. The day fighters were extremely busy immediately following D-Day. By 10 June, a hastily constructed forward landing strip between Ste. Croix and Ver-sur-Mer was ready to accept aircraft, and did so on a transitory basis for the next five days for aircraft from both Johnson's and Keefer's Wings. It was an effective and efficient filling station for squadrons doing routine sweeps over the beachheads and battlefields.

On 13 June, the RCAF day fighter community was particularly saddened by the loss of one of its greatest and most highly respected leaders. The ebullient Lloyd Chadburn died, not from enemy action, but from a mid-air collision over the Normandy beachhead. A fine fighter pilot and an extremely capable leader, Chadburn had been an inspiration for all who knew him and served with him.

By 15 June, forward airfields were ready to garrison Spitfires on the Continent. Gord Ockenden, then serving with 443 Squadron of Johnson's Wing, recalls:

Our groundcrew landed on the beachhead in Normandy around D+3 and started to set up camp; Mess tents, hangar tents, jerry can refueling dumps, and ammunition areas, while the army engineers used road graders to level a farmer's field near Ste-Croix-sur-Mer, and laid steel tracking for our field, known as B.3. German dead, snipers, and lots of incoming artillery rounds made our boys aware of the battle.

Our Wing celebrated the departure from Ford on D+9 (15 June) with a going away lunch at Arthur King's pub in Chichester. We subsequently squeezed as much bread and as many quart bottles of beer as we could into each cockpit as we "merrily" left Ford in a three-squadron (54 Spitfires), loose — very loose — formation flight to B.3. Despite the joyful condition of some of the pilots, we got all the aircraft safely on the ground and distributed the beer and bread to our grateful groundcrew. The place was a dusty mess and every landing was almost under instrument conditions.

The Wing arriving at B.2 (Crepon) the next day (127 Wing, now commanded by Wing Commander R. C. Buckham) incurred several accidents — obviously they hadn't started from a pub . . .[1]

Action on the Continent was quickly forthcoming, as Ockenden notes:

Dawn Patrol the next morning was an unusual one. England was socked in and unable to provide fighter support to the beachhead. The Normandy coast was obscured in low stratus, and a six-plane Dawn Patrol from our Wing over the U.S., British, and Canadian beachheads rapidly degenerated into a two-plane — Flight Lieutenant Don Walz and me. The heavy dust on takeoff caused unserviceabilities to the rest of the Flight.

After a half-hour beachhead patrol that was confined to between the front line and the bay where the ships had barrage balloons in the clouds, our Section control, on board a warship, advised us that 20+ Huns were inbound above the stratus. Our two-plane Section, Don leading, was vectored to intercept. The stratus was breaking up and we engaged a gaggle of Bf 109s as they descended to strafe and run. My guns jammed on the first round (the heavy dust in the chambers formed a block to the bolts as they went forward). Then Don, with me acting as his faithful "I-won't-lose-you-Number-Two," engaged a '109, and Don got him. The other Huns strafed troops as well as our airfield, then ran for it . . . (Thank God!). Control then ordered "guns free" over the beachhead as all aircraft there appeared to be unfriendly. Our troops actually engaged us with fire right into the circuit . . . (poor shots!).

An extract from the Hun's debriefing (the German was captured by Canadian troops after bailout) stated: "When I came out of clouds, there were two aircraft in front of me. For a moment I thought they were Bf 109s, but I soon made them out to be Spitfires. Right beside me were six more Spitfires. Escape at low altitude was unfortunately not possible since I was surrounded by the enemy . . ."

I know that Don and I were very busy, but for two Spits to "surround" someone shows that he was panicking just as much as we were.

The Dusk Patrol on the same day by six 443 Squadron aircraft was a disaster. I was busy in our campsite helping to bury bloated German soldier bodies, when Flight Lieutenant Hugh Russel stated that he would take my place in the air so I could finish the burial duties. Besides, I'd had a rough morning. Four of the six-plane formation climbed up through cloud near Sassy, Normandy, and were jumped. All four were shot down. Squadron Leader Hall, Flight Lieutenant Russel, and Flying Officer Perez-Gomez (a Mexican volunteer) were all killed. Flight Lieutenant Don Walz bailed out, suffering facial burns in the process, and was rescued by the French Underground.

After several transfers of location, Don was hidden by the Hervé family in Malicarne. They kept him in the attic of the Hotel Boule d'Or and the owner's two teenage daughters took care of him.

Don was rescued by the Americans when the breakthrough came in August, and he returned to the Squadron, and then back to flying. He and I subsequently visited Malicarne and I met the Hervés, including Janine and her sister. Why he left them to return to the Squadron has always been a mystery! (Don has visited the families that rescued and hid him three times in the last fifteen years, and he is still considered their close friend and "hero.")

It should be noted that we pilots were soon wearing army battledress. After a couple of days in Normandy, where the dust made

Air Force blue look like German blue and our troops shot at us, we were all put into khaki with Air Force rank, badges, etc., and stayed that way for months until we got to either Belgium or Holland.[2]

Meanwhile, the Canadian Typhoons of 143 Wing, along with counterpart RAF Typhoon wings, were extremely active in Normandy, decimating bridges, supply dumps, rail targets, and all manner of enemy things that moved. They were meeting very little opposition, although the air-to-ground environment was always hazardous. Both 438 and 439 Squadrons' losses were relatively light during the invasion period, but 440 Squadron lost eight aircraft during June alone. The Wing and the entire Typhoon community would be extremely active later in the summer over Falaise and during the German retreat that followed.

During the third week of June, the Spitfire and Typhoon Wings were formally tasked with "strafing anything that moved"[3] — a task they would pursue with particular zeal throughout the rest of the drive across Europe, though not without considerable losses. The day fighter squadrons, however, still retained the primary task of destroying the Luftwaffe in the air, and air combat encounters were a near-daily occurrence over Normandy during the latter half of June. On the twenty-eighth, the RCAF had a scoring field day, their best day of the war. Of thirty-four enemy aircraft destroyed in the theatre, twenty-six confirmed kills and twelve probables fell to the guns of Spitfire pilots from the Canadian wings.

Major reorganizational changes were in store for the day fighter wings in July, along with significant changes in the hierarchy. George Keefer's second operational tour ended that month, a highly successful period for him during which he had added four more confirmed kills to his previous successes in the desert. On the thirteenth, Johnson's 144 Wing, which had been the highest-scoring fighter Wing on the Continent, was disbanded; 441, 442, and 443 Squadrons were broken up and transferred to 125 (RAF), 126, and 127 Wings respectively. Johnson became Wing Commander Flying of 127 Wing, while Group Captain Bill MacBrien assumed overall command from Deane Nesbitt. Keefer's place at the flying helm of 126 Wing was deservedly given to Dal Russel, and titular leadership passed from Keith Hodson to Group Captain Gordon McGregor. A popular and charismatic leader, Russel had been in the thick of things since his outstanding showing with 1 Squadron during the Battle of Britain.

He was a skilled warrior who had demonstrated an even greater capacity for leadership and command. Bill Olmsted remembers meeting this fine officer when joining 442 Squadron as a Flight Commander, just prior to Russel's promotion to command 126 Wing:

After loading my gear onto a waiting truck, I stomped through mud and rain to Dal Russel's tent, where I had been directed to report, and hammered on his tent flap. A shouted, "Come on in," welcomed me as I entered a dimly lit tent to see a tall, blond, handsome, and half-naked officer in the process of shaving. Shaking my hand, he bade me have a seat while he continued with his ablutions.

"You should know the history of the Squadron, Bill," he said, "so that you know the problems we've had and why I asked for you." This last bit of information excited me more than a little.

He then proceeded to detail the Squadron's story from its original formation in Canada under his command through to the present moment. He emphasized that all of the groundcrew were from the original group, while most of the pilots had been with the Squadron before coming to England as an autonomous flying unit. The pilots were keen, daring, and aggressive with many hours of flying experience, but with little operational experience to go with their flying ability. To offset this shortcoming, several experienced leaders had been added to the Squadron strength, but it was still difficult to control the extremely spirited and intrepid pilots. Despite only six weeks of operational experience, the Squadron was the highest scorer in the Wing and, he added, "I intend to keep it that way."

With a twinkle in his eyes, he concluded, "I feel that in order to get the most out of these keen pilots, still more leadership is needed. That's why you are here. You'll fly as a Flight Commander for awhile, and I'd appreciate you passing on as much gen as possible to the fellows."

I was greatly impressed with Dal's presentation and even more so with the man himself. As one of the earliest RCAF pilots to go to England, Dal was among the few RCAF who flew fighter aircraft in the Battle of Britain. While with Number 1 Squadron he destroyed five of the enemy, for which he was awarded the DFC. Along with MacGregor and McNab, he was among the first Canadians to be so decorated. After completing his first tour, he returned to Canada, serving for a time as CO of the forerunner of

442 Squadron. Later he went back to England to complete a second tour with 411 RCAF Squadron, earning a Bar to his gong and promotion to the rank of Wing Commander, completing his second tour on October 18, 1943.

After another rest period he became one of the few Canadians successful in obtaining permission to fly a third tour of operations. To do so he had to accept a rank demotion to Squadron Leader in order to take over 442 Squadron. During the six months I was to serve under him, I watched and participated as he built the highest-scoring Wing in the Second Tactical Air Force. Dal was a superb organizer, a fine pilot, and a great leader. I admired his understanding of human nature and how his personality inspired confidence and cooperation in every man who served under him. He was never too busy to talk to the most junior airman on the station or to pause and chat with some pilot who sought his advice or understanding. His open personality and friendly, spontaneous nature got the best, and the most, out of every man in the Wing.

Within a week of my meeting him, Dal was posted to command 126 Wing, which he had originally formed at Redhill in July, 1943. Our present 144 Wing was dissolved and Johnson moved to command 127 Wing. 442 Squadron was happily incorporated into Dal's new Wing with Squadron Leader Harry Dowding taking over as my new CO.

During my months with the Squadron, I learned more and more to appreciate the opportunity to work for Dal. He had an infectious laugh and a great sense of humor, which we came to know well because he was constantly mingling with the pilots. His brother Hugh had been shot down and killed on June 16, which explained the dark circles around his eyes I noticed during our first meeting, but that was the only sign of the grief he kept bottled up within himself. Time and again I was to observe and even experience his compassion and understanding.[4]

From now on, enemy fighter activity over the Continent would gradually become more sporadic, due to pilot and fuel shortages as well as a Luftwaffe inclination to husband resources for an occasional attack in force. Infrequent airborne encounters with large Luftwaffe formations would occur, however, right until war's end. Cec Brown describes one such event, during the evening of 16 July:

Andy MacKenzie and I were leading separate groups of six aircraft, just out looking for trouble. One pilot had engine trouble and headed back to our base at B.2, leaving us eleven aircraft. Our groups were about one mile apart and just cruising along when I noticed four Typhoons below heading for our territory at a high rate of speed. I knew they must be running from something, and just then I saw a bunch of Me 109s on their tails. I called to Andy to invite him to join the fun but he replied that he had all he could handle where he was.

Without checking the number of '109s, we tore into them at about 5000 to 6000 feet. Suddenly the sky seemed to be full of aircraft, with everyone shooting at someone. In the midst of all this, I twice saw Harry Boyle clobbering a '109, and eventually he claimed three destroyed. Andy MacKenzie got two, and Jim Collier got one. In addition, there were claims of two probables, and one damaged. I was never known for my shooting accuracy, and I got none; although I'm sure I scared a couple and even had a pretty good "go" at a long-nosed FW 190 that appeared in the scramble. We lost one pilot.

When we returned to base, we were told by Intelligence Officers that they had been monitoring by radio and confirmed that we had tangled with "Matoni's Circus," which consisted of fifty-four '109s led by Walter Matoni in an FW 190.[5]

While the Tactical Air Force was living under canvas and advancing across France during the last summer of the European war, meals and living conditions were generally less than sumptuous. Innovative ways were sought to improve the daily fare, and successful provisioners were able to get away with a lot, as Art Jewett discovered.

At Tilly-sur-Seulles, the meals served in the Mess tent weren't the most appetizing. This wasn't the fault of the cooks in any way. They did their best with what they were supplied — mostly Bully Beef, dehydrated potatoes and anything else that wandered by, with or without fur or feathers. Occasionally they tried to make an Irish Stew out of the corned beef. The tiny little pieces of red meat floating around in the rehydrated, dehydrated potatoes looked somewhat unsightly, and some wag named it "Boiled Pilot After a Crash." Pretty awful, but that's the way it was!

One day I was tasked to fly a Spit with a couple of bent wings

back to the support unit at Bognor Regis, in exchange for a
replacement aircraft. Before I left, the outfit got some money
together and I was asked to bring back a good quantity of lobster
in the new aircraft. It was then in season and this would be a real
treat for the Squadron . . .

Anyhow, I took off in the late afternoon with bent wings,
money, high anticipation of good food, a night on the town, and
even the possibility of meeting a WAAF or two. After arrival at destination, I got a drive into Bognor to a nice hotel, got cleaned up,
went out on the town and had a wonderful evening — good food,
good booze, after which I don't remember very much until I got
up in the hotel in the morning, showered (or bathed), shaved, and
went down for breakfast. The waiter asked me if I would like to
have breakfast on the terrace facing the English Channel. It was a
beautiful summer morning, clear fresh air, no fog, and good visibility. I struck up a conversation with an English Captain, who was
also there for a few days. A couple of Supermarine Walruses were
stooging up and down over the Channel, and the Captain asked
what they were doing. I explained that possibly some of the
bomber boys had gone "into the drink" returning from a raid the
previous night, and the Air/Sea Rescue Walruses were searching for
survivors. After breakfast, I went into town, bought a great bunch
of lobster, and went back to the airfield to pick up my new aircraft
and return to the Continent.

At the airfield, I picked up my helmet, parachute, etc., and with
the lobster, got a lorry driver to take me to the flight line. The new
aircraft was clean, gassed up, and armed, but there didn't seem to
be any place to put the lobster. So I asked the driver (an RAF
Corporal) to take the lobster out to a spot on the perimeter taxi
strip where there were a few trees, and to wait for me there. I taxied out and parked the aircraft beside the lorry. I then told the
Corporal to unload the ammunition trays and throw the ammo (20
millimeter and 50 caliber) into the woods and reload the trays with
the fish. He was somewhat reluctant to do this, explaining that I
was throwing away the King's ammunition. I quite forcefully told
him to do it, and that he could tell the King where the ammo was
and he could come and get it, if he wanted it. Besides, I had my
.38 Smith & Wesson, and he didn't have one.

I soon took off and arrived back at B.19, parking in my usual
spot. When taxiing in, I noticed two or three airmen waving

"hello," which I cheerfully returned. As I stopped the engine, the groundcrew Sergeant hopped up on the wing, stuck his hand in the cockpit to shake hands, and said, "We're sure glad to see you back, Sir." I said, "Why? I was only in Bognor overnight." "But you were reported missing last night, Sir," he said. I thought, "Holy Christ!" I got so excited about being in England that I forgot to sign in at destination — which was Standard Operating Procedure — and therefore no signal went back to take-off point, saying that I had landed safely at destination. At this point, my Flight Commander showed up and said, "Brannagan (S/L Tommy Brannagan — the Squadron Commander) wants to see you — you were reported missing last evening." I thought, "Holy Christ; those Walruses were looking for me!" Before I got to Brannagan, the armourers showed up and reported that there was no ammo in the machine gun or cannon trays — only lobster. This had to be reported also. By the time I got to Brannagan's truck/office, I figured I would be shot well before sunset, and that was if I was lucky! I got there and saluted. I well remember his remark: "Jewett, I don't want to talk to you — but Group Captain Malan does — he's waiting for you at Wing headquarters." Sailor Malan, the legendary South African ace, was well known for a pretty good temper. I again thought, "Holy Christ! I won't even make it to lunch . . . I'll probably be shot on sight." Anyway, I went before him and it was kind of dicey for a few minutes, but I survived. I had learned from Johnny Conlin not to lie. It was now lunch time. I got back to the Mess tent and most of the lads were enjoying lobster, but I couldn't eat a bite. I did enjoy the stew though, with all those little pieces of red meat floating around, knowing that, at least for the time being, the boiled pilot wasn't me . . .[6]

While June and July in Normandy were typified by many intense air-to-air engagements, August's operations stood out in sharp contrast. Only twenty-five enemy aircraft would be downed by all the Spitfire squadrons during the entire month — almost as many as had been felled on one day in June! The German air force in the West had been decimated in the air and bombed out of their airfields. What scarce resources they did have were largely being kept for mass attacks against the relentless strategic bombing missions of the Eighth Air Force, and seldom appeared over the tactical battlefield.

By late July, the U.S. Army had made a breakthrough between St. Lô and Coutances and were driving towards the Loire River, westward into Brittany and eastward towards the Seine River, cutting behind the German Seventh Army in the process. By 13 August, they had reached Argentan. At the same time, British and Canadian troops attacked southward from Caen towards Falaise, cutting across General von Kluge's line of retreat in the process. Slowly, inexorably, giant Allied pincers were closing on the Germans in Normandy.

During the first two weeks of August, the Typhoon squadrons were particularly active. On the second, Judd's "Bombphoons" caught the 9th Panzers attempting to retreat from the Conde-sur-Noireau area and fell upon them four separate times over a six-hour period.

After diving through the usual intense curtain of flak to release their bombs, the pilots came down again to strafe. One pilot pulled out of his dive so sharply that many rivets popped out of the Tiffy's mainplane. Another levelled out in a valley, looking up into the startled faces of flak gunners on the hill beside him . . .[7]

And on it went, with the Typhoons decimating enemy armour, gun emplacements, troop concentrations, headquarters buildings, bridges, and other key positions. A typical example of the outstanding support they provided to the army was an attack by nine 439 Squadron aircraft against a particularly resilient and bothersome enemy position in the village of Jean Blanc on 9 August.

The heavy haze had dissipated somewhat by this time and the target was quite easily approached from the north-west at 6000 feet. An almost vertical dive attack was carried out from the south-east, right down to 1000 feet. All bombs landed where they were aimed and the entire west half of the village seemed to rise in the air. F/L Scharff led the boys back in a beautiful strafing attack from the south-west at 1000 feet, right down to the tree tops. All fields, bushes, and roads leading into the village of Jean Blanc from this direction were sprayed by cannon fire. At this point, our own artillery dropped more red smoke shells on the north-west corner of the target so we roared in again with cannon talking! This time, the attack was pressed home until some of the aircraft were in danger of being hit by ricochets as they zoomed over the town. A small orchard at the north-west corner of the town was sprayed unmercifully. A large wooden house at the edge of the orchard was burning furiously, and the entire village was cloaked in a mantle of smoke and dust.[8]

Left devoid of air-to-air targets, the vulnerable Spitfires were tasked more and more frequently with air-to-ground sorties, which they performed with great alacrity and skill. Art Sager recalls the period:

> The major task of the Wing in August is to delay the retreat on these two fronts by doing as much damage as possible to the Hun, his transport and armour. Spitfires are no longer air fighters but ground attack aircraft and most of the shows are "armed reccos," some with bombs slung under the fuselage.
>
> It's a necessary job, but not a pleasant one. The hunting for targets and quick planning of attacks are exciting, but the strafing of despatch riders, soldiers in lorries or scrambling into ditches, turns the stomach. It's less revolting to drop a bomb on a tank or shoot up a mobile gun or armoured vehicle, but even this leaves a bad taste. My revulsion is eased somewhat by the knowledge that there is some risk. When identified and attacked, the Germans open up with flak and anti-aircraft fire against which the soft-bellied Spit has little protection. Attacking ground targets is definitely not "a piece of cake." In my first two weeks on operations, three pilots are shot down and a dozen return with damaged kites.
>
> I get my introduction to this new kind of fighting by flying Number Two to the Squadron Leader and Flight Commander. Intelligence gives the area to be covered and the current bomb line and, flying usually in Sections of four or six at between 6,000 and 8,000 feet, I search the roads and byways between map coordinates. When the Hun is sighted — a flash of metal, sudden movement, grey-green forms under trees — I dive singly into the attack, drop my bomb if carrying one on the first pass and return for other passes with cannon and machine gun. When, six days later, I'm leading my own Section, I find the searching more productive at 5,000 feet or lower as I discover that the Hun seldom fires until flushed out.
>
> In the seventeen days of service with 403, I fly on fourteen armed reccos and two front-line patrols, and my total "score" is six "flamers," seven "smokers" and eight "damaged," including two tanks. Not included are two or three dead horses harnessed to guns, and a frightened Frenchman in a field, who identifies himself in

time by waving his arms. I do not fire on any of the lorries with red cross markings, though many claim that they're fake ambulances; and indeed on one sortie, the occupants jump into a ditch and bravely fire away with machine guns. By the seventeenth of August, the Wing is credited with over 500 MT (mechanized transport) destroyed or damaged, and the roads are jammed with burnt-out vehicles.[9]

But the killing was not all one-sided. The Germans were innovative, and although they ran out of many things during the latter months of the war, something they seldom seemed to lack was anti-aircraft support for their troops. If life for a Spitfire pilot attacking ground targets wasn't inherently dangerous enough, the Germans deliberately increased the threats by establishing "flak traps." They would set up a few old trucks or abandoned vehicles in a clear area at the edge of a wood, then fill the woods with flak and wait for an unsuspecting fighter pilot to commit to an attack. Art Jewett remembers one such event:

During an "armed recce" on 13 August 1944, I spotted a group of trucks at the edge of a wooded area at about my "nine o'clock." It appeared to be a good target, and so I reported it to Flight Lieutenant Bill Brown, my Flight Commander. He said, "It's your target, Art. Go get them and we will give you cover." I broke down from the Squadron, lined up on the trucks, and when I was in range, opened up with cannons and machine guns. As I did so, the Jerries opened up from the ground. I never saw so much tracer — everything they had in those woods, they used. I yelled to the Squadron, "It's a flak trap!," and broke port over the woods, stayed low for a few seconds and then pulled up to rejoin 441 Squadron. As I was pulling up, Brownie's voice came over the radio, "I'm hit. I'm going home." It wasn't standard R/T form, and from the tone of his voice I felt that the "home" he was going to wasn't Tilly-sur-Seulles (B.19) or Canada, but somewhere else. We never saw Brownie again. He must have followed me down to attack, drew fire, and was hit. The whole thing lasted only a few seconds. He was a hell of a fine Flight Commander . . . .[10]

By 15 August, the Canadian army was within a mile of Falaise, and two days later the town was captured. Meanwhile, the Americans were pressing in from Argentan, trapping the Germans in a narrow pocket between the two towns. On the seventeenth, they started streaming eastward from Falaise in hundreds of vehicles massed in enormous convoys, and that's when Allied air power fell upon the Germans with an iron fist. On the seventeenth and eighteenth, Dal Russel's Wing, working in concert with Johnnie Johnson's, destroyed almost 1,200 enemy vehicles, and the Typhoons also took an awesome toll. In this killing zone, time and date lost their meaning, as Art Jewett recalls:

> It was a turkey shoot. We laid it to them, much as they had done to us in the first years of the war. On August 18, I flew in three attacks. We didn't have to hunt for targets; they were right there and, being in a hurry, they hadn't had time to set up flak traps. Their air force didn't show up for the "party," no flak, nothing but lines of trucks and various types of transport. It was on this day, in between raids, that I was sitting under an old apple tree, waiting for my aircraft to be refueled and the guns cleaned and rearmed. The Padre came by and must have seen me sitting there. He came over and asked me if I was going to the service. Without thinking, I said, "What happened . . . did somebody get killed?" He looked at me and very quietly said, "No, young man. It's Sunday." I had lost touch of the fact that it was the Sabbath. This realization, coupled with my flippant remark, really bothered me for a while . . .[11]

Viewed from the ground, the carnage at Falaise was almost beyond description. The fierce destructive power of the Allied air forces was driven home dramatically to an advance ground party of 39 Reconnaissance Wing, which happened along that way shortly thereafter:

> . . . most terrible of all were the fields of Chambois near Falaise, where entire German convoys had been caught by the "Eyes of the Army," and then came the Typhoons and dive-bombing Spitfires to sow death and chaos amongst them. In lanes, on open fields, under hedges, they lay dead in groups. These men had died for Adolf Hitler. It was a terrible sight, and yet more sorrow was expressed for the poor horses that lay dead by the hundreds in this carnage. A few German prisoners had been rounded up and they were burying their dead comrades.[12]

All told, RCAF wings had attacked and destroyed or seriously damaged over 2,600 enemy vehicles in the Falaise pocket. Weather had
hindered operations on the nineteenth and twentieth of August, and
suspended them completely on the twenty-first. When flying resumed
again on the twenty-second, the Germans had fled eastward to the
Seine River between Elbeuf and Bernay, and were not nearly as concentrated as they had been at Falaise. Still, some action was possible,
and over 175 additional vehicles were destroyed by a combination of
Spitfire and Typhoon attacks during daylight hours.[13]

The rapidity of the German retreat quickly situated the Spitfire airfields much too far to the rear for effective, sustained contact with
the enemy. Accordingly, Dal Russel's 126 Wing moved forward from
Cristot to a new base near Evreux, while Johnnie Johnson's 127 Wing
traded Crepon on the Norman coast for lodgings at a former German
airfield northwest of Dreux and, best of all, a relative "stone's throw"
from Paris. The City of Light was liberated by Allied troops on 25
August, and simultaneously, British and Canadian troops occupied
Honfleur at the mouth of the Seine River. Two days later, these
troops had established four bridgeheads across the river and were driving hard to Rouen, which capitulated on the thirtieth. The
Canadian army then struck out toward Dieppe, while, on their eastern flank, the British Second Army took Amiens on the thirty-first
and crossed the Somme.[14] Gord Ockenden of 443 Squadron remembers those late summer days during the period of the move to Dreux:

When Patton got on the roll from Normandy, he received priority
on gas. Since we got assigned to B.26 Illiers l'Evêque near Dreux,
around 60 km from Paris and well within the American sector of
operations, we couldn't get the fuel to fly much.

For many members of the Wing, our first road sortie was into
Paris, where we helped celebrate the liberation. Our patrol area was
the Montmartre, and it was impossible to pay for a drink. Our all-
night champagne party resulted in few fit to depart the next day.
My Number One, Don Walz, persevered in getting me into the
Squadron jeep, only to have one delightful girl kick him several
times on the shins while her girlfriend dragged me back to the
party. After a considerable display of willpower, Don rescued me
and we left for our Wing. To this day he says I owe him a life. I'm
not sure whether he means mine or the girl's!

While at B.26, we scrounged a lift into Dreux. Being short of wheels, we commandeered a U.S. Army jeep from outside the gate at a very busy brothel. We left one pilot there, who shall remain nameless, helping the Madame keep score on a blackboard in the foyer. Four of us, one being Fred Kearnes, who later became President of Canadair, pushed the jeep silently down a hill, then started it and took off for B.26. Fortunately, the sub-machine gun on board jammed before we hit any pursuers!

On arrival back at the Wing at around midnight, we turned the vehicle, complete with full battle gear as well as the personal gear of its rightful owners, over to our groundcrew. "Camouflage it," we said. The next morning, they handed it back to us with the colors, decals and serial numbers on the sides being an exact duplicate of Wing Commander Johnnie Johnson's personal jeep!

We used this little number to get gas, loaned it to Squadron Leader Wally McLeod, toured the area (while assiduously avoiding U.S. Army police checks) and just generally enjoyed the vehicle for a couple of weeks. Johnson eventually saw it parked next to his and wondered where the "twin" had come from. Shortly thereafter, Johnnie's batman wrote off our Wing Commander's vehicle. The wreck was bulldozed into a bomb crater and then "ours" became "his" . . .[15]

————◆•◆••◆————

By early September, the Allies had overrun the port of Antwerp and were doggedly advancing along the coast and through northern Belgium. As the armies moved, so did the Spitfires and the Typhoons. On 1 September, Russel's 126 Wing moved from Evreux to Poix, and then in quick succession to Brussels. The airfield there was intact but extremely congested, since it was being used simultaneously as a logistics airhead and a combat base. Meanwhile, the stubborn German resistance in the Channel ports was delaying the Allied advance, since many commodities, particularly fuel, were in short supply. Although the port of Antwerp had been captured relatively early, supply ships would not reach it until January 1945. This was due to the tenacious German defence of the island of Walchern in the Schelde River estuary, which denied passage to Allied shipping. Generally speaking, for the first six months of combat on the Continent, the Allies were forced to move their supplies through the innovative Mulberry Harbours, towed from the United Kingdom to the Normandy beaches. There is no doubt, however, that Allied control of the air significantly helped move the vital supplies "along the chain" during this logistically challenging period. Had the Germans been able to attack the supply lines in strength, those attacks could have had a disastrous impact on the Allied drive across the Continent.

The members of Johnson's 127 Wing would cool their heels at B.26 Illiers l'Evêque for the first three weeks of September, since all ground transport had been requisitioned to support the forward area — another effect of the supply problem. On 22 September, the Wing finally moved deep into Belgium to B.68 Le Culot near the university town of Louvain, and then, at the end of the month, to B.82 Grave in Holland. On 27 September, in an engagement over the Nijmegen-Arnhem area of Holland during which Johnnie Johnson scored his thirty-eighth and final kill of the war, the popular Commander of 443 Squadron was killed. Wally McLeod would be sorely missed by the RCAF fighter community. A born scrapper, he had led 443 Squadron from the organization of 144 Wing in England, through the reorganization into 127 Wing, and throughout the first four months of action on the Continent. His score of twenty-one confirmed kills was the highest for any member of the RCAF, and he had been deservedly recognized for his fine fighting spirit and leadership with a DSO and a DFC and Bar. Number 443 Squadron was quick to avenge the death of their leader, as recalled by Gord Ockenden.

On 28 September 1944, Flight Lieutenant Gordie Troke, DFC, was leading a patrol between the Maas and Nijmegen bridge area in support of Operation Market Garden, the "A Bridge Too Far" fiasco. Then, Control reported painting 60+ Huns just as we were turning south to head back to B.68 (Le Culot) in Belgium. Short of fuel, we engaged the massive force of '109s and '190s, five miles northeast of Nijmegen under a 5000 foot overcast. All hell broke loose as we asserted Spitfire superiority with little maneuvering room. 'Twas a real scrap! 443 Squadron got seven destroyed and four damaged with one Spit down and three others with holes in them, but no pilots lost. I got two. We landed at several temporary fields due to low fuel . . .[16]

The airborne landings at Arnhem and elsewhere in Holland were bringing the Germans out in force; something which hadn't happened for many weeks. At the end of August, after less than three months of combat on the Continent, the nine Canadian fighter squadrons claimed 262 victories for relatively minimal losses. Number 401 Squadron was in the vanguard with forty-seven and a half kills, 441 Squadron next with thirty-five. Johnnie Johnson was the highest individual scorer of the campaign with nine kills since the landings, and 401's CO, Hugh Trainor, was close behind with eight and a half, then G.W. Johnson (401 Squadron) with seven, and W.T. "Grizzle" Klersy (401 Squadron) and Wally McLeod of 443 Squadron with six each. Pickings were lean through late August and early September, but new aces began emerging in the leaden autumn skies over Belgium and Holland. No star shone brighter than that of Flight Lieutenant Don Laubman of 412 Squadron, who claimed four victories on 27 September alone. Of his eventual score of fifteen confirmed victories, which made him the highest individual scorer of the 2TAF, fourteen and a half were scored after D-Day — a remarkable performance.[17]

On 4 October, 126 Wing moved to Rips in southeast Holland, where they were knee deep in mud, and then ten days later to Volkel in the Dutch Corridor. Nevertheless, the brief stay at Rips yielded a very colourful engagement.

Squadron Leader Rod Smith was to have a very distinguished second operational tour with the Second Tactical Air Force on the Continent, augmenting the six kills he scored in the skies over Malta with a further seven and a half confirmed victories and adding a Bar to his DFC. During the first week of October, he would lead 401 Squadron on what was thought at the time to be an historical event, the first airborne destruction of a German jet fighter. Though it was subsequently determined that on two occasions, Thunderbolt pilots of the USAAF had edged Rod and his Squadron out for that particular honour, it was nonetheless a "first" for fighter pilots from the Commonwealth.

On the afternoon of 5 October 1944, Smith was leading 401 Squadron on a patrol at 13,000 feet over the Nijmegen road bridge in Holland. All was quiet until the 83 Group controller (Kenway) called and said that their GCI radar was painting an aircraft to the northeast, headed towards them at co-altitude. Rod then turned the Squadron, which was in an open battle formation, to the northeast, climbed 500 feet and levelled off in a position three or four miles northeast of Nijmegen. Almost at once he spotted the aircraft at dead 12 o'clock to the formation, 500 feet below, travelling head-on to them southwest towards Nijmegen at a great rate of knots. He quickly identified the aircraft as an Me 262, the extremely elusive German jet, and reported his sighting to the Squadron, while simultaneously building in some manoeuvring room for a hard slice turn to port, should they be so fortunate as to remain undetected. Several of the other Squadron pilots replicated his positioning move and it soon became apparent that the enemy pilot had not seen them, in all likelihood because they were positioned between him and the sun to some degree.

As Rod closed on the '262 during his final swing back left around to the southwest, he drank in the aircraft's marvelously futuristic lines. His thrill factor rapidly intensified as he closed to position behind it for a perfect shot. However, that perfect shot was not meant to be, since another Spitfire, in a turn similar to his own, ended up sandwiched between Smith and the Messerschmitt. Frustrating as it was, if Rod fired, he would obviously risk hitting the other Spitfire, piloted he found out later by John MacKay. Shortly thereafter, the '262 pilot half-rolled into a rather steep dive, then began fishtailing from side to side, still in the dive and still headed in a generally southwestward direction. After some hesitation, which prompted a rather impatient radio call on Rod's behalf, MacKay opened fire, and several cannon strikes appeared on the trailing edge of the Messerschmitt's wing near one of its engine nacelles. Those strikes were accompanied by a stream of strange-looking vapourous grey smoke. At least two other Spitfires then fired on the '262, which by now had pulled out of its dive at around 3,000 feet over Nijmegen, still heading southwest. Since it was no longer trailing smoke and was accelerating away from the pursuing Spitfires, the 401 pilots thought that they had been robbed of a kill. Then, the '262 pilot zoomed into an extremely impressive vertical climb, which left the pursuing Spitfires even further behind, but to Rod's and Tex Davenport's great surprise and delight, brought it soaring up to where they happened to be. Since the zoom climb had killed some of the Messerschmitt's speed advantage, with his throttle wide open Rod was able to pull up behind it in a near-vertical position to within around 350 yards, the maximum effective firing range. He fired an eight-second burst at both engines, saw strikes on both nacelles, and noticed a plume of fire streaming from one of them. By now the '262 was rapidly decelerating and Rod's range quickly closed to around 200 yards. Meanwhile, unbeknownst to Rod, Tex Davenport was behind him and firing at the German jet. Eventually, both the '262 and Rod's

Spitfire fell off in stall turns to the right in unison, but this did not bode well for the Canadian, since on the completion of the stall turns, the two pilots' relative positions were reversed and the German ended up on *his* tail! Rod was in an extremely helpless position, nose down and to the right with not enough airspeed for control for quite a few seconds to come. Furthermore, due to the limited rearward vision in the Spitfire, the enemy jet was completely out of sight on his tail; probably just as well under the circumstances, for Tex later reported that the German was firing at Rod at the time! After what seemed like an eternity, during which time Rod wondered if cannon shells were going to come crashing into him from behind, the '262 appeared a few yards off his starboard side, also diving almost vertically, but was in obvious trouble as the trailing plume of fire had become much larger. It then crashed in a field within Allied lines, sending up a tremendous column of smoke and fire in the process.

Rod called up Kenway right away and told him that they had shot down a German jet, just to the southwest of Nijmegen. Kenway then replied, "I know, we've seen it; good show!" By the time the 401 pilots got back to their field at Rips, they were understandably elated, chattering like magpies and comparing notes on their individual recollections of the engagement. Since five of them had actually shot at it, and since the encounter was rather confusing at best, they decided that it would be fairest all around to share the kill five ways. A day or two later, they learned that the pilot had managed to get out of his stricken aircraft prior to ground impact, but too low for his parachute to open.[18]

Whenever weather permitted, the Typhoon units were now thoroughly mauling a highly bewildered and demoralized German army. By October, 143 Wing was garrisoned at Eindhoven in Holland, and popular Wing Commander M.T. Judd was replaced by Wing Commander F.G. Grant, the previous CO of 438 Squadron. Elsewhere, Canadian pilots were serving with distinction on RAF Typhoon units. Withering ground fire was by no means the only hazard to fighter-bomber operations, as Jake Coupland recollects:

Our Typhoon Squadrons were rocket projectile equipped and our operations were in the ground support role, rather than a purely fighter role. Flying at very low levels most of the time, we attacked road and rail transportation, tanks, shipping, cross-Channel gun emplacements, V1 and V2 rocket sites, and other "targets of opportunity." Typhie casualties were high for a period of air superiority, due of course to our operations being at very low levels.

Wing Commander W. Dring, DSO, DFC, was Wing Leader of 123 Typhoon Wing in France. I met him at 84 GSU; he had me posted to his old Typhie Squadron, 183. I arrived there on 1 September 1944. We flew "Cabranks," supporting the Canadian Army as it cleaned up the coastal ports of France. The Jerries feared being rocketed. Sheltered in the large concrete cross-Channel gunpits, the German garrison at Boulogne surrendered when threatened with attack by the Rocket Typhies of 123 Wing orbiting over their heads.

On my last flight but one I was leading a Section of four on Cabrank. Troops of the Canadian First Army were trying to cross a narrow canal but were held up by gunfire directed at them by a German spotter from his position in a church steeple. The Air Contact Team in its Jeep located with the stymied troops called on R/T, "Boswell Yellow leader, 'winkle' that bastard please!" In line-astern, we went in at 50' just above the small hay stacks, behind each of which Canadian troops were trying to keep out of sight from the German spotter. They were about 200 yards from the Germans and normally we fired rockets at about 700 yards short of the target. Our rockets would roar just over a bunch of very scared Canadian heads!

Firing my four 20mm cannon to keep the Jerries' heads down, I got to within 400 yards of the church before letting all eight rockets go in one salvo, breaking away sharply to avoid my own rocket explosions and flying debris. I had been concentrating so hard on the target that I failed to heed the trees between me and the target! My Typhie flew through the tree tops, scattering leaves and branches everywhere. When I gained altitude to reform with my Section, I found that I couldn't throttle back, so I pushed it forward, hoping it might loosen. It made matters worse. I called my Number 3 and told him to lead the Section home, as I was obliged to go on ahead!

Reaching my aerodrome, I called up the controller, explaining my situation. After a short delay, during which I was tearing full-bore around the aerodrome, Wing Commander Dring came on the R/T. He told me to climb to 2000' and bail out! I got to 2000' very quickly, but on looking over the side, decided to attempt a landing. I dropped to deck level, and on the downwind leg, pulled the nose up to lose speed, then downed the undercarriage. On the landing approach, the speed was climbing fast, so once again I pulled the nose up, and when the speed dropped, I lowered my flaps. The speed was increasing rapidly as I descended, but I was nearly at the runway, so I switched off! Immediately, seven tons of Typhoon began falling like a brick. I was going to hit the fence at the end of the runway. I flicked the switches on and 24 cylinders generating 2400 horsepower snapped into life. Before my psyche and my anatomy could suffer a second twitch, I switched off. Happily the sudden burst was enough to get me over the fence and to make a perfect three-pointer.

"Wingco" Dring was across the field in his Jeep before I had pulled off the runway. He pulled out a large stick protruding from my air scoop, and we just missed being doused in glycol. "Close call, Coup, but nice flying," said Dring as we climbed into his Jeep for the drive to Dispersal. A few days later, I was sent to No. 8 RAF General Hospital in Brussels with stuffed and inflamed sinuses, and while there applied for transfer to the RCAF. I returned to London on 22 December for documentation and became a member of the RCAF on 24 December, 1944. With three operational tours completed, the RCAF grounded me.[19]

The fighter-reconnaissance boys of 39 Wing were practising their essential craft all over the battlefield during the Allied advance across the Continent. After the Normandy invasion, 39 Wing truly became "the Eyes of the Army" when they assumed all reconnaissance responsibilities for both the British and the Canadian armies in northern Europe. They generated a staggering amount of photographic production and interpretation work. For example, during a two-week period from the start of the German rout at Falaise, the Wing averaged the development of 32,000 photographic prints a day! While 400 Squadron continued to ply their high-altitude trade in their Spitfire XIs, 414 Squadron flew the Spitfire IX in the low-level tactical reconnaissance role and 430 Squadron soldiered on in a similar role with their aging Mustang Is until November; their patience was rewarded that month when they re-equipped with new Spitfire XIVs.

The change from static to fluid warfare introduced a new type of mission, the contact reconnaissance, on which the pilots worked in cooperation with a patrol car moving with the forward elements on the ground. The car assigned tasks which the troops required — searches of areas immediately ahead, the presence of defences or road blocks, the condition of bridges, etc. — and in this way helped both to speed up the advance and keep Army headquarters informed of the location of its forces.

To keep in touch with the rapidly moving Army, the Squadron (414) advanced from St. Honorine to Illiers l'Evêque (B.26) in the last days of August, watched enemy transport "on the run" to the crossings over the Somme, and then, as the battle front again drew out of range, moved ahead to Poix (B.44), and thence, on 7 September, to Evere (B.56) on the north-eastern outskirts of Brussels. From this base, the pilots carried out missions in support of the airborne landings at Eindhoven and Arnhem. During this period of rapid advance, Flight Lieutenant J. C. Younge was lost while strafing barges near Ghent, and Flying Officer J.W.H. McEachern was killed in the crash of his Spitfire. After a fortnight at Evere, the Squadron moved again to Blakenberg (B.66) near Diest, where it rejoined No. 39 Wing after three weeks' separation. While operating from this field, the pilots destroyed another FW 190 and also had their first views of the new enemy jets with which, in the weeks that followed, they had a few inconclusive brushes.

Blakenberg proved to be a mudhole in the damp autumn weather, and on 2 October, the Wing pulled out to settle down at Eindhoven (B.78) for a long five-month stay, ending a mobile life which had seen six moves in seven weeks. Squadron Leader Hutchinson completed his tour at this time and was succeeded by Squadron Leader Gordon Wonnacott. The battle lines had now become stabilized along the line of the Maas, and the pilots spent the long weeks of autumn and winter reconnoitering over the front from Cleve to Roermond to report on enemy defensive activities, road and rail traffic, the condition of bridges, etc. — in brief, to gather the information which the Army required to ascertain the enemy's intentions. Repeatedly, the Army expressed its appreciation of the pilots' work. Artillery reconnaissances, or "shoots," against hostile batteries became more frequent now as the battle again became static along the Maas front. Beyond the lines, the pilots kept close check on enemy freight yards and recorded the progress of the campaign to strangle all rail traffic to the battle area.

Persistent fog and rain greatly hampered the work of reconnaissance during these months. Increased opposition was also encountered from the flak defences, which had got well dug in, and Flying Officers H. J. S. O'Brien and G. G. McLean were victims of the enemy's accurate fire.[20]

***

Although the ubiquitous Spitfire Mk IX remained the backbone mount of the Commonwealth day fighter arm on the Continent during 1944, by autumn several new Marks and aircraft types were starting to appear in the combat zone. The Spitfire was undergoing another major evolution, which resulted in the excellent Mk XIV series. This fine aircraft was essentially a standard Mk VIII airframe, beefed up to accommodate the massive, 2,050-horsepower Griffon 65 engine, which drove a five-bladed Rotol airscrew. Later variants were fitted with the cut-down rear fuselage and the superb "teardrop" rear-vision canopy. Possessing 400 more horsepower than the production Spitfire IX, the XIV series was 25–35 mph faster than its predecessor, with a correspondingly superior rate of climb. A separate production batch, called the FR XIVE, was fitted with clipped wings for low-level work, an oblique F.24 camera in the rear fuselage, a teardrop canopy, two .5-inch Browning machine guns, and two 20-mm cannon. Number 414 Squadron of 39 Wing would be fortunate enough to fly this outstanding aircraft during the closing month of the European war, while 430 Squadron received earlier variants of the Mark in November 1944.

Near the end of September, 125 Wing exchanged their Spitfire IXEs for 126 Wing's older IXBs, and at that time, all four of the Wing's Squadrons (including 441) rotated back to the U.K. to make the transition to the Mk XIVs. The re-equipped Wing, which now included 402 Squadron, was rotated back to the Continent under the capable leadership of George Keefer, beginning his third tour of operations. He would add four more confirmed kills to his previous victories during the latter months of the European war, bringing his final total to thirteen confirmed kills.

As surely as the Mk XIV was a significant improvement in an established line of thoroughbreds, the Mk XVI was, in the words of one distinguished veteran who flew it, a "dog's breakfast." This troublesome variant was a marriage of convenience between the Mk IX airframe and the low-altitude Packard-Merlin engine, built under licence by the Americans and available in surplus numbers at the time. Producing 1,705 horsepower, it was slightly more powerful than the standard Mk IX, but exhibited treacherous performance characteristics and was prone to catching fire and throwing connecting rods in flight. Still, this variant would be widely used in the low-altitude ground-attack role during the waning months of the European war.

One new British fighter aircraft was introduced to front-line service in 1944: the Hawker Tempest. This fine aircraft was a developmental derivative of the Typhoon, and it married the fuselage, Sabre II engine, and front radiator of a standard Typhoon with a new thin wing and a larger fin and tailplane. The result was an enormous reduction in aerodynamic drag, and the Tempest proved to possess all the ruggedness of the Typhoon while being extremely fast and manoeuvrable in the bargain. A versatile aircraft, it was a fine air combat fighter but was equally suited to ground-attack duties. Due to its extremely fast low-level speed, it was also used extensively to combat the V1s during the summer of 1944. Although none of the Canadian squadrons were equipped with the Tempest, many Canadians in service with RAF units were able to fly this fine aircraft. John Garland of Richmond, Ontario, was a seasoned veteran of tactical operations in the desert and in Italy. In 1944, he would enjoy considerable success with the Tempest on the Continent, winning the DFC in the process before being shot down and taken prisoner in February 1945. John remembers his early operational impressions of the Tempest:

In August '44 at RAF West Malling where I had been posted, Tempest Mark Vs were being flown in by the ladies of the ATA. These big fighters looked a bit daunting after the comparatively tiny Spits, but we thought that seasoned fighter pilots like us should have no problem. We moved to Manston on 29 August and I had my first Tempest flight on 6 September, then had one more flight in it before going on my first operation (total time on type, 1:45). The first two missions were probably of little operational value as we were sent to strafe an area near The Hague, designated by map reference as a suspected launch site for V2s. The next two missions on 15 and 17 September were also in the Hague area and on both days, we set vehicles on fire. I think I began to appreciate even then the exceptional capabilities of this aircraft. The normal cruising speed of 300 mph was a good 60 mph more than the Spitfire IX.

It was much steadier in a dive and with the four short-barreled 20mm cannon, which had a much higher rate of fire than the older cannons (around 850 rounds per minute compared to 550 rounds per minute), a short, one-second burst would put small vehicles out of action. A very stable gun platform with excellent firepower. Certainly a long step ahead of the old Hurricanes of only two years prior . . .[21]

Back in England and in command of 274 Squadron, Stocky Edwards saw his unit through its re-equipment with Tempests in early August, and he was certainly influenced by the female ATA pilots who flew the aircraft in from the factories.

When the Squadron converted to Tempests there was, as usual, some anxiety among the pilots in having to give up their Spitfire IXs. None of us had been very close to a Tempest before. It looked bigger, higher off the ground, sturdier, and it was much faster; but not so genteel. The Tempests were delivered to the Squadron by the Air Transport Auxiliary, a group of women pilots. After landing and shutting down the engines, they removed their helmets and before doing anything else, took out their compacts to powder their noses and apply lipstick. It was too much for my boys, and they immediately decided there was nothing to flying the new aircraft. The Tempest took off and landed very similar to the old Hurricane, but much faster. It was a fine aircraft to fly and fight, and it also had tremendous acceleration for the time period.[22]

By early October, Russel's 126 Wing was bogged down in mud at Volkel in the Dutch Corridor, but just before leaving Rips, 411 Squadron rotated back to the U.K. for gunnery camp and dive-bombing practice. The standard bomb load on the Spitfires when on ground-attack missions was now a 500 pounder under the fuselage centreline and a 250 pounder under each wing. There was now markedly reduced Luftwaffe opposition in the air, although the Germans still made their presence felt from time to time. Number 401 Squadron was similarly rotated shortly after arriving at Volkel, which left the Wing with only 412 and 442 Squadrons. At Grave, Johnson's 127 Wing was a "partner in misery" with 402 Squadron and the rest of Keefer's Wing. All concerned endured appalling conditions for their three-week tenure in the area, and there was near-continuous rain for a fortnight of this period. To add to their misery, the Dutch Corridor was a narrow (twenty-mile) finger of land running between Eindhoven, Nijmegen, and Arnhem, surrounded by isolated pockets of German resistance. This resulted in frequent enemy shelling of the airfields and their access roads — a thoroughly demoralizing state of affairs. The airfields were also bombed and strafed by Me 262s in the ground-attack role, inflicting a number of casualties. Gord Ockenden recalls these unpleasant events:

On 22 October 1944, 127 Wing was evacuated from B.82 Grave, in Holland. This airfield was on a grass area in an oxbow of the Maas River, just south of Nijmegen and near the tip of the Allied advance along the Corridor from Eindhoven to Arnhem. We had moved there on 30 September to give direct support to the Nijmegen stand. German artillery could reach us, Me 262s started dropping anti-personnel bombs on us, the Germans flooded the area, and the dry oxbow filled up. "Mary of Arnhem," the German broadcaster, stated that we would be driven out, etc. She was right. An RAF Wing was located on the east side of this grass/mud airfield, and it left also. We had lost aircrew, groundcrew, and aircraft due to the Me 262 "out of the sun" APB deliveries. Time to retreat!

Eighteen Spits of 443 Squadron taxied out with two groundcrew on the tail, ready to do emergency take-offs from the soggy grass field. I noticed all the groundcrew abandoning the tails, saw an AP cannister burst above us, and called, "Red Leader, airfield under attack."

The eighteen Spitfires went to full boost; some cleared the dispersal, others went through maintenance, some crossed paths on the airfield, others leap-frogged over other Squadron aircraft parked on the perimeter. However, all did get airborne in one piece and we assembled for the flight to our new home at Brussels-Melsbrock (B.58). 'Twas one of life's most exciting takeoffs!

It is interesting that 127 Wing and 126 Wing were in Holland early at "Grave" and "Rips" respectively — both lost people on the ground and both had to evacuate. With names like that for airfields, why stay?[23]

Just two days before this rather abrupt and disorganized departure, however, 443 Squadron's morale had been rekindled by a party of gargantuan proportions. Art Sager, Squadron CO at the time, recalls:

The weather closes in and it starts to rain, heavily and continuously. There is little flying as the airfield is only partially serviceable; in parts it's a lake, in other parts a bog.

I get permission from the Group Captain to go to Eindhoven to collect the champagne for the Squadron party. A big blow-out is needed to lift the spirits of both pilots and airmen. I leave in the jeep with Gordie Troke at noon.

At 83 Group the Catering Officer says, "You're 127 Wing Bar Officer, I suppose?" I reply, "Well, yessir, for the day anyway," muting the last four words. He agrees to let me have the complete allotment for the Wing — 275 bottles at 2,146 guilders, which, in pounds, is more than I want to think about. But they're not all for 443 — we'll sell some of them to pilots of other Squadrons.

A very comfortable and well-furnished building, Group Headquarters. None of these boys go short. I collide with AVM Broadhurst and an Air Commodore going out the front door, salute them smartly and, as we were wearing battledress and dirty boots, we both feel like country bumpkins.

Thence four miles south of the city to the AOC's Mess, here to collect the champagne from its huge "cave." Cunningham has his headquarters in the clubhouse of a golf course, his Fieseler Storch parked beside the eighteenth green. The Mess is located in the home of the President of the Philips company, a hundred yards into park-like woods beside the course. Here the brass has taken full advantage of the luxuries available, of which there are many, including very pretty waitresses.

When we finally load the jeep and rope the cases on securely — I wonder if the chassis will hold — I inquire politely if it would be possible to have a bite to eat before starting the long journey back to Graves. The officer goes to inquire and returns. "I'm very sorry but the PMC says it's impossible as there are too many visitors and not enough food. He gives you his sincere apologies." The PMC, poor fellow, must indeed have a trying time finding enough food for the hard-working members of Group, who live in such hazardous conditions near the front line!

I spend much of the day on arrangements for the party. Down at Flights, Mike the Sergeant reports that the collection of eight guilders from each man for champagne has been completed. I line up the entertainment to be provided by the airmen. There'll be a hillbilly band led by Corporal Scarfe, gags, sketches, and a singsong.

There's a lot of talent in the outfit. I look around for a hall in which to hold the party — schools in the village and a cafe near the airfield — but decide the risk is too great as at all places there are too many windows that could be broken. We'll have to settle on the airmen's Mess tent after all.

The Canadian Army Show arrives on camp in the afternoon. Their concert is held in the airmen's Mess as it's the biggest. The floor is as muddy as the road outside, but with canvas chairs for the upper class and petrol cans for the erks, it's made quite comfortable, at least for the former. It's a high-spirited show with humour and originality. The four girls add considerably to its success, for here in the mud, all members of the gentle sex are Dorothy Lamours. And it is damn nice to see girls' legs occasionally!!

Operations continues to promise that "It'll clear up tomorrow," but I'm sure that tomorrow will never come. All the roads are ankle-deep in mud, passable only with four-wheel drive. With the jeep and ten men, I pull a thirty-hundredweight out of the ruts and the Padre in his fifteen-hundredweight out of a hole. The airfield is unsafe, even for taxiing.

No party anywhere could be more timely than 443's on 20 October. The Wing has been grounded for three days, it is raining solidly, and morale is low. I circulate an invitation to all the men, unfortunately having to restrict it, because of space, to Squadron personnel. The turnout is 100%, pilots and men in battledress and gum boots, many wearing tin helmets against the rain, all carrying mugs.

Free beer is served first as a primer and then, at nine sharp, myself, Terry, Ocky, Stevey, and others hand out bottles of champagne, still wrapped in paper, in return for a receipt of eight guilders. Cork-pulling time is nine-fifteen, before which I demonstrate how it is done with minimum loss of the precious fluid.

The popping of corks sounds like gunfire. Then there is silence as the men start to drink from their mugs or straight from the bottle. Most have never tasted champagne before. I can practically feel their initial disappointment as they take huge gulps and find this nectar of the Gods no stronger than ginger ale. And then, all of a sudden, as the alcohol takes effect, there's an outburst of yelling and laughter and the party is on the way. Second bottles are available on payment, or more free beer.

The party goes on until midnight, well after the last corks have been popped and the beer kegs drained, and the participants are clearly feeling no pain. It has been a riotous and successful blow-out, doing more in three hours to strengthen relations between officers and men than any amount of talking, and restoring in one fell swoop, Squadron morale and ésprit-de-corps. The miracle of the evening is that all the boys get safely back to their billets, particularly the pilots who have to navigate in jeep and truck through flooded roads and over a swollen river to reach the village. Stories are recounted the following day of how they almost didn't make it.[24]

Brussels-Melsbroek constituted a considerable culture shock for the Canadians after their austere existence at Grave. The citizens of this beautiful city were bubbling with enthusiasm and gratitude for their Allied liberators, eager to show their appreciation after spending so many dark years under the yoke of Nazi tyranny. Bill Olmsted describes Brussels and its charming inhabitants from the perspective of a leave period spent there during the autumn of 1944:

While the Belgians were under German domination, the black market had carried on a flourishing business, and the Belgians, in a way, were thankful for it. The poor did not get a great deal to eat, but at least their money could buy the bare essentials. The wealthy, on the other hand, were able to buy almost everything they needed and lived quite well, although at great expense. The Germans had imposed a curfew, which started at eleven o'clock at night and lasted until five the following morning. Those who wished to spend an evening at a nightclub started their parties before curfew hour and stayed until the curfew was lifted the next morning. That arrangement seemed to have been satisfactory to both the Belgians and the Germans.

When the Allies arrived, they abolished the black market, but omitted to bring in the food which the black market had ordinarily supplied and which the population had relied upon. Thus the city began to go hungry as it never had before. The curfew now didn't begin until midnight, but all nightclubs and cabarets were ordered to close at half past ten and to ensure that they did, the electricity was turned off. This forced the clubs to carry on with candles because they were raided nightly by the Belgian military police, who forced the patrons to leave. What might have been an indignity became a common occurrence in Brussels, because the Belgians were a gay people who like to wine, dance and romance in their city's many smart cabarets and luxurious nightclubs.

In order to smash the black market, all money used during the German occupation was made worthless after a suitable warning period, each individual being allowed to cash or exchange a relatively small amount of the old money for the new Belgian currency. This move produced the desired result, although it caught many, whose small fortunes plummeted rapidly in value. Despite these strict measures, the Belgians did not grumble, although they might have preferred a little less Allied control. They obviously accepted the measures as the necessary medicine for the restoration of Belgium.

Brussels became a rest center for the British and Canadian Twenty-first Army Group and for all the RAF and RCAF stationed in Belgium and Holland. Hotels, cinemas, restaurants, and cabarets were commandeered by the Allies, and the city soon became one massive stronghold of troops on furlough. All passes for leave in Brussels were issued with a special pamphlet devised and issued by Army Welfare Services and Education Branch, Headquarters Brussels Garrison, containing much useful information and a variety of restrictions. Each of us required a special Leave Scheme Pass, all cafes were to be emptied by 2300 hours, curfew was in force from midnight to 0500 hours, and all brothels were out of bounds to service personnel. We also had to be suitably dressed, were not allowed to carry personal firearms, and were required to salute senior officers as well as the tomb of the Belgian Unknown Soldier. We could not change money for civilians or speculate in currency and we had to vacate our hotel rooms by 1100 hours on the day of departure. Among the general notes was a warning not to talk about or identify our unit, nor were we to discuss equipment, losses, or battle experiences: "The people of Brussels are very hospitable and will do all they can to make your leave enjoyable. Enjoy yourselves with them, but do not tell them anything." We were also told of the high prices of casual refreshments, and informed that we must not buy food in civilian restaurants. The pamphlet included a large-scale map of Brussels clearly indicating the hotels, bars, theaters, and points of interest.

Our leave lasted only a couple of days, of which I retain one memory. One afternoon, as Jack and I were sitting in a popular cafe enjoying a drink, a waiter approached with a message that a lady and her granddaughter would like to join us, if it was not inconvenient. More out of curiosity than the need for companionship, we agreed. Soon a magnificent creature, like a ship in full sail, marched up to our table, accompanied by a very shy young girl. The lady was something from a different era, dressed totally in black in a very ornate dress, which I guessed was high fashion before World War I. Wearing an enormous black hat, smoking a cigarette through a long black holder, she used her cane as if it were one more ornament. I felt this imperious person was in her late seventies and she exuded an air of confidence, although I thought I could detect a slight nervousness. In broken English, she introduced herself as Madame Spaak and the twelve-year-old girl with her as Catherine. After ordering ice cream, she got around to inviting us to dinner that evening to their home on the Avenue Louise. We politely refused, pleading previous engagements, something I have since regretted, for her son, Paul Henri Spaak, became Prime Minister of Belgium and the young girl achieved international recognition as the movie star, Catherine Spaak.[25]

Number 127 Wing remained at Brussels-Melsbroek for nearly two weeks. On 4 November they moved a short distance to B.56 Brussels-Evere. Number 126 Wing was destined to remain at B.80 Volkel until 7 November, at which time they moved north to Heesch and closer to the front. At roughly the same time, Keefer's 125 Wing left the misery of Grave for Diest. The Typhoons of 143 Wing had been garrisoned at B.78 Eindhoven since October, while the Spitfires and Mustangs of 39 Wing moved there in stages throughout October and November. These unit locations would remain constant for the rest of the calendar year and, in most cases, a significant portion of 1945. By way of exception, 402 Squadron would join 127 Wing on 29 December, in order to fly with the other Canadian units stationed at Heesch.

Sullen, late-autumn weather, coupled with a certain stagnation of the Allied advance, brought about drastically reduced flying operations in November. Then, on 16 December, *Generalfeldmarschall* von Rundstedt launched a major offensive with twenty-four divisions. Known as the Ardennes Offensive, this took place in southern Belgium between Monschau and Echternach against the U.S. First Army, in a last-ditch attempt to turn the tide for the Germans in the West. The element of surprise, coupled with bad flying weather for the first four days of the operation, initially worked in von Rundstedt's favour. But excellent flying weather on Christmas Eve which continued through the last week of the year brought 5,000 Allied fighters and fighter-bombers to the aid of the beleaguered First Army. By 28 December, the German initiative had been stymied.

The Luftwaffe had husbanded its meagre resources during the bad weather period, and the good weather brought them out in droves. The result: a significant late-year scoring spree for the RCAF wings. Both 126 and 127 Wings were in the thick of it, claiming twenty-eight additional victories by year's end, including thirteen by 411 Squadron alone. On Christmas day, overhead the Squadron's home base at Heesch, Flight Lieutenant J.J. Boyle exhibited tremendous showmanship when he shot down an Me 262 right over the field while the troops were queuing for their turkey dinners. This unit also possessed an extremely able Flight Commander, Flight Lieutenant R.J. Audet, who was about to make RCAF history. A long-time flying instructor with consummate flying skills, Audet was a relative latecomer to the war with no previous combat engagements in spite of being in theatre since 1943. He would rectify that, however, by scoring ten and a half kills in a little over a month and winning the DFC and Bar. Although one of his victories would be an Me 262 jet, he is much better known for his exploits of 29 December, when he shot down three FW 190s and two Bf 109s in a single engagement, a Commonwealth record. Furthermore, four of the five kills occurred within less than two minutes of combat time! Dick Audet's rising star was abruptly extinguished when he was shot down and killed on 3 March 1945. This tragedy occurred while he was attacking a train — yet another victim of the murderous German flak.

John Garland was having an extremely productive year-end with 80 (RAF) Squadron in his high-performance Tempest V. On 3 December, he was fortunate enough to gun down one of the highly sought-after Me 262s, and with a minimum expenditure of ammunition at that.

Probably my most vivid memory of any engagement was the one that occurred on 3 December 1944. I had broken away from the Squadron formation with my Number Two and had strafed the locomotive of a freight train a few miles south of the town of Rheine. As I pulled up from the attack, I saw an aircraft flying at low level along the tracks towards the town. I applied full power, turned port and dove to intercept. I quickly closed and the other aircraft started weaving violently. I identified it as an Me 262. As I got close enough to fire, he started a sharp turn to port and appeared to flick roll. As he completed this, his cockpit canopy came off. I fired a short burst. I saw no strikes but apparently he was already out of control and crashed immediately. Looking back, I suppose the whole engagement only lasted one or two minutes at most.[26]

Even the reconnaissance squadrons were making impressive air-to-air scores during the Ardennes Offensive. On 24 December, over a German marshalling area, Flight Lieutenant Bill Sawers of 414 Squadron won a DFC by destroying three Me 109s and damaging two others. His Squadron mate, Flight Lieutenant "Sammy" Hall, who was later awarded the DFC and Bar, also destroyed two '109s.

John Garland tangled with another '262 on Christmas Day while on an armed reconnaissance, although this time the results were inconclusive. Nevertheless, he and his Squadron mates celebrated on 27 December in fine style.

Garland and five other Tempest pilots ran into four very determined Focke Wulf pilots, who were not ready to admit that the war was over. Garland's flight was at 8000 feet when they spotted the FW 190s ahead and above them. The Germans dove to the attack. The ten aircraft roared towards each other with guns firing, then the neat formations broke up into a dogfight. Garland found himself meeting one of the FW 190s head on. He fingered his firing button and the guns chattered. As the Focke Wulf swept past, Garland cranked around in a tight turn, ready for anything, but there was nothing more to be done. Garland watched the aircraft slam into the ground. The fight was over. All four FW 190s had been shot down.[27]

All over liberated Europe, soldiers, sailors, and airmen of the Allied forces were being welcomed with unfettered enthusiasm and joy. As Christmas of 1944 loomed nearer, 39 Wing at Eindhoven felt that they would like to do something to reciprocate for the warm hospitality extended to them by the Dutch nation in general and the citizens of Eindhoven in particular. Jim Prendergast, who was at the time a very experienced reconnaissance pilot with the DFC, and a Flight Commander on 430 Squadron, recalls:

We arrived at Eindhoven piece by piece during mid-October through November and were treated in a most hospitable fashion by the citizens of the city, particularly the Mayor. He frequently apologized however, that their life and living standards were rather spartan, having lived under four years of occupation by the Germans when they were quietly resisting all the time. They didn't have some of the same freedom or benefits that the citizens of France and Belgium had experienced. Matter of fact, when we arrived, we were rather startled at the amount of sheer hunger that existed amongst the young children as we saw them on the streets of the various towns and villages. Nonetheless, they were prepared to share everything they had with us, and this helped us because we had been living in tents and temporary quarters since before we left England and all through France, Belgium, and Holland. Pretty rough conditions with frequent moves. To come into ready-built, permanent buildings, inside plumbing, and things such as the entertainment services of the RAF, it became a much more pleasant existence for us. In response to the attitude of the citizens, an ad-hoc group from our Wing approached the Mayor during the middle of November with the thought of having a Christmas party for the children. All of us were particularly interested in children, although few of us had any, but seeing them on the streets and in chatting with them, it was a treat to see how relieved they were that we were there. We left it up to the Mayor to decide what children should come, but immediately there was the question of how many children we could cope with. He said there were probably 1,500–2,000 children in Eindhoven that he thought would enjoy a party. However, we realized that with the facilities we had available and whatever we could put together in five or six weeks, we probably couldn't cope with much more than 500, and that was the capacity of one of the small theatres we were going to use. So we arbitrarily decided that we could manage about 500, providing them with a Christmas meal (Canadian style), an individual present, and entertainment.

The presents were no problem because we drew upon our sources of friends and family, both in the U.K. and in Canada, and the gifts started to barrel in. We then searched for appropriate food preparation facilities so we could give the children a truly Canadian Christmas dinner, and that was obtained. But again, we ran up against numbers. The Mayor then decided that he would limit the group to ages five and six. He thought there were probably about 500 or so children in that age bracket.

. . . As our preparations proceeded, 39 Wing extended a request to get cooperation from the other Wings on the base for food, presents, clothing, etc. At this time somebody came up with the brilliant idea of having all the aircrew give up their weekly ration of one orange, which we could accumulate and give to each child coming. The Mayor had said that they hadn't seen oranges for five or six years in Eindhoven, so it would be a real treat. As the invited guests arrived in the theatre for the party, all nicely dressed and well-mannered, we found that following them was a large group of scrawny, hungry ragamuffins, but we welcomed them as well. This was going to press our food and presents, we realized, but such was the case. The meal went off extremely well, as did Santa Claus and all the Christmas entertainment we could provide. Then the time came to give out the oranges, because we wanted to make sure that every child had one. They didn't know what to do with them. They had never seen an orange. So the master of ceremonies, in his wisdom, decided to tell them that they were to be eaten. Well, despite the fact that they had had a full meal, they were still hungry and began to eat the oranges, skin and all. We had to stop that very quickly, as we felt that would spoil the real enjoyment of having an orange. The adults in attendance scattered among the children and showed them how to peel the oranges and eat them properly.[28]

The law of averages finally caught up with Hedley Everard on Christmas Day, when he was forced to abandon his aircraft after it was critically damaged in the fragmentation blast of an Me 109 that he had just destroyed. Even something as serious as capture by the enemy in wartime, however, can provoke a humorous reaction.

Back in that forest clearing where I had lain, the sound of rifle bolts warned me that live rounds were rapidly being rammed into the breeches. Grey-green Wehrmacht uniforms suddenly surrounded me, and at a sharp command, I was seized. Two soldiers grabbed my legs, two my arms, and a fifth had a hammerlock around my neck from behind. An officer approached me from the front with a pistol in his hand and shouted, "Hands up!" Instinctively I tried to raise my arms, but they were tugged down roughly by the soldiers holding them. The young officer stepped closer, placed the weapon against my forehead and repeated the order, whereupon I again tried to raise my pinioned arms. My fear of immediate death vanished at the thought of this ridiculous tableau, which reminded me of an old slapstick scene from a Laurel and Hardy comedy. Involuntarily, I started to laugh. Perhaps it was a nervous reaction. After a few hesitant seconds, the young officer's face slowly relaxed into a half-grin. There were a few grunts of low laughter from the soldiers further away, and the handholds on me relaxed. A curt order was barked and after a rapid, professional search, my captors stepped back. The young officer returned his sidearm to its holster. I was surprised to see my battered officer's cap in a soldier's hand. I jerked it away and placed it on my head. Since this bold action was not met with a blow from a rifle butt, I then calmly retrieved my packet of cigarettes from another soldier's hand, and starting with the officer, I proffered a cigarette to each of my captors. As we lit up, I felt a sense of relief all around me . . .[29]

As the sixth year of the European war drew to a close, Allied victory seemed close at hand, and a dangerous complacency was settling in regarding some operational practices. Many combat aircraft were left unprotected in the open air, and were literally parked wingtip-to-wingtip on the 2TAF bases. It was an arrogant, presumptuous beddown of valuable equipment in an active war theatre, an arrogance which would cost the Allies dearly in very short order.

In Italy, 417 Squadron continued its nomadic existence in the relentless drive northward to oust the Germans from the country. Shortly after the liberation of Rome, Squadron Leader O.C. Kallio, a battle-hardened American with the DFC, succeeded Squadron Leader W.B. Hay as Commanding Officer of the Windsors. Since virtually all aerial opposition had been driven from Italian skies, 417 was retasked as a fighter-bomber squadron, and was destined to spend the balance of the Italian campaign dropping 500-pound bombs on road surfaces, buildings, rail lines, bridges, culverts, radar stations, gun posts, and enemy strong points. The Squadron members also raked these targets, as well as locomotives, freight cars, and other special objectives, with cannon fire. Throughout the summer and autumn, the Squadron advanced rapidly northward through Fabrica, Perugia, and Loreto, finally ending up in Fano in early September, where they would spend most of the rest of the calendar year. Rail facilities were a priority target, and if Mussolini made the trains run on time, 417 Squadron certainly put a kink in their schedules. The period from July through September was particularly busy. During that time, approximately 450 tons of bombs were slammed into enemy installations. In early July, the Windsors moved to Perugia.

The campsite at Perugia was a pleasant one, the tents being pitched in an orchard away from the landing field. Liberty runs into the city enabled the men to go sightseeing or shopping, and they soon found a friend . . . a Canadian woman whose husband was manager of a hotel in Assisi where the Windsors and all who wore "Canada" flashes were welcomed with open arms. Mr. Wadland, the "Y" supervisor, made frequent visits to the Windsor camp, bringing with him films, suppliers of cigarettes, and other comforts. One of the most attractive features of Perugia was its laundry service. No longer did the men have to depend on their own skill with soap and scrub brush; for a few lire, the peasant women provided 24 hour clothes cleaning service, a great boon. There were other diversions too, such as the motorcycle instruction a certain Canadian officer in the RAF attempted to give the CO and one of the Flight Commanders. Under normal circumstances, this would probably have caused little comment, but 3:00 am is hardly a normal time for such proceedings. As a motorcycle with its novice riders threaded its way uncertainly through the rutted camp, the staccato of its engine was all but drowned in the murderous imprecations that rose from the tents.[30]

As in northwest Europe, flak was a major threat to Canadian Spitfire pilots in Italy. Four Squadron pilots were killed in July due to anti-aircraft fire. In August, the "Rover" mission was introduced, where Squadron aircraft were directed to tactical targets by ground controllers situated with the spearheading troops in reconnaissance vehicles.

Autumn operations diminished as the bad weather rolled in, characterized by extensive rain, fog, mist, frost, and snow. Several stalwarts became tour-expired, including Kallio, who received a DSO for his outstanding leadership of the Windsors during the preceding five months.

Dave Goldberg had been posted to 417 Squadron in August as a Flight Commander after his harrowing escape from Occupied Europe. He performed yeoman service in that position, and was later chosen as a logical candidate to succeed Kallio as "King of the Windsors." It was a position he would hold until the end of hostilities in Europe and in which he would win the DFC. Goldberg gives his general impressions of 417 Squadron during this late stage of the war:

During my service with 417 Squadron, we initially carried out bomber escort operations without encountering any enemy aircraft, and soon converted to fighter-bombers in order to support the Eighth Army.

Much of our time was spent in "cab-ranking," where we were directed on to ground targets by ground controllers. At times, we would range as far afield as Yugoslavia, where we carried out shipping attacks and train busting.

[No.] 417 Squadron was quite unique in that it was the only Canadian fighter squadron operating in Italy, and as a component in the Desert Air Force, the Squadron was self-contained in that it had its own motor transport, medical doctors, intelligence staff, groundcrew, and other ancillary services, which was quite unlike those fighter squadrons which served in the Second Tactical Air Force.

This Squadron had its own particular Canadian characteristics, reflected by comfortable informality on the ground but with air discipline and enthusiasm of a very high order. We operated within an RAF Wing consisting of five squadrons, whose Commanding Officers and other personnel were made up of many different nationalities. These included Canadians, Australians, South Africans, and other citizens of what was then the British Empire. Being with such a variety of nationalities from different countries was always very interesting and exciting.[31]

The RCAF could justifiably derive great pride from 417 Squadron's accomplishments in Italy during 1944, and the Windsors' combat exploits during the closing months of the war in the following year would be equally outstanding.

---

1   Gord Ockenden, letter to author, July 1993
2   Ibid.
3   Leslie Roberts, *There Shall Be Wings*, p. 203
4   Bill Olmsted, *Blue Skies*, p. 169
5   C. T. Brown, letter to author, March 1993. Major Walter Matoni was a 44 victory ace, decorated with the Knights Cross. He survived the war. — DB

6   Arthur Jewett, letter to author, August 1993
7   *RCAF Overseas: The Sixth Year*, p. 262
8   Ibid., p. 263
9   Art Sager, letter to author, April 1993
10 Arthur Jewett, letter to author, August 1993
11 Ibid.
12 *Flap: The History of 39 Reconnaissance Wing RCAF*, January 1945, p. 7
13 *RCAF Overseas: The Sixth Year*, p. 268
14 Ibid.
15 Gord Ockenden, letter to author, July 1993
16 Ibid.
17 Christopher Shores, *The History of the Royal Canadian Air Force*, p. 66
18 R. I. A. Smith, personal recollections to author, September 1993
19 John D. Coupland, letter to author, August 1993, and Allan Simpson, *We Few*, p. 38
20 F. H. Hitchins, "The War History of 414 Squadron," *The Roundel*, Vol. 6, No. 7, July–August 1954, p. 43
21 John Garland, letter to author, July 1993
22 Lavigne and Edwards, *Kittyhawk Pilot*, p. 286
23 Gord Ockenden, letter to author, August 1993
24 Art Sager, letter to author, April 1993
25 Bill Olmsted, p. 215
26 John Garland, letter to author, July 1993
27 Tom Coughlin, *The Dangerous Sky*, p. 161
28 Jim Prendergast, tape to author, August 1993
29 Hedley Everard, *A Mouse in My Pocket*, p. 10
30 Keith Robbins, *417 Squadron Official History*, p. 26
31 David Goldberg, letter to author, May 1993

9

CHECKMATE

1945

"Write my 'chute off! Write my 'chute off!"
— CHUCK DARROW, 416 SQUADRON

The first day of the last year of the Second World War dawned cold, crisp, and clear over central Europe. Perfect flying weather for the Allied air forces — and for the Germans as well. *Unternehmen Bodenplatte* (Operation Baseplate) was a boldly conceived plan to attack simultaneously sixteen Allied tactical airfields in Belgium, Holland, and eastern France. The main architect of the plan was Adolf Galland, and the intent was to launch the operation coincidentally with von Rundstedt's Ardennes Offensive. Atrocious flying weather characterized the early days of the ground offensive, causing *Bodenplatte* to be stillborn. Although 1,500 fighter aircraft had been carefully marshalled for the operation, intense air fighting during the last week of 1944 had attrited at least a third of them. By the time the green light was finally given for the mission, the Ardennes Offensive had been contained and *Bodenplatte* had lost its *raison d'être*.

Undeterred by logic and reason, with Galland on leave in disgrace, the German High Command ordered *Bodenplatte* for the morning of 1 January, when it was hoped that the Allies would be nursing monumental hangovers. Though well planned, the mission was poorly executed. Nearly 900 fighter aircraft from thirty-three *Jagdgruppen* and one *Schlachtgruppe* launched at dawn, but the generally poor quality of the pilots doomed the mission to failure. A full ten *Gruppen* never found their targets, while a further nine made completely ineffectual attacks. Only a third of the force, eleven *Gruppen*, succeeded in attacking their designated targets in strength, on time, and with the element of surprise intact. Even then, poor shooting considerably limited the damage done.

Worst hit of the RCAF bases was Eindhoven, home of the Typhoon and Reconnaissance Wings, although the defenders were not caught as much by surprise as hoped for by the Germans. At the time of the attack, 400 Squadron pilots were enroute from their billets to the field in preparation for takeoff, eight aircraft of 414 Squadron were already airborne on patrol, 430 Squadron pilots were awaiting orders in their dispersal, two Typhoons of 438 Squadron were just in the process of taking off, and six others were about to do so. Also, four 439 Squadron Typhoons were entering the landing pattern, and an additional eight Typhoons of 440 Squadron were holding short of the runway, in preparation for takeoff.[1] It was 9:20 a.m.

Out of a clear, crystal sharp Dutch sky they came. More than 50 Messerschmitt 109s and Focke Wulf 190s flashed out of the sun, and for twenty minutes, wove an exact pattern of destruction over the Eindhoven field.

Stung into action by our aerial smashing at the Ardennes salient, the Luftwaffe was making one of its last stands in simultaneous attacks on Allied airfields in Holland and Belgium.

For twenty endless minutes, the black-crossed attackers whipped over the drome, strafing at will but concentrating on the parked aircraft. Again and again they returned to the attack as smoke belched up from burning and exploding planes.

Feeling like huge targets, everybody hugged the frozen earth or found scanty shelter in ditches, some full of cold water. Coming so long after Normandy, the attack had the unreality of a movie newsreel. In white faces and shock-glazed eyes, danger left its mark and many a prayer was muttered amid the curses at the multi-coloured Jerry kites.

But things were not altogether one-sided in the air. Squadron Leader Gordon Wonnacott, DFC, returning from a 414 sortie in the Ardennes, went into action at the tail-end of the raid. In double-quick time he shot down two Messerschmitt 109s and a Focke Wulf 190, winning an immediate Bar to his Distinguished Flying Cross.

In the meantime, Flying Officer "Wally" Woloschuk, later to win a DFC, caught the homebound Nazis in the Venlo-Roermond region. The 414 pilot mixed in immediately, scoring a kill on a FW 190 and damaging an Me 109.

On the ground, Warrant Officer Ron Beatty, then a Flight Sergeant, got going as soon as the Jerries attacked. He grabbed a Bren gun, mounted it on a partly broken-down wall, and practically unprotected "proceeded to engage all and sundry aircraft as they approached within range." Thus read the official report of his action, which won him a Mention in Dispatches.

Amid the whining bullets and cannon shells, death came to two of the Wing's groundcrew. Due to leave for Canada the next day, LAC Ross Bell, a fitter of 6414 Servicing Echelon, was showing his replacement the ropes when the attack began. They dived under a Spit for protection but a Jerry unleashed a burst which killed Bell and wounded his replacement. LAC Len Williams, a rigger of the same outfit, had just completed his DIs (daily inspections) when he was hit seeking cover in the centre of the field.

In all, some fifteen were injured slightly, while a considerable number of aircraft were rendered unoperational and a score of trucks damaged.

Death was ever close all over the field, especially in the corner which housed the armament and maintenance sections. Caught in the cross-fire from every angle of attack, the tail-end of bursts whipped through their work shacks.

Loaded with enough high explosive, gun cotton and detonators to blow up the whole area, the bomb disposal truck took a direct hit from a burst, but the bullets missed the explosive by a scant four inches. Inside the armament section, a 20mm cannon shell smashed through some files and through a wall, leaving a snowstorm of paper behind.

Meanwhile, in all parts of the drome, weird experiences were happening every minute. A 414 mechanic was enveloped in flames when a plane blew up behind him. His overalls, leather jerkin and pants were burned and his winter underwear singed, but he was untouched. Another came out of his shack to have one bullet tear a pair of pliers out of his hand and another strike him in the leg. Sitting in a gasoline tender when the first wave swished over, an "erk" dived under the truck. Suddenly realizing it was a gas "bowser," he scrambled over barbed wire and broken concrete to a small gully. The moment he reached comparative safety, the bowser went up in flames.

Finally the attack was over but danger was still present. Planes of neighbouring Wings were blowing up, and exploding ammunition crackled through the air. Tense nerves found relief in swift action and soon the Wing was operational again.[2]

Approaching the circuit, 439 Squadron Typhoons intercepted fifteen FW 190s on target egress from Eindhoven. Flying Officers R. H. Laurence and A. H. Fraser each downed two of the raiders, and one of Laurence's victims was the German leader, an *Oberst* (Colonel). Laurence was shortly thereafter awarded a DFC, his performance on New Year's Day being a repeat of some fine shooting on 29 December when he also destroyed two FW 190s.

At both Heesch and Evere, the Germans were less fortunate. Number 126 Wing got off virtually unscathed, since many of the Heesch Spitfires were airborne when the attack occurred.

The Grizzly Bears (441) and the Caribous (442) were on sweeps. Two Sections of the Winnipeg Bears (402) were out on patrol. The Falcons (412) were just getting ready to go on their first operation and the Rams (401) were at the end of the runway waiting to take off, when forty or more FW 190s and Me 109s swept over the airfield and made passes at the aircraft on the ground. They inflicted neither casualties nor damage.

The Rams hurriedly scrambled into the air, most of the pilots getting separated. On his return, Flying Officer Cameron, who was awarded the DFC in February, reported that he had destroyed three Me 109s. Flight Lieutenant W. E. Foster damaged an FW 190, while Johnny MacKay (now a Flight Lieutenant) destroyed two FW 190s and an Me 109. MacKay stated that shortly after take-off he was vectored into the Reichswald area, where he saw an FW 190 on the deck. He fired and it exploded, crashing in flames. Returning alone, he saw an FW 190 trying to get on the tail of a Tempest. He fired a few short bursts at the Focke Wulf but his ammunition was exhausted. He closed in and, as the enemy pilot attempted to do a shallow turn, the FW's port wing struck the ice on the lake below and the aircraft blew up. On pulling up, MacKay then sighted an Me 109, which again by bluff he forced down into a field where it bounced into some trees and broke up. For this achievement, MacKay was awarded the DFC.

On their sweep, the Grizzly Bears saw two FW 190s in the Twente area, both of which Flight Lieutenant Dick Audet shot down, bringing his score to seven in two days. The only damage the Hun inflicted on the Bears was to put a hole in the thatched roof of the Squadron's dispersal. Similarly no damage was done to the Falcons who, on the other hand, shot down four aircraft during the morning blitz, and three more later in the day. The Squadron had left Heesch at 1930 hours, just before the enemy arrived. West of Venlo they encountered upwards of thirty FW 190s, which were already being engaged by Tempests. Flight Lieutenant Doak fired at one, which flicked and exploded on the deck. Later that day, Doak was himself shot down by an FW 190. Flight Lieutenant B. E. MacPherson forced the pilot of another to bale out. A third, attacked by Flying Officer V. Smith, piled up in a wood, and a fourth was destroyed by the joint efforts of Squadron Leader Dover and Flying Officer E. D. Kelly.

The Caribous had been airborne at 0850 hours on a fighter sweep, but Flight Lieutenant R. C. Smith had to return because of trouble with his jettison tank. As he neared base, he heard that the Huns were heading for Eindhoven and shortly thereafter found himself at that place, the only Allied aircraft among forty enemy planes. He made some ten attacks in all, but never stayed anywhere long enough to watch results. On return to base, he ran out of petrol at 7000 feet and was forced to make a dead stick landing. He made no claims but it was not long before Group Headquarters and Eindhoven airfield were telephoning in their congratulations for damaging one Me 109 and forcing the pilot of a second to bail out. Another pilot of the same Squadron, Flight Lieutenant D. C. Gordon, also was returning early when, as he neared base, he saw a mighty gaggle of Huns on the deck. He destroyed two FW 190s and then was wounded by flak in the head and back. He was forced to crash land. He climbed out gingerly and was promptly clapped on the back by an enthusiastic Dutch woman, who ran up to wish him Happy New Year. In all, seventeen pieces of shrapnel were removed from his torso. He was awarded the DFC for his work on this occasion. Meantime Flight Lieutenant Keene's Section met a number of enemy aircraft west of Venlo. Flight Lieutenant Pieri destroyed two FW 190s and probably destroyed two more, while the Section Leader destroyed one. Pieri's achievement was cited when his DFC was awarded in 1946. Further north Flight Lieutenant Lumsden, recently awarded the DFC, damaged an FW 190 and shared in the damaging of another with Flying Officer J. A. Cousineau. An Me 262 was damaged by the joint efforts of Flight Lieutenant R. K. Trumley, Flying Officer W. H. Dunne, RAF, Flight Lieutenant J. N. G. Dick, and Pilot Officer E. C. Baker. Unfortunately, Flying Officer D. A. Brigden was killed.

Far from hampering the efforts of the Wing, the enemy attack on their airfield seemed to spur our pilots on to greater achievements. In the course of the day, they destroyed on all operations twenty-four enemy aircraft, probably destroyed three and damaged seven for the loss of two.[3]

At Evere, the Wolves (403 Squadron) had gotten a two-ship element airborne at 8:48 a.m. and a second pair at 9:28 a.m. Icy ground conditions delayed operations, but at 9:39 a.m. the Oshawas (416 Squadron) were taxiing out when a "mixed bag" of forty FW 190s and Bf 109s appeared overhead.

There was no warning and only one aircraft of the Oshawas was able to get airborne. Flight Lieutenant Harling was the pilot of the leading aircraft as the Squadron was moving along the perimeter track preparatory to takeoff. He had almost reached the runway when the Germans fired bursts into the aircraft immediately behind him. The aircraft of Flight Lieutenant Nault, Pilot Officer Ken Williams and Warrant Officer Lou Jean were all shot up. Since the ground on either side of the track was soggy, it was impossible for the rest of the pilots to taxi round the damaged aircraft and follow Harling onto the runway. This did not deter Harling, who took off and, single-handed, immediately engaged the enemy. He was shot down and killed, however, over Brussels.

The four aircraft of the Wolf Squadron, returning from patrols, engaged the enemy, Pilot Officer Reeves destroying two FWs, Pilot Officer Steve Butte destroying another and two Me 109s as well. Butte was later awarded the DFC for these victories. One FW 190 was destroyed and an Me 109 probably destroyed by Flight Sergeant G. K. Lindsay.

The enemy had succeeded in wiping out eleven aircraft of the MacBrien-Johnson Wing on the ground and damaging a dozen more. Nine men were wounded and one was killed among the groundcrew, one of the wounded dying in hospital the next day.[4]

For many of the attacking German pilots, their problems did not begin until the egress from their respective target areas. *Unteroffizer* Norbert Risky of JG 26 numbered among them, his Focke Wulf being hit by ground fire over Evere.

During my second attack my aircraft shuddered — a flak hit! Oil blinded me. I tried to wash the oil off without success. To the side of the field a large plume of smoke was rising. Fleeing into this, I tried again to clean my canopy — still no luck. Escape was now uppermost in my mind. My engine was running somewhat roughly, but its power and the instruments were all right. I set course over the roofs of Brussels . . . About ten minutes later I saw aircraft in front of me. I stalked them slowly; as soon as I could identify them as our own, I breathed easier. It was Oblt. Glunz with four or five planes. Hopefully my engine would keep running until I reached our lines. I was slowly losing oil; the oil temperature crept upward. I flew over the ocean at low altitude and was again taken under fire by the picket boats. This obstacle was overcome at full throttle . . . Oil was flowing everywhere; it turned to smoke whenever it hit hot metal. My comrades disappeared slowly over the horizon. Alone, I crossed the meadows.

Suddenly my oil pressure dropped away to zero; there was a loud noise, and a long flame came out from under the cowling. The hot metal began to crackle. Things looked bad — I was too low to bail out and had too little speed to climb. Beneath me, only trees . . . Ahead was some flat ground suitable for a crash landing. I tightened my straps, put my head down, and braced for the crash. Unfortunately, the landing site had some holes; one wing broke off, and the engine likewise. It began to get hot in the cockpit. Just as I emerged, the hot ammunition started to go off, and I had to hit the ground. A half-hour later, an army Volkswagen picked me up and brought me to Zwolle. By late evening, I was back in Nordhorn.[5]

Tempest squadrons would score heavily on 1 January. John Garland was truly in the thick of it, in both the air-to-air and air-to-ground disciplines. He was on his way back to base after a successful morning train strafing mission with 80 (RAF) Squadron in the Münster area of Germany when things got really exciting.

On 1 January '45, we were returning from a patrol north of the Ruhr at about 8000 feet when I spotted an aircraft on the deck, going in the opposite direction. The only reason I was able to see it was because it happened to be passing over a patch of snow. My Number 2 followed me as I made a diving 180-degree turn to ground level. Fortunately, when I got down to about 100 feet, I was still behind and picked up two aircraft approximately 1000 yards ahead. As I closed to about 200 yards, I identified them as FW 190s. A couple of short bursts put the first one out of action, and I recall his under-fuselage tank bursting into flames. The second aircraft became aware of my presence and took some evasive turns, but I was very close, and again a few bursts of the 20mms sent him crashing on fire into some trees. I doubt if either of us was over fifty feet during the final stages of the combat. My Number 2 stuck with me and we went directly back to Volkel. As I shut down the Tempest in dispersal, the groundcrew pointed to a stream of glycol spurting from the radiator. It had been holed by debris from one of the '190s and I was lucky to have made it back to base.[6]

Shortly thereafter, Garland destroyed a Ju 188 just as its wheels touched down on an airfield near Aachmer in Germany, thereby denying himself an air-to-air kill and the coveted distinction of being an ace. He was then awarded a well-deserved DFC, but on 8 February he went the way of so many others when enemy anti-aircraft fire felled him just after he strafed a train near Rheine. He spent the remaining few months of the war as an "all-expenses-paid" guest of the Third Reich.

When the sums were done, *Bodenplatte* was a bold concept that suffered from weak execution. Three hundred of the 900 German aircraft that participated were lost, including 214 pilots. Furthermore, nineteen of those casualties were senior formation leaders, including three *Geschwaderkommodoren*, six *Gruppenkommandeure*, and ten *Staffelkapitaene*. They were losses the German Fighter Arm could ill afford. On the other hand, although the Allies lost nearly 300 Commonwealth and USAAF aircraft, manpower losses were light overall and had absolutely no effect on their ability to engage the reeling German forces with relentless determination.[7]

While stories abound of the warmth and generosity of liberated European people towards Allied soldiers, the economic conditions on the Continent, coupled with the massive influx of men and materiel to the region and a misplaced sense of business acumen, produced a flourishing trade for some of the seamier characters of the war — the black marketeers and profiteers. It is a particularly sad fact of life that many of these shameless individuals were in Allied uniform, and their victims were often fellow servicemen. Parachute silk was a highly prized black-market commodity, and Chuck Darrow, who flew with 416 Squadron out of Brussels-Evere during the winter of 1944–45, recalls a chilling incident which could easily have cost him his life. His primary concerns regarding the event are a wonderful testimonial to his youth.

At the time on 416 Squadron, we used to leave the parachutes in the aircraft overnight. Apparently on one of the other bases, two guys bailed out and, their 'chutes being damp, they only streamed but did not open. After that we used to put them in a tent, and in this tent they had a kerosene heater. When you got up early for first ops in the morning, it was damn dark. You would go into the tent, grab the parachute, go for a Squadron briefing, then away you'd go, and it would *still* be dark when you took off. When I landed after the first op in the morning, I left my 'chute in the aircraft. Then I went up on a second op, and after the mission, the groundcrew were waiting for me and said, "Your parachute is due for a repack." So they took my parachute and gave me another one. I wasn't supposed to be doing another trip, but someone was sick, so I volunteered and away I went . . . I came back and after landing from that op, the groundcrew were waiting for me again. They said, "We'd like to show you something here." I went into the warming tent and found out that when they had opened up my regular parachute, which was originally a silken effort, in its place they found some blankets! Someone had swiped the parachute itself. I wasn't upset because nothing had happened, but what *did* upset me was the fact that I was going to be charged £165–£200 for the loss of "parachute, one, aircrew, for the use of . . ."! *I was ticked off!!* Anyway, on New Year's Day when the Huns strafed the aerodrome, I said to the CO, "Write my 'chute off! Write my 'chute off!" He said, "Your 'chute's written off, but I've got *enough* damn problems, never mind worrying about your damn 'chute, Chuck!" So I never did pay for it, and the 'chute was written off . . .[8]

When the Ardennes Offensive commenced in mid-December, all Commonwealth aircrew were issued sidearms and told to wear them at all times, not just on combat operations. On 31 January 1945, the danger of running into rapidly advancing Germans while on a pass in downtown Brussels and elsewhere was considered negligible, and the order was rescinded. Dick Reeves, by now a Flight Commander on 403 Squadron, drove his jeep to Brussels-Maelsbroek from Brussels-Evere on the night of the thirty-first, unarmed and unafraid, for a rendezvous with destiny.

We were at a club, generally enjoying life, and I had driven the jeep in from the base. On arrival, as was standard practice, I removed the rotor arm and the high-tension lead. The reason we took these out of the jeeps was because they were being stolen at such a rate that you had to disable them or they would disappear. There were lots of courts of inquiry going on, and our CO at one point went to the town major (a senior military policeman) with the court of inquiry about a previous incident involving his jeep. *This* jeep was then in turn stolen, the court of inquiry report was stolen, and they had to have a court of inquiry on the loss of the court of inquiry and the loss of the second jeep! It was getting pretty wild! At any rate, as I went outside the club to check the jeep during the course of the evening, I noticed that two soldiers dressed in American uniforms had its hood up. I said, "What the hell are *you* doing?" and they turned and stuck a 9-mm pistol in my guts. It was now the first day that they told us we didn't have to carry a sidearm anymore and I didn't have one with me, or I might have come out of this confrontation a little differently. At any rate, I reacted to them, shoved the gun down, and a bullet went through my foot! I stood there for a minute; they *ran*. A British officer then came along and I told him that I had been shot. He ran into the club and, fortunately for me, both the CO and Squadron doctor were there and they came out to the jeep. My pals had already replaced the rotor arm and the high-tension lead, and these folks started arguing over who was going to take me to the hospital; so about *this* time I said, "Hey, this thing *hurts!*" Anyway, the doctor picked me up and drove me to Edith Cavell Hospital, where I spent about a month listening to the buzz bombs going over . . .[9]

In January 1945, 443 Squadron re-equipped with the troublesome Spitfire Mk XVIs, and soon all of 127 Wing was flying this disappointing aircraft. The majority of the Squadrons within 126 Wing would finish the war in the Spitfire Mk IXE, while 402 Squadron got to keep their excellent Spit XIVs. Name changes were also in store for the fighter Wings in January. Dal Russel had by now completed an extremely rare third tour of operations. He was replaced as Wing Commander Flying at 126 Wing by Wing Commander Geoff Northcott. The other Canadian day fighter Wing also changed names when, in the same month, Group Captain Stan Turner replaced the tour-expired Group Captain Bill MacBrien as Commander. Also in January, command of 143 Wing, the Typhoons, passed from Group Captain Paul Davoud to Group Captain Deane Nesbitt. Thus it came to pass that an impressive array of 1940s novices held the most senior operational flying commands in the RCAF day fighter and fighter-bomber Wings during the twilight of the war in Europe.

In terms of air combat, which would be a relatively rare event from now on, a highlight for 126 Wing occurred on the twenty-third of the month, when the Squadron caught some Me 262s operating from a field near Osnabrück and shot three of them down in the landing pattern. Another one was shot down later that same day in the same vicinity by 411 Squadron, while in March both 401 and 402 Squadrons would bag an additional '262, bringing the total RCAF claims against the elusive jets to nine. It was eventually discovered that the otherwise-potent jets were extremely vulnerable and predictable during their long final approaches to landing. This was due to very poor turbine response time and a subsequent need to handle the throttles gingerly when in the landing configuration. Unlike piston-engine fighters, the jets of the era could not have their throttles "firewalled" when in trouble, or else an engine compressor stall, flameout, or meltdown would occur. In more asset-rich times, they had been provided fighter caps of Messerschmitts or Focke Wulfs when in the vulnerable landing pattern, but by 1945 they could rarely get that type of protection, since the German piston-engined *Jagdgeschwadern* had been largely decimated.

In February, the weather greatly improved and the final push into Germany began. The First Canadian Army under General Harry Crerar had struck out eastward from Nijmgen and the Reichswald Forest to overrun all territory in their path to the west of the Rhine River. Further to the northwest, the British Twenty-first Army

Group was pushing relentlessly forward. The Reconnaissance Wing found itself extremely busy supporting all these activities, and early in the year, a detachment of 414 Squadron in their Spitfire IXs moved to Kluis near s'Hertogenbosch in Holland, where it was intensely involved in supporting the spring ground fighting for the Reichswald Forest.[10] By now, the Wing was entirely equipped with Spitfires, 430 Squadron having given up its trustworthy but war-weary Mustangs for Spitfire XIVBs in November.

The Typhoons were very active during the winter-spring period, and were greatly beloved by the army for smashing German strong points prior to the endless series of infantry advances.

As with all low-level operations, these assignments resulted in peculiar and risky personal experiences. The most remarkable was perhaps that of Squadron Leader "Bing" Crosby of 439. His aircraft was hit by flak and exploded, throwing the pilot clear. Twice Crosby tried to pull his parachute rip-cord with his right hand, but a dislocated shoulder made the normal drill impossible. At last he managed to pull it with his left hand, landed safely and made for a nearby copse, where he lay in severe pain, wrapped in his parachute, for almost two days. At one time, German soldiers were at work within a few feet of his hiding place. Subsequently, Allied aircraft attacked and bombed nearby, covering the hidden man with debris. That was enough for Crosby. He knew the British lines were not far away and made for them, successfully eluding German patrols and sentries. At last he encountered a patrol from the British 43rd Division and was evacuated to hospital, suffering from frostbite as well as his shoulder injury. Soon afterwards Crosby was awarded the DFC.[11]

Throughout the course of 143 Wing's operational wartime service, more than 100 Typhoons were lost in action, but only eight of these losses were the result of air-to-air combat. The Wing was scoring an increasing number of air-to-air kills over the Luftwaffe, a fact driven home in dramatic fashion on 14 February. As a Valentine's Day present to the German Fighter Arm, 439 Squadron's Flight Lieutenant Shaver and Flying Officer Fraser each felled an Me 262 in a very rare encounter with the German jets.

During this final drive for Germany, the Spitfires and the Typhoons became more specialized in ground-attack missions. Typical targets included the obliteration of anything that moved on enemy lines of communication, the cutting of rail lines, the destruction of trains and communications facilities, and the destruction of canal bridges in the Germans' immediate rear area. Much of this essential work was done in support of the First Canadian Army, and though the losses were relatively light, flak was still taking its toll of men and machines, and would do so right until the end of hostilities. Complaints were frequently made that enemy aircraft were nowhere to be seen, and the principal danger to the life and limb of Allied pilots rested squarely in the hands of German anti-aircraft gunners. Dick Audet was killed by flak on 3 March, and Don Laubman, then CO of 402 Squadron, was also caught by flak on 14 April. Unlike Audet, Laubman would parachute to safety and, after a brief incarceration, would return to his Squadron by 5 May.

On 2 March, the Turner/Johnson Wing (127) moved from Evere to B.90 Petit Brogel near Bourg-Leopold.

There they were housed in Nissan huts, which they found better than tents but not as good as the quarters they had occupied in Brussels. The weather was cold and they had difficulty getting wood for the small stoves — coal was unobtainable. Many of the pilots made trips to nearby German towns, München-Gladbach, Roermond, and Cologne, from all of which they returned with tales of desolation and irrepressible German arrogance.

Uneventful operations and bad flying weather characterized the first week of the month, and in the second week, things hardly improved.[12]

After a relatively slow time of it in February, the McGregor/Northcott Wing (126) at Heesch got things off to a highly respectable start in March.

On the 1st, the Rams (401), on their only show of the day, an armed reconnaissance, were bounced in the Dorsten area by about forty Me 109s and FW 190s. Squadron Leader Klersy called a break and got behind an Me 109, which he brought down in flames. A second one similarly went down in flames and then, as his Section reformed, Klersy met some FW 190s, one of which he destroyed. It went into the deck and exploded. Klersy now had ten destroyed, an achievement for which he was awarded the DSO. Flight

Lieutenant MacKay obtained strikes on an Me 109, damaged an FW 190, which spun towards some cloud, and then similarly damaged another FW, which likewise spun towards the cloud. This last shed its starboard wing, and Johnny chased it down until he saw it crash in flames. Flying Officer A. E. Sawyer probably destroyed an Me 109. These victories gave the Wing the honour of being the first formation in Second Tactical Air Force to chalk up a total of 300 enemy aircraft destroyed. The Squadron's success was somewhat offset by two casualties. Flight Lieutenant O. E. Thorpe, on his last operational trip, was forced to crash-land at Volkel, where he escaped with nothing more than a bad shaking up, but Flight Lieutenant Harry Furniss, whose aircraft was damaged in the combat, failed to return, and was later reported a prisoner of war.[13]

On 7 March, 39 Wing moved from Eindhoven to B.90 Petit Brogel and joined company with 127 Wing in preparation for the assault on the Rhine River at Wesel. The Wing pilots really liked B.90. Although they would be under canvas once again for the next three weeks, the pine forest in which the base was situated provided excellent natural camouflage. Also, the runways were made of metal planking, and fresh eggs appeared on the daily menu after a long hiatus.

———

The final assault on Germany was about to begin. Operation Varsity, the codename for the airborne crossing of the Rhine, was launched on 24 March 1945, and it would demonstrate many facets of tactical air power at their finest. Naturally, the recce Wing was intimately involved before, during, and after this massive operation.

All this seemingly uneventful routine of noting positions on the ground and taking photographs was put into perspective for the pilots of the Wing on the night of the 23rd, when they were briefed for operations on March 24th. The briefing officer, from the Second British Army, told the pilots of the magnificent pictures they had taken of the projected crossing points on the Rhine. In the period 17–24 March, their photographs had been developed as soon as they could get them out of the cameras. What was of immediate importance was phoned in advance to the army and then, a trace was made showing full details of all flak positions in the zones of artillery and air responsibility. Every 24 hours, amendments to this trace were signalled to the army and thence to First Allied Airborne Army Headquarters. Apparently, the Germans built up their flak defences, but these could not be concealed from the all-pervading eye of the camera. One sortie, flown by Paul Barton of the Toronto Squadron (400), (a pilot who was later awarded the DFC for his work), resulted in the discovery of many well-hidden camouflaged positions of light flak batteries, as well as the presence of a mine belt. Sorties flown by this Squadron for the preceding three months, over 100 in number, covered the area from the Rhine to Hanover. As a result of these sorties, defence overprints were prepared and distributed to each division of the army concerned. These overprints in turn were annotated and distributed amongst all officers down to platoon commanders, who were thus able the more easily to locate their objectives. Special mosaics of the Rhine were also made, and a photostat of the Rhine floodings was prepared daily for the army. Delivery of reports and prints was made each day to Sixth Airborne Division in England, the Eighteenth Airborne Division in Dreux, the 8th, 12th and 30th Corps, and the First Allied Airborne Army Headquarters in Paris. By using Auster aircraft, delivery to mobile corps headquarters was made possible, since these aircraft were able to land in any available grass field. In addition, motor transport did two runs of 200 miles each twice every 36 hours; the two vehicles covering 5000 miles in three weeks. Enlargement and reprints were frequently received in England within 24 hours of the placing of an order. On March 23rd, special sorties were flown over the battle area in the morning and the photographs were developed, printed, interpreted, and flown to England by Dakotas, so that they were in the hands of the General Officer Commanding Sixth Airborne Division by 2100 hours. This meant that each army platoon commander had a 24-hour-old photograph of his objective to carry with him on the morning of the 24th. As a result of these photographic reconnaissances, it was decided that there had been no increase in the flak defences in certain areas and the army was able to proceed with the operation as planned. The pilots were interested to hear the briefing officer explain that certain units would cross the Rhine at points which they had photographed. It was equally interesting to have the operations officer explain the next day how this had been carried out . . . .[14]

Although the day fighter Wings were successful in destroying numerous ground targets during Varsity, their primary task was to provide an impenetrable air umbrella over the vulnerable transports and gliders. It was generally felt that the Luftwaffe would defend the Rhine to the death from the air. For that reason, the Spitfire umbrella was constant, but the German fighter pilots simply didn't show up for the party. Bill Gould, now with 443 Squadron, recalls the spectacle from his perch on high:

On March 24, "Plunder Day," General Montgomery crossed the Rhine. An armada of aircraft and gliders crossed over our heads for three hours, and 30,000 men were dropped across the Rhine River. We caught up with much of the operation at the Rhine, and the sight of paratroopers landing, gliders and aircraft crashing, death and destruction everywhere, was an unforgettable experience. I was very happy to be in the air instead of on the ground . . .[15]

During Varsity, the aircraft most popular with the troops were the beloved Typhoons, and they were very effective during the operation.

The Squadron was awakened at 0400 hours for breakfast, briefing and then battle. It was a hectic day for us: the kites were going up all the time. Those who did not fly were playing horseshoes, eating or sleeping. The boys were fagged out in the evening after having carried out nine operations, which totalled 48 sorties . . . It was really an amazing sight, Tiffies all over the sky, also heavies, mediums, Spits and all the Daks coming out of Germany around 1030 hours after dumping their loads of paratroopers, who were subjected to terrific flak . . . The (Typhoon) pilots take off their hats to these fellows, who must have a lot of intestinal fortitude.

The Westmount Squadron (439) attacked the flak positions and bombed a town in preparation for the arrival of the airborne troops. Late in July, the Squadron learned of the importance of this operation when the following communication was received from their Group Headquarters:

At approximately 0650 hours on the 24th March 1945, (Rhine, D-Day), the Westmount Squadron put 22 thousand-pound bombs in a group of buildings in the Dorsten area. The target was laid on by the Army as a possible headquarters. In May 1945, *General der Fallshirmtruppen* Schem (GOC First Paratroop Army) was found in a hospital on Sylt. He had been under a collapsed wall in the Typhoon attack, suffered severe concussion and internal injuries and had to give up his command on the 27th of March 1945, as soon as a deputy was made available.[16]

During the period of 28–30 March, 143 Wing moved its Typhoons to Weeze in Germany, a few miles to the west of Wesel. With this act, the Nesbitt/Grant Wing staked its claim as the first RCAF unit to enter the Third Reich. Number 439 celebrated by wiping out two formations of enemy tanks near Osnabrück, strafing a train, and attacking some defensive positions in a wood. Meanwhile, 440 Squadron bombed a headquarters and strafed trains, barges, an ammo dump, and various types of transports.[17] For the next month, the Wing would operate at only two-Squadron strength, since 438 Squadron had deployed back to England for, of all things, a gunnery camp! It makes one wonder what the battlefield east of the Rhine was considered to be, if not ample opportunity to practise weaponeering. On 8 April, 143 Wing moved on to Osnabrück for a brief, one-week stay, then pressed on to Hustedt, where they would finish the war. The Wing continued to bring relentless pressure to bear on the reeling Germans throughout April, but not without twelfth-hour costs.

An unusual target was provided on the 17th. After attacking rails between Bremen and Hamburg, the attention of the Tiffies was directed to some shipping on the Elbe. The Wildcats (438) dive-bombed an anchored cargo ship and some oil storage tanks, while the Beavers (440) scored a direct hit on the stern of a minesweeper. They were less successful in attacking other ships and a submarine, which had reduced evasive tactics and the use of anti-aircraft fire to a fine art.

It was a pleasure on the 18th to attack SS troops at the request of the army, though other ground targets were also successfully strafed. Again, shipping came in for some close attention the next day. This time, it was a mysterious light cruiser anchored off Wilhelmshaven. Though the flak was intense, one direct hit was obtained on the superstructure, two more amidships, and three on the stern. The ship listed to port and was emitting smoke as the aircraft left the scene. An attack on three or four merchant vessels produced no tangible results. For his part in this operation, the newly-appointed Commanding Officer of the Wildcats, Squadron

Leader Beirnes, DFC, who was responsible for two hits on the stern of the cruiser, received a Bar to his decoration.

The army called for action again on April 21st, and the two Squadrons answered with an attack on Achim, east and south of Bremen, bombing the roads and causing confusion, enabling the British to capture the town.

The Westmount Squadron (439), now replacing the Beavers, celebrated their return to operational flying on the 23rd by strafing rail and road targets and a number of barges. They poured ammunition into some Ju 88s they saw on the ground, but were chagrined to learn that the enemy aircraft were dummies. Flight Lieutenant McCullough was forced to crash-land, but called up to say that he had got down safely. On the same day, the Wildcats lost Pilot Officer T. Hartnett, who was last seen entering a cloud over a wood, and was subsequently posted as killed. For the rest of the month, rail targets received major attention, though on the 24th the Westmount Squadron, after cutting some rails, sighted a six-engined BV 222 resting on the water and left it in flames. Credit for this (victory) was awarded to Flying Officers W. Kubicki, J. Black and M. Hallford. In the evening, the same Squadron saw thirty enemy aircraft parked on an aerodrome. These too they attacked, seeing strikes on eight of them, though some of them burned. The Wildcats had the misfortune to lose another pilot on the 25th, when Flying Officer T. M. Jones crashed after his aircraft had been hit by flak. On April 26th, Flying Officer E. D. Brydon flew too low in an attack on some transport and collided with some trees. This was the seventh casualty sustained by the Wildcats in the course of the month.

. . . The Wildcats opened the month of May with a blind bombing operation against an enemy airfield. Vectored by control over their objective, they released their bombs, only to discover that they had hit a point a half mile northwest of the target. They had better success against rails later in the day, claiming three cuts in all. The Westmount Squadron carried out two operations against the enemy railway system, bombing and strafing three trains, but failing to cut the rails.

For the next three days, enemy shipping was the primary objective. After successful attacks on rail and road transport on the 2nd, the two Squadrons were directed to dive-bomb a troop ship with 1000 pounders. They obtained a direct hit on the bow, two hits amidships, and one hit on the stern, causing a large explosion amid-ships. The Westmount Squadron on their noon operation in search of road convoys east of Lübeck got three motor vehicles and three goods trucks, damaging five others. They then sighted a Fieseler-Storch flying at fifty feet. It attempted to land but was shot down by Flight Lieutenant Tex Gray. In approximately the same position, an FW 44 was seen and shot down by Flight Lieutenant Jack Cook. In the afternoon, they immobilized a train by cutting the line in front of it and behind it, while on later sorties, they had more successes on both rail and road transport. Wing Commander Grant accidentally blew up an ammunition dump when bombs that had hung up came away while he was returning from an anti-shipping strike.[18]

Air-to-air kills were few and far between for the night-fighting 409 (Nighthawk) and 410 (Cougar) Squadrons on the Continent during the first three months of 1945. Both units were quite successful during April, however, as many high-ranking Nazis attempted to "desert the sinking ship." Number 409 Squadron remained at Lille-Vendeville from 12 October until they moved forward to B.108 Rheine in Germany on 19 April — the first RCAF night fighter squadron to garrison east of the Rhine River. Within four days of their arrival, on 23 April, they established a Squadron record by shooting down six enemy aircraft in one night. Furthermore, they followed this highly successful night with three more kills on the twenty-fourth. During its operational career, 409 Squadron had accounted for sixty-seven enemy aircraft destroyed, nine probably destroyed and twenty-four damaged. Forty-seven officers and men had been killed on operations. On 15 May, they joined 410 Squadron at B.77 Gilze-Rijen, before moving one last time to Twente for disbandment on 1 July 1945.

Number 410 Squadron left the Nighthawks at Lille-Vendeville on 6 January and returned for the next three months to Amiens-Glisy. Operations remained relatively quiet through March, and three enemy were downed for the loss of two Squadron crews. On 4 April, the Squadron moved to B.77 Gilze-Rijen. Joe Schultz, after completing a six-month instructing tour in the U.K., had rejoined the Squadron in France and crewed up with a new navigator, Flying Officer J. S. Christie. This able night-fighting team would account for all three of 410's air-to-air victories after the move to Gilze-Rijen, and when

Schultz was awarded a Bar to his DFC during the summer of 1945, he was officially credited with eight enemy aircraft destroyed.

Jack Christie was a really fine navigator and we had a profitable second tour together. However, there was no really serious action for us until almost the end of the war. It was mostly just boring patrol work, though patrolling at 28,000 feet on New Year's Eve 1945 over Holland and watching the V2s being launched towards London was a rather interesting pyrotechnic display.

In early April, 1945, we moved to Gilze-Rijen in Holland, where we remained until the end of the war. In the last part of the campaign, 410 Squadron finally got the opportunity to get some good patrols, and we were fortunate enough to get a Junkers 188 in the Hanover area about a week after the move to Gilze. At this stage of the game, the Germans were evacuating Berlin, with some of their VIPs trying to get out and head for South America, etc. There was a lot of air activity at times over the city's airfields, and on the night of April 22, we got into the thick of it and ended up getting two Junkers 88s. I saw the last of these crash straight into the perimeter track of one of the Berlin airfields in the Fehrvellen area near Templehof . . .[19]

Number 410 Squadron's victory log at war's end totalled seventy-five and three quarters enemy aircraft destroyed, two probably destroyed, and eight damaged. Fifty-nine officers and men were killed while on wartime operations with the Squadron, and the unit disbanded on 9 June 1945.

For both 406 (Lynx) Squadron and 418 (City of Edmonton) Squadron, role changes would occur during the last year of the war. The Edmontons had performed second to none in the intruder role, and for the period of operations ending in November 1944, they had destroyed 103 enemy aircraft in the air and seventy-five on the ground. They had also accounted for seventy-nine and a half V1 flying bombs between June and September, 1944, a remarkable accomplishment.

On 1 November, 418 Squadron was posted to 2TAF and joined 605 (RAF) Squadron as 136 Wing at Hartford Bridge. For the rest of the war, their mission would be to provide close support to the army, and no further air-to-air victories would be forthcoming. They would continue to operate from Hartford Bridge in their Mosquito VIs until

15 March, at which time they moved to the Belgian coast at B.71 Coxyde. Their targets were anything that could be bombed and strafed from the air at night. The Squadron's impact in this role was highly significant, although not without considerable losses as they too fell prey to the ubiquitous German flak batteries. In February alone, 418 lost a record seven aircraft to enemy ground fire. In April, they made their last move of the war to Volkel in Holland, where mud and boredom prevailed. They disbanded on 7 September, still at Volkel.

Meanwhile, 406 Squadron crews under Russ Bannock were operating their Mosquito Mk 30s with the potent Mk X AI radar to telling effect from their coastal base at Manston. Bannock had brought several 418 Squadron luminaries with him on the move to 406 Squadron, including Don MacFadyen and J. T. Caine. Both Bannock and MacFadyen would post four more air-to-air victories while with 406, and MacFadyen would also add two more air-to-ground kills to his score. In fact, the Squadron would tally twenty-three air-to-air and nine air-to-ground kills from December 1944 until the termination of hostilities. By war's end, 406 Squadron had destroyed fifty enemy aircraft in the air, and also accounted for many more on the ground. They were disbanded in England on 1 September 1945.

On 6 April, the Turner/Johnson Wing changed nomenclature for the last time when Stocky Edwards, now DFC and Bar, DFM, replaced Johnnie Johnson as Wing Commander Flying. Almost immediately, the Wing moved from Eindhoven, where they had been since the end of March, to Goch in Germany. On the thirteenth, they moved to Diepholz, thirty-five miles to the north of Osnabrück, and finally two weeks later to B.154 Reinsehlen, thirty miles south of Hamburg, where they would remain until July. Their accommodations were as varied as the moves themselves. While the Squadron had to go under canvas at Goch, German barracks were available at Diepholz, and Reinsehlen turned out to be even better.

At this last place, they found undamaged wooden buildings for use as barracks. Excellent camouflage had hidden the place so successfully that Allied bombers had apparently never found it. The Germans had set large numbers of booby traps before they left and they had attempted to plough up the landing strip, but lacked sufficient time to complete the job. Camp water and lighting systems were soon in working order and the furrows on the strips were quickly turned down so that operations could begin almost immediately.[20]

From now on, the German military situation would degenerate very quickly. Air-to-air kills during the first three weeks of April were infrequent, but air-to-ground missions abounded. Although the Allied air forces would fly more than 30,000 individual sorties during the last week of April alone, and suffer a loss rate of less than one-half of one percent, flak took its toll right to the very end. Stocky Edwards recalls the general mood of all going into the last months of the war in Europe:

> The war seemed worn out by then. Every mission in the last two months visibly indicated the Jerries were finished, but they wouldn't give up. Now they had nowhere to go — they were bottled up, but like us, they had been fighting so long they couldn't visualize it being over — not having to get airborne and fire the guns in anger and dodge the flak anymore. The whole dismal war effort had become our lives and careers for so long, we just couldn't appreciate any way of peaceful co-existence.[21]

Number 126 Wing under Gordon McGregor and Geoff Northcott was also on the move in April, leaving Heesch for Rheine in Germany on the twelfth. The stay at Rheine was, however, a brief one, and two days later the Wing moved on to B.116 Wunstorf, where they would finish the war. For the next few days, the priority target was the German transport system, and their efforts brought excellent results. On the sixteenth, the four Squadrons accounted for forty-five locomotives, 139 rail trucks, and eleven barges, along with several air-to-air kills. The next day, 401 and 411 Squadrons combined to damage twenty-nine locomotives and destroy 103 railway cars. Number 401 also accounted for sixty-six motor transports. Over the following four days, the Luftwaffe mounted a feeble attempt to defend the motor transports from the Spitfires. It was a desperate stand by desperate men, and German losses were heavy. On the nineteenth, at Hagenow airfield, the Wing destroyed many motor vehicles and locomotives. Then, 412 and 402 Squadrons, working in concert, downed seven enemy aircraft and damaged three others, most of the German adversaries being FW 190s.

As the "Eyes of the Army," 39 Wing found itself frequently on the move during the last weeks of the war. On 30 March, the Wing's ground party crossed the Rhine via a pontoon bridge at Xanten:

The convoy rolled through battered Wesel, still burning and housing fighting Nazi fanatics, past the hundreds of gliders used in the airborne landing and so to B.104, Damm airfield, fifteen miles northeast of Wesel. Just before reaching the field, the trucks halted to let the airport construction machinery clatter by! It was an omen for this field with the descriptive name. B.104 was just mud and water.

Meanwhile, back at B.90, the terrific pace continued with tactical, contact, and artillery reconnaissance sorties flying every possible minute.

On all its moves, the Wing was divided into two parties, which were complete airfields in themselves. Thus, the first group would push on to a new site, get operational, and the planes would fly in without losing a moment. Then the second group would move to the new 'drome.

A current of tenseness underlay all our actions at Damm, with extra sentries at night, special guards on M.T. runs and ration trips, which took endless hours. We moved about the countryside in groups of at least three. At night, the huge searchlights beamed on the sky at the Rhine spread an eerie glow over the dark fields. In the distance, red tracers laced the sky as Nazis fought on in Wesel.

But there were compensations in many ways. German civilians, still dazed by the speed of our powerful drive, were evacuated from the airstrip locality with the result that a farm came into the Wing's possession. In no time, chicken, geese, pork chops and roast pork turned up on the menus. Hunting of all sorts was very good in the neighbourhood, and soon venison and souvenirs appeared.

An enemy jet fighter zipped over the field shortly after we arrived, but got a hot reception from the ack-ack batteries. Constant rain and the speed of the army's advance eventually "washed out" B.104, so on April 8, we moved to Rheine.

Keynote of a network of German airdromes, Rheine, 25 miles north of Munster, had been well plastered by our bombers. Runways gaped with huge holes, hangars were piles of twisted steel, and the remaining buildings wrecked by demolition. The Wing again became a complete unit when the aircraft and the rest of the field pulled in from B.90.

During this period, every available kite was in the air checking for indications that the Wehrmacht would mass and fight. A daily watch also was kept to see if the Nazis were pulling out of Holland. Bremen and Hamburg were everyday targets as our pilots answered the army's incessant calls for information.

The swift pace of the Allied advance resulted in "leap frog" tactics on April 16, when over 60 sorties were flown. The planes took off from B.108, completed their missions, and landed at B.116 Wunstorf near Hanover, where "A" party was ready for them. Wunstorf was in good condition with hangars, aircraft and supplies intact. Here "requisitioning" hit a peak with the discovery of a champagne warehouse![22]

The claim that "A" party was ready to receive Wing aircrew is a debatable point. Jim Prendergast, the new CO of 414 Squadron, remembers:

On April 18, 1945, I had returned from leave in Canada after having completed a full tour of fighter reconnaissance with 430 Squadron. I arrived at B.116 in Wunstorf near Hanover on the eighteenth to take command of 414 Squadron, a sister squadron of the one I had flown in before. I was given a briefing at Group Headquarters before arriving, which said that the Squadron personnel, both groundcrew and aircrew, were rather tired, having had many frequent moves since crossing the Rhine a few weeks earlier, and having had quite a few changes in command. They also thought that the discipline had slipped somewhat, and one of the jobs I would have would be to try to get this back in line, and to maintain an anti-fraternization policy while we were in Germany. This request to tighten up the discipline bothered me a little bit, because the last thing I wanted to do was to move into a squadron and get into trouble with the established practices within the unit, having come from a sister squadron where I thought I had a reasonably good reputation for fairness. On April twentieth, on the day of this particular mission, Bud Loveless and myself took off to do a harbour reconnaissance of Harburg and Hamburg along the north coast of Germany, checking particularly for any submarine activity, as Hamburg had been one of the main points of embarkation for submarines during the entire war. We completed our mission, and as I flew back, I began reflecting upon the warning I had been given regarding discipline on the Squadron. Before I took off that morning, I thought that there had seemed to be a bit of apprehension among some of the groundcrew in talking to me, and there were none of the NCOs around me when I actually left to take off.

However, upon relanding at the aerodrome (which was a very dicey job because the main runway was still pocked with damage from our own bombers, who had been hitting Hanover quite regularly), the practice was that you would land and then taxi towards the entrance of your own dispersal area. There was about a half-mile of taxiing to the dispersal itself, and normally we would wait at the end of the runway until some members of the groundcrew came out to sit on the edges of our wingtips and guide us through the taxiable area. Nothing happened . . . I had been on the ground for at least five minutes, which seemed like half an hour to me, with the engine ticking over, and no sign of anybody coming up from the dispersal to acknowledge that we were waiting to be brought in. In my impatience, I turned the aircraft around and headed it towards the dispersal area and fired all the cannons and machine guns, the shells of which passed over the dispersal itself. Well, that certainly shook up everybody . . . Within minutes, people were barreling out to meet us. My thoughts went immediately to how I would take care of what I considered to be poor service in something which was absolutely essential, had we been attacked on the runway by any Luftwaffe that were still around. However, I was met by the senior NCO when I pulled up in front of the dispersal hut. He invited me to come into the office as he wanted to show me something. I went in and looked, and here was my desk completely covered in some of the finest champagne, cognac, and wine that I had seen during all my earlier experiences in France and Belgium. As I was told, the evening before, the groundcrew, while they were inspecting the ammunition bays that the Luftwaffe had beneath the dispersal hut, had found a door which they thought led somewhere else. They didn't get it open until sometime early in the morning, but they already had some inkling that it was a hidden storage for just such things as wine, champagne, and cognac. They then proceeded to "liberate" some of it by breakfast time, and after I took off, they apparently got into it pretty well because by the time I returned, nearly all of it had been sampled, and they had found it all most enjoyable. My anger was softened by the fact that they did think about me first and had arranged to get storage containers for it, so we could retain as much of it as possible before we had to share it with the other units on the airfield. There was quite a good celebration that evening because of this, and I think there was a certain bonding that took place between myself and the groundcrew, who had not had a chance to get to know me from earlier days. The officers agreed that although a good portion of it would go to themselves, we would share it with the groundcrew, who had found it, and we would make sure that we kept some, anticipating that the victory in Europe would be coming along very shortly. Therefore, we carefully stashed some away in all sorts of places where we didn't think it could be found by anybody who was above my rank. The date to enjoy it came a little faster than we thought. May fifth was a rather eventful day . . . Bud Loveless had gone missing shortly after we had done our mission on April twentieth. He returned to the unit after having been a POW for two weeks. We celebrated appropriately, and shortly afterwards, we moved to B.156 Luneburg to become an occupational air force on an interim basis. Insofar as bar supplies and other niceties [were concerned], we were able to find more of this as we moved on to Luneburg, which was one of the top Luftwaffe bases. They hadn't had time to completely evacuate the base of all their storage before we arrived there, and some of our original supplies from Wunstorf were still available, when on August twelfth we moved back to the U.K. to officially disband the Squadron.[23]

Even at this late stage, Jim Prendergast's war was far from over. In keeping with the expression, "There's always a critic," his mission on 2 May was memorable in more ways than one.

At B.154 Reinsehlen, located about thirty miles southwest of Hamburg, we were flying Spitfire XIVs, which were specially outfitted for low flying, and armed with five camera settings for photography, two 20-mm cannons and four .50-calibre machine guns. That day my Number Two was Doug Fuller, and our mission was to go up to the Wismar harbour area and do a reconnaissance of any troop movement and shipping activity that appeared to be either arriving at or leaving the harbour. I had been there the day before, so I was fairly well informed about what we might expect up there. I had noticed that south and east of the harbour there was a German airfield. However, on that particular day, there was no activity on it, and that puzzled me a little bit. We normally flew at about 3,000 feet and cruised at 300 miles an hour, but on this day I decided to fly at between 500 and 1,000 feet to avoid as much attention from the airfield as possible as we approached Wismar

harbour. I did all my reconnaissance from the northwest side, notic-
ing a tremendous amount of troop movement within the town and
many vessels being loaded with equipment, armament, and vehicles,
etc. It almost appeared as though there was an embarkation getting
ready to leave from the harbour very shortly. After reviewing this
situation visually, I decided to take a photo run with an oblique
camera running fairly close to the edge of the harbour, at which
time I attracted a fair amount of flak. This was according to my
Number Two, who told me it was getting close. I finished that
mission, then I decided that we would dive down to around 300
feet and swing north and west, do a slow right turn over the Baltic
Sea, and wind up passing the airfield east of the city, popping up
to have a look at it as we went by. When I popped up, I noticed
there was a '262 jet fighter being towed into a hangar and two
Focke Wulf 190s taxiing out to take off. I called Fuller and he had
a quick glimpse of what I saw, so we did a slow 360-degree turn,
while getting our cannon and machine guns ready for firing, as well
as our gyroscopic sights. Just as I came over the perimeter of the
airfield, the whole sky was lit up by what appeared to be a wall of
light flak, which we flew through. I could see that the '190s had
taken off and that the '262 was no longer visible. I told Fuller that
I would take the aircraft on the left (the first one) and that he could
take the aircraft on the right. As I slowed down to get it in my
sights, I had an opportunity for a three-second burst and it just
exploded in the air. I looked around to see where Fuller was. He
called to say he had lost sight of me because the flak was so bad.
He had climbed up to 3,000 feet and was getting away from the
airfield. The second aircraft seemed to be climbing away at this
point, so I cut in behind it, when it suddenly turned sharply and
dove for the water. I followed him and got off a two-second burst,
whereupon I saw strikes appear along the engine cowling. Two
pieces fell off the aircraft, and it crashed into the water. I then realized that I was only about 100 feet above the water in a tight turn
and in a stall position in my own aircraft, so I had to clear that up
right away — it seemed pretty stupid to spin in when there was so
much joy in my mind, having shot down two aircraft after several
years of not even having a good shot at one. On returning to the
airfield that day, I found that I had been outdone by Sammy Hall,
who had bagged three Focke Wulf 190s, one Messerschmitt 108,
then damaged a '190 and another Messerschmitt 108. However, this

just encouraged us to have a worthwhile celebration that evening as a well-earned reward.

A good friend and neighbour of mine who had been flying Spitfires had been shot down and was a POW for a couple of years . . . On the particular day that I had my fun at Wismar harbour, he had been sitting, watching the airfield for some time as an escapee from a POW camp, trying to figure out how he could steal an aircraft and get away. He had his eye on the '262, and his ambitions were somewhat dashed, because after I came along, they significantly increased the guard at the airfield and he had to get out of that area. However, he did say that he admired the first aircraft I shot down, but thought I could have done a better job on the second one of blowing it up, instead of just damaging it, before it went into the harbour.[24]

Even as the Continental-based RCAF day fighter Squadrons were savouring the taste of victory in their ubiquitous Spitfires, two RCAF day fighter Squadrons were back in the U.K. converting to a potent new type of aircraft, the long-range North American Mustang Mks III and IV. Number 442 (Caribou) Squadron was the first RCAF unit to convert to the Mk IV, at Hunsdon in early April, while 441 (Silver Fox) Squadron was sent to Digby for a similar conversion to Mustang IIIs later in the month. Although the war in Europe ended before 441 Squadron could participate in any operations in their new aircraft, the same could not be said of 442 Squadron.

On March 21st 1945, the Caribous, commanded by Squadron Leader Johnston, left Heesch for Hunsdon to spend the few remaining weeks of the war in England. At the beginning of April, they converted from Spitfires to Mustangs for long range bomber escort and returned to operational flying on the 9th, accompanying Lancasters to Hamburg, where an oil refinery was bombed. On the 10th, they undertook a similar mission to the Leipzig marshalling yards, a single Me 163 being the only enemy aircraft encountered. The next day they accompanied bombers to Nuremburg, the only opposition of any kind being a moderate amount of flak. On their fourth, fifth and sixth operations with their new aircraft, they escorted Bomber Command Lancasters to Swinemünde. As they were returning from one of these operations, some strange aircraft were sighted which, on investigation, turned out to be Russian Air Force. On April 15th, Flight Lieutenant Dick failed to return, being last heard of over the Enschede-Münster area, but the next day the Squadron scored twice. Northeast of Berlin, some FW 190s were bounced. Flight Lieutenant W.V. Shenk, trying to scare off an FW that was on the tail of another Mustang, chased the enemy down to 2000 feet, scoring strikes on the starboard wing. The FW straightened out, rolled over on its back, and took a gentle dive upside down towards the deck. This was claimed as a probable, since Shenk did not actually see the enemy crash. Meantime, Flying Officer L.H. Wilson and Flying Officer R.J. Robillard chased another FW 190, both firing at it until it took fire, dived into a wood and blew up. These were the last Squadron victories.

On April 18th, the Caribous patrolled enemy airfields in northern Germany and southern Denmark while Lancasters bombed Heligoland. Acting as Wing Leader was Lieutenant-Colonel W.H. Christie, who had flown with the Squadron on occasion. Fifteen miles southwest of Handorf, he experienced engine trouble and had to bail out, his parachute being seen to open. He was thought to have landed safely but behind the enemy lines.

The next day, as the Squadron was taking off on an escort to Lancasters bombing Munich, Flying Officer Robillard had a very narrow escape. When his aircraft was only ten or fifteen feet in the air, it dropped a wing and crashed, but the pilot walked away from the wreck without a scratch. As the Squadron was returning, Flying Officer D.J. Jeffrey was forced to make a belly landing near Canterbury, but he too got away without injury. A hundred Lancasters bombed the oil refinery at Regensburg on the 20th, and the Caribous were again called upon for escort duty. Two days later, as the marshalling yards at Cuxhaven were raided, the Squadron patrolled between Zeven and the target. Nothing eventful marked either occasion. Similarly, there was an attack on Flensburg on the 23rd.

The 25th provided one of those operations to which every pilot must have looked forward. At 0650 hours, the Caribous took off to escort Lancasters in an attack on Hitler's chalet at Berchtesgaden. The fighter pilots merely noted that the bombing was heavy and concentrated, no opposition being encountered.[25]

For the day fighters, the honour of having the last significant engagement of the war with German aircraft fell to the Turner/Edwards

Wing on 1 May 1945. On an early patrol over the Elbe River bridge-head, 403 Squadron intercepted and destroyed two FW 190s. Some-what later, three 421 Squadron pilots accounted for another FW 190 near Schwerin.

In spite of the absence of an airborne enemy during the last days of the war, heart-stopping experiences were still common for RCAF fighter pilots. Procrastination can, however, sometimes be the best policy, to which Murray Lepard of 412 Squadron will attest. While he was attempting to decide what degree of difficulty he wished to assign to a graceful exit from his Spitfire, unforeseen events overtook his deliberations.

On May 4th 1945, I was on an armed recce north of Hamburg to the Kiel area when my engine quit. I had experienced limited flak in the Hamburg area and I suspected I had been hit in the under-belly tank. I tried to restart the engine but nothing happened; therefore, I called on R/T that I was bailing out, since it was not hospitable below for a forced landing. I trimmed the aircraft for a glide, threw the coupe top back and the side door down, then threw off my helmet, undid my harness and, holding onto the canopy, I got out on the wing. I held on and debated how best to go off — rolling backwards or sliding off feet first. I don't remem-ber a slipstream at all, possibly due to an increase in adrenalin from the moment. I had hung on a few seconds, debating, when in front of my face I heard the Merlin start up. I couldn't believe my ears at first, but it continued running and I climbed back in, eased the throttle up a couple of times and got good response. I did up my harness, fastened the side door, and tried to pull the coupe top up, but it seemed jammed by something. I looked back and there was my helmet still attached to the cord, flailing about in the slipstream. I pulled the helmet in and put it on. I noticed the Squadron cir-cling above, waiting to see what would happen, so I closed the canopy, called up to say I was joining the Squadron, and did so. We proceeded to complete our mission. When I landed, I discovered the cause was a suspected airlock. It had happened on the previous trip, but the engine had restarted alright and so it was not reported.[26]

As surely as someone had to be the first RCAF combatant during the European portion of the Second World War, someone also had to be the last. Bill Gould of 443 Squadron remembers that moment, on 4 May 1945:

I was leading an armed recce from Diepholz airport, Dummer Lake, to an area close to the Danish border. At the briefing, I was given dire warning of what would happen if I strayed across the border into Denmark. The flak on that trip was deadly, but the roads were covered with German vehicles. My log book shows that I attacked five vehicles, two of which were flamers. On our Wing, a vehicle could only be claimed as destroyed if it burst into flames; otherwise it was claimed as damaged. One of my targets was a large grey bus. When my shells hit it, the whole back end of the bus exploded. Someone told me later that the Germans were burning wood to make some kind of fuel to drive the buses, and that the explosion was probably caused by one of those tanks of fuel blowing up. Either that or the bus was carrying ammunition. On returning to base with a very good Squadron score for the day, I felt quite pleased with our work. While taxiing in towards the dispersal, I saw a group of people standing around as if they were waiting for us. As I got closer, I could see that at least two of them had scrambled eggs on their hats. One looked almost as if he were wearing a yellow hat. "My God," I wondered, "What have I done? Surely I didn't get across the border into Denmark." I had paid particular attention to my map reading but something must have gone wrong somewhere. As I taxied closer, it became obvious that they were waiting for me. Whatever it was, there was nothing I could do except surrender myself to my fate. I climbed out of my aircraft, walked up to the senior officer and came smartly to attention, fearing the absolute worst. Instead, he thrust out his hand and said, "Congratulations, Gould, you have flown the last flight of the war." It is a strange thing, but for forty-eight years I have been trying to remember the identity of that senior officer. At a recent 443 Squadron reunion in Victoria, British Columbia, we were discussing this last flight and someone mentioned that Air Marshal Wilfred Curtis was visiting our Wing the day the war ended. I guess it must have been Air Marshal Curtis who gave me the biggest fright of my life . . .[27]

Throughout the drive across the Continent, the RCAF contribution to the overall success of the 2TAF in defeating Hitler's Third Reich had been tremendous. Number 126 Wing was the top scorer of the Tactical Air Force with a balance sheet of 361 air-to-air victories, twelve air-to-ground victories, 131 aircraft losses, and ninety-eight pilot losses. Number 127 Wing had a final tally of 184 air-to-air victories, eight air-to-ground victories, 105 aircraft losses, and eighty pilot losses. Within the RCAF fighter community, 401 Squadron (126 Wing) was the top unit with 112 air-to-air victories. Number 126 Wing was destined to remain in Germany with the Occupation Forces throughout the summer. On 12 May, the Wing moved to Fassberg, and then on 5 July to Ütersen, a few miles south of Hamburg. Number 127 Wing remained at Reinsehlen until July, but started selectively disbanding in June.

From D-Day until VE-Day, thirteen RCAF fighter pilots in service on the Continent accounted for more than 120 German aircraft. Top scorer was Squadron Leader Don Laubman of 412 and 402 Squadron with fifteen kills, followed closely by Squadron Leader Bill Klersy of 401 Squadron with fourteen and a half. Johnnie Johnson was third overall in the 2TAF with thirteen confirmed, and his total wartime score of thirty-eight air-to-air victories was tops not only for the Commonwealth but for all the non-Soviet Allies in the European theatre of operations. Other high scorers included John MacKay of 401 Squadron with eleven and one fifth confirmed victories and Dick Audet of 411 Squadron with ten and a half kills. A summary of 2TAF RCAF unit results and losses is transcribed below:

	126 Wing	127 Wing	143 Wing	39 Wing	144★ Wing	TOTAL
SORTIES	22,372	20,084	12,043	11,915	2,482	68,896
500-lb. bombs	5,067	1,171	21,994		107	28,348
TANKS						
Dest.	7	5	12			24
Dam.	82	51	25		1	159
MECHANIZED TRANSPORT						
Dest.	1,407	1,267	509	6	57	3,246
Dam.	3,061	2,559	1,026	8	123	6,777
LOCOMOTIVES						
Dest.	61	17	22			100
Dam.	435	126	283	4	2	850

	126 Wing	127 Wing	143 Wing	39 Wing	144* Wing	TOTAL
TRUCKS						
Dest.	172	60	379			611
Dam.	1,397	421	1,409			3,227
SHIPS						
Dest.		1	4			5
Dam.	5	12	23			40
BARGES						
Dest.	2		10			12
Dam.	52	59	92		11	214
RAIL CUTS	426	108	1,264		3	1,801
SIGNAL BOXES						
Dest.	2	1				3
Dam.	1		2			3
ENEMY AIRCRAFT						
Dest.	361	184	17	201/2	56	638 1/2
P.D.	12	8	1		1	22
Dam.	156	103	6	11	13	289
LOSSES						
Pilots	98	80	104	27	8	317
aircraft	131	105	132	42	11	421

* No. 144 Wing disbanded in July 1944.

To this may be added that twenty-five pilots destroyed six or more enemy aircraft *in the air* while serving with 2TAF. Of these, thirteen were members of the RCAF, and another, an RAF pilot, was leader of an RCAF Wing (Johnson).[28]

———◆•••◆———

In Italy, 417 Squadron continued to make life something less than a picnic for the *Wehrmacht*. On 5 December, the Squadron moved to Bellaria on the Adriatic coast, about seven miles north of Rimini. There it would remain until the war was over, and 417's primary task would be to support army operations in the region west of Ravenna. In January, the Windsors continued their relentless pounding of German rolling stock and transport, claiming 116 freight cars and thirteen other vehicles. Unfortunately, they also lost three pilots, as flak continued to be a serious problem, just as it was in northwest

Europe. Flying Officer T. R. Wilson was awarded a DFC for the courage and fortitude he displayed in bringing his stricken aircraft back to base after having been wounded by flak over Vicenza.[29]

Early in the new year, Karl Linton joined 417 as a Flight Commander, where his considerable operational experience from northwest Europe was greatly appreciated. He recalls life amongst the Windsors during the last months of the Italian campaign:

In Italy we flew mostly in groups of four, doing *very* close work with the army. That was a nasty bit of war, which required dive-bombing specific buildings where civilians lived. In fact, my first mission on this second tour was to take out a church, wherein snipers were located. We did . . . I felt bad about destroying a church, but by this time maybe the feeling didn't last so long. I never saw an enemy aircraft in the air during my second tour of sixty-nine trips, practically all of which were dive-bombing and strafing trains, stations, boats, buildings, and tanks. The small arms fire was almost like flying through hail at times. My aircraft got hit on seventeen separate trips, but I never got a scratch!

We did not see much of the Italians in uniform at that stage, but we bartered with the Partisans; old boots for revolvers, candy, gum, cigarettes for paintings, and once, four of us traded our monthly ration of a 26 oz. bottle of rye whisky for a captured German jeep . . .[30]

While the pace of operations was somewhat subdued in January and most of February due to unfavourable winter weather, late-month activity picked up considerably as the predominately foggy skies began to clear. By March, the sun was out in strength, and so was the Squadron. That month, 417 dropped nearly 106 tons of bombs on German lines of communications and defended areas, made forty-three rail cuts, and claimed one locomotive, eighty freight cars, seven passenger coaches, forty-seven other vehicles, and sixteen barges, plus other strong points and gunpits. Two pilots were lost to flak, one of whom was killed.

In April, the pilots in 417 Squadron traded in their Spitfire Mk VIIIs for Mk IXs and redoubled their efforts for the last full month of the war. A total of 938 flying hours were flown on 723 individual sorties, during which over 244 tons of bombs were dropped. The Windsors made three rail cuts and claimed one locomotive, twenty-four freight cars, eighteen tanks, 148 motor vehicles, 121 horse-drawn and ox-drawn vehicles, eight barges, seven pontoon bridges, and seven gun emplacements. From 8 April onward, most operations were flown to support the army in its final thrust across the Senio and Po Rivers and into the plains of Venetia. Two more pilots were killed by flak during the month. Flying Officer F. A. Doyle was also hit by flak on the twenty-third and crash-landed in flames behind enemy lines. Italian peasants mercifully sheltered him for two days before he could reach Allied troops.

One amazing incident marked these operations. On the 25th, as Flying Officer G. H. Slack was racing down the airfield on his take-off run, a tire on the Spitfire blew out. The aircraft cartwheeled and the 500-pound bomb broke free and went hurtling down the runway, fortunately without exploding. The aircraft was a complete write-off, but Herb Slack emerged from the dust and confusion unscathed. A few hours later, he was in the air on another sortie . . .[31]

On 2 May, the German forces in Italy "called it a day." The out-standing work done during the latter stages of the campaign resulted in DFCs being awarded to three of the Windsors, including the CO, Dave Goldberg. On 4 May, the Squadron moved 130 miles north to Treviso, where it would remain until disbandment at the end of June.

While most Germans in Italy surrendered on or about 2 May, some in remote mountain regions didn't seem to get word of the Allied victory until considerably later. Karl Linton recalls:

It was a bit cold when I arrived in Italy, but it certainly became beautiful in April and stayed that way through June. Two or three weeks after VE-Day (May 8), four of us decided to take a trip up into the Alps. We got about halfway to our destination when we met a few German soldiers walking down the mountainside, absolutely loaded with rifles, revolvers, etc. We continued on a bit further 'til we now found the road completely choked by armed German stragglers . . . and they did not eye the four of us in a friendly way at all. So, being bright for a change, we turned tail and got down those Alps very quickly. Our four on-hip Smith and Wessons didn't impress them at all! I found out later as I flew back to Bellaria, where I was first stationed in Italy, that many thousands of German soldiers had marched down the runway and had simply flung all their rifles, revolvers, and other arms into a pile that I later estimated to be 400'–500' long x 40'–50' wide x 3'–7' high. Such is the waste of war . . .[32]

After a slow start in North Africa, 417 Squadron had matured to become one of the most outstanding units of the Desert Air Force. Along with a formidable record of ground targets decimated, the Windsors had accumulated a fine air-combat scoresheet, consisting of twenty-nine enemy aircraft destroyed, eight probably destroyed, and a further twenty-two damaged. Twenty-two Squadron pilots had been killed on operations, and the Windsors had served at over thirty different locations during three and a half years of war — truly indicative of the nomadic nature of their existence. Number 417 Squadron had made a very substantial contribution to the victories of the Eighth Army, both in Sicily and in Italy.

In Burma, the great re-conquest of the country was occurring on three fronts: on the west coast by XV Corps, in the centre by the Fourteenth Army, which was driving towards Mandalay, and in the northwest by forces under the command of General Stilwell. Akyab fell on 2 January without a gun being fired, after the town had defied capture for such a long period of time. The high point of its capture occurred when six Japanese aircraft suddenly arrived in the area and five of them were promptly shot down by patrolling Spitfires. By the third week of the month, in a combined operation that included smokescreens laid by Hurricanes and air cover provided by Spitfires, Thunderbolts, and Mitchells, a successful amphibious landing and assault were carried out on Ramtree Island, seventy miles to the south of Akyab.[33]

Dave Bockus had to be hospitalized for malaria and dengue after his harrowing experiences as a Chindit. By July 1944, however, he was fully recovered and flying Spitfire Mk VIIIs with 67 (RAF) Squadron. Dave adds a personal twist to the saga of the capture of Akyab, and also suggests that there were other things just as scary as falling into the hands of the Japanese:

On 11 January 1945, on an operation against the Jap coastal base at Myebon, I lost my engine and hurt my neck in the subsequent bailout. After experiencing previous jungle walks, my intention this time was to end up in the ocean. I delayed too long, trying to slide out the door, and the Spit flick-rolled. The radio and oxygen cords caught, jerking my head. I broke loose and a few seconds later, experienced that great feeling of descending under an open 'chute. Great, that is, as long as the crotch straps are in the right place . . . However, blowing up my dinghy within sight of shore and in waters known for crocodiles, sharks, and stingrays was definitely "twitch time." Soon, I had the uneasy comfort of having a 1/8" thickness of dinghy rubber keeping me from being something's dinner. Things were looking very bad when I heard a single plane, which seemed to be searching the shoreline a few miles to the south; then some Spitfires and later an air/sea rescue Sea Otter arrived overhead. After landing, the Otter's hatch opened and the first face to appear was that of my friend, Squadron Leader Bob Day.[34] Nip fighters had shot down a Sea Otter in the same area a few days earlier, so the flight back, at what I thought was a steady taxiing speed, was touchy. When the Otter was shot down, 67 Squadron caught and blasted five Oscars out of the air. Those air/sea rescue guys sure had a lot of guts. We made fun of their slo-mo planes, but here is one person who has a lot of respect for them.

I was none the worse for wear, with just a sore neck and a whopping headache. One day later, we were back over Myebon with some USAAF P38s, and two Nip fighters were shot down. A short time after that, both Myebon and Ramtree Island fell to the Allies. The tide had turned. The Nips had held the area since 1942 . . .[35]

Along with these coastal successes, the Fourteenth Army was pounding the Japanese in the central region. Most of the enemy's armour was destroyed by Hurricanes at Myinmu on 19 February, and this action was pivotal in clearing the way for the recapture of Mandalay on 21 March. The push south to Rangoon was a race against the impending monsoon season. The Allied drive prevailed, however, greatly assisted by RAF airpower, and Rangoon was occupied on 3 May. Soon the rest of the nation would be in Allied hands. It had been an extremely difficult campaign, which could not have been won without airpower, and Canadian fighter pilots had made a significant contribution in the theatre. By the end of July, victory in Burma was absolute. The theatre campaign of 1944–45 had cost the Japanese nearly 180,000 casualties, most of them fatal. In this fifteen-month period, the RAF element had dropped 36,000 tons of bombs and destroyed around 900 enemy aircraft, along with airlifting over half a million tons of supplies to a highly fluid front.[36]

Although Canada had no fighter aircraft units serving in the Pacific during the Second World War, Canadian navy fighter pilots served proudly and with great distinction as members of the British Pacific Fleet. One Royal Canadian Navy Volunteer Reserve pilot, Lieutenant Don Sheppard, flew Corsairs from a Royal Navy carrier and scored five victories over the Japanese, winning a Distinguished Service Cross in the process. Another Canadian, Bill Atkinson, scored five and a half kills flying Hellcat night fighters with the British Fleet, and was also awarded the DSC.[37]

No documentation of Canadian fighter pilots during the Second World War would be complete without mention of Lieutenant Robert Hampton Gray, Canada's only fighter pilot winner of the Victoria Cross during the conflict. Hailing from Nelson, British Columbia, and educated in Vancouver, "Hammy" Gray joined the RCNVR in 1940. In 1943, he received a Mention in Dispatches for his execution of daring attacks in Norwegian fjords on the German battleship *Tirpitz*, and on three destroyers. In April 1945, Lieutenant Gray was aboard HMS *Formidable* flying Corsairs with the Pacific Fleet. By July, *Formidable* was within striking distance of Japan, and Gray led several strikes with cool professionalism and great dash, winning a DSC. On 9 August, he led his Flight in a daring raid against the Japanese naval base at Onagawa Bay. He selected a destroyer as his target, and dived to attack through a hail of gunfire. On the final run-in, his Corsair was holed repeatedly and burst into flames. Still, Gray never wavered on his target run, and at fifty-feet range, released his bombs. One of them struck the destroyer amidships and it sank almost immediately. Meanwhile, Gray's blazing Corsair funeral pyre thundered into the waters of Onagawa Bay. Six days later, on 15 August 1945, the Second World War was over.

And so, the longest global "shooting war" of all time had drawn to a close. From Coltishall to Cologne, and from Manston to Myebon, Canadian fighter pilots had fought with great skill and courage, contributing in no small measure to the war effort and to ultimate victory for the forces of democracy. Not only on RCAF units, but with even greater representation on RAF units, they helped forge for Canada a proud legacy of honour and accomplishment in battle. At least 134 Canadian fighter pilots reached the coveted "ace" status, and many rose to command not only RCAF formations but many RAF units as well. Their selfless contribution to victory, which includes many hundreds of the official 14,541 RCAF war dead, will not be forgotten.

1 Leslie Roberts, *There Shall Be Wings*, p. 212
2 *Flap: The History of 39 Reconnaissance Wing RCAF*, August 1945, p. 4
3 *RCAF Overseas: The Sixth Year*, p. 240
4 Ibid., p. 241
5 Donald L. Caldwell, *JG 26: Top Guns of the Luftwaffe*, p. 319
6 John Garland, letter to author, July 1993
7 Donald L. Caldwell, p. 324
8 Chuck Darrow, tape to author, July 1993
9 Dick Reeves, tape to author, July 1993
10 Christopher Shores, *The History of the Royal Canadian Air Force*, p. 58
11 Leslie Roberts, p. 217
12 *RCAF Overseas: The Sixth Year*, p. 253
13 Ibid., p. 250
14 Ibid., p. 281
15 Bill Gould, letter to author, July 1993
16 *RCAF Overseas: The Sixth Year*, p. 297
17 Ibid., p. 298
18 Ibid., p. 302
19 R. D. Schultz, tape to author, September 1993
20 *RCAF Overseas: The Sixth Year*, p. 265
21 Edwards and Lavigne, *Kittyhawk Pilot*, p. 294
22 *Flap: The History of 39 Reconnaissance Wing RCAF*, August 1945, p. 14
23 Jim Prendergast, tape to author, August 1993
24 Ibid.
25 *RCAF Overseas: The Sixth Year*, p. 275
26 Murray Lepard, letter to author, July 1993
27 Bill Gould, letter to author, July 1993
28 *RCAF Overseas: The Sixth Year*, p. 304
29 Keith Robbins, *417 Squadron Official History*, p. 31
30 Karl Linton, letter to author, May 1993
31 Keith Robbins, p. 33
32 Karl Linton, letter to author, May 1993
33 John D. R. Rawlings, *The History of the Royal Air Force*, p. 173
34 Squadron Leader R. W. R. "Bob" Day, RCAF, commanded 67 (RAF) Squadron, and would be the only member of the RCAF to claim five air-to-air victories over the Japanese. — DB
35 Dave Bockus, letter to author, June 1993, and Lloyd Hunt, *We Band of Brothers*, p. 4
36 John D. R. Rawlings, p. 175
37 D. J. Sheppard, conversation with author, July 1993

Bibliography

Bader, Sir Douglas · *Airforce* magazine · Ottawa: Air Force Publications, September 1979.

Baker, E. C. R. · *Fighter Aces of the RAF* · London: William Kimber, 1962.

Beurling, George, and Leslie Roberts · *Malta Spitfire* · Toronto: Oxford University Press, 1943.

Bishop, William Arthur · *Courage in the Air* · Whitby: McGraw-Hill Ryerson, 1992.

Brickhill, Paul · *Reach for the Sky* · London: Collins, 1954.

Brown, George, and Michel Lavigne · *Canadian Wing Commanders of Fighter Command in World War II* · Langley: Ballentine, 1984.

Caldwell, Donald L. · *JG 26: Top Guns of the Luftwaffe* · New York: Ballentine Books, 1991.

Carlson, Don · *RCAF Padre with Spitfire Squadrons* · Ottawa: DND, 1969.

Collier, Basil · *The Battle of Britain* · London: Batsford, 1962.

Coughlin, Tom · *The Dangerous Sky* · Toronto: Ryerson Press, 1968.

Deighton, Len · *The Battle of Britain* · New York: Coward, McCann & Geoghegan, 1980.

Edwards, James F., and Michel Lavigne · *Kittyhawk Pilot* · Battleford: Turner-Warwick Publications, 1983.

Everard, Hedley · *A Mouse in My Pocket* · Picton: Valley Floatplane Services, 1988.

Galland, Adolf · *The First and the Last* · London: Methuen, 1955.

Godefroy, Hugh · *Lucky Thirteen* · Toronto: Stoddart, 1987.

Green, William · *Famous Fighters of the Second World War* · New York: Hanover House, 1960.

Grinsell, Robert · *Focke Wulf FW 190* · London: Jane's, 1980.

Halliday, Hugh · *242 Squadron: The Canadian Years* · Stittsville: Canada's Wings, 1981.

Hitchins, F. H. · "The War History of 414 Squadron," *The Roundel*. Vol. 6, No. 7 · Ottawa: DND, July–August 1954.

Hunt, Lloyd · *We Band of Brothers* · Ottawa: The Canadian Fighter Pilots' Association, 1992.

_____ · *We Happy Few* · Ottawa: The Canadian Fighter Pilots' Association, 1986.

Johnson, J. E. · *Wing Leader* · New York: Ballentine, 1956.

Lucas, Laddie · *Flying Colours* · London: Hutchinson, 1981.

Mayer, S. L. · *The Russian War Machine 1917–1945* · London: Bison Books, 1977.

McIntosh, Dave · *High Blue Battle* · Toronto: Stoddart, 1990.

_____ · *Terror in the Starboard Seat* · New York: Beaufort Books, 1980.

Milberry, Larry · *Sixty Years* · Toronto: CANAV Books, 1984.

Nolan, Brian · *Hero: The Buzz Beurling Story* · Toronto: Lester, 1981.

Olmsted, Bill · *Blue Skies* · Toronto: Stoddart, 1987.

Oxspring, Bobby · *Spitfire Command* · London: Grafton, 1987.

Quill, Jeffrey · *Spitfire* · London: Arrow Books, 1983.

Rae, Jackie · *Airforce* magazine · Ottawa: Air Force Publications, Spring 1989.

Rawlings, J. D. R. · *The History of the Royal Air Force* · Feltham: Temple Press, 1984.

RCAF Historical Branch · *AFP 49* · Ottawa: DND, 1946.

_____ · *Flap: The History of 39 Reconnaissance Wing RCAF* · Ottawa: DND, 1945.

_____ · *RCAF Overseas: The First Four Years* · Toronto: Oxford University Press, 1944.

_____ · *RCAF Overseas: The Fifth Year* · Toronto: Oxford University Press, 1945.

_____ · *RCAF Overseas: The Sixth Year* · Toronto: Oxford University Press, 1949.

Reader's Digest · *The Canadians at War 1939/45* · Westmount: The Reader's Digest Association of Canada, 1986.

Robbins, Keith · *417 Squadron Official History* · Stittsville: Canada's Wings, 1983.

Roberts, Leslie · *There Shall Be Wings* · London: George Harrap, 1960.

Scott, Desmond · *Typhoon Pilot* · London: Arrow Books, 1982.

Shores, Christopher · *The History of the Royal Canadian Air Force* · Toronto: Royce Publications, 1984.

Simpson, Allan · *We Few* · Ottawa: The Canadian Fighter Pilots' Association, 1983.

Sweetman, Bill · *Spitfire* · London: Jane's, 1980.

Terraine, John · *The Right of the Line* · London: Hodder and Stoughton, 1985.

Toliver, Raymond F., and Trevor J. Constable · *Fighter Aces of the Luftwaffe* · Fallbrook: Aero, 1977.

Williamson, Murray · *Strategy for Defeat: The Luftwaffe 1939–1945* · Chartwell: Secaucus, 1986.

INDEX

INDEX

INDEX

INDEX